AMERICA'S GREAT PATRIOTIC WAR WITH SPAIN

*Mixed Motives, Lies and Racism
in Cuba and the Philippines, 1898-1915*

By

JOHN TEBBEL

MARSHALL JONES COMPANY
Publishers Since 1902
Manchester Center, Vermont

Marshall Jones Company, Publishers
P.O. Box 2327, Two Main Street
Manchester Center, Vermont 05255

Manufactured in the United States of America

Tebbel, John William
   America's great patriotic war with Spain : mixed motives, lies, and racism in Cuba and the Philippines, 1898-1915 / by John Tebbel.
1st ed.
      p. cm.
   Includes bibliographical references and index.
   1. Spanish-American War, 1898.   2. Spanish-American War, 1898-Causes.   3. Spanish-American War, 1898-Influence.
4. Spanish-American War, 1898-Propaganda.   5. Racism-United States-History-19th century.   I. Title.
E715.T43   1996
973.8'9--dc20

                                                              96-16825
                                                                   CIP

I.S.B.N. 0-8338-0229-1

10 9 8 7 6 5 4 3 2 1
First Edition

Photos, Illustration and Reproductions:

Cover: Raising of the flag at Santiago.
Reproduced from the Collections of the Library of Congress
by Scott Mattern

For Bea and Aggie,
who know why–
and for Jack,
wherever you are

No war the United States has fought was launched with so much patriotic fervor, and none faded so fast from national memory. It was gone before it was over. "This was our most quickly forgotten war," the historian Richard Welch observes, "the war least celebrated in legend and song, least marked by cenotaph and monuments." The short conflict with Spain in Cuba, and its cruel, much longer extension to the Philippines is also remarkable for other reasons.

It "divided America more than any other between Appomattox and Vietnam" says the military historian, Geoffrey Perrett. "From this one small war would flow a century of consequences," not least among them the racist aspects of the war with the Vietnamese, which the conflict in the Philippines foreshadowed in several respects.

Some recent historians of the war believe that what happened in Cuba and the Philippines should be separated as two separate wars, and while there may be some scholarly arguments for that conclusion, the war is best understood as a continuous conflict. First blood was drawn on May 19, 1898, at Manila Bay by Commodore Dewey, nearly two months before actual hostilities began in Cuba, where the struggle lasted a scant six weeks. Action began concurrently in the Philippines and it was 1915 before resistance was finally snuffed out there. Many of the officers and troops who served in Cuba fought in the Philippines as well, and certainly for them, it was a continuous war.

I have tried to re-create the war in terms of those at every level who were involved with it. I have used the same present tense, you-are-there technique I found so useful in an earlier book I wrote on the Revolutionary War (1993). This time, in addition to the letters of soldiers, officers and civilians, I have had the advantage, in the Cuban section, of reports from the field by correspondents who accompanied the troops. Some of these, like Harry Sylvester, were superb reporters. Others were legendary writers like Richard Harding Davis, and one was Stephen Crane, who brought the great talent of his fiction writing to reporting the war, and used the materials of these reports to create some of his best fiction. Few wars have been better reported. William Randolph Hearst may not have started the war, as he and others liked to think, but he did mobilize public opinion and, with Joseph Pulitzer, saw to it that the war in Cuba was thoroughly covered by the most remarkable group of correspondents ever assembled.

Ostensibly the Spanish-American War was fought for the liberation of Cubans from Spanish rule, and most of those who fought in it thought that was what they were doing. But there were also political, commercial, and even religious motives involved, and to an even greater degree in the Philippines phase. At the time this was seen as a struggle between Republicans who believed in establishing America as a world power, "imperialism," as the anti-imperialist Democrats called it, and those who wanted no part of national expansion, especially the annexation of poor, helpless countries. It was an argument symbolized at one extreme by President William McKinley and, at the other, by Mark Twain.

On closer examination, the war proves also to be a study in developing racism. To conduct a racist, expansionist war, it was necessary for politicians and other interested parties to lie until it was difficult to tell sometimes where the truth might exist, if anywhere.

From a purely military standpoint, the Spanish-American War was, by all odds, the most confused, mismanaged, and generally incompetent military adventure we have ever carried out. In its Philippine phase, it was also a sickening chapter of racist brutality, a story glossed over for years and it is certainly not among the brightest pages in the American story. By way of contrast, the interservice rivalries among generals provide high comedy of a kind that would be truly amusing if the consequences hadn't been so frightful.

Finally, it was a war that mirrored the times. While it was being fought, America was going through a period of buoyant prosperity, recovering from the Panic of 1893 and soaring toward a seemingly bright and profitable future, making the conduct of the war, and the fact of the war itself, seem as distant as it was disturbing. No wonder it was rapidly put out of the national mind as soon as it was safe to do so.

Coming so relatively soon after the Civil War, it sometimes seemed like a postscript, since the presumed object was human freedom, and since many of the generals who fought on both sides in the Civil War appeared for curtain calls in Cuba and the

Philippines. It was, in short, a war with a cast of characters and an explosive series of events involving notable figures that would shame a Hollywood epic. The literature of the Spanish-American War is slight by comparison with that of the Civil War, the Revolution, or World War II, let alone Vietnam, but there have been notable contributions from academic historians and from writers of popular history as well. I have drawn extensively on both. Some have been particularly helpful. Joyce Milton's recent *The Yellow Kids*, for example, is by far the best and most thoroughly researched of any account dealing with journalistic coverage of the war, and I am much indebted to her for that phase of the conflict. Frank Freidel's *The Splendid Little War,* a picture-text account by this noted historian, was also singularly useful for its quotations from officers, soldiers, and correspondents, and for its eyewitness accounts. Margaret Leech's *In the Days of McKinley*, was also indispensable for its account of the war's political aspects. I am grateful also to Dorothy Geismar for pointing out to me the significant study by her late husband, Maxwell Geismar, of Mark Twain's contributions to the anti-imperialist movement. Nor can I neglect to offer abundant thanks and gratitude to Sarah Miles Watts, who has been collaborator as well as researcher with me on previous projects, and for this volume was once again my indispensable researcher and valued friend.

John Tebbel
Durham, North Carolina
March, 1996

TABLE OF CONTENTS

America's Great Patriotic
War With Spain

PART ONE

INVENTING A WAR

1

THE GREAT FILIBUSTER WAR

ON A MARCH DAY IN 1895, THE AMERICAN STEAMSHIP *ALLIANCE* is plowing ahead peacefully in Cuban waters, six miles off Cape Maysí, on her way from Colón to New York, when a swift Spanish gunboat, the *Conde de Venadito*, suddenly overtakes her and commands this blameless ship to "heave to." The captain of the *Alliance* considers this presumptuous and refuses to halt. Instead, he pours on the coal and flees. In pursuit, the Spanish vessel fires repeatedly on the *Alliance*, but she escapes intact.

So the Age of Hysteria dawns. Hot, or reasonably hot, exchanges ensue. The Spanish argue that the *Alliance* was in the process of transferring arms to shore as supplies for the perennial Cuban rebellion--in other words, it was filibustering. The *Alliance*'s captain denies it, and also says he wasn't within the three-mile limit, as the Spanish are charging. The State Department backs him up. All this happened in the Windward Passage, it says, and that's a natural highway between American and Caribbean ports; interference can't be tolerated, especially when no state of war has been declared in Cuba.

It isn't the first time such a flap has occurred, and it won't be the last, but somehow this one hits a raw nerve, or at least the nerves of editors and editorial writers who have a clear vision of the connection between patriotism and circulation. "OUR FLAG FIRED ON!" is the most popular headline of the day, and in New York, where the competition for readers is at its fiercest, Joseph Pulitzer's *World* screams that our flag has been insulted on the high seas, and the lives and property of Americans endangered. The commander of the Spanish vessel is "stupid," if not worse.

In the New York *Sun*, an editorial writer embellishes this theme. "It is evident," he writes, "that the Spanish government, whose arrogance and brutality provoke its Cuban subjects to rebellion, requires a sharp and stinging lesson at the hands of the United States...The next vessel ought to be pursued and blown out of the water. Let it [the State Department] bring

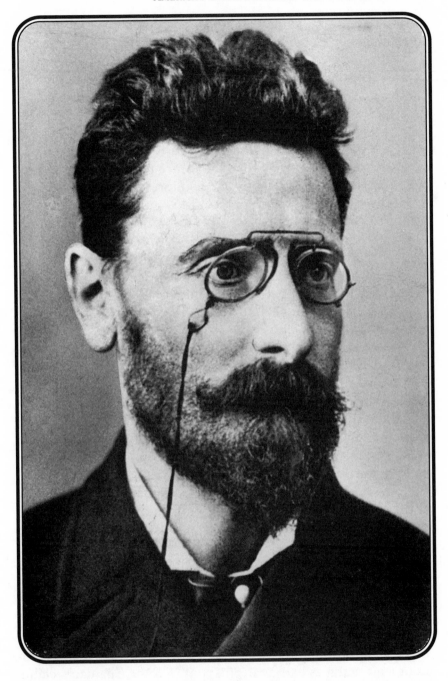

Joseph Pulitzer, publisher, New York World

– Corbis-Bettman

Spain to her knees, or punish her by the destruction of her navy and the loss of Cuba." A fateful forecast of things to come.

Nor is this the product of overheated New York journalism. In Chicago, the *Tribune* reminds its readers that it isn't the first outrage committed by the "hot-blooded Spaniards, but it is high time they should be stopped."

In fact, filibustering--the illegal supplying of arms and other aid to Cuban rebels--began as early as 1823, when revolt against Spanish rule first broke out. Since then, Americans have been industriously supplying, at a comfortable profit, goods and services to the rebels. The source of this activity is in New York, where Cuban leaders have set up the Junta, an organization of unnaturalized Cubans and their sympathizers. The Junta raises money, helps to fit out filibustering expeditions, and propagandizes Americans on behalf of their cause. Its members include Cubans who came up to New York, took out naturalization papers, then went back home as Americans to help fight for freedom from the inside.

The filibustering expeditions have made no particular effort to hide their traffic, which irritates President Grover Cleveland, who wants nothing to do with what's going on in Cuba. When Spain, whom he considers a friendly power, complains about filibustering, he responds in June 1895 by issuing a proclamation pointing out that the filibusterers are in violation of American neutrality laws, and he shakes a heavy finger at them or anyone else who's thinking of violating them.

The filibusterers don't listen. They keep right on sending ships, and Spain keeps right on complaining, until Cleveland, with an election coming up, instructs the Navy to prevent the sailing of these illegal ships if it can, and if it can't, to capture them. Soon Coast Guard cutters begin to appear in Florida ports, and others are sent out on patrol. The government calls this a diligent guarding of its coast, but the Spanish say it isn't much of an effort and send some ships of their own to prowl off Florida, an act the citizens of Key West call an invasion.

On the whole, however, the figures show that the government isn't being as half-hearted about it as the Spaniards claim. From 1895 until the end of 1896, seventy-one filibustering expeditions start out for Cuba, but only twenty-seven get there. About thirty-one vessels are involved constantly on behalf of the Junta.

All this commotion, following on the heels of the *Alliance* incident, wakes up public interest among Americans, who haven't thought much about Cuba until now. All they know is that on February 24, 1895, following the sporadic rebellion that those involved call the Ten Years' War, a little band of tattered revolutionaries gathered somewhere in the Cuban interior and elected a "president of the republic," although they control no port or city in Cuba and spend much of their time on the run from Spanish soldiers.

Is anyone willing to recognize this freshly minted government? Not the United States, certainly, but in New York, where William Randolph Hearst has just arrived from San Francisco to establish the *Journal*, the new republic acquires an ally who not only solemnly "recognizes" it in the pages of his newspaper but will do more than any single individual to push Americans into war with Spain to liberate the island, although not with the results the rebels anticipate.

At least the insurgents have a leader who is the essence of revolution, Máximo Gómez, whose shining ambition is to become the George Washington of Cuba. Gómez is a tough old bird, a Santo Domingan, stocky, with a flaring white mustache, short and unassuming, but the fire is in his eyes and often on his tongue. Another commander, General Antonio Maceo, is a mulatto who cuts a dashing figure. Beyond them in Cuba are ragged bands, hardly an army, carrying on a vicious guerrilla warfare, terrorizing the planters on their plantations, and the workers as well, burning their sugar cane fields and steadily reducing the sugar and tobacco industries which are Cuba's livelihood.

Farther away, in New York and other American cities, is the propaganda army whose intent is to keep the revolution going with all the money and supplies it can get and, if possible, to involve the United States. These former Cuban citizens are, many of them, cigar makers who have settled down in Key West, Jacksonville, New Orleans, New York, and other cities. They have a lobbyist in Washington, Gonzalo de Quesada, who calls himself "Cuban Revolutionary Chargé d'Affairés," although he has no diplomatic standing. Far more formidable, even if he doesn't look it, is Tomás Estrada Palma, once a schoolteacher but now heading the Junta in New York, dwelling modestly on Bleecker Street, living from hand to mouth, working night and day to raise money and to spread thick layers of propaganda on the public consciousness.

With no funds to rent an office, Palma works in rooms at 66 Broadway graciously shared by a sympathizer, Horatio Rubens, a New York lawyer. There the Junta operates on a more or less twenty-four-hour basis, organizing filibustering expeditions and acting as a "news agency," which translates to "propaganda mill." It supplies stories, a few of them actually true, about what is going on in Cuba and the reporters gather to hear them every afternoon at an informal briefing. They call it the "Peanut Club," because Rubens thoughtfully supplies them with peanuts as refreshment. The "news" they get is divided into two categories: tales of rebel victories and stories of Spanish atrocities. Estrada Palma's sources, he keeps telling them, are heroic Cubans who have risked their lives to bring the truth to Americans.

Since, in these days of intense competition, the reporters are not devoted to confirming stories, they print the tales as given; but most of them have nagging doubts, and they itch, as any good newsman would, to get down to Cuba and see for themselves. It won't be easy. Neither the Cuban nor the American government thinks this is a good idea. There's always the chance that the real truth, whatever it is, will leak out.

As for publishers, they don't want to rely on propaganda alone, even though it sells papers, and they're constantly embarrassed by printing stories that turn out to be blatant lies. General Maceo is reported killed--several times. Once it's a suicide. Gómez is said to have been killed in battle every few weeks, and Havana is regularly declared to be in the hands of the rebels. No wonder an American participant in the conflict says this war contains "a larger amount of lying than any before or since."

If there's any lying to be done, the newspapers and their correspondents intend to raise it to a new level. At least it will be *their* lies. They know that Cuba is now a gold mine of happenings. Stories trickle out, one of them about an American, Frederic Funston, who will shortly become a general and bring both glory and wrath on his head in the Philippines, but who is now fighting as a volunteer with the rebels in Oriente Province. Funston isn't entirely sympathetic to the insurgents, after he sees them scouring the country, "taking from the miserable people the last sweet potato, ear of corn, or banana that could be found."

A 21-year-old correspondent for one of the London papers, Winston Churchill, gives us a picture from the other side, after he charges with a small Spanish force across a clearing, on whose edge Cubans are skulking in the underbrush. "The insurgents are bad shots," Churchill advises his readers. "It appeared to me that tons of lead passed over the heads of General Valdez's staff, with whom I was. Three orderlies were wounded. My general conclusion is that European methods of warfare are almost out of the question in a wild countryside." As his British ancestors discovered when they came to America to fight another revolution.

With the public more curious every day to know what in the world is going on in Cuba, the press finds itself frustrated. The Spanish authorities are already irate at the few American reporters who have managed to get to Cuba and are sitting in comfortable chairs in Havana hotels, writing "eyewitness stories" supplied by obliging Junta informants, in which the Spaniards invariably emerge as jungle beasts. Even if the correspondents wanted to move out of the lobby, the authorities rigidly restrict the movements of reporters and censorship is tight. It's forbidden to travel inland, or to have anything to do with the rebel army.

In that case, the reporters are going to have to circumvent the authorities somehow, and that will require an ingenious kind of war correspondent who has no intention of sitting in a hotel lobby, taking handouts. Almost as though ordered, Sylvester "Harry" Scovel comes upon the scene. There will be bigger names covering this war--Richard Harding Davis, Stephen Crane, among others--but Scovel is the quintessential nineteenth-century reporter, a man without fear who will go anywhere and do anything to get a story.

Scovel's previous career has hardly prepared him for derring-do in Cuba. An Ohioan, he had been manager of the Cleveland Athletic Club and toyed briefly with the life insurance business at his father's insistence, but all the time he wanted to write. Only twenty-six in 1895, Harry came into the newspaper business at a time that author Irvin S. Cobb called "the era of the great reporter." He had begun by freelancing as a critic for Pittsburgh and Cleveland papers, but he yearns for the far larger drama of the foreign correspondent, or "traveling commissioners," as Hearst wants to call them. A few are already celebrities.

Harry Scovel gets into the Cuba affair by mere chance, covering a Liberty League rally in Pittsburgh, where he senses the rising public interest in the island's struggle and learns that not much accurate news is coming out of Cuba. He hears that it's a crime to consort with rebels, and already a New York *World* reporter has been arrested for trying to interview an insurgent commander. To the rescue! Scovel sees his opportunity and wastes no time grasping it. With just $200 in his pocket, he takes the train to New York and beards the *Herald*'s editor in his den, asserting that he will get the truth out of Cuba regardless of all difficulties. Amazingly, the editor believes him and says he will pay $24 a column for anything Scovel can smuggle out. Scovel says he intends to interview Gómez himself, although there's a small problem: he doesn't know Spanish. No matter. Harry immediately shows an astonishing grasp of how to be a big-time correspondent. He goes to Horatio Rubens at the Junta office, tells him what he intends to do, and gets a letter of introduction to Gómez.

But he still has a lot to learn. He takes a regular passenger boat to Cuba, and in a week he's back. Customs officials smelled a newspaper rat, searched him, and refused him entry--but not before he had chewed and swallowed the letter of introduction.

Rubens is consoling, writes him another letter, and suggests that he take the steamship *Niagara* to Cienfuegos, on the southern coast, where the officials are less alert. For good measure, Rubens gives him the name of a contact who will help him see Gómez. So Harry boards the *Niagara* and nobody hears a word from him for three months--the *Herald*, his family, or the Junta.

What has happened to him is a radical initiation into his chosen profession, as Joyce Milton, the best historian of the "yellow kids" of the "yellow press," tells us. Arriving at Cienfuegos in mid-October, Scovel finds that his contact has left town--"indefinitely." With only a little cash, he decides to get through the Spanish lines himself before the money runs out. This intrepid rank amateur simply tries to walk out of Cienfuegos at night and is stopped by a Spanish patrol on the edge of town. "The night was dark, I was much excited," Scovel recalls later. "I pretended to be an officer of the steamship *Niagara*, ashore on a toot." Incredibly, they accept his story, but they escort him back to his hotel, relieving him of his wristwatch and his remaining cash on the way.

Ten days later, Scovel tries it again, leaving luggage and an unpaid hotel bill behind. This time he makes it, and for the next two weeks wanders through the countryside, walking by night and hiding in the daytime, relying for food on the generosity of those he meets. By luck, he encounters a stranger who knows enough English to understand who he is and what he wants to do. The stranger gives him directions to Gómez's mountain hideout.

Harry turns up there on November 1, in desperate condition, ragged and half starved--but just in time to hear Gómez announce that he intends to invade the western provinces, with the immediate intention of destroying the cane crop. He expects much resistance, since 15,000 Spanish soldiers have arrived during the summer.

Scovel marches off with the rebel troops and on November 30 they encounter the new Spanish army near Sancti Spíritus, in southern Santa Clara Province. Scovel is not the only reporter to witness the ensuing battle. Young Winston Churchill is there for the London *Daily Graphic*, and has no high opinion of Gómez's little army. "They neither fight bravely nor do they use their weapons effectively," he reports. "They can neither win a single battle or hold a single town. Their army, consisting to a large degree of colored men, is an undisciplined rabble."

But Harry sees something Churchill doesn't. If the rebels are so inefficient, why have the Spaniards retreated back to their base, leaving ten of their number dead and abandoning a twenty-mule supply train? Granted, the rebels may not be able to fight in the approved fashion, but Scovel, who has read a little military science, understands that in guerrilla warfare the object is not to take territory but to demoralize the enemy. To him, the advance is "a march of intimidation and propagandism," and he's impressed by how much Gómez is able to do with so little.

Traveling with the general and his men, sharing their lot, Scovel witnesses the plundering of Matanzas Province, in central Cuba, where the rebels scorch the earth as they pass, not even sparing the property of American citizens, some of whom when the commander lashes out with his sword at a young porter, and at dinner one night Rea is taken aback by Gómez's frank opinion of his still unofficial allies. "You Americans don't know how to fight," he says. "You never did. You have been thrashed in every war since gaining your independence." It doesn't help that Gómez is equally brutal with fellow Cubans, who've been fighting by his side for years. Of course the general's incivility may be induced at times by the brandy he drinks to alleviate his chronic sciatica, but there are those who think what he really wants is to be a dictator.

When the troops move out on a raiding expedition, Scovel has a chance to get some mild revenge for Rea's initially denouncing him in Havana, which still rankles. Hoping to waylay a Spanish troop train, the rebels tear up a railroad track, but when the train appears it turns out to be the regular Havana express. Having looted the freight cars, they climb into the engine cab, trying to find out how it can be put out of commission. Scovel whispers to Gómez that Rea is actually an "expert engineer," who knows "more about railroads than any man on the island." The general then gives Rea the job of dismantling the engine.

Rea not only knows nothing of railroad engines, but he fears losing his noncombatant status. Seeing that the boiler pressure is only twenty pounds, he tells the rebels to destroy the blow-off valve, which releases a cloud of steam, taken as a sign of the engine's demise. Gómez immediately offers to make Rea his chief engineer.

The rather uneasy truce between Scovel and Rea continues as the two men march on with General Gómez. At one point they're ambushed by Spanish troops and nearly killed. Scovel, thrown from his horse, runs after his mount in a hail of bullets, almost tripping over the ankle-length mackintosh flapping around his calves. Somehow he catches the horse.

As time goes on, the two reporters learn still more about the rebel commander's personality, which will soon come in conflict with those of American generals. On a Santa Lucía ranch in Hoyo Colorado, Gómez sits in the living room of the ranch house, calmly working his way through a stack of American newspapers while a Spanish column 2,000 strong is marching down the main road. When an artillery shell nearly knocks him out of his chair, he gives his troops the order: "Scatter!"

only what he says he is but, like Bowen, is also the son of a college president. Bowen asks Scovel what he wants to do, and Scovel tells him simply, "I want to make a reputation as a war correspondent."

Fair enough. Bowen cables his managing editor and gets permission to hire Scovel, who is immediately released and ordered deported, but that's only to soothe the Loyalists. While Scovel is waiting for papers from the military court, George Rea comes to visit him, full of apologies. He's heard from Bowen who Scovel really is, has cabled the *Herald* editor who had hired him, and heard a dismaying story.

Not long after Scovel was hired, this editor was fired, it appears, so that when the new correspondent's dispatches arrived, they were either destroyed or sent on to the deposed editor. One story managed to get through, and appeared without a byline, standard *Herald* practice. Realizing its mistake, the New York office now tells Rea to pay Scovel $27 for the story that was printed--more than twice the usual rate. Scovel sees the grim humor in the situation, especially when Rea tells him that a few days earlier *he* had almost been thrown into jail, suspected of being El Inglesito. But Harry doesn't forgive the *Herald*, and a lengthy feud is born.

This tall, lanky redhead from Brooklyn, in his twenties, who studied electrical engineering at Stevens, tells Harry that he's about to go in search of Gómez himself to get an interview. "I wish you luck," Harry says, as the two sit in a café drinking whiskey. "I'd be glad to introduce you to the old man."

Rea leaves Havana on January 18, a week later falls in with Colonel Pedro Díaz, who is on his way to meet Gómez at temporary headquarters set up in an abandoned sugar plantation in the southwestern part of the province. When Gómez's army arrives, Rea is impressed by these several thousand mounted men, ill dressed and ill equipped though they are. From Scovel's enthusiastic description of the general, however, he expected to see an impressive elder statesman, but his first glimpse of Gómez is disappointing. The general, he wrote later, is a "chocolate-colored old man, who gave me the idea of a resurrected Egyptian mummy." That's one shock. The second is more severe. Riding behind Gómez is Harry Scovel.

Further acquaintance doesn't improve Rea's opinion of the general. He sees an exhibition of the famous Gómez temper when the commander lashes out with his sword at a young porter, and at dinner one night Rea is taken aback by Gómez's frank opinion of his still unofficial allies. "You Americans don't know how to fight," he says. "You never did. You have been thrashed in every war since gaining your independence." It doesn't help that Gómez is equally brutal with fellow Cubans, who've been fighting by his side for years. Of course the general's incivility may be induced at times by the brandy he drinks to alleviate his chronic sciatica, but there are those who think what he really wants is to be a dictator.

When the troops move out on a raiding expedition, Scovel has a chance to get some mild revenge for Rea's initially denouncing him in Havana, which still rankles. Hoping to waylay a Spanish troop train, the rebels tear up a railroad track, but when the train appears it turns out to be the regular Havana express. Having looted the freight cars, they climb into the engine cab, trying to find out how it can be put out of commission. Scovel whispers to Gómez that Rea is actually an "expert engineer," who knows "more about railroads than any man on the island." The general then gives Rea the job of dismantling the engine.

Rea not only knows nothing of railroad engines, but he fears losing his noncombatant status. Seeing that the boiler pressure is only twenty pounds, he tells the rebels to destroy the blow-off valve, which releases a cloud of steam, taken as a sign of the engine's demise. Gómez immediately offers to make Rea his chief engineer.

The rather uneasy truce between Scovel and Rea continues as the two men march on with General Gómez. At one point they're ambushed by Spanish troops and nearly killed. Scovel, thrown from his horse, runs after his mount in a hail of bullets, almost tripping over the ankle-length mackintosh flapping around his calves. Somehow he catches the horse.

As time goes on, the two reporters learn still more about the rebel commander's personality, which will soon come in conflict with those of American generals. On a Santa Lucía ranch in Hoyo Colorado, Gómez sits in the living room of the ranch house, calmly working his way through a stack of American newspapers while a Spanish column 2,000 strong is marching down the main road. When an artillery shell nearly knocks him out of his chair, he gives his troops the order: "Scatter!"

They do, and in minutes a thousand rebels and several hundred of their horses have disappeared into the cane fields.

Scovel thinks this is pure genius. Rea calls it "a Coney Island handicap," and "shameful." He takes an upper-class view: gentlemen don't run from a fair fight even if they're outnumbered, and some of the general's glory-seeking younger officers agree with him.

As for the general, during the retreat he suffers a cavalry officer's ultimate insult: his horse is shot in the rump. This doesn't improve the Gómez temper. That night at dinner, he looses a frontal assault on Rea. "By what right, Mr. Rea," he says, "do you sit at my table and eat? How do I know you are not a Spanish spy in disguise?" Obviously he intends to get rid of Rea, and even offers him ten gold pieces if he'll join General Maceo's army. Rea can hardly avoid the hint. Maceo arrives the next morning and Rea leaves with him later, while Scovel departs for Havana.

This is the first time we've had a good look at Maceo, the revolution's other major leader. They call him "the Bronze Titan," and in many ways he is Gómez's superior. A son of peasants and self-educated, Maceo is a man without fear. He has been wounded a dozen times in the Ten Years' War. Celebrated for never refusing a fight, off the battlefield he's a philosopher. Rea gets along much better with him than with Gómez for the next two and a half months of thirty-five skirmishes and guerrilla tactics.

Rea even manages to overcome, a little, the racism that's going to permeate this war. "I could not help but feel a certain admiration," he writes, "for the man who, despite his color, was so far the superior of the many 'opera bouffe' generals in the Cuban Army of Liberation. When the enemy did not bother him for a few days, he went out looking for them, to remind them that he was still alive."

Scovel arrives in Havana to find that everything has changed. Up to now, the American public has been reading the kind of stories he and Rea, among others, have been sending back, describing what's happening in the interior while their colleagues sitting at the curbside tables of the Inglaterra Hotel retail whatever they can get by the censors, much of it highly unflattering to the Spaniards, which is ironic because the hotel is owned and operated by middle-class Spanish Loyalists.

What has changed is the arrival on February 10 of Valeriano Weyler y Nicolau, the new military governor. Madrid has decided that Arsenio Martínez Campos, his predecessor, has permitted things to get out of hand and recalled him. Weyler, an ambitious politician and military tactician, has been instructed to do whatever needs to be done to put down the rebellion.

The new governor is actually of German descent, as his blue eyes attest. Soon he will be known as "Weyler the Butcher," thanks to the *World* and the *Journal*, but first impressions don't justify the portrait of him painted by the Junta in advance of his coming. A series of atrocity stories (planted first in the New York papers, then widely circulated across America) depict Weyler's alleged conduct during the Ten Years' War, especially an incident known as "the dance of Guáimaro." This is supposedly described in a history of the conflict written by Manuel de la Cruz, now dead, and quoted in a "press release" written by the Junta lobbyist, Gonzalo de Quesada. De la Cruz wrote, if in fact he did: "The Dance of Guáimaro is famous in Puerto Principe. He (Weyler) captured a number of ladies of the best society of this province. They were taken to the village of Guáimaro. Around a large bonfire in the public square, he placed the defenseless women. The ferocious hordes of negros [sic] who comprised the fourth company of the command were ordered to violently undress the prisoners. They then played an African dance, and the unfortunate Cubans who refused to participate were whipped by Weyler himself."

Quesada followed up this scare story with a letter to the New York *Post*, asserting that survivors of the dance were still alive in Puerto Principe Province. If so, none of them came forward to confirm the story.

Gómez is no doubt one of the few people delighted by Weyler's arrival, because, with the help of Junta propaganda, he believes the "butcher" can be counted on to stir the sympathies of America. "Our Philip II," he calls the new governor.

The general's hopes are rapidly being realized. In New York, Hearst's *Journal* and Pulitzer's *World*, with the *Sun* trailing after, have been spreading atrocity stories on their front pages for some time, and with Weyler's arrival, they burst out in full cry, their sensational accounts picked up and reprinted by newspapers across the country.

William Randolph Hearst, publisher, New York Journal

– Corbis-Bettman

The *Journal* is the worst, as the idea grows in Hearst's mind that his unfeigned sympathy for the Cubans is also a boon to circulation, and in time he will believe that it's really his and the *Journal*'s war. His reporters stop at nothing. The paper declares that it's "the daily practice of the Spanish jailers to take several prisoners from the forts and prisons and shoot them." A headline proclaims: "FEEDING PRISONERS TO SHARKS." Another story describes how captives are drowned at night. Still others tell of how the brutal Spaniards are attacking hospitals, raping women, poisoning wells, throwing nuns into prison, and "roasting twenty-five Catholic priests alive."

Weyler's arrival stirs the paper to an even higher pitch. The *Journal* is first to call him "the Butcher," and describes him to its horrified readers as "Weyler the brute, the devastator of haciendas, the destroyer of families, and the outrager of women...pitiless, cold, an exterminator of men. There is nothing to prevent his carnal, animal brain from running riot with itself in inventing tortures and infamies of bloody debauchery."

Can this be the same man the paper's own reporter, Kate Masterson, a celebrated sob sister, describes when she somehow manages to ingratiate herself with the general and gets an exclusive interview? He takes her into his private suite in the governor's palace and proudly hauls out pictures of his wife and children he had to leave behind in Spain. He shows her around and confesses he has a secret place he's proud of--a superbly appointed bathroom with a huge tub, complete with a shower activated by a brass pull chain. Since she's writing for Hearst, Kate has to pretend that she's scandalized by the piles of Turkish towels and the lavish use of hot water when the poor Cubans are suffering, but she has a hard time working up even a mild outrage. In her story, Weyler comes out, in Joyce Milton's words, as a "lonely, rather monkish old man."

Is this the same chap the New York papers have been describing? Is *he* the one responsible for killing "defenseless, harmless people hiding in their own homes?" Somehow a dispatch from William Bowen slips through and puzzled readers of the *World* learn that Weyler is really just a good soldier, with an undeserved reputation for cruelty, "a man of extraordinary energy and great intelligence."

Heresy! Pulitzer at once dispatches a young correspondent named James Creelman, who gets things back on track, writing from Havana that "no man's life, no man's property is safe, American citizens are imprisoned or slain without cause, American property is destroyed on all sides." Somehow he also obtains an interview with Weyler, and the portrait that emerges is anything but "lonely" or "monkish." Weyler is no less than "the most sinister figure of the nineteenth century," as Creelman recalls later in his memoirs. He even finds Weyler repulsive physically. "His head was too large for his body. His forehead was narrow, the nose and jaws prominent and bony; the chin heavy and projecting. The sharp lower teeth were thrust out beyond the upper rows, giving the mouth a singular expression of brutal determination. The eyes were gray and cold. The voice was harsh and guttural...and he jerked out his words in the curt manner of a man accustomed to absolute authority. It was a smileless, cruel face, with just a suggestion of treachery in the crows' feet about the eyes; otherwise bold and masterful."

The interview does not go well. Weyler tells him that his government "will not yield an inch to force or to threats of force," and "We shall crush the insurgents like that," closing his hand "as though he were strangling something." Weyler says he would have no problem at all if it weren't for the Americans: "The Cubans are fighting us openly; the Americans are fighting us secretly." Then he falls back on the common complaint of politicians: "The American newspapers are responsible. They poison everything with falsehood. They should be suppressed."

When Creelman attempts to argue that the newspapers didn't organize or arm the insurgents, and asks why the Cubans are fighting at all, Weyler says they are lawless, and when Creelman reminds him that Spain has controlled the island for four hundred years and inquires who made the Cubans lawless, Weyler strikes the table furiously with his fist and snarls, "Men like you, who excite rebellion everywhere--meddlesome scribblers." Then he warns Creelman: "I have a long arm. The penalty for trafficking with the insurgents is death; do you understand that--death!"

At this moment, they're interrupted by a small, pale man who slips in and lays some papers on the general's desk. Creelman recognizes him as a rebel spy, a mole in the palace. As the man leaves, he glances over his shoulder at Weyler, whose back is turned, smiles at Creelman, and raises his eyebrows.

Then the interview ends with another threat: "Remember," says Weyler, "you will be watched in all that you do here. My eyes will be on you night and day."

Creelman leaves the presence, a little shaken. He needs a drink. Sitting in the Café Inglaterra having one, he is abruptly joined by another American wearing a business suit badly in need of pressing and an aging derby--a sharp contrast to the Spanish officers in their full-dress uniforms who occupy most of the tables.

"Nice evening," the stranger offers.

Creelman takes a second look. It's Harry Scovel. "Great God!" he says. "Don't you know they're looking for you?"

"Yes, I know," Scovel says conversationally. "They're looking for me, but this is the last place they'll expect to find me. But don't whisper. It will excite suspicion. I've dropped my identity for the present. I'm Mr. Brown--Mr. Brown of New York--traveling about in search of a chance to make good investments."

Disguise is certainly necessary. Scovel has filed truly scurrilous stories about Spanish oppression and Butcher Weyler, besides an exclusive interview with Gómez and a personal message from the general to the American people which the *World* published on February 22. Weyler has put a $25,000 price on his head, dead or alive.

Until now, Creelman supposed Scovel had been hiding in the hills. Instead, the wanted man says, he's been in New York for six weeks. On February 4, while he was with General Maceo, observing a skirmish between the general's bodyguard and a Spanish patrol, he had suffered a leg wound. When it became infected, he was smuggled into Havana, where a United States Health Service consular official got him onto a tramp steamer, disguised as an American businessman going home to be treated for tropical fever.

In New York, Scovel has met his *World* employers for the first time--Bradford Merrill, the editor, and Pulitzer himself. He's been offered $60 a week and $400 expense money to go on doing what he's been doing. His friendship with Gómez now has real value. So he's returned to Cuba via Key West, and we get an idea of how the correspondents and the Junta are working together, although with different motives, to advance the rebel cause.

On April 1, 1896, José Dolores Poyo, who's the Junta's agent in Key West, informed New York: "Last night, eleven of the expeditionaries who were here embarked for Cuba, armed, equipped with 100 cartridges each, and serving as the escort of my good friend, the *World* correspondent, Sylvester Scovel, who is once again marching to the front of the revolution."

This time Harry didn't get to the front. The schooner *Martha*, carrying him and the "expeditionaries," was met by a Spanish gunboat patrol and they were lucky to get back to Bahía Honda, the *Martha's* home port. Undiscouraged, Scovel went to Key West and borrowed the clothes and identification papers of Harry Brown, a *World* reporter there, and has slipped back into Havana unchallenged on a regularly scheduled Ward Line schooner.

As he finishes unfolding this story to Creelman in the Café Inglaterra, he adds that Pulitzer wants them to investigate reports of Spanish atrocities against civilians and "document" them. From what follows, it seems that the publisher and his reporters may have different notions of documentation, which is not to say that there isn't enough oppression and cruelty going on in Cuba.

Scovel and Creelman begin to send back horrible stories to the *World*, supposedly sworn to by witnesses, of food and water poisoned by the Spanish, wounded prisoners butchered, Cuban women raped, a drunken Spanish major who killed fifty Cubans single-handed, old men and little boys cut down and their bodies fed to hungry dogs, and other atrocities that have become "almost a religion" to the Spanish soldier.

Scovel writes of slaughtered prisoners: "The skulls of all were split in pieces down to the eyes. Some of these were gouged out. All the bodies had been stabbed by sword bayonets and hacked by sabers until I could not count the cuts; they were indistinguishable. The bodies had almost lost semblance of human form. The arms and legs of one had been dismembered and laced into a rude attempt at a five point [sic] Cuban star. The tongue of one had been cut out, split open at the base and placed on the mangled forehead. Fingers and toes were missing. The Spanish soldiers habitually cut off the ears of the Cuban dead and retain them as trophies."

No wonder Weyler imposes a strict censorship and deports the reportorial offenders he can lay hands on. He denies all the horror stories, of course, but at the same time he grumbles, "How do they want me to wage war? With bishops' pastorals and presents of sweets and money?"

He has an ally in George Rea, who is so indignant over Cuban coverage that he writes a book titled *Facts and Fakes About Cuba*, exposing scores of frauds. Nevertheless, as William Swanberg notes in his biography of Pulitzer, "Millions of words of pure fiction appeared in print."

By mid-1897, Weyler has quite a crowd of correspondents to deal with. There are nearly forty reporters in Key West, representing papers from all over America, most of them trying to get into Cuba, some content to exploit rumors. Eight of them are what Hearst calls "journal commissioners," and among them is the legendary Richard Harding Davis, the beau ideal of the war correspondent, and an altogether remarkable figure in his own right. Davis had agreed to sign on for a month as a commissioner, at the unheard-of figure of $3,000--and expenses, which in his case are likely to be heavy.

Americans already know about Davis. For one thing, he's lent his tall, square-jawed, pink-cheeked body to his friend, Charles Dana Gibson, who has drawn him as the male equivalent of the elegant, romanticized, aloof Gibson Girl. To those who view the results in the old *Life* magazine, he seems the epitome of "muscular Christianity." A less hypnotized critic writes that on a typical day Davis experiences "shrapnel, chivalry and sauce Mousseline, and so to work the next morning on an article."

Davis has the habit observed in highly egocentric men of referring to himself in the third person. He's a born snob, too, but underneath it all there's something else, as his friend Augustus Thomas, the playwright, has pointed out. "At his very best," says Gus, "he was in heart and mind a boy grown tall." Davis is a son of privilege, whose mother, the popular novelist, Rebecca Harding Davis, idolizes him, refers to his younger brother Charles as "a sequel to the story--an afterpiece," and scarcely mentions his sister Nora.

As a student at Lehigh, Davis appeared at classes dressed in suits of the finest English woolens, wearing kid gloves and carrying a cane. Already an opportunistic writer, he got out press releases about his academic accomplishments and sent them to the papers, so that even before they handed him a diploma, he was the best-known undergraduate in the country. After graduation, he began his journalistic career on the Philadelphia *Record* and the New York *Sun*, where Arthur Brisbane, in his pre-Hearst days, became his close friend. No newspaper could contain Davis, however. He branched out into fiction and created a character called Courtland Van Bibber, who wore a top hat and Inverness cap and was an obvious projection of Davis himself.

Attracted quite naturally to the most romantic aspect of newspaper work, the life of a foreign correspondent, Davis had become a roving reporter for *Harper's Weekly*, covering brush fires in the Middle East and Central America. His prose might be arrogant but it's never boring once you accept his basic premise that only Anglo-Saxons are fit to run the world. Before he went to work for Hearst, he proved himself human by suffering from sciatica and what he calls "nervous storms," which inexplicably were accompanied by feelings of worthlessness.

Milton believes that part of Davis' psychological problem was the fact that, at thirty, he was still a virgin. That did not prevent him from having unconsummated (presumably) affairs with Helen Benedict, one of the day's better-know-heiresses; the blossoming actress Maude Adams; and Ethel Barrymore, a promising teenager.

But certainly there's something wrong. He can't even kiss the bride at a friend's wedding, and complains that women he meets are simply not fastidious enough for him. Until he encounters Princess Alex of Hesse at the Acropolis. Alex is fastidious enough for anyone, but the dashing correspondent found himself too shy to ask for an introduction. Instead, he projected her as the heroine of a popular novel about a young American writer who falls in love with a photograph of his dream woman. Naturally, the book was titled *The Princess*.

Recovering from this distant infatuation, Davis fell under the spell of Yvette Guilbert, the French singer of whom the music critic of the *World* said, "She has the loveliest neck in New York." She was also having a full-time affair with her business manager, whom she eventually married, but in the meantime, she was not above using poor, mooning Davis for all the publicity value that could be extracted.

Disillusioned again, Davis was ready to listen when Hearst asked him if he'd like to go to Moscow and cover a wedding. It was a shock when he heard that the bride was Princess Alex, but he wanted to see Moscow even if he had to suffer. As it happened, the trip proved to be disastrous from every standpoint, and back in New York again, he jumped at the chance when Hearst inquired if he'd like to cover the Cuban insurrection.

The transportation is to be Hearst's own yacht, the *Vamoose*, a 112-foot super fast steam vessel. She fairly skims out of New York Harbor, but then her crew, who were hired in Newport, learn for the first time that this is not a pleasure cruise but a trip to the war zone where Spanish torpedo boats are lurking. The men wait until they get to Florida and then go on strike. Davis retires to the veranda of the Key West Hotel. He's beginning to think Hearst is a jinx.

While he's sitting there, his new boss fields another war correspondent whom he entrusts with a mission which tells us a great deal about the madness that is developing. Ralph Delahaye Paine, a minister's son from Jacksonville, whom Milton describes as a "muscular six-footer, with jug ears, and a pleasant but slightly goofy smile," has been going nowhere on the Philadelphia *Press*. Somehow he hears the name of the Junta's Jacksonville organizer, José Huau, and it strikes a distant chord of memory. José owns the corner cigar store and soda fountain where young Paine used to buy his ice cream cones.

When Paine suggests to the *Press*'s editor that this connection might lead to Cuba, he's rejected out of hand and consequently comes up to New York to see Hearst, who welcomes him. The publisher has just heard that Davis and the illustrator, Frederic Remington, who's with him, are stranded in Key West. Maybe Paine will do better. Besides, he has an idea with all kinds of circulation possibilities.

Rummaging around in a closet, Hearst pulls out a large mahogany case and removes from it a dress sword fit for an emperor, gold-plated, with a diamond-encrusted hilt, and a scabbard with elaborate decorations. Hearst tells Paine that at a recent Cuban-American fair in New York the *Journal* had conducted an auction, giving visitors a chance to vote for the "world's greatest living soldier." No one is surprised when General Gómez wins hands down. In recognition of this exalted position, the Cuban leader is to be given this $2,000 token of Hearstian and Cuban-American esteem. The problem is how to get it to him. Paine is the solution, Hearst decides; he will be the messenger--if he agrees.

Pulling out the sword, Hearst shows Paine that the blade is inscribed with "Viva Cuba Libre," and "To Máximo Gómez, Commander-in-Chief of the Army of the Republic of Cuba," which of course doesn't exist. Paine admires the sword but he's momentarily chilled by the idea of delivering it.

"I suppose," Hearst says meditatively, "that these inscriptions would be devilish hard to explain to the Spanish army, if you happened to be caught, wouldn't they? I swear, I don't know what else to do with the confounded thing. Of course, if you're nabbed at sea, you can probably chuck it overboard in time."

Getting into the spirit of the thing, Paine replies, "And if I get surrounded on land, perhaps I can swallow it." But he can't let the opportunity go. "Never mind," he adds, "I'm the damn fool you're looking for."

Meanwhile, back at the Key West Hotel, Davis and Remington have negotiated a deal with the crew of the *Vamoose* to take them on to Cuba, but when the ship gets into open seas, it wallows around so badly that Davis can see it's not a reliable craft. Worse, when they sight Cuban shores, the captain makes three passes at the island and has to turn back every time because of engine trouble. Davis sits in his cabin and writes to his mother: "I lay on the deck and cried when he refused to go ahead." Back in Tampa, the intrepid "commissioners" take a regularly scheduled Plant Line boat to Havana without any trouble.

Once there, boredom sets in. Weyler is severely restricting all the correspondents, after booting out a few, and there is nothing much for the press to do except transform Junta handouts into atrocity stories. Remington is so bored that he begins drinking heavily, until one day in desperation he sends a famous telegram to Hearst: "EVERYTHING IS QUIET. THERE IS NO TROUBLE HERE. THERE WILL BE NO WAR. WISH TO RETURN. REMINGTON." To which Hearst fires back an equally famous reply: "PLEASE REMAIN. YOU FURNISH THE PICTURES AND I'LL FURNISH THE WAR. HEARST." He means it, too, and millions of Americans will go on believing he did, but inventing this war will take more than Hearst's rabid journalism.

Davis encourages Remington to leave anyway, for reasons he explains to his mother after the artist disobeys orders and departs--soon to return, however. Davis writes: "I am so relieved at getting old Remington to go that I feel as though I had won $5,000. He was a splendid fellow but a perfect kid and had to be humored and petted all the time."

By now, all the principal actors in the correspondents' war are on the scene or about to be, but one who is not present, after a false start, will come back later and overshadow even the great Davis. Stephen Crane is a most unlikely newspaperman. The city editor fired him from his first job as a *Herald* stringer because, as he said, the man couldn't write. He was not careful with the facts, grammar sometimes eluded him, and his style tended to be overblown. Never mind; he could write fiction, and by 1894 his career as a short-story writer and novelist was well under way. *The Red Badge of Courage* was an instant success and an authentic classic.

Crane has an avid fan: Theodore Roosevelt, then New York City police commissioner. They met at the Lantern Club, a hangout for young and literary newspapermen, and became casual friends. Crane sent him a Western story he'd written, which T.R. was mildly critical of because a "Mexican greaser" outwits a noble frontiersman. Someday, Roosevelt told him, he should write a story where the outcome is reversed, because "it's more normal that way."

In late 1895, as things are beginning to heat up in Cuba, another Lantern Club friend, Irving Batcheller, who's running a struggling news syndicate, invites Crane to be his correspondent in Cuba.

Hoping to see a real war, Crane accepts. He arrives in Jacksonville in the middle of November with $700 in gold as expense money and checks in at the St. James Hotel, the city's best. Jacksonville, he finds, is instant boredom. Later he writes: "The town looks like soiled pasteboard that some lunatic babies have been playing with. The same old women are sitting on the hotel porches saying how well the climate suits them and hurling the same lances with their eyes to begin bloodshed." Bored, Crane turns to a real time-killer, Tolstoy's *"Peace and War,"* as he calls it, and delivers a verdict echoed by thousands: "He could have done the whole business in one third the time and made it just as wonderful. He goes on and on like Texas."

There are other diversions, however. Making a friend of the man who runs the lobby newsstand, "Cap" Norton, he accepts the retired skipper's invitation to inspect "the line," town's red-light district, and there, at the Hotel de Dreme, which masquerades as a nightclub, he meets his soulmate, thirty-one-year-old Cora Taylor, known to everyone as "Miss Cora," whom Milton calls one of "the most exceptional and fascinating women of her time." Her body is lush, her clothes elegant, and her mind brilliant. She's just read Crane's novel, *George's Mother*, which he autographs for her, and it's now a toss-up whether he will ever leave Cora for Cuba.

In the weekend following Thanksgiving, another guest checks into the St. James Hotel. It's Harry Scovel, accompanied by Horatio Rubins, who's there for a meeting of Junta men. Scovel is looking for a boat that will get him to Cuba. Waiting for the *World* to send him a filibuster craft, he passes the time with Crane and Cora, and the two men become close friends.

Then, early in December, Ralph Paine checks into the St. James, on his way to Cuba with Gómez's ceremonial sword. It turns out that he's an old acquaintance of Crane from the days when Stephen was stringing stories from the Jersey shore and Paine was working for the Philadelphia *Press*. Things are now getting a little crowded at the Hotel de Dreme, because Scovel and Crane are making it clear they want as little as possible to do with Paine.

A miniature war breaks out. Paine tells them about the sword and Scovel, Gómez's friend, is outraged. The money it represents would rescue a Cuban village from starvation, he says, and provide shirts for the general's entire army. "I hope for your sake you never get to deliver that sword," he tells Paine, "because the Old Man will know where to stick it."

This jolly little group breaks up when Paine finds that a tug called the *Three Friends*, most famous of the filibustering craft, is loading in port, with cases marked "prime lard" which really contain prime munitions, along with other containers of condensed milk and salted codfish equally lethal. Paine hops on board this boat on the night of December 13, convinced he's going to beat his colleagues at the Hotel de Dreme.

Scovel has other things on his mind. After five false alarms, it is confirmed that General Maceo is really dead this time, although how it was done is a mystery. Rumors are thick. Some say poison. Others simply "killed in action." The *World* doesn't believe anyone at first and carries, instead of an obituary, one of Scovel's interviews, now months old. All of this fills Harry with the determination to get to Piñar del Río and find out for himself how his friend Maceo died.

While he's looking for transportation, Paine and the motley passenger list of the *Three Friends*--including Cuban volunteers, some mercenaries, and two American deserters--are in trouble. The ship was followed down the St. James River from Jacksonville by a suspicious United States revenue cutter. "Dynamite Johnny" O'Brien, the skipper, tries for four days to shake his pursuer, rambling up and down the coast, and just after he breaks away cleanly, the *Three Friends* takes on one more passenger--Scovel.

Harry's presence often means trouble, and this is no exception. A Spanish gunboat ambushes the *Three Friends* at the mouth of the San Juan River. The Cuban volunteers, delighted to find war so easily available, fire off their new Mausers, while the mercenaries ready the Hotchkiss gun. It proves to be the decisive weapon. The first shot is a direct hit, the gunboat sends up distress rockets, and is ready to surrender. But then another gunboat appears, and Dynamite Johnny escapes by sending out a lantern on a makeshift raft, decoying the Spaniards.

Having escaped, Captain O'Brien has no wish to take his cargo back to Jacksonville, so he deposits it, along with most of his passengers, on a tiny island called No Name Key, off Florida. Paine and Edward McCready, another correspondent, are furious to be left high and dry while Scovel returns to Jacksonville with O'Brien. A small schooner arrives at No Name nine days later, bringing supplies and a message from O'Brien. He's chartered another filibustering boat, the *Dauntless*, and will try again. But Paine and McCready, whose only object is to file stories, persuade the supply boat's skipper to take them to Key West. There they find that Scovel's account of their frustrated voyage has appeared in the *World* on Christmas Day, billed in the headlines: "FIRST NAVAL BATTLE OF THE CUBAN WAR." It's no consolation to Paine and McCready that well-wishers give them a banquet at Palacho's Café.

Next day, Paine gets a copy of his own paper, the *Journal*, and finds alarming headlines: "THREE FRIENDS FILIBUSTERERS IN FEAR FOR THEIR LIVES. If Convicted of the Crime They Will Be Sentenced to Death. The Hotchkiss Gun Plays an Important Part in Charges. Administration Will Prosecute." Shaken, Paine goes to the barbershop and finds

Davis there, buried under a pile of hot towels, getting a facial. Davis generously offers to lend him the *Vamoose* to take him back to No Name so he can catch O'Brien and the *Dauntless*, renewing the assault on Cuba.

There had already been another bizarre incident in this already bizarre war. As the *Vamoose* steamed into Key West, some Cuban seamen who were ferrying guns and ammunition to the *Dauntless* mistook Hearst's yacht for a revenue cutter and they panicked, throwing some of their cargo into the sea. Emilio Numez, a Cuban general in command of the *Dauntless*, was so furious that now he won't let Paine and McCready come onto the ship, relenting only under threat of bribery. But when the ship gets to a safe landing in Cuba, he refuses to let them leave the boat and takes them back to Jacksonville.

The news there is not good. Several members of the failed *Three Friends* expedition, including Dynamite Johnny, have been indicted for piracy. Scovel and McCready have slipped the net, since their stories of the venture were published anonymously, but Paine got a byline from the *Journal* and now he's on the lam, hiding out first in an obscure hotel. Then, with the help of his father and false papers, he moves from one hideout to another until it appears that the case will never be tried because of sheer inertia. This happy circumstance derives from the fact that the tug's owner, Napoleon Broward, is also the Jacksonville sheriff and no witness can be found who'll appear before a grand jury.

Coming out of hiding, Paine gets his old job back in Philadelphia, and with the help of his friend José Huau at the cigar store, he arranges to have the ceremonial sword delivered to Gómez's wife, who is in Santo Domingo.

It's quite a chore getting to Cuba, obviously. Crane leaves Jacksonville for the island on December 29 on a small, elderly steamer called the *Commodore*, commanded by another valiant Irishman, Edward Murphy. It is carrying a cargo of cased guns and a ton of cartridges, besides the usual complement of Cuban recruits. Her departure has been attended by threats shouted from the pier, and an overheard muttered threat, "It's all fixed. She will sink."

Passing from the St. James River into open sea, the *Commodore* runs into a squall and, by the time she's off St. Augustine, begins to take on water. The Cubans are already seasick, and Crane was ill when the voyage began. The ship begins to founder, and as Crane writes later, she "shifted and settled as calmly as an animal curls down in the bush-grass." Everyone piles into the ship's three dinghies, and watches as the *Commodore* slips under the waters without a struggle.

In the ten-foot dinghy, besides Crane, are the captain, who's been injured, the ship's cook, and an oiler, all of whom appear later as characters in one of Crane's best-known stories, "The Open Boat." With the help of wind and oars, they row toward Mosquito Inlet, whose lighthouse they can see every time the dinghy crests on a wave. People on the beach see them and wave, not realizing they're in trouble. Night comes on and there's still no rescue; sharks are circling the craft. At first light, the refugees head for shore and eventually they have to swim for it. Everyone gets there safely except for the oiler, killed by a crashing wave.

Crane survives but he's not in good shape. Still suffering from intestinal problems, he's been fifty hours without sleep or food except diluted whisky and biscuit. His brother says later that this event was the turning point and Crane never regained his health. He's given up on Cuba for the time being, but there are other lands, other wars, and before long he'll be off to cover the conflict between Greece and Turkey for the *Journal*. When the real war in Cuba begins, with America's declaration, he'll be back.

Events are now rushing everyone toward a conflict that no one except the American public and the yellow press seems to want. Weyler, carrying out his order to take strong measures, does so and it is the key to what follows. He decrees: "I order and command that all the inhabitants of the country now out-side...the towns, shall, within...eight days, concentrate them-selves in the towns. An individual who after the expiration of this period is found in the uninhabited parts will be considered a rebel and tried as such."

What Weyler has done is to invent the concentration camp. He's moving the entire rural population into what he calls *zonas de reconcentración*, areas clustered around fortified cities and towns. To make this horrendous mass movement possible, he recruits a little army of cub *guerrilleros*, as they're termed, who will do what no one else wants to do. Then he orders the building of a twenty-three-mile-long barrier of barbed wire, supplemented by earthwork fortifications, from Mariel in the north to Majana in the south. That keeps the *reconcentrados* in and the rebel armies out, and those who try to cross it will have to deal with a barrier electrically lighted, complete with artillery and 15,000 troops.

News of this development, splashed all over America in newsprint, escalates public rage and puts more pressure on Congress and the White House to do something about it. The newly elected President William McKinley calls it "not civilized warfare but extermination," and on the eve of his inauguration in March 1897, says fervently to retiring President Cleveland in the White House: "If I can only go out of office at the end of my term with the knowledge that I have done what lay in my power to avert this terrible calamity with the success that crowned your patience and persistence, I shall be the happiest man in the world."

The war will be over in Cuba before an assassin's bullet strikes McKinley, but its end will bring him no happiness, and from the beginning of his first term, he's going to be in a state of siege as the events of 1897 guarantee the war of 1898.

For what Weyler has done is to commit a fundamental error. By reconcentrating the rural population, who make the economy of Cuba workable, he has sharply diminished the island's food supply, which has already been much diminished by Gómez's burn-and-destroy campaigns, so now everyone will have trouble getting enough to eat. The failures of such filibustering craft as the *Three Friends* and the *Commodore* lead the Junta to suspend deliveries for a few months, and that worsens matters. A crisis approaches inexorably. Weyler's strict censorship not only complicates the problems of the correspondents, but leads them into even wilder attempts to evade it and encourages pro-rebel reporting, which in turn elevates the public blood pressure in America.

In short, the stage is set for a series of events in 1897 and early 1898 that will push the United States into a war whose outcome is never in doubt but whose results reverberate today.

2

ESCALATING THE PROPAGANDA WAR

WEYLER IS IN A STATE OF GROWING FRUSTRATION. IS THERE NO way to stop these American scribblers from telling lies about him and his administration? He's tried deporting them, but either they sneak back into the country or they're replaced. Worse, the New York papers have discovered that by reporting his persecution of journalists they've astonished and alarmed Madrid. The authorities there may find it hard to comprehend why so much public excitement exists in America over the jailing or deporting of a few reporters, but they're not yet contemplating war with the United States and they regard this as dangerous agitation. They instruct Weyler to stop.

This requires more restraint than the general is capable of, particularly when he reads what Hearst's new correspondent, Frederick W. Lawrence, is writing. Lawrence has developed the job of covering an insurrection from a table at the Café Inglaterra into a fine art. His laziness is surpassed only by his imagination. He's producing vivid stories about a wholly imaginary campaign, reporting, for example, how General Maceo (not yet dead, of course) makes a joke of crossing and recrossing the great Mariel barrier. In one glorious night, Lawrence reports, he captured and burned two cities, Piñar del Río and Santa Cruz--a truly incredible feat considering that they are 300 miles apart. On another day, he reveals the existence of Amazons in the insurgent army. Gómez, he says, has appointed Colonel Adele Pilotro to command a regiment, while her husband is serving simultaneously as a Spanish Army colonel. Lawrence titillates his readers with the suggestion that they may meet in battle.

The Amazon story is quickly picked up by other papers and improved even more by imaginative writers. When Maceo is campaigning in Piñar del Río, the *World* also extols the ingenuity of the illiterate peasants who constitute the rebel army.

They make cannons out of tree trunks, the paper says, and in Havana Province, they destroyed an entire cane field by dousing black snakes with kerosene, igniting them, and turning them loose.

Editors consider such stories entertainment, but uncounted thousands of readers want to believe them. In any case, since these tales are printed as straight news, there's no way to distinguish them from ordinary publicity handouts. To cover themselves, editors often follow such accounts with denunciations of them as propaganda—sometimes on the same day.

Creelman and Scovel are easily the stars (so far) in the coverage of Cuba. Now working for Hearst, Creelman was already a celebrated correspondent, his short, stocky figure and black goatee familiar sights all over the world. His ego is even more monumental than Davis's. When he interviews noted people, it's hard to tell sometimes who's the celebrity. He didn't hesitate to give Pope Leo XIII some instructions on Protestant-Catholic relations, and questioned Tolstoy sharply about modern marriage. Sitting down with Sitting Bull, he showed no reluctance in giving his views on the brotherhood of man. No wonder Hearst says of him: "The beauty about Creelman is the fact that whatever you give him to do instantly becomes in his mind the most important assignment ever given any writer. He thinks that the very fact of the job being given to him means that it's a task of surpassing importance, else it would not have been given to so great a man as he."

Scovel, too, is rapidly becoming a celebrity in his own right. As one who has seen more of the war in Cuba at first hand than perhaps anyone else, he's determined to rise above the kind of fanciful coverage the correspondents (not omitting himself) have been giving their readers. The truth, he believes, may be the best propaganda of all, especially if he can authenticate what he writes.

Just as the Great Cuban American Fair opens in New York, the *World* carries his story of a ride through the Cuban countryside, a series of articles in which he is explicit about names and places. In San Pedro, where he found fifty vultures in the village square, he saw the visible evidence of the slaughter of unarmed men, and concluded that the stories he once thought were exaggerated he now believes to be true. For six weeks, working his way through Piñar del Río Province, he collected

196 affidavits from people who have been victims of Spanish brutality, resulting in 112 deaths.

These affidavits have a devastating effect on the sensibilities of American readers. Here is Doroteo Delgado, a middle-aged woman, who testified: "Yesterday in the morning at the approach of the column of Colonel Frances from Mariel to the place called 'La Merced' they spoke to my son, eighteen years old, asking for insurgents, and as he answered that he did not know, one of the soldiers, in the presence of the chief, struck him five or six times with the barrel of his carbine, leaving him much injured." She said she went from house to house trying to find a rebel hospital, but then the soldiers came back to her home and beat her with a cane.

Florina Espinosa, another Cuban woman, tells Scovel: "My two nephews were killed by the troops for no reason whatsoever. They went to visit some friends, and when they arrived at La Vigia...they were caught by the irregulars attached to a column of infantry. Francisco Espinosa tried to run and the irregulars killed him with a shot to the head. They then took Pelaya Espinosa to San Sebastián, where they hacked him to pieces with an infantry bayonet. Neither of my nephews are insurrectos and they had nothing to do with the war. One was twenty years old, the other nineteen."

This is a different kind of narrative than people back home have been accustomed to reading. The names of those who gave depositions are withheld from published articles, but otherwise the places and the people are specific, as are the names and ages of witnesses. Scovel even managed to get the names of the leaders of a death squad.

This fact-finding trip was also the last time Scovel saw General Maceo, and in four long interviews, he gave the *World's* readers a full-length portrait of this charismatic, remarkable man. No doubt of it, he was the revolution's hero and shortly would be its martyr. Scovel learned that upper-class civilians in the revolutionary movement didn't like Maceo. They were thinking of Haiti and of how Toussaint L'Ouverture's bloody rebellion against France was followed by a general massacre of white slave holders and a black republic. They don't want this to happen in Cuba. That's why they were quietly abandoning the general and his army, and also why the later theory that Maceo was poisoned had some credibility.

But Maceo had a last trick up his sleeve. Through Scovel, he sent a message to the Junta in New York that it would be a terrible blow to morale in the revolutionary movement if he were cast aside. At that, the Junta sent down a filibuster boat loaded with supplies and volunteers, including Gómez's son Panchito--an unmistakable sign that the general was on Maceo's side against the civilians.

After his interview with Maceo, Scovel returns to Havana, a horrendous trip, helped by Cuban guides through the bayous of Majana Swamp. It takes three days and nights, without food or anything to drink but dangerous "green water" from the swamp. This infects the gunshot wound that sent Scovel to New York earlier. It's never healed, and soon he's too ill to walk. Safely smuggled into Havana, his friends in the consulate get him shipped off once more to New York, again disguised.

At home, Harry finds that his dispatches have made him something of a folk hero, and in the four months it takes him to get well again, he basks in his fame. Still, he gets mixed reviews from those who think he's more of a dangerous agitator than a hero. Convalescing, Harry improves his time by falling in love with a St. Louis society girl of old stock and old money, whose family is stricken by the thought that their Catholic daughter might marry a mere reporter who says he's Protestant but is far more likely to be an atheist. Before the situation can be resolved (he'll marry her later), Pulitzer calls Scovel and assigns him to Cuba again. Harry is now a ranking pundit. The *World*'s front page carries his four-part series analyzing the present state of the Cuban crisis. In it, he dismisses all those stories about Amazons and other Café Inglaterra tales. Spain, he points out, has 200,000 men in the field and therefore possesses a decisive advantage, since Gómez has only about 50,000 soldiers he can count on. He even compliments Weyler, in a left-handed sort of way, observing that he "has never been credited with military genius, but he handles his columns better than Martínez Campos." Scovel concludes: "The struggle to free Cuba will soon be worthy of the bloody name and fame of war."

On the day after New Year's, 1897, Harry sneaks back into Cuba via the coast of Piñar del Río. He's a celebrity there, too, with a price on his head, and he creates his own persona. His public image, as Milton tells us, is of "a sort of Wild West cowboy, very tall, very blond, with beaded buckskin shirt and white ten-gallon hat, or sombrero." Actually, Harry is now operating on a much more sophisticated level. He has grown a precise little mustache, plucked his eyebrows, carries his own English saddle, and calls himself Harry Williams. It's too much competition for Davis. Hearing about the plucked eyebrows, he remarks that *he* hasn't found it necessary to do that to get a story.

For nearly two weeks, Scovel investigates the circumstances of Maceo's death, determining that he was not betrayed by civilians. Then he slides unobtrusively into Havana and immediately is closeted with the American consul, Fitzhugh Lee, who has asked to see him. Lee wants Scovel to be an unofficial messenger to Gómez, carrying with him an even more unofficial American plan for peace. The essence of it is that an armistice will be declared if the rebels accept a promise of home rule. The United States will guarantee the armistice through a treaty with Spain.

No one, it appears, has made any attempt to keep this epic meeting a secret. In New York, the *World* reports that Harry is on a mission for the State Department, and then, as it so often does, indignantly denies this story as a rumor. In Cuba, what Scovel is up to has become so well known that when he meets Gómez again at his mountain hideaway, the general says, only half-joking, "So now you have to come to demand my surrender."

For the record, Gómez says that an armistice must be based on independence if he's to surrender, but talking privately with Scovel, he intimates that he is not as unmovable as he was. The death of Maceo, and of his son not long after, along with the terrible damage Weyler has done, has sobered him considerably. He intimates that if the United States works out something with Spain and then sends a delegation to him with terms for a settlement that he can endorse, the revolution might be over.

Scovel returns to Havana, and his career as a *sub rosa* diplomat, which has proved to be no secret at all, is cut short abruptly by the unforgiving Weyler. Some off-duty police officers, with their eyes on the reward, plan to ambush him, shoot him, dump his body in a cane field and collect the money. Somehow this plan reaches the ears of an Associated Press reporter, who passes it on to Thomas Alvord, Jr., the *World*'s man in Havana.

Now it's a real-life thriller. Alvord hurries to Scovel's hide-away, eluding possible tails by changing carriages three times, and tells Harry he must get out of Cuba at once. The marked man demurs, although he admits that filing dispatches in Havana may be too dangerous. But Alvord has another plan. Go by train to Trinidad de Cuba, on the southern coast, he says, and I'll meet you at the station. Scovel agrees, but when Alvord arrives at the station, there's no sign of Harry. Frantic, Alvord tries to cable Lee to find out if the consul knows any-thing, but there's no answer so he assumes that his message has been intercepted and the authorities know where Scovel is hiding.

Alvord has to assume that Harry is somewhere in Trinidad, and he appeals for help to a wealthy American planter named Stillman, who's been known to aid reporters. Stillman doesn't want to get involved in this tangled plot, but he agrees to go into Trinidad and find Scovel, which he does, and while he's at it, starts a rumor that the wanted man is hiding out at his planta-tion, passing himself off as Alvord.

At this point, Scovel takes matters into his own hands. He steals two boats, and by means of a little bribery, sails away into the night, making an obscene gesture at the Spanish fort as he passes by. Alvord covers his departure, paying the boat owners $25 each so they won't talk. Reporting on this escapade to his boss in New York, Bradford Merrill, Alvord says of Scovel: "He is the coolest, most daring fellow I ever knew."

Just how cool is demonstrated anew the next day while 300 soldiers are searching the Stillman plantation as Alvord watches. During the search, a servant brings him a letter from Scovel. He hasn't gone far. In fact, he's hiding in a nearby house. Once more it's up to Alvord. He finds some sympathizers who aren't being watched and they manage to take Harry some clothes, provide him with a guide, and give him $25 to buy a horse. That's all he needs. He makes a last trip to Gómez's camp in the hills and then heads south, planning to escape Cuba by boat, the same one that got him out of Trinidad, but the skipper is too nervous. The dragnet is out and he feels it tightening.

Scovel winds up in the fortified town of Zaza, a port at the moment full of elite Guardia Civil troops. He's near exhaustion, and he's lost his derby, replacing it with a hat called a Jipijapa he's picked up at Gómez's camp. He's also filthy and his shoes are collapsing. But he still has his guide, who tells him what he should do next.

Knocking on the front door of a well-known elderly landowner named Francisco Thome, Scovel represents himself as Harry Williams, an American who has come to Cuba to buy scrap metal, which will be delivered when the war ends, at a substantial profit. Thome is enchanted by the idea and promises to go on the train with him to nearby Tunas, where he has friends with heaps of metal to sell. After Scovel cleans up, the two men get on the train and Harry thinks he's going to pull it off, but a heavy hand descends on his shoulder. A Spanish officer demands his military pass. This sharp-eyed man has noticed Scovel's hat, a style that is seldom seen on the southern coast.

Taken up to the baggage car, Scovel listens while the soldiers guarding him try to decide whether it wouldn't be better just to shoot him rather than deliver him. (Apparently they don't know about the reward.) Fortunately, they decide on delivering; it's doubly fortunate for Harry because Alvord is covering his capture and Americans are reading the details in the *World*. Harry Scovel has become an international incident.

Big headlines announce it: "WEYLER FEARED AND HATED HIM--WILL NOT DARE TO SHOOT HIM, BUT MAY TRY TO KEEP HIM IN PRISON AS LONG AS POSSIBLE." Editorially, the *World* is outraged. Spain has affronted the United States again, it proclaims. Matters rapidly get worse. Alvord can't find a lawyer willing to represent Scovel, who is taken up to Sancti Spíritus, a provincial center, where he is arraigned on several capital charges. It's hardly consoling to read the *World*'s headline: "SCOVEL MAY DIE BUT HIS DEATH WILL FREE CUBA."

He won't die if Americans can help him. Harry is a *cause célèbre*. There's an outpouring of support for him from around the country. Politicians and noted public figures issue letters of support; eighty-seven correspondents (including Davis and Remington) join noted editors in support of Scovel; seventeen state legislatures pass resolutions demanding his release. They are joined by the Territory of Oklahoma, the city council of Columbus, Ohio, and the alumni association of the University of Michigan. On the floor of Congress, his arrest is denounced, and the Senate passes a unanimous resolution calling on the

State Department to inform Spain that there is an "imperative necessity" to transfer Scovel back to Havana where Lee can monitor his treatment.

Are there any exceptions to this chorus of indignation? Yes: the *Journal* and Hearst's West Coast newspaper, the San Francisco *Examiner*. Their policy is never to print Scovel's name. There are a few exceptions. Conservative newspapers call the whole affair just another example of yellow journalism.

Even at this high level, the *World* can't help embroidering the facts. They assert that Scovel is "imprisoned in a vile jail, in a filthy and smallpox infected town," without a lawyer, and "in imminent danger of butchery by a decree of a drum-head court-martial." Not to despair, says the *World*, reporting that there are "Free Scovel" mass meetings being held all over the country and justice will be done.

In fact, Scovel is living better than he has for some time. His cell is carpeted, he sleeps in a bed, his furnishings even include a rocking chair. These amenities have been provided by Señora Madrigal, the wife of an American consular official, Rafael Madrigal. The other prisoners learn that they are in the same boat with a real celebrity and they shower him with hand-crafted gifts, including leather bridles and belts, straw sculptures, paper flowers and what are called "decorated toothpicks." When Alvord comes to visit him, their conversation is constantly interrupted by bevies of young girls come to view the celebrated prisoner. No wonder Scovel is in excellent spirits. He's writing daily letters to the *World*, datelined "Calaboose No. 1," which Señora Madrigal tucks into her bodice when she leaves after her daily visits.

In Washington, the State Department is quietly worrying about all this. If there's a trial, it's certain to come out that Scovel was the messenger from Lee to Gómez, bearing a peace proposal from the United States Government, which everyone concerned is prepared to deny ever existed. In a Spanish court, however, especially a military one, the mere accusation will lend some credence to public charges already made by the Spanish ambassador, Enrique de Lome, that Scovel is an American spy who is also a commissioned colonel in the rebel army (an honor Gómez would have been happy to confer). Hoping to avoid any such embarrassment, State puts quiet pressure on Madrid to release Scovel.

As for the prisoner, he doesn't know *what* to think. The body of the guide who was with him before his capture, badly mutilated, has been found lying on the road near Tunas. Since his captors are now giving him numerous and obvious opportunities to escape, he fears they may be setting him up for the same kind of execution. Rafael Madrigal thinks this is quite possible, and warns Alvord that some of Weyler's officers are irate to think that Madrid might give in to American pressure, and Scovel's "accidental" death could well be the result of their anger. He has, unfortunately, become a symbol of American support for the rebels.

Eventually Weyler himself calls on Harry, but when he sees the piles of gifts and flowers, and the comfortable furnishings, he turns and walks away without talking to anyone. His iron hand is felt at once. The warden loses his job and the pretty girls who come to visit are turned away.

Gómez, meanwhile, hoping to help his American friend, takes a hostage, Luis Morote, a reporter for the Madrid paper, *El Liberal*. If they kill Scovel, Gómez says, he will dispose of Morote, but that proves to be unnecessary. Still hoping to avoid any further trouble with the United States, Madrid instructs Weyler to release Scovel and to see that he leaves Cuba safely. Heralding his return to New York, the *World* headlines that this is "Another Triumph for Publicity," but in fact, the whole affair has had a chilling effect on the press. The correspondents in Cuba are considerably more careful about what they do and write for the next six months and, as a result, the national blood pressure at home temporarily recedes.

Not for long. This time it's Richard Harding Davis who precipitates a new cry of outrage. Shortly after Remington left for New York, Davis decided to take a short sabbatical too. He'd had a frustrating time in Havana and felt that, even though Hearst didn't deserve it, he ought to give the publisher a big exclusive story. In January 1897, he had written to his mother: "All Hearst wants is my name and I will give him that only if it will be signed to a different sort of story from those they have been printing. I am not writing for the Journal. The Journal is printing what I write."

The prospect for "a different sort of story" suddenly appears as he is preparing to leave for New York on the American steamer *Olivette*. Before the ship leaves, customs officers come aboard and search three young women who are traveling together, looking for letters they might be smuggling to the Junta. Observing this procedure with distaste, Davis whips off a dispatch to the *Journal* accusing the customs men of demanding a cabin to which they took the girls for a strip search. In New York, this story absolutely delights Hearst and Davis's friend Remington asks to illustrate it, producing a drawing depicting a naked girl shrinking in terror on deck while leering Spanish officials watch, none of which is in Davis's story.

Always skeptical of anything the *Journal* prints, and hoping to embarrass its rival, the *World* sends a reporter to Tampa, where the three girls get off the boat. One of them, a Señorita Arango, denies Davis's story, and her two companions agree. She says a matron conducted the strip search privately. When this revelation appears in the *World*, Davis writes a letter to the paper's editor denying that he ever wrote the account that way; he blames Remington. It's true that his story only suggested that there was a strip search by the officials, but Remington's picture has done the damage, and it's the picture everyone remembers. The *Journal* plays the story for all it's worth to steam up the public, and Davis issues a statement asserting that he will never write for Hearst again.

By this time, Hearst and the *Journal* are in full cry. Davis's story and Remington's picture ran under a five-column headline: "DOES OUR FLAG PROTECT WOMEN?" and has set off a national resolution directing the State Department to provide any information it has about the incident, and the Senate passes a similar resolution. But when the *World*'s story appears, Congress drops the matter.

Hearst shows no embarrassment about being exposed as a barefaced liar. He's now working both sides of the street in his campaign to invent and promote a war with Spain. Creelman has been posted to Madrid as a special correspondent, and sends back stories depicting Spain as preparing for war. "Great activity continues in all Spanish ports, particularly in Cartagena," he reports, "where the full available strength is now employed in fitting out six ironclads and three cruisers, which, with the Glasgow torpedo boat destroyers, will make a powerful flying squadron."

The *Journal* encourages him by printing an article headed, "Does Spain Mean War?" and declaring that Madrid was "stung to shame and blind rage" by Weyler's failure to put down the rebellion, and means to revenge itself on the United States. The paper polls senators to find out how many of them would support a joint resolution that declares it will be "mandatory on the president to protect the struggling Cubans from being exterminated by the Spanish." Fourteen senators would be willing, the *Journal* reports. Then the state governors are polled to determine how many favor intervention by either recognizing the rebels or giving them material aid. The questionnaire also asks how many volunteers each state might provide in case war is declared.

Hearst is steadily building in the *Journal* the idea that the public wants war. In Madrid, Creelman is busily promoting the notion that the Spaniards are in a critical state of mind. One of his dispatches appears on the front page, headed: "CRISIS IN SPAIN ALMOST AT HAND; WHOLE NATION IS THRILLED WITH AN OVERPOWERING SENSE OF IMPENDING DISASTER." Spain is almost bankrupt, Creelman says, and "she can neither prosecute a war of the first class, nor even long sustain her strife against Cuban patriots."

This is all part of what the *Journal* is calling "the new journalism," which sounds a lot like the old journalism of an earlier nineteenth century. There is a primitive quality about it which has an antebellum flavor. A cartoon depicts "Uncle Sam" raising a toast to a young man labeled "Journal," who stands on a stack of newspapers with a card saying "Scoop" suspended from him. This is, the *Journal* tells its readers, "the journalism that does things," and whose slogan is, "While others talk, the *Journal* acts." Other papers are given short shrift. The *Sun* proclaims, "If you see it in the *Sun*, it's so," but the *Journal* says, "If you see it in the *Sun*, you're lucky."

What Hearst and his paper want is war with Spain, and successive events in 1897 which it exploits bring that outcome ever nearer. The first concerns Dr. Ricardo Ruiz, a Cuban dentist but a naturalized American, who's found dead in a cell at Guanabacoa, just a few miles east of Havana. Investigation discloses that he was a revolutionary in the Ten Years' War who fled to the United States when that part of the long revolt failed. Returning later as an American citizen, his political convictions unchanged, he was arrested for train robbery after a rebel raid on a railway. Two weeks later, Ruiz was found dead in his cell and the Spaniards say it's a suicide, brought about by pounding his head against the wall. George Eugene Bryson, a *Journal* correspondent, is permitted to view the body, and his subsequent story bears the headline: "AMERICAN DIES IN SPANISH JAIL." That's enough to start the hounds baying. Bryson writes that there is strong evidence Ruiz was murdered.

Hearst exploits this tragedy to the limit. In the *Journal*, he demands war with Spain. He sends money to Ruiz's widow and urges her to use it as steamship fare to New York, which she does. Then he instructs one of his Washington reporters, Alfred Henry Lewis, whom Swanberg describes as "a former drunk, who had effectively smeared Senator Mark Hanna," to interview Senator John Sherman, of Ohio, who is soon going to be Secretary of State. Lewis obliges, and his story is headlined, "SHERMAN FOR WAR WITH SPAIN FOR MURDERING AMERICANS." Those who read the story observe that Sherman is not that definite about it. He admits that all he knows is what he reads in the *Journal*, and says that "if the facts are true, as reported, and American citizens are being murdered in Cuba in cold blood, the only way to put an end to the atrocities is to declare war on Spain."

Now Bryson files another dispatch from Cuba, asserting that he has examined the chair in Ruiz's cell and found, "as though from the grave," a message scratched on it declaring he was "being killed." This precipitates such an uproar, following the Sherman interview, that the senator feels he'd better cover his posterior. He disclaims the entire interview and calls it "a lie from beginning to end." Not everyone in Washington swallows the disclaimer. People know this seventy-four-year-old senator as a man who appears to be losing his mental faculties, often not knowing what he's said or done, or even where he's been--and he's about to be Secretary of State!

Hearst counters Sherman's disavowal by sending Mrs. Ruiz and her children to Washington, where his bureau men see that she gets to meet the senator and the President himself, who has already said, "We want no wars of conquest. We must avoid the temptation of territorial aggression." In the end, Hearst's ploy is only partly successful. Americans sympathize with Mrs. Ruiz and regret her husband's death, but they're not about to go to war over it. Hearst realizes he's going to have to produce something more dramatic. In the fall of

1897, that something turns up in the delectable teenage person of Evangelina Cosio y Cisneros, the Cuban Joan of Arc, a.k.a. "The Flower of Cuba."

3

THE SHORT HAPPY CAREER OF EVANGELINA CISNEROS

"WHY DO THEY ALWAYS CALL ME THAT?" THE FLOWER OF Cuba sometimes protests. "I am Evangelina Cosio." To the pro-rebel American press she is always "Miss Cisneros," but that's because Hearst and the others don't want anyone to forget that her great-uncle was the first president of the Provisional Republican government. Her father was a well-known revolutionary.

It's not surprising, then, that when first seen Evangelina is a political prisoner. The Havana correspondents know a little about her but not much. They know she's young and beautiful and that's enough for some of them, but it takes George Bryson, on his rounds for the *Journal*, to visit her in prison and to see, rather dimly at first, another object of Spanish persecution. Bryson, who is somewhat old-fashioned for a Hearst reporter, finds himself genuinely shocked by the spectacle of this lovely convent-educated girl living under the same roof with prostitutes, murderers, and madwomen in the notorious Casa de Recojidas prison, where the abandoned females of Havana are tossed together.

Bryson tells his *Journal* colleague, George Clarke Musgrave, what he's seen, and Musgrave goes to see for himself. It's a snake pit, he reports, with psychotic women parading around, some in the nude, screaming obscenities, along with a varied collection of prostitutes, all of whom are regularly raped by the guards.

Appealing to Fitzhugh Lee, Bryson asks him to look into the situation. After this inspection, Lee sniffs the beginning of another Hearstian crusade. Conditions in the prison are certainly appalling, he finds, but Evangelina has a private room, hardly a cell, quite apart from the other prisoners, and enjoys at least a few amenities. For the moment, she's not in the slightest danger. But Bryson is far from satisfied. He's heard one of her jailers make a sexually harassing remark to her, and he fears the worst. Time for action.

When Hearst learns about Cisneros from Bryson's dispatches, his agile mind grasps the possibilities at once. "We've got Spain now!" he exults to his managing editor, Sam Chamberlain. Creelman is called in to take charge of the "Free Evangelina Cisneros" campaign, and naturally, he conducts it in grand style. A petition to the Queen Regent of Spain, Maria Christina, is drawn up, asking her to intercede to obtain a pardon. Copies are sent to more than 200 Hearst correspondents and stringers scattered across America to be circulated, and thousands of people sign up.

In the *Journal*, Creelman writes: "This tenderly nurtured girl was imprisoned at eighteen among the most depraved Negresses of Havana, and now she is about to be sent in mockery to spend twenty years in a servitude that will kill her in a year. This girl, delicate, refined, sensitive, unused to hardship, absolutely ignorant of vice, unconscious of the existence of such beings as crowd the cells of the Casa de Recojidas, is seized, thrust into a prison maintained for the vilest class of abandoned women of Havana, and shattered in health until she is threatened with an early death."

There's scarcely a word of truth in this description. Evangelina, as Joyce Milton tell us, is not "a pale-skinned upperclass virgin waiting to be rescued by a broad-shouldered American hero." She's a tough little revolutionary who's already had quite a career in the insurrection. Her father, a rebel from Camagüey, had been charged with forming a cavalry company (guilty as charged) and sentenced to death. This sentence was commuted to life in the Spanish penal colony in Ceuta, Africa, whose horrors were well known. Evangelina had gone to Weyler and pleaded with him not to send her father to a place where he might well die, and the "Butcher," in spite of his reputation, showed compassion and sent him to the Isle of Pines, where he was under little more than house arrest. Since her mother had died, Evangelina went along to keep house for him.

They were no sooner settled than Evangelina was busy with plans for his escape. In this she had the help of her boyfriend, a member of the noted Betancourt clan. Using the oldest device in the world, Evangelina raised her eyelashes and sent a look in the direction of Colonel José Berriz, the prison camp commander, who naturally assumed this was an invitation and followed her to her room, where he was set upon by Evangelina's fellow conspirators, tied up, and would have been used as a hostage if a few passing soldiers had not heard the commotion, rushed in, freed him, and arrested everybody. Before this skirmish with the armed conspirators was over, several innocent bystanders were killed. That's why Evangelina finds herself in the Havana prison, charged with sedition and awaiting trial.

Not if Hearst can help it. The national campaign is soon under way, and in Havana, Bryson and Musgrave are taking some bold and potentially disastrous steps on their own. Bryson finds a military judge who says he'll free Evangelina for $2,000, but while George is trying to raise the money, Weyler finds out about it and deports him. Musgrave is afraid to continue any such efforts for fear that Evangelina will be transferred to the African prison colony. At this point, Fitzhugh Lee steps in and makes a personal plea to Weyler: surely, he says, all this can be negotiated.

Weyler isn't unreasonable about it, but he points out that he's in an impossible position. If he sees that Evangelina gets a harsh sentence, she will immediately become a heroine of the revolution. If he lets her go, the Junta propagandists will say that this is proof she's innocent. Then, reverting to a familiar theme, he tells Lee that if the American press would stop making this case an international incident, an agreement could be reached, possibly sending Evangelina back to Spain where she could live with her relatives and go back to school.

Fat chance. Hearst and the *Journal* are well launched on their national crusade on behalf of the Flower of Cuba. Hearst even has the chutzpah to ask Weyler to be merciful--Weyler, the man his paper has called "the prince of all cruel generals this century has seen." Weyler doesn't even bother to answer. Meanwhile, the crusade is in full cry, and news of its progress is reported everywhere in the country by the Associated Press.

The response to the *Journal*'s petition campaign is overwhelming. It's directed at women, and it soon lists President McKinley's mother, Senator Sherman's wife, Mark Hanna's wife, Ulysses S. Grant's widow and, keeping the Civil War balance even, Jefferson Davis's widow. Not to mention Julia Ward Howe, Frances Hodgson Burnett, Clara Barton, and thousands of anonymous women who want to get Evangelina out of jail. The *Journal* fills twelve columns of one edition with the names of petitioners, classified by states.

Hearst carries the crusade to England, where Lady Rothschild and Mrs. Ormiston Chant, the well-known London temperance worker, undertake a drive to get 200,000 signatures on a petition. In America, Julia Ward Howe addresses a petition to Pope Leo XIII, which the *Journal* forwards along with the others. By this time, it's obvious that the United States and much of Western Europe is in a state of high indignation.

In Washington, Depuy de Lome, the Spanish Ambassador, is trying desperately to head off this juggernaut of public opinion. He sends out a batch of open letters addressed to prominent women, who don't answer them. Nothing he does works, because Evangelina is now, as Swanberg puts it, "a symbol of wronged innocence," her name adored at hundreds of mass meetings. Hearst cables the names of petitioners, beginning with the most prominent, to the Queen Regent, who is so alarmed she suggests to Weyler that he should treat Evangelina gently and put her in a convent, but the "Butcher" has had enough of American scribblers and Americans in general. He flatly refuses.

For more than two weeks, the *Journal* keeps elevating the intensity level of its campaign. Hearst knows it can't go on much longer, however. Something more sensational is required to keep the cause alive, and it occurs to him that the answer is to rescue Evangelina.

That solution had already occurred to Musgrave before he ever wrote his first story about the beautiful prisoner. Had he fallen more than a little in love with the Flower of Cuba? He had visited her every day, taking her small comforts, until the guards were so used to his presence that a daring plan evolved in his mind. He would send these now unsuspicious guards out to buy cigars, then overpower the jailer and flee with Evangelina to a rebel agent's house nearby. The agent had already arranged with an engineer on the Matanzas railroad to smuggle her out of Havana. After that, it would be improvisation. When Musgrave disclosed this plan to her, Evangelina had agreed to it eagerly, but at the last moment, he lost his nerve. That was when he and Bryson had turned to the only other alternative: making Evangelina's story known to the American public.

Hearst has nerve enough to spare. He isn't in the least disturbed by the arrival in New York of Fitzhugh Lee, come up to visit his son at West Point, from which he also graduated, and to take a month's rest. As soon as he arrives, he's interviewed by a reporter from the *Commercial Advertiser* and takes the opportunity to denounce Hearst's campaign as "tommyrot."

Then he issues a public statement: "I wish to correct a false and stupid impression which has been created by some newspapers. I refer to Señorita Cisneros. This young woman has two clean rooms in the Casa de Recojidas, and is well clothed and fed. It is all tommyrot about her scrubbing floors and being subjected to cruelties and indignities. She would have been pardoned long ago if it had not been for the hubbub created by American newspapers. I do not believe for one moment that the government intended to send her to the penal colony in Africa or elsewhere. I believe her name is now upon the roll for pardon. That she was implicated in the insurrection on the Isle of Pines, there can be no question. She herself, in a note to me, acknowledged that fact, and stated she was betrayed by an accomplice named Árias."

This statement creates some nervousness among the crusaders. The *World* prints a statement from Weyler denying that he ever intended to deport Evangelina to Africa, and the paper adds that if Weyler changes his mind, it will be the *Journal*'s fault. Even some of Hearst's minions are made uncomfortable by the crusade's underlying cynicism, but Hearst can't be stopped now. He's committed to freeing the prisoner and he means to do it.

To engineer the Great Escape, he calls upon a reporter in the *Journal*'s Washington bureau, Karl Decker, whom Milton describes as a "blond, six-foot-plus, square-jawed Virginian," whose father was a Confederate colonel. Although he's only thirty-three, Decker feels that he might be a little too old for such shenanigans when Sam Chamberlain first tells him about his new assignment, but Hearst won't take no for an answer. Given a choice between his job and his boss's intentions, it's no contest. Besides, Sam has told him he will be well rewarded. Hearst sits him down in his office and tells him what to do.

Decker has worked in Cuba before and knows Havana well, so he checks in at the Hotel Inglaterra (where else?) as soon as he arrives. He visits Evangelina and tells her what he's about to do. She says she's ready. Then Decker recruits two accomplices: William McDonald, an American who's in the shipping business in Havana, and Carlos Carbonelle, a Junta agent, another of those naturalized American citizens.

Surveying the landscape around No. 1 O'Farrell Street, where the prison is located, Decker observes that there's a vacant house directly across the narrow street and he instructs Carbonelle to rent it. The house's flat roof is only eight feet away from the second-floor parapet of the prison, and Evangelina is on that floor.

On the night of October 6, the conspirators climb to the roof of the rented house, slide a twelve-foot plank across to the parapet, and cross over in stockinged feet. They look toward Evangelina's cell and even in the darkness they can see the white handkerchief she's tied to the bars, the prearranged signal that she's ready to be rescued.

Writing about it all later, Decker recalls that as soon as he began working on the bars with the hacksaw, "she gave a glad little cry and clasped our hands through the bars, calling upon us to liberate her at once." This touching moment may well be doubted, as may Decker's claim that he had supplied her with drugged bonbons to be given to her cell mates so they would be asleep. Another and far more accurate version is that the guards were bribed and drunk.

In any case, Evangelina slides through the bars, makes the perilous journey back to the safe house on the plank, thirty-five feet above the street, and descends through the dark house to the street where Decker whisks her away in a waiting carriage. After hiding out for three days, Decker has her dress in a sailor's uniform, tucks her telltale hair under a cap, and gives her a cigar which she smokes as she walks boldly down Obispo Street to the wharf and the American steamer *Seneca*, which will take her to New York. After he files a cable bringing Hearst up to date, Decker takes another boat and follows her.

When the *Seneca* nears its New York pier, Evangelina comes on deck and is at once terrified by a huge crowd waiting to welcome her. Many of them have read the headline: "EVAN-GELINA CISNEROS RESCUED BY THE JOURNAL. An American Newspaper Accomplishes at a Single Stroke What the Best Efforts of Diplomacy Failed Utterly to Bring About in Many Months." In the following story, the *Journal* explored human history and concluded that only the rescue of Mary Queen of Scots could rival it.

Her well-wishers on the dock don't see much of Evangelina because the ship is met in the harbor by a steam launch carrying Bryson and a covey of *Journal* men who take her over. She's Hearst property now and he means to make the most of it. They take her to a flower-filled suite in the new Waldorf Hotel on Fifth Avenue and Thirty-fourth Street. An interpreter keeps the bewildered girl more or less abreast of what's going on.

Never has anyone been exploited as ruthlessly by a newspaper as Hearst and the *Journal* exploit Evangelina in the next few weeks. With the publisher's money oiling the way at every step, she's whisked through the best New York shops and outfitted in a style to which she has never dreamed of being accustomed. Arrayed in a white couturier dress, she leaves the Waldorf on Decker's arm, chaperoned by Mrs. J. Ellen Foster, of the Ladies' Cuban Relief Association of New York, and makes a triumphal procession down Fifth Avenue, preceded by an honor guard of naval cadets, soldiers, and policemen, while thousands cheer along the route to Delmonico's at Twenty-sixth Street, where she is to be the guest of honor at a banquet.

The ballroom fairly glitters with the rich and prominent--a remarkable tribute to a daughter of the revolution who only a few days ago was sitting in the Casa de Recojidas. Everyone's there except Hearst. These occasions aren't his cup of tea. On the other hand, he can't stay away, and just before the banquet begins, his French racer rolls up to Delmonico's and he hurries inside. An observer writes: "The man who footed the bills came into the room where [Miss Cisneros] stood among the palms, shyly shook hands with the heroine whom his wonder machine had created, and then excused himself and hastened away in his automobile."

The evening progresses with speeches by politicians and by Dr. Lincoln de Zayas, of the Cuban Legation, as they like to call it. Then everyone moves down to Union Square, where the peasants are invited to join in the celebration. Thousands of people are waiting to see the Flower of Cuba, searchlights play over the scene, fireworks are bursting above, and bands play on. Henry George appears and gives a moving speech praising the courage and enterprise of the *Journal*.

After this ball is over, Evangelina is taken on a celebrity tour, chaperoned by General John A. Logan's white-haired widow. They stop first in Washington, where she is presented to a somewhat reluctant but polite President McKinley. Then she's taken on a nationwide tour, a revolutionary heroine speaking to middle-class audiences, while the *Journal* records every movement from the beginning--"Her First Elevator Ride," the buying of her superb trousseau (somewhere along the line she and Carbonelle have fallen in love), her favorite color (black)-- 375 columns of such trivia. Her dearest wish, the *Journal* reports, is to become an American citizen: "I do so want to march and sing, 'I am an American.'" To further that wish, the government, under Hearst pressure, permits her to take out naturalization papers less than twenty-four hours after her arrival.

What did you want to be when you were growing up? they ask her. A nun, she says simply. What is your ambition? To be an English teacher. But what was going through your mind, as a television interviewer would have asked her in later years, while you were reciting this Hearst-manufactured litany, believing that it was all being done to free Cuba? Charles Michelson, one of the *Journal*'s correspondents, says later that she knew Hearst was exploiting her, but having gotten on the merry-go-round, she couldn't get off.

Abruptly, everything stops. The speaking tour is over, and Evangelina is no longer useful; the campaign has run its course. The country is no closer to war with Spain, but its blood pressure has been raised once again. It's shocking even to some Hearst people who've been part of this charade that Evangelina is suddenly dropped cold and left to shift for herself. For a time, she lives in Lee's Virginia home, and then is passed around to other high-level sympathizers. But then, relief at last. She marries Carbonelle in May 1898, and after he's done service in the American army during the war as a captain, she will settle down with him in Havana, where he will practice dentistry for many years.

If Evangelina is quickly forgotten, so is Decker, the one-time hero of the piece. Hearst never pays him the promised reward for his daring rescue. He submits an expense account, including bribe money he says he paid the guards, but the *Journal* simply ignores it. The bribe money is the difficulty. Hearst wants to believe the jail break was a glorious exploit and no one dares tell him that the bribe made it a snap--except, of course, for the walk across the twelve-foot plank. Not one to give up easily, Decker is still trying to get his money out of the Hearst corporation thirty years later, without result.

If Hearst didn't achieve a declaration of war out of this episode, he got something else he didn't expect. The incredible story has been spread all over the Spanish papers too, and the result is that Spanish public opinion, never much concerned before, is now thoroughly aroused, and war is not quite so unthinkable.

4

THE MAINE REMEMBERED

IF WE CAN'T PERSUADE THE SPANISH TO STOP DOING WHAT they're doing to the Cubans, and if we can't find some way to satisfy the *insurrectos* without eliminating the Spaniards, is there any way to prevent war?

In the corridors of high finance, the answer seems simple enough to some people. Good old American private enterprise will do what Hearst and the politicians cannot. It will buy Cuba from Spain on behalf of the insurgents. There will, of course, be a profit. A New York financial syndicate agrees to do all the financing and negotiating, and when the deal is completed, it will skim some off the top--more than enough to make it worthwhile.

This scheme originates in the head of Samuel M. Janney, of Christy and Janney, a Wall Street banking firm, but he is only the front man. The moving figure in the audacious adventure is Colonel John J. McCook, a noted corporation lawyer in New York, as well as a powerful figure in the Republican Party. McCook could have been Secretary of Interior in the new McKinley Administration, since the President is his friend, but he prefers the arcane life of the Street.

McCook first lays out the plan in the spring of 1897, on a visit to the White House. He suggests to the President that the banking syndicate negotiating the deal would operate under the government's supervision. Washington correspondents hear about this visit and duly report it, but McCook denies everything. Apparently he has a green light from the White House, however, because he begins at once to negotiate with the Cuban leaders in New York, and on August 5, signs a formal agreement with the Junta's American leader, Tomás Palma. Janney signs for the syndicate.

If nothing else, it's an ingenious scheme. According to the contract's terms, the syndicate will pay part of the enormous debt Spain has run up in Cuba, and in return, Spain will with-draw from the island and give the Cubans their independence. The syndicate's cut will be $150 million Cuban in public bonds, only a little less in United States currency. The bonds will pay four percent interest annually, and the principal is to be paid off in fifty years. But are these bonds really any good? To make sure, the syndicate secures them with a lien on Cuban customs receipts. The American government, acting as a financial trustee, will supervise the servicing and collection.

A splendid little idea for the syndicate, and for the Cubans too, but how about Spain? The contract states blandly that the United States will use its influence to secure Spanish accep-tance, and will also act as a guarantor of the contract's terms. Naturally, there's a catch clause. McCook is designated as the man delegated to secure the American government's accep-tance, and if he can't do that by October 1, the contract will be null and void.

There is also a significant omission in this document. Nowhere does it say how much money the syndicate is required to pay Spain. It only guarantees to make the best bargain it can, and since the amount of the Cuban bonds is fixed, that means the syndicate won't know how much money it's going to make until after it has negotiated with the Spanish government.

The October deadline goes by, and a month's extension is granted, but it's another month and the year is running out before the syndicate gets final approval from the Cuban Council of Government. Meanwhile, however, Janney and Palma have signed *another* contract, and there are some major changes. Now the syndicate will get Cuban bonds worth $37.5 million in return for getting Spain out and the Cuban Republic in, with formal recognition by both the United States and the Spanish government. In this new version, Spain doesn't get anything.

What's happened is that the push toward war has become even stronger in these early days of 1898. The syndicate believes that its primary ally is Washington. But things are a lit-tle confusing. The first contract remains in force, but the second will be void if the first can be implemented. Still, the Cuban Council of Government approves the second document on January 27, 1898.

Everyone involved has made strenuous efforts to keep these negotiations secret, but of course that's impossible, and early in March the *Journal* gets wind of what's going on and breaks the story, describing the first contract and assessing its prospects as hopeless. It also charges that the scheme is a plot to "transfer the Cuban question into a commercial transaction," and for once, the *Journal* is correct. But then, only a few days later, Hearst suddenly reverses his course, claims it was his idea in the first place, and in front-page headlines declares: "CUBA, THROUGH THE JOURNAL, OFFERS TO BUY HER FREEDOM." The story quotes Bartolomé Maso, who will be President of the Cuban Republic (if it ever exists), as saying Spain will be paid a substantial indemnity if it agrees to independence.

It's all too late. By this time, events are moving much too rapidly for anyone's scheme, even Wall Street's, to avert war. At least one irritant has been removed. The Spanish government has concluded that Weyler has failed to bring anything approaching order to Cuba, and late in October, he's recalled. Scovel finds out about this coming event in a peculiar way. Arriving in Havana at the time Decker is preparing to rescue Evangelina, he's recognized on the street, arrested, arraigned, and ordered expelled from Cuba, all within six hours from the time he disembarked. As he's being pushed up the gangplank of the *Seneca*, a Spanish officer, who's making a pretense of giving him a rough time, whispers in his ear: "You are officially deported, but you might as well turn around and come right back. Weyler is done for." The recall comes next day, and Scovel is soon back on the scene with his new wife, Frances, matters of religion having been overcome.

What has happened is a political turnover in Madrid, with the Liberal Party coming to power. As a replacement for Weyler, the new ministers send Captain-General Ramón Blanco y Eranas. His orders are entirely different from Weyler's. He's to prepare Cuba for home rule (good news) and in effect sign a peace treaty with the American press (incredible news).

Blanco's first act is to pacify the *World* by reinstating Scovel on the basis of a plea bargain. He's to appear in court and be given a six-year sentence, with a fine of $600, after which he'll be paroled and accredited as a correspondent. By the middle of November, he and Frances are ensconced in a suite at the Inglaterra and Frances writes home that Cuba is like "champagne and ice cream." Well, yes and no. On the surface,

Blanco's arrival has resulted in the creation of an artificial world in which everyone is nice to everyone else. Scovel is even called upon by the general who had him arrested, and who half apologizes for doing his duty.

But nothing can gloss over the abject misery in which most of Cuba's population lives. Harry is permitted, almost invited, to take a tour of Havana Province, and Frances makes her debut as a foreign correspondent while she travels with him. Writing in a letter to the St. Louis *Post-Dispatch*, she reports: "In some places, these poor people would get on a train, their feet swollen and sore and their bodies nothing but skeletons. They cried around the café so that one cannot eat a mouthful of food and the waiters shut the doors and windows so that we could eat in comfort. In one town before ten o'clock in the day, Mr. Scovel had seen twenty-three dead people and in Havana a woman was dying right on the street, another dying under the portico of the palace."

Harry Brown, another *World* correspondent, who's been traveling with the Scovels, doing a series on the miseries of the *reconcentrados*, estimates that 30,000 people have died in the past several weeks, most of them women and children. Brown has taken hundreds of pictures showing children shrunk by malnutrition to ghastly images of themselves, and one of the *World*'s staff artists has translated these pictures into graphic illustrations. The sketches have a profound impact on Americans, who are not accustomed to seeing such realism in their newspapers. The pictures are also viewed by Cabinet members in Washington.

Maybe that's why another officially unofficial peace feeler is put out to Gómez by John Sherman, who is now Secretary of State. Once again Scovel is a messenger. Harry, of course, is delighted; it will be a sensational honeymoon trip. When he applies to Blanco for permission to travel, the new governor is so astounded by the idea "of a woman going out there" that he consents. Rafael Madrigal is recruited for the expedition, and in New York, the *World* denies that there's anything official about the trip. But Scovel is, in fact, charged with finding out how Gómez feels now about accepting a settlement negotiated by the United States, if it guarantees home rule.

Carrying a 10" x 12" American flag as a safety precaution, the party makes a perilous four-day journey, complicated by the fact that three-hundred-pound Madrigal has a heart condition and has trouble keeping up. Halfway there, they arrive at the camp of a rebel brigadier general, where Frances, carrying the flag, salutes the lone-star banner of the Republic, for the first time ever.

This ceremony is repeated at Gómez's headquarters on a stock farm near Arroya Arenas, enhanced this time by a nearly unrecognizable version of the "Star-Spangled Banner," attempted by a Cuban bugler. Madrigal goes so far as to dip the flag, an implied recognition of the Republic.

After all this, the mission is a flat failure. Gómez wants no part of home rule. Knowing Spain is nearly bankrupt, he believes it can't afford to keep an army in Cuba very much longer. He tells Scovel: "In a few weeks, Spain will either evacuate Cuba or fight the United States. I think the United States will only want Cuba commercially. Frankly, if Cuba were annexed tomorrow, I don't think there is an American statesman that would know what to do with her." A shrewd analysis.

Back in Havana, a state of near hysteria prevails as the day of autonomy, January 1, 1898, promised by Spain's Liberal Party approaches. The middle ground is melting away on both sides. Moderates are ready to accept autonomy, but the separatists say "Never!" and the Loyalists look toward the United States as their only hope of retaining power.

The international game is also acquiring further complications. German warships have been seen cruising around the Caribbean, and in far-off Manila they keep nosing around the harbor. Young Theodore Roosevelt, who is now Assistant Secretary of the Navy, orders the North Atlantic Squadron to begin maneuvers in the Gulf of Mexico. Someone in the State Department (surely not the Secretary) has conceived the idea of negotiating with Spain to trade peaceful visits of battleships to help calm things down and send a message that normal relations are not yet impossible. The idea is that the Spanish battleship, the *Vizcaya*, will visit several ports on the East Coast, while the second-class American battleship, the *Maine*, will pay a call on Havana, acting as a symbol not only of hope for peace but of American power.

Controversy immediately surrounds this plan. Fitzhugh Lee says blandly that the object of the *Maine*'s visit is to protect

American property from the turmoil taking place in Havana, but American non-interventionists accuse the government of trying to encourage the Loyalists to ask for American protection. There's also the question of whether anyone, especially American sailors on shore leave, will be safe in Havana, which teems with plots and counterplots. Dynamite has already been found in the Casa Nueva, an office building where both the American consulate and the *Journal* have offices.

This internal pot boils over on January 12, when anti-government supporters riot in the streets, shouting, "Down with Blanco!" and "Long Live Weyler!" a sound it's too bad the Butcher can't hear in Madrid. Offices of the four papers supporting autonomy are ransacked. Alarmed, Lee cables Washington requesting that the *Maine*'s visit be postponed. At the moment, she's docked in Key West, and Captain Charles D. Sigsbee has orders not to leave for Havana until he gets a coded message from Lee carrying the words "two dollars." No one expects any real trouble, however, until late February, when elections are scheduled. At this critical juncture, Washington double-crosses Lee. On January 24, John R. Caldwell, the *Herald*'s chief Havana correspondent, enters Lee's office and shows him a cable from his paper: "SEND REPORT CUBAN CANE CROP. WANT FOR MAIN SECTION." What's this? Lee inquires. Caldwell explains that it's a code telling him the *Maine* is on its way to Havana and he wants to confirm it.

"Nonsense," Lee says briskly. "The government would never send a naval vessel here unless I requested it, which I haven't done." But after Caldwell leaves, he's disturbed enough to query the State Department, and it confirms that the battleship is indeed steaming toward him. Lee is stunned. He can't find out, because no one knows, what led McKinley to issue this order. Is he worried about those four German warships nosing around Haiti? Who knows? Lee can't do anything but tell State that the timing of this visit couldn't be worse, and he won't guarantee anything.

On January 25, the *Maine* duly arrives in Havana Harbor, all 319 feet of her, smokestacks amidships belching thick smoke into the Cuban air. Her hull has been painted white, the traditional peacetime color, and she's an imposing sight to the excited crowds who greet her with mixed emotions on the waterfront.

Her arrival shows some evidence of haste. Spanish officials discover that the ship doesn't have the required documents certifying the crew is free of yellow fever. No matter. The Spanish commander sends out a case of excellent sherry to Captain Sigsbee and his officers. They come ashore, have dinner with Lee, and are invited to see a bullfight next day. In New York, the *Journal* salutes the *Maine*'s safe arrival with a triumphant headline: "OUR FLAG IN HAVANA AT LAST."

Meanwhile, another blow to relations between Spain and the United States is being manufactured by--this time--a Spanish journalist. Don José Canalejas, editor of *El Heraldo* in Madrid, has been visiting Havana, hoping to find out what's really going on, and early in February, as he's getting ready to return to Spain, a Cuban acquaintance named Gustavo Escoto drops in on him. What Canalejas doesn't know is that Escoto is an agent of the Junta. Seeing that the editor's private secretary is busy packing papers, Escoto offers to help. While he's doing so, with both the editor and his secretary out of the room, Escoto sees a letter from Depuy de Lome, the Spanish Ambassador. Reading it quickly, he stuffs it in his pocket and hops on the next boat to New York, where he turns this document over to Horatio Rubens at the Junta office.

It's a letter de Lome should never have written, and it's going to be enough not only to do him in but to create another international incident. In it, the ambassador gives his frank opinion of McKinley, which is devastating: "...Besides the natural and inevitable coarseness with which he [McKinley] repeats all that the press and the public opinion of Spain have said of Weyler, it shows once more that McKinley is weak and catering to the rabble and, besides, a low politician who desires to leave the door open to himself and to stand well with the jingoes of his party." That's bad enough, but de Lome goes on to call Governor Blanco's plan for autonomy a fraud, a sentiment with which many Cubans will agree.

Horatio Rubens knows what to do with this incriminating letter. He makes a copy and gives it to the *Journal*, and Hearst devotes an entire front page to it under a blazing headline: "THE WORST INSULT TO THE UNITED STATES IN ITS HISTORY." De Lome's immediate resignation is demanded. Doing a little research, the *Journal* turns up a book the ambassador wrote twenty-two years earlier, in which he made disparaging remarks about American women. Another gross insult! That inspires some *Journal* writer to contribute a few lines of doggerel, duly printed:

"Depuy de Lome, Depuy de Lome, what's this I hear of you? Have you been throwing mud again, is what they're saying true?"

"Get out, I say, get out before I start to fight. Just pack your few possessions and take a boat for home, I would not like my boot to use but--oh--get out, De Lome."

All this is accompanied by one of Homer Davenport's inflammatory cartoons, depicting De Lome being booted out of the country by the figure of Uncle Sam, with a caption: "The Flag of Cuba Ought to Float Over Morro Castle."

De Lome has been around long enough to know when he's finished, and he resigns at once, leaving Washington on February 11. On the same day, he gets a sort of revenge when the *Journal's* 138-foot yacht, the *Buccaneer*, the *Vamoose's* successor, is boarded by the Havana harbor police as she attempts to dock, right under the nose of the *Maine*. The police are still looking for Decker, and they've heard a rumor he might be on board, but all they find is Nathaniel Hawthorne's son, Julian, the author of best-selling novels, whom the *Journal* has just assigned to Cuba. Looking around, however, they spot a few artillery pieces and take them away, to the paper's outrage. Next morning, the *Journal* declares "The Spanish-Journal War," which is hardly news by this time.

So we come to the fateful night of February 15. It's the second day of carnival, and the whole city is deliriously drunk with revelry in the hours before Lent. To avoid any possible trouble, the crew of the *Maine* has been forbidden shore leave and the men are already in their quarters. They've been denied any on-shore recreation for three weeks, and the only thing that has kept them docile is the prospect that by Mardi Gras time, on February 17, they will be in New Orleans. This hope was dashed a few days earlier by notification that their departure has been postponed. The reason is that Lee, his initial fears of anti-American riots calmed, has decided it wouldn't be a good idea to let the *Maine* leave just now, before it can be replaced.

On this cloudy, moonless night in February, the sultry air scarcely moving, Sigmund Rothschild and a friend are sitting at the rail of the Ward Line steamer, *City of Washington*, anchored near the *Maine*, and they agree that the big battleship is a

for an Immediate Court of Inquiry---260 Men Dead

DESPATCH TO THE STATE DEPARTMENT, THE CAPTAIN SAYS THE ACCIDENT WAS MADE

on, Just Arrived from Havana, Says He Overheard Talk There of a Plot to Blc ;i, the Dynamite Expert, and Other Experts Report to The World that the Wre \ccidental---Washington Officials Ready for Vigorous Action if Spanish Respon Can Be Shown---Divers to Be Sent Down to Make Careful Examinations

New York World, February 17, 1898

courtesy, New York Public Library

comforting sight. On shore, John Caldwell files his nightly report to the *Herald*--this time one word, "tranquil"--and goes to join other reporters sitting in a dockside cantina.

On the *Maine*, Captain Sigsbee is in his cabin, writing to his wife, telling her that he's just found a letter in his uniform pocket, addressed to her from an old friend, that he's been carrying around for ten months and forgot to give to her. As he finishes his own letter, he hears the bugler blowing taps; it's nine-thirty. All but four of his officers, who have gone ashore, are lounging about the deck or reading in their bunks. Sigsbee puts his letter in an envelope, seals and addresses it. In the junior wardroom, naval cadet W. T. Cluvarius has also finished a letter at the same time and has also sealed and addressed it. Both men glance at their watches and, as they report later, note the time. It's nine-forty.

At that moment the *Maine* blows up in a burst of flame and destruction. Lieutenant John Hood, the chief watch officer, who's been sitting on the port side of the deck, testifies later that he felt rather than heard the explosion, which seemed to him to be coming from underwater, near the forward section of the starboard deck. "I instantly turned my head," he testifies, "and there was a second explosion. I saw the whole starboard side of the deck and everything above it as far as the aft end of the superstructure spring up into the air with all kinds of objects in it--a regular crater-like performance with flames and everything else coming up."

In the Café Inglaterra, windows shatter and the Scovels, along with the rest of the patrons, duck for cover as they see the sky over the harbor flare with a brilliant white light. On the *City of Washington*, Rothschild and his friend, deafened by the blast, stagger for cover from the debris beginning to fall from the sky. Captain Frederick Teasdale, sitting in his cabin on the British boat *Deva*, tied up to a wharf about a half mile away, is shocked from deep sleep by the explosion, which knocks out the transom of his stateroom door.

At the Spanish navy yard's quarters on shore, Lieutenant Julio Perera is reading in his bunk when the shock wave of the blast throws him to the floor, and at that moment, every light in Havana goes out. In the darkness, a bugle sounds, calling out the garrison. Turmoil on the streets. A cavalry troop riding back from maneuvers is momentarily staggered by the shock wave, and then the frightened horses begin galloping through the dark streets, now crowded with people.

On the *Maine*, the lights are out too and Sigsbee, leaving his cabin, bumps into someone coming in. "Who's there?" he calls. From the darkness, a voice: "Ensign Anthony, sir. I have to report to the captain that the ship has blown up and is sinking." There's nothing like Navy discipline.

Only one man saw the explosion at first hand and lived to tell about it, according to A. C. M. Azoy, a historian of the event. That was fireman William Gartrell, who was on the ship's lowest deck in the steering engine room in the far stern. He happened to be looking through a compartment when the brilliant blue flame of the explosion suddenly dazzled him. He and Frank Gardner, a coal passer who was with him, say later that they felt scarcely any shock, but they ran to the ladders along the starboard side.

Beginning the long, perilous climb to safety, Gardner hits his head on a steel beam and can't go on, but Gartrell pushes toward safety, up two ladders and along a passageway, then past a door leading to the junior officers' wardroom, and at last up one more ladder to the wardroom itself, with the rising water lapping at his feet through the whole horrendous climb. He finds a mess attendant, Westmore Harris, and they begin to pray until they hear an officer yelling, "There's hope, men! Follow me!" Guided by his voice, they tumble out at last on deck, where Gartrell faints. He's rescued later.

Captain Sigsbee and his orderly, meanwhile, have reached the main deck, already awash. In the light from the flames, they can see that the deck farther aft is still above water and they reach its momentary safety. Standing by the starboard rail, Sigsbee takes stock. The entire forward part of the ship is a ghastly wreck. Two funnels are hanging over the side, and beyond them he can see a jumble of twisted steel plates, rigging, davits, fittings--and bodies. He feels the ship slowly sinking, and hears an eerie whistle, telling him that there's water in the watertight compartments, pushing air up through cracks in the deck.

Dazed officers gather around him. They've found safety after groping through darkness and wreckage, and they'll all have frightening stories to tell later. One of the worst tales from a crewman is messman John Turpin's story. He had been serving a meal before bedtime in the senior officers' mess when the blast threw him and others to the floor, where he was briefly unconscious. Getting to his feet, dazed, Lieutenant Fred Jenkins calls, "Which way out?" and Turpin answers dutifully, "I don't know, sir." At that point the second explosion occurs, and Turpin sees Jenkins make a despairing gesture and disappear in the shoulder-deep water. Miraculously, Turpin feels a rope swing against his face, and climbs up it to the deck. Jenkins is gone.

On the sinking ship, Sigsbee quickly organizes rescue and salvage parties to answer the cries for help that seem to be coming from everywhere, on the ship and from those already swimming in the shark-inhabited waters. They will be rescued by the *City of Washington*, the *Deva*, and the Spanish cruiser *Alfonso XII*.

It takes less than fifteen minutes for Sigsbee to determine that all the wounded have been taken off and there's nothing more to be done. Only then does he give the order, "Abandon ship." One more lifeboat is waiting for him at the rail of the quarterdeck. Rowed over to the *City of Washington*, his first act is to scrawl a message on the back of an envelope to Secretary of the Navy John Davis Long, in Washington: "Maine blown up in Havana Harbor at nine-forty tonight and destroyed. Public opinion should be suspended until further report."

The makers of public opinion are already at work. Scovel and George Rea find themselves in a rescue boat with Havana's chief of police, Colonel José Paglieri. The chief has made a career of arresting Harry, who is soon able to scribble an eyewitness account. "The superstructure alone loomed up, partly colored by the red glare of flames glancing upon the black water," he writes. As a searchlight sweeps the water around the chief's boat, he and the others can see parts of bodies floating, and Rea hears Scovel exclaim, already coming to a Hearstian conclusion, "Great God! They're all gone. This is the work of a torpedo, and it marks the beginning of the end." Actually, it's more like the end of the beginning.

The chief's boat arrives at the *City of Washington* and everyone climbs aboard. Sigsbee is there, recognizes Scovel, pencils another message to Washington, and asks him to see that it gets on the cable. Appropriating the chief's boat, Scovel and Rea hurry back to the cable office, which is awash with reporters because the clerk who operates it has gone home and has to be retrieved.

When he arrives, everyone lines up, but Scovel and Rea get priority because they have Captain Sigsbee's message, so they're first. Harry also, as usual, has something else up his sleeve. Some time ago a friendly Cuban had filched and given to him a blank cable form, pre-stamped by the censor. He's been saving it for the rainy day that has just arrived. Sigsbee's cable goes off first, but Scovel's purloined form is next. It's not a clear scoop, however. Fred Hilgert, the Associated Press's Havana man, sent the first bulletin before the clerk went home. Nevertheless, Scovel is only minutes behind, and his is the first account of the tragedy. It will take a later cable to give the American public the worst news: 260 of the *Maine*'s 350 officers and men are dead.

In Washington, Secretary Long gets Sigsbee's first cable shortly before 1 A.M. and the Navy Department's windows on Seventeenth Street light up as though it, too, is exploding. Messengers begin running in and out. Helen Long, the Secretary's daughter, coming home from a ball, finds one of them at the doorstep and takes the dispatch to her father in bed. He lets McKinley sleep a little longer before, at dawn, he sends a Navy officer to wake him up. McKinley comes down to have breakfast with his house guest, Myron Herrick, looking gaunt and depressed.

A sense of calamity grips Washington that day. Nothing like it has been seen since the assassination of President Garfield. Flags are lowered at half-mast, all official functions are canceled, silent crowds gather outside the White House, as well as in the lobbies of the War, Navy, and State buildings. Those at State gaze mutely at a scale model of the *Maine*, outside Long's office, until workmen come in, open the glass case, and take down the tiny ensign from its peak, meanwhile placing one at half-mast on the stern. A mingled sense of grief, anger, outrage, and fear sweeps from coast to coast. As Guy Perret tells us, the governor of Texas dispatches a company of Rangers to guard the border--from what, no one is clear. A Broadway musical comedy, *The Bride Elect*, reaps an unexpected benefit when one of its songs, "Unleash the Dogs of War!" elicits nightly cheers from the audience. Even the conservative *Atlantic* magazine, which has been fighting adamantly against the interventionists, feels compelled to spread an American flag on its cover.

If anyone is happy about the *Maine*'s sinking, it's Hearst. He's no monster, so his regret over the loss of life is genuine enough, but when he hears the news, his first reaction is an exultant, "This means war!" and, as Swanberg describes it, his subsequent coverage of the disaster "still stands as the orgasmic acme of ruthless, truthless newspaper jingoism." To him, the *Maine*'s sinking means that his wish for war is going to be fulfilled. The Junta is happy, too, because their cause has been flagging, and they know that unless the United States goes to war, they may be out of business.

In Havana, the reaction verges on chaos. When he hears the news, Blanco bursts into tears, imagining at once the dreadful consequences that are sure to follow. He does what he can for the moment, sending a delegation of officers to express official regret and then organizing every kind of assistance possible.

What Blanco and everyone else wants to know is: "Who did it?" There is a reasonable explanation and many unreasonable ones. On the side of reason is the Spanish contention that the explosion was an accident. There's plenty of evidence to support that theory. These coal-powered ships like the *Maine*, whose keel had been laid in 1888, have a design flaw. The coal bunkers are close to the ship's magazine, and the heat from the bunkers is a threat to it. Already, in 1897, there had been a dozen or more fires on American ships, and on one, the cruiser *Cincinnati*, wooden ammunition crates had caught fire but catastrophe was averted in time.

It isn't just the Spaniards who advance this theory. The Navy's Bureau of Ordnance believes from the start that this is what happened. Answering the public cry that the *Maine* was sunk by a Spanish torpedo, Philip R. Alger, the Navy's leading explosives expert, asserts: "No torpedo, such as is known to modern warfare, can of itself cause an explosion as powerful as that which destroyed the *Maine*. We know of no instance where the explosion of a torpedo or mine under a ship's bottom has exploded the magazine within." The non-interventionists seize on this statement and Thomas Reed, Speaker of the House, declares it proves that battleships are dangerous and we should stop building them. Roosevelt denounces Reed and says the blast was "an act of dirty treachery."

It will be eighty-nine years before Philip Alger and the Spanish Board of Inquiry are vindicated. In 1976, for reasons not clear, the Navy's foremost experts on the subject will study the *Maine*'s sinking and conclude that she was sunk by internal explosion, presumably caused by a fire in a coal bunker which reached the ammunition. The Spanish Board had also pointed out that, if a mine or torpedo had been the cause, a geyser of water, which no one saw, would have been thrown high in the air, and the harbor next day would have been covered with dead fish, also unreported.

Meanwhile, in Havana, Scovel and his fellow correspondents are fairly sure the explosion was an accident, but on the other hand, they know how many Loyalists, hoping to provoke war, are possible suspects. Blanco orders an immediate investigation, and divers are soon busy in the harbor. Scovel writes that the mystery will be cleared up in twenty-four hours, but of course he's off by decades.

There are immediate problems, too. Since Blanco's divers haven't the authority to remove bodies from the wreckage, the afternoon of the explosion finds a cloud of vultures sitting on the hull, still protruding above the water, and horrified spectators on shore can see them swooping in to pick at American flesh. Next morning, this horror is compounded when charred bodies begin to surface and the tide washes them up against the seawall.

The lighthouse tender *Fern*, whose senior officer is Roosevelt's brother-in-law, Lieutenant Commander William S. Cowles, has arrived after a quick trip from Key West, but it has no divers, and no further help is expected for another day. Some of the sailors from the *Fern* try to approach the wreck, but the Havana harbor police turn them away.

Blanco wants a joint inquiry into the affair, and says he will take charge of the recovery work, but Lee tells him that the prospect for cooperation is slight, considering Washington's and the nation's present state of mind. Lee urges Sigsbee to take temporary command, but the captain is still too dazed, sitting on the deck of the *City of Washington*, hour after hour, watching what's left of the *Maine* rising up from the water. Sympathetic correspondents defend him, but they know he's out of it. Scovel and the others are quick, however, to belabor the Navy for not moving faster. The four officers on

$50,000 REWARD—WHO DESTROYED THE MAINE

MAINE
NEW YORK JOURN
EXTRA

NEW YORK, THURSDAY, FEBRUARY 17, 1898.

WAR! SURE!

MAINE DESTROYED BY SPANISH; THIS PRC
ABSOLUTELY BY DISC

FORTUNE
OFFERED BY
THE JOURNAL.

TORPEDO

Cable Cut Between Havana and Key West an the Navy Department Unable to Obtain News—Fleet Mobilizing off Florida.

VIZCAYA ORDERED NOT TO ENTER THIS PORT.

Señor Du Bosc Charge d'Affaires of the Spanish Legation has sent instructions to New York to hire a tug and get word to the Command-
of New York harbor until further notice from him
the Charge d'Affaires that the presence of the Vizcaya might precipitate serious trouble

TORPEDO HOLE FOUND IN THE MAINE.
BY GEORGE EUGENE BRYSON

The Maine was destroyed by a torpedo; the whole city knows it, and is waiting almost with a bated breath for what must follow. This morn
have been [so entirely] ignorant of the [nature] of the lost battle ship reported the discovery of the evidence of design in the Maine's destruction. One
made soundings just under that portion of the Maine where the men had their bunks, was badly shattered. There was an eight-inch hole and th
head inward. On the larger scale the wound just like what would be inflicted by driving the point of a lead pencil through a bit

DIVERS ELUDED SPANISH GUARD AND EXAMINED THE HULL
made the discovery eluded police guard last night and made their investigation privately. It is not known whether they are agents of Captain
American Government An uncertain rumor ascribes the authorship of the enterprise to the English Consul. England would naturally
affair for its own purpose. General Bollam denies that he put the divers to work.

DISCOVERY CAUSES GREAT EXCITEMENT IN HAVANA.
throughout the city, and the wildest excitement prevails, though as yet has not taken the form of popular tumult. The Palace officials are par-
CONTINUED ON SECOND PAGE.

New York Journal, February 17, 1898

shore leave and the uninjured survivors have been evacuated to Key West, but no hospital ship or nurses have arrived, and there's also a problem of what to do with the dead bodies. The injured are lying in Havana hospitals, where the nurses don't speak English and so are unable either to console them or to forward messages to families. Frances Scovel and the wives of other correspondents come to help them out.

But the bodies won't wait, and on February 17, Sigsbee accepts Blanco's offer to bury them in a military cemetery, with full honors and the Bishop of Havana attending. It takes nineteen hearses to convey the bodies. The Catholic chaplain of the *Maine*, Father Chadwick, conducts the services, during which Sigsbee reads from the Episcopal prayer book. American mourners present are incensed that Washington has no idea that Protestant pastors don't exist in Havana and haven't sent one down.

While the funeral is going on, the harbor is full of divers, not only Blanco's but teams from the *Journal*, the *Herald*, and the *World*, with Navy divers arriving a day later. The harbor police won't let anyone approach the wreck, however, and the authorities won't even permit Sigsbee to examine the remains of his ship unless he gets a pass from Blanco. Lee and Sigsbee go to see Blanco, protesting that, even though sunk, the *Maine* is still an American ship and Sigsbee has a right to visit her. The governor is trying hard to extricate himself from this nightmare without any more difficulties so he suggests that each nation should investigate separately, and promises to restrain the harbor police. Later, an American ensign rows out and puts a flag on the upthrust hull of the sunken ship.

Talking it over, the correspondents are skeptical. After all, the Spanish divers have been out there for three days, and if they've found anything incriminating, they have no doubt removed it. Scovel and the others poke around the debris that's been piled up on the dock, and they find a piece of the forward compartment from the berth deck which has an eight-inch hole in it, with the flanges bent in--the kind of tear a torpedo would make. Bryson thinks that it's enough evidence. He writes: "The *Maine* was destroyed by a torpedo," and his story runs beneath a *Journal* headline, "WAR! SURE!" with the subheads, "Maine Destroyed by Spanish. This Proved Absolutely by Discovery of the 'Torpedo Hole." What follows is "the most hysterical newspaper campaign in American history," as Joyce Milton puts it. Hearst is now screaming for war at the top of his journalistic lungs.

Into this overheated atmosphere, only three days after the *Maine*'s disaster, the innocent *Vizcaya* anchors in New York Harbor, the other half of the exchange State had negotiated. Captain Antonio Eulate is profoundly shocked by the news of what's happened. He orders the ship's flag flown at half-mast and cancels any appearances at the festivities the Junta has been planning. That isn't enough to satisfy the paranoid public. A cordon of patrol boats has to be thrown around the ship after the *World* warns that she might have "treacherous intentions," and gloomily predicts: "While lying off the Battery, her shells will explode on the Harlem River and in the suburbs of Brooklyn." The Spanish authorities in New York and Washington don't take this seriously, but they're so suspicious of *Journal* reporters that they won't permit them to board the *Vizcaya* and also temporarily cut them off from the cable office in Havana.

Hearst attacks anyone who opposes war with Spain, including presidential advisor Senator Mark Hanna. According to the *Journal*, his and McKinley's efforts to avoid war are just an attempt to protect the profits of their Wall Street friends. As anger rises to a new pitch around the country, Hearst recruits a posse of senators and congressmen to go see for themselves what's happening in Cuba, inviting each of them to write his impressions for the *Journal*.

All of these junketers come home deploring in print the terrible devastation, but the wife of Senator John Thurston, of Nebraska, pens a special letter to "Journal mothers," pulling out all the stops: "Oh! Mothers of the Northland, who tenderly clasp your little ones to your loving hearts! Think of the black despair that filled each Cuban mother's heart as she felt her lifeblood ebb away, and knew that she had left her little ones to perish from the pain of starvation and disease."

If there's anyone capable of really denouncing what Hearst is doing, it's E. L. Godkin, nearing the end of his notable career as editor of the New York *Evening Post*, whose influence far surpasses its meager circulation. Godkin has been watching the press carnival in Cuba and at home with disgust, and he writes: "When one of [the yellow journals] offers a yacht voyage, with free wine, rum and cigars, and a good bed, under the guise of philanthropy, or gets up a committee for Holy purposes, and promises to puff it, it can get almost anyone it pleases to go on the yacht voyage and serve on the committee--senators, lawyers, divines, scholars, poets, presidents, and what not. Every one who knows anything about 'yellow journalism' knows that everything they do and say is intended to promote sales. No one--absolutely no one--supposes a yellow journal cares five cents about the Cubans, the *Maine* victims, or any one else. A yellow journal is probably the nearest approach to hell, existing in any Christian state."

It isn't hard to agree with Godkin when the *Journal* proposes to raise a regiment of muscular athletes, including the boxers "Sunny Jim" Fitzsimmons and James Corbett, baseball player Cap Anson, hammer thrower Jim Mitchell, and Red Water, an Indian football player. All of them agree to join up for what the paper promises will be "a war of revenge."

Inspired by this action, Jesse James's brother, Frank, offers to head a cowboy company. There are plenty of other recruits in the Wild West: 600 Sioux Indians, for instance, and representing the good guys, according to the *World*, 30,000 Indian fighters under the leadership of Buffalo Bill Cody, who promises they will clear out the Spaniards in two months. Hearst has been claiming it's "our war," but it's beginning to look like everybody's war.

To those who might accuse Hearst of egging others on to possible loss of life and limb while he lives in luxury, the publisher writes to the President offering to arm and equip a cavalry regiment, including himself as a volunteer, disclaiming modestly that he seeks no more than to be "a man in the ranks." McKinley thanks him, coolly, and declines. Not to be put off, Hearst tries to get into the Navy, offering the *Buccaneer* as well as himself. The yacht would be armed and manned with sailors Hearst would enlist himself and pay out of his own pocket. This offer is accepted, with the provision that the ship be manned by Navy men and officers. The Navy offers to examine Hearst as a possible line officer, but the publisher is suddenly coy.

Through it all, after the *Maine*'s demise, McKinley maintains calm in the face of public pressure. He appoints a Navy Board of Inquiry, led by Captain William T. Sampson, the *Iowa*'s commander, to investigate the sinking, and he accepts Madrid's regrets and sympathy. To Senator Charles W. Fairbanks, of Indiana, he says: "I don't propose to be swept off my feet by the catastrophe. My duty is plain. We must learn the truth and endeavor, if possible, to fix the responsibility. The country can afford to withhold its judgment and not strike an avenging blow until the truth is known. The Administration will go on preparing for war, but still hoping to avert it. It will not be plunged into war until it is ready for it."

But a great emotional surge toward war is already sweeping the country. Public opinion generally doesn't believe the *Maine* was sunk by accident, and when the Spanish Board of Inquiry decides it was, they're even more certain of foul play. The facts may lead the Navy Board of Inquiry to the same conclusion, but they're not likely to reach it because such a verdict would be an admission that there was something wrong with the ship's design, or with the way it was operated. Not to mention that a battleship had been lost through negligence while it was on a most sensitive mission.

But the Navy Board has an escape hatch. It's asked only to determine whether there was any negligence on the part of officers or crew, not what caused the explosion. Sigsbee comes off badly in the inquiry. Still possibly in some kind of post-traumatic shock, he can't remember details, leading Admiral Hyman Rickover to observe in the 1976 study of the sinking that Sigsbee's testimony depicted "an individual who was unfamiliar with his ship. Whatever the reasons, he appears to have been isolated from the day-to-day routine."

As the inquiry progresses, the evidence seems to show (erroneously) that the *Maine* was blown up by a mine, either planted or floating. Lee sends a staff member, Henry Drain, to testify that a letter signed simply "An Admirer" had been received at the consulate, outlining a conspiracy by Morallo Street merchants to plant a mine. But it turns out that the letter was passed to the consulate by none other than Carlos Carbonelle, Evangelina's soon-to-be husband, who as a Junta agent is hardly the reliable source Lee thinks he is.

For eighteen days the Board goes on taking testimony, in Washington, Key West, and Havana. Then, in four more days, it produces its report, wrong in every particular, as we know now. It says a submarine mine destroyed the *Maine* but doesn't say how it happened, and is unable to pin responsibility on anyone.

While this verdict only raises more questions, it has one positive result: it moves Spain as well as America closer to war.

How can the public help it? William James, the eminent psychologist, recalled years later that "in 1898 our people read the word 'war' in letters three inches high for three months in every newspaper." On some days, according to Lawrence I. Berkove, the Ambrose Bierce scholar, "it was possible to read the first four or five pages of a Hearst paper without finding any article of substance except war stories."

War fever is running high in Havana, too. As the *Maine* hearings drag on, preparations for war are everywhere. The harbor batteries are made ready for action, and for the first time in years, the army takes gunnery practice. Anti-Americanism is rife. Correspondents are suspected of being spies, and some of them might as well be. The inimitable Scovel, for example, sneaks out of the city before daylight one day and, hiding in the hills, looks down on the Santa Clara battery, which is practicing firing at targets being towed two miles offshore. They aren't very good at it, he notes. Scovel doesn't know what to do with this information, since Captain Sampson, who is sitting with the Navy Board in Havana at the moment, has refused to speak with either reporters or witnesses.

In fact, Scovel is thinking of setting up a spy ring, using the work of the *World*'s Havana bureau as a cover, and goes so far as to send George Rea, who's now working for him and the paper, to Puerto Rico to gather military information while he's presumably writing articles.

In New York, nearly all the papers are crying for war, in one degree or another. Madness prevails. The *World* takes a survey of women in ten cities and finds that nine out of ten favor war. The Brooklyn *Eagle* hires teams of operators who will monitor all 7,500 telephone subscribers in Brooklyn and Long Island if war is declared. Somewhat ruefully, the *Wall Street Journal* admits that the lower end of Manhattan is still anti-war for the most part.

In the Junta's New York office, where peanuts are still being served, there is deep suspicion of the American government. These activists have come to believe that the United States has done nothing for three years except to extend sympathy, and now intends to intervene and snatch away Cuban independence just at the moment it seems possible.

President William McKinley

reproduced from the collections of the Library of Congress

But even *they* don't grasp the mixed motives that are stirring the pot to a boil in Washington. The truth is that the Administration fears Spanish withdrawal because the Germans, who have been hovering around on the periphery, might step in as they had in Haiti. In any case, America isn't particularly interested in seeing a democratic regime set up in Cuba, and never has been. Liberals may be bleeding for the Cuban people, but the conservatives who control the government are hoping the Spanish Empire will keep on falling apart and the United States will gather up the pieces, the Germans notwithstanding. A similar division of opinion in Congress isn't going to make a declaration of war easy. All we can be sure of at this point is that inevitable war is sticking its black nose around the corner.

5

TO THE BRINK--AND OVER IT

SINCE THE WHOLE COUNTRY IS EAGER FOR WAR AFTER THE *Maine* disaster, a good many people can't understand why McKinley is so reluctant, why he continues to resist. Is he just an aging, weak man who doesn't want to take on the responsibilities of war? Or does he have some kind of secret agenda---some Wall Street deal or sinister hidden motive?

None of the above. The roots of the President's extreme caution lie in his life and the character shaped by it. As the historian Gerald F. Linderman observes, "The Civil War was McKinley's bridge to manhood." When it began, he was only eighteen. The nation was alive with partisan passions, but young William felt no great exaltation, no stirring call to arms. His view of the conflict was strictly cerebral. After watching the first volunteers entrain, he talked the matter over dispassionately with a cousin and decided "in cold blood" that he should enlist as a private because it was his duty. Considering the awful carnage, McKinley served through it all as though he were being protected for posterity. During the four years of the conflict, he rose from private to brevet major, fought in a dozen of the bloodiest battles, was never wounded, never even had a serious illness, and was cited at least three times for courageous action. One of those times occurred at Antietam, when, as a commissary sergeant in the 23rd Ohio Volunteer Infantry, he drove through heavy musketry fire with a team of mules to take food and coffee to the front lines. His colonel, Rutherford B. Hayes, another future President, gave him a commendation for this action.

Again, as Union troops retreated from Kernstown, Virginia, McKinley braved heavy enemy fire to deliver a message that gave an exposed regiment the opportunity to retire before being annihilated. By this time he was a staff officer. In the same battle, he led a volunteer force to retrieve abandoned cannons.

Through all the four years of conflict, one thing characterized McKinley: a turning inward, not outward. His concern was for the safety and welfare of his comrades, not the destruction of the enemy. He never killed a Confederate soldier, as Linderman points out, and would have thought it "a burden, not an honor" if he had. Always a religious man, he attended camp services as often as he could.

McKinley discovered that he wasn't alone in these feelings. Watching a Union surgeon treating a wounded Confederate soldier with special care, he inquired and found that the doctor was a Mason, and that other Union Masons were helping their Southern lodge brothers whenever they could. This good deed took place near Winchester, Virginia, and McKinley immediately joined the lodge in that village and was a Mason for the rest of his life, as George Washington had been.

Young McKinley came out of the war with a hatred for everything he had seen. He never talked about military accomplishments, and the horror never faded from his memory, as it did for so many of his comrades. At the time of their discharge, they may have agreed with Sherman that war was hell, but their feelings began to dissolve in a haze of reconciliation at G.A.R. encampments, patriotic speeches on the Fourth of July, and frequent wavings of the bloody shirt. By 1890, even such intellects as Oliver Wendell Holmes, Jr., along with millions of lesser Americans, had come to believe that to fight in a war was somehow a test of a young man's virtue as he fought against someone else's moral values.

In the days before the conflict with Spain begins, the President is not one of these people. He doesn't believe personal qualities can only be tested by battle, and when the papers call for war, he stops reading them. He suffers when his name is hissed by crowds in the music halls, and when it's reported that he's been burned in effigy. But he simply can't bring himself to lead the country into war until there is no way to avoid it. As the last Civil War soldier to occupy the White House, he tells his physician Leonard Wood, not long after the *Maine* disaster: "I have been through one war, I have seen the dead piled up, and I do not want to see another."

But he can't avoid his responsibilities as a political leader either. A committee of nearly fifty Republican caucus members call on him and inform him that the party is facing disaster if he persists in resisting war with Spain. His Vice-President, Garret A. Hobart, takes him on an afternoon carriage ride and tells him the blunt truth: "Mr. President, I can no longer hold back action by the Senate; they will act without you if you do not act at once." Disunity in the party and his country--how much longer can he hold out?

The Cabinet and his other advisers aren't going to be much help. Every Tuesday and Friday morning he looks around his improvised desk at the eight old men he is supposed to rely on for advice. Here is his Secretary of State, John Sherman, gaunt in a loose black suit that doesn't fit him, and often not quite with it. In author Margaret Leech's words, "He looked baffled and insulted, like a workman asked to perform a delicate task with a blunt and damaged tool." Yet he's the only member of the Cabinet with any experience in foreign affairs. For Cuba's suffering population he has merely perfunctory sympathy; Sherman believes only commercial considerations are important. On the other hand, he feels public pressure and has come to believe war is unavoidable, although he won't support any action, like enlarging the Navy, that would bring it nearer. Yet this is the same man who once advocated acquiring Canada. At Cabinet meetings, he usually sits silently, his mind confused.

Who will act for him then? Unfortunately, it's the First Assistant Secretary, Judge William R. Day, a lawyer from Canton, Ohio, "thin and pale, with melancholy red mustaches," as Leech describes him, a man who hates Washington and his job. This bureaucrat is now taking direct charge of the most important matters at State, and he's doing it out of simple loyalty to McKinley.

Somebody has to mind the store and do the hard work, however. That's the Second Assistant Secretary of State, Alvey A. Adee, a career diplomat who does the dogsbody work of drafting instructions, deciphering secret messages, analyzing communications from other governments, and generally representing State. He does command respect even though he's extremely deaf and his voice is a falsetto.

Surveying the command structure at State, one diplomat is moved to remark privately: "The head of the [State] department knows nothing, the First Assistant says nothing, and the Second Assistant hears nothing." Whitelaw Reid, a Civil War reporter turned diplomat, who will eventually become publisher of the

New York *Herald Tribune*, is rumored to be Sherman's successor. He has an even more wounding thing to say about the Secretary, whom he calls "a little ragged boy in Cincinnati."

Such men are not capable of dealing with the national mood, many people think. In America, a whole generation has grown up since the Civil War, knowing nothing of the dreadful realities that their fathers and uncles faced. Young firebrands like Theodore Roosevelt are the essence of this new breed. Nor is the present crop of intellectuals immune to war fever. Brooks Adams writes about war as though it's a noble endeavor in itself, taking the Darwinian view that such conflict is nature's way of improving the breed.

But other millions of people disagree, and the struggle is exemplified by John Long, Secretary of the Navy, who was a leading figure in the Peace Society before he got his Cabinet job, and whose assistant is Roosevelt, the most pugnacious advocate of war. In a speech at the Naval War College, T.R. has already declared that "no triumph of peace is quite so great as the supreme triumph of war."

This view is supported by the reform elements in the population--the Populist followers of William Jennings Bryan and those who will later become Progressives, along with moralist crusaders of every variety. Politically, to oppose war is suicide. Senator Henry Cabot Lodge tells McKinley: "If the war in Cuba drags on through the summer with nothing done, we [the Republican Party] shall go down to the greatest defeat ever known."

There are all kinds of mixed motives involved in this rush to war. Former abolitionists envision the freeing of slaves in Cuba when Spain is defeated, and some diehard Southerners deplore this possibility. Black people idolize mulatto generals like Maceo and their sympathies are naturally with the rebels. Organized labor supports *Cuba libre* because it fears an influx of refugees looking for jobs if Spain wins. Their leader, Samuel Gompers, who began his career as president of the cigar makers' union, knows something about Spanish exploitation. But Cuban liberty also has strong support in the Middle Western business community, which expects new markets for American goods in Cuba and Latin America. Consequently the Bryan liberals who are pushing for war are joined by the National Association of Manufacturers and leading trade journals, who are convinced the end of Spanish rule means a rapid economic development.

This mixture had already been demonstrated in May 1896, when the Cuban-American Liberty League, founded the year before by a businessman named William O. McDowell, held its Great Cuban-American Fair in Madison Square Garden. For two weeks, everything was sold there, as Milton records--"tropical produce, potted plants, specialty food items, Havana cigars, smoking accessories, and Cuban handicrafts." Society matrons supported this enterprise and ran concessions. The *World* reported that debutantes were recruited to stroll through the crowds selling bouquets of roses.

A particularly riveting feature of this event was Mrs. W. H. Jenny's tableau vivant, "Gypsy Camp in a Rocky Grotto," with the lady herself as queen of the gypsies, whose court included a bevy of Broadway showgirls. Mrs. Jenny appeared to be under the impression that the Cubans were gypsies. She was overshadowed momentarily on opening night, however, by the fiery General Daniel Sickles, the Civil War hero who lost his leg at Gettysburg. Forty-three years earlier, as a legislator, Sickles had been one of the engineers of the Ostend Manifesto, an early attempt by the United States to acquire Cuba. He was less celebrated for this diplomacy, however, than for his later notoriety as the man who killed his wife's lover, Philip Key, the son of Francis Scott Key, composer of "The Star-Spangled Banner."

By the spring of 1898 the Cuban-American Fair has been all but forgotten, lost in a sea of conflicting ideas. Fitzhugh Lee, on the brink of the conflict, comes out strongly for self-determination for black Cubans, and the New York *Tribune* points out that this seems peculiar, since blacks in Lee's own state, Virginia, can't vote. How does it happen, the paper inquires editorially, that men like Lee, who never protested "the lynching of the 'nigger' in the South," now seem so hell-bent on "loving the nigger" in Cuba? "Can it be that they regard 'niggers' in Cuba more favorably than in Georgia or Mississippi?" Racism is only beginning to show its ugly face in this conflict.

If there's anything everybody can agree on, it's the financial necessity to get the war over with if we're going to have it. This insurrection has cost American traders and investors millions of dollars already, and neutrality is increasing the cost every day. It hasn't escaped some observers that much of the destruction in Cuba has been caused by the *insurrectos* themselves.

McKinley can understand the financial necessity well enough, but it only worsens his moral and political dilemma. He needs a good negotiator in Spain in these critical months, and it's not easy to find one. He settles on General Stewart L. Woodford, a New York lawyer, who goes to Madrid with instructions to stop the conflict in Cuba if there's any reasonable way to do it.

Before he can even get there, the Spanish premier, Canovas del Castillo, is assassinated by an anarchist, and this absolutist is succeeded by a liberal, Práxedes Mateo Segasta, who has never liked the Cuban war. He assures Woodford that what he wants is pacification and eventual home rule. It was Segasta who recalled Weyler and sent Blanco. However, he intends to carry on the war "by humane and Christian methods," whatever that means, and he so instructs Blanco. Woodford does secure permission for America to send down food, medicines, and other supplies. The public contributes generously to a relief fund, to which the President himself makes an anonymous contribution of $5,000.

If attempts at peacemaking are still going on in Madrid, contrary moves are being made in the American government, particularly by T.R., who is carrying on a confidential correspondence with Alfred Thayer Mahan, the influential naval historian who advocates the use of sea power. Roosevelt works out with him a plan for a two-ocean Navy capable of dominating a not yet built canal that would join the Atlantic and Pacific. Roosevelt believes war is imminent and he thinks that will be a good thing because it will give the armed forces some "actual practice." War, he is certain, will elevate America to a higher moral plane, far above its preoccupation with making money. As Leech describes him, his mentality is "somewhere between that of a Boy Scout and the young Kaiser Wilhelm."

Secretary Long carries on a running war with T.R. and succeeds in calming him down somewhat, but Long's health compels him to take a holiday of several weeks, and Roosevelt finds himself, to his exuberant delight, in command of the ship. The first thing he does is to make sure there will be an instant attack on the Philippines if war breaks out. Most Americans are not aware of this vulnerable Spanish possession; that includes

McKinley who, like many others, doesn't even know exactly where they are. One American who does know and has ambitions to use the islands as a vehicle to fame is Commodore George Dewey, who at the moment is president of the Navy's Board of Inspection and Survey. He's a white-haired Vermonter, nearly sixty, whose fierce mustaches and general demeanor give him an authoritarian appearance. He had been a young lieutenant in the Civil War, serving under Admiral Farragut on the Mississippi, a commander who became his role model. What Dewey wants from this prospective war is command of a squadron, and he's going to get it. Specifically, he wants the Pacific Squadron, remote from Washington's interference, and T.R. is "de-lighted" (as he would say) to provide it.

There will be a vacancy in the command of the Atlantic Squadron, too, and the man who wants this one is John A. Howell, "a plump old officer with spaniel's eyes and splendid sideburns," as Leech describes him. His résumé looks good: commander of the League Island Navy Yard in Philadelphia, an authority on steel and ordnance, inventor of a gyroscopically guided torpedo. Best of all, he ranks Dewey. On the debit side, he's been passed over repeatedly and can't get along with superiors--but he *does* have friends in Congress.

Before Long gets back from his vacation, T.R. finds a letter in his mail from one of those friends, Senator William E. Chandler, of New Hampshire, who urges that Howell get the next command available, which is going to be the Pacific Squadron. Roosevelt, who is not one of Howell's admirers, is determined to prevent any such appointment. He prods Dewey into calling on one of his congressional friends, Senator Redfield Proctor, of Vermont, the marble king and a former Secretary of War. Proctor, a friend of the President, is happy to help when Dewey calls on him. That same day he talks to McKinley and gets his promise to appoint Dewey--over seven other officers ahead of him.

Now that the Navy has given the Asiatic command to Dewey and the Atlantic to Howell, everyone should be satisfied, but the decision was so clearly a patronage deal that Dewey is indignant. He wanted the job, but he wanted it on merit. Worse, the Navy has refused to elevate him to the customary rank of rear admiral, and that makes him a bitter man. Just the same, he takes the job.

One thing this episode has accomplished is to bring Roosevelt closer to the President, who begins to see some merit in him, as T.R. does in McKinley. They are very different people, but Roosevelt sometimes dines with the President, goes with him on his afternoon drives, and is careful to laugh at his jokes. When T.R. talks about going to war himself, the President laughs indulgently, as though it's something he can't take seriously. T.R. also gives him little talks about preparedness, meanwhile flooding him with tides of data about the Navy.

Armed with his new command, Dewey sails in December 1897 for San Francisco, to take charge of the Asiatic Squadron. His instructions are to strike at Manila if war is declared. McKinley certifies this order, but as Herman Kohlsaat, publisher of the Chicago *Times-Herald*, says later, "He could not have told where those darned islands were within two thousand miles."

McKinley's mind is on Cuba, not the Philippines, wherever they are. He wants negotiation with Spain, even in the present atmosphere of nearly total distrust, but Spain is refusing to negotiate. Someone has to move the situation off its deadlocked center, and the surprising person who does it is Senator Proctor. Improbably, he turns out to be the catalyst for war.

Born in Cavendish, Vermont, Proctor has already done much to serve the country. His grandfather was lieutenant of the militia who fired a musket in the affair at Lexington, and young Proctor, after graduation from Dartmouth and an unsuccessful effort to seek his fortune in Minnesota, returned to his native state and fought in the Civil War as an officer in a Vermont regiment. After the war, he practiced law in Rutland, established his highly successful marble business, and became governor in 1878. Ten years later, he was Secretary of War in President Harrison's Cabinet, and in 1891 was appointed to the Senate, filling a vacancy.

In the spring of 1898, Proctor is one of those senators who takes a trip to Cuba to inspect the situation for himself. Most of those other politicians who went there have expended their conclusions in the *Journal*, but Proctor has something more to say and he says it on March 17, interrupting a boring debate in the Senate on the quarantine powers of the Marine Hospital Service. He rises to speak, as Linderman describes it, "tall and graybearded, with Lincoln's economy of body and a bearing conveying calm and dignity." He speaks for only a half hour, and it's anything but an outburst of passionate oratory. He gives a chronological and detailed account of Cuba's suffering under Spanish rule--dry, statistical, without emotion. Instead of putting everyone to sleep, he somehow galvanizes the chamber. Another senator says later, "It's just as if Proctor had held up his right hand and sworn to it." Speaker Reed is less charitable: "A war will make a large market for gravestones," he says.

At the end, Proctor sums up the situation. The war in Cuba, he says, has polarized the population of this island. There is no movement at the moment because each side has enough strength to resist any compromise, but neither is strong enough to impose its will on the other. There's something so compelling about his recital that former President Benjamin Harrison, who hears it, declares later, "No speech in any legislative assembly in the world in fifty years so powerfully affected the public sentiment."

There's nothing unusual in Proctor's speech, no new facts or perspectives, no specific course of action urged, but the combination of the senator's quiet personality and his words strikes a deep, resonant chord in America as well as the Senate. Proponents of the war are carried to new heights of enthusiasm by it and even many anti-interventionists are converted. It proves to be the final push toward war.

One of Proctor's most trenchant statements in his recital is a confession of his own conversion: "I went to Cuba with a strong conviction that the picture had been overdrawn; that a few cases of starving and suffering had inspired and stimulated the press correspondents, and they had given free play to a strong, natural, and highly cultivated imagination. Before starting I received through the mail a leaflet published by the *Christian Herald*, with cuts of some of the sick and starving reconcentrados, and took it with me, thinking these must be rare specimens, got up to make the worst possible showing. I saw plenty as bad or worse, many that should not be photographed and shown."

Of the situation outside Havana, he says: "It is desolation and distress, misery and starvation." The fortified towns are "virtually prison yards, and the hospitals are indescribable." He finds the plight of the reconcentrados heart-wrenching: "Torn from their homes, with foul earth, foul air, foul water, foul food or none, what wonder that one-half have died and that one-quarter of the living are so diseased that they cannot be saved? Little children still walking about with arms and chest terribly emaciated, eyes swollen, and abdomens bloated to three times the natural size. The physicians say these cases are hopeless.

"Cubans have been found dead about the markets in the morning, where they had crawled, hoping to get some stray bits of food. Most important is the spectacle of a million and a half of the people, the entire native population of Cuba, struggling for freedom and deliverance from the worst misgovernment of which we ever had knowledge."

Americans have heard all this from the newspapers, and they're already in an emotional state, but Proctor's calm matter-of-fact words carry the conviction that Hearst has never quite achieved through superlatives. Proctor's phrases, as Mark Hanna says, are like "so many fire brands thrown broadcast over the country." Floods of letters swamp the White House and congressional mail rooms. The Chicago *Post* declares: "The blood of innocents is on our doorsteps, and it must be wiped away."

The *Vermont Standard*, proud of its native son, sums it up succinctly: "For months and months the people of this country have heard almost incredible stories of the destitution and misery resulting from Spanish barbarity, but the majority of people did not know how much was true and how much exaggeration, and they failed to grasp the awful reality of it all. Senator Proctor's testimony is worthy of perfect confidence. It makes the matter real and tangible. It arouses the people to the necessities of the case and it should be followed by action through the land." Woodrow Wilson will echo this verdict years later when he calls the speech "one of those rare utterances which have really shaped public policy."

Proctor's speech proves to be the peak of his political career. His public utterance during the war tells us much more about what kind of man he really is. Of the Caribbean people, including the Cubans, he will say, "Of course they are very different from Americans, and far inferior." During the war he will lose interest in the cause and come to regard it as an irritating obstacle to a European vacation he's been planning. He does gear himself up to one personal crusade--a proposal to form a Cuban regiment that will be sent to fight the Filipinos. In the end, Proctor will find himself derided by both Cuba and the

Administration. But he has done what no one else has been able to accomplish, and has pushed even McKinley closer to the brink. The President confers constantly with Senate and House leaders amid rising excitement.

On March 24, the report of the Navy Board of Inquiry on the *Maine* is due to be delivered, and thousands of people gather at Union Station in Washington, since the evening train from the South is expected to be bringing the messengers with the report.

It's nine-thirty before the train arrives and four tired officers step out, guarding the pouch they have carried all the way from Key West. It's in the hands of Lieutenant John Hood, a *Maine* survivor. For some fouled-up reason, no carriage is waiting for these messengers and they have to cross the tracks through the baggage room to a hackstand on Sixth Street.

As they reach it, the crowd spots them and surges forward; someone even jostles Hood, whose hand makes a warning move toward the pistol at his hip. Space is cleared, the officers get into a carriage and roll up Pennsylvania Avenue, with five cabloads of reporters in hot pursuit. They're disappointed, though, when the officers vanish into the Ebbitt House and send word that the report will not be delivered until the following day.

Next morning, a Friday, McKinley receives it in the library of the White House, and at ten-thirty the Cabinet retires to consider it, a conference that takes all day, with time out for lunch. Since the report finds no evidence of a Spanish conspiracy, contrary to popular belief, McKinley thinks it's better to let matters rest over the weekend before he sends the document on to Congress. His emphasis is still on negotiation. Day cables Woodford that night: "Peace is the desired end." But that means the report on the *Maine* has to be glossed over.

It isn't going to be easy. Conservatives hold the Republican majority in the House and they can be counted on to uphold the President's policies, but they're divided in the Senate, where Senator Lodge leads the demand for war. In the country at large, war fever has been allowed to flourish because McKinley has virtually cut himself off from the press and has made little attempt to defend himself. Of course he can't discuss secret diplomacy in any case but, on the other hand, he can't remain noncommittal forever.

In his report to Congress on the inquiry, McKinley once more calls for "deliberate consideration," but there's no statement of purpose, only his reiteration that he wants to do the right thing--that is, what is just and honorable. He makes the error of trying to keep the actual contents of the *Maine* report secret by locking it up in the executive office safe, but the early Monday morning editions of papers carry a full and accurate account by the Associated Press. Instant outrage. Who's leaked? How did the AP get it? The White House damage controllers summon the AP's veteran Washington bureau chief, Colonel Charles A. Boynton, while the safe is opened, disclosing that the document is still there, intact. Boynton has to sign a statement swearing that his information did not come from the White House, and in fact the source will never be disclosed.

The damage has been done, however. From what they read in the papers, the public comes to its own conclusions and decides that Spain is guilty as hell. From that morning, the country feels itself already at war, aching for revenge. The New York *Times* sums it up: "There is no stopping place short of the absolute independence of Cuba. It would have been as easy to end the War of the Revolution at Bunker Hill or the Civil War at Bull Run as to turn back now."

In that kind of atmosphere, Congress gets the President's own report and sends its leaders to the White House to tell McKinley it won't do. By Tuesday, there's rebellion on the Hill. Democrats want to recognize the Cuban Republic at once. Republicans are still divided, but the turmoil in the Senate is so great that Vice-President Hobart has trouble keeping order. Speaker Reed, in the House, attempts to suppress the warmongers but a caucus of fifty Republicans protest that he's trying to thwart the will of the majority. It's the exclusive right of Congress to declare war, they say, an argument still resonating in our time.

While McKinley begs for a delay of even two days before taking any action, people in his own party are accusing him of acting as a front man for financial interests, declaring, as Leech tells us, that he is "frightened by the wheeling vultures of Wall Street, enticed by ghouls to mortgage prostrate Cuba for the benefit of investors in Spanish bonds." When the word "peace" is heard in the House, hisses fill the air.

While all this is taking place, temperatures are also rising in Spain, and in Europe generally, where there is little, if any, sympathy for self-righteous America. Stephen Crane was in London, still reporting for the *Journal*, when the *Maine* was sunk, which he accepted with his customary fatalism, but now he reports that there is a general European dislike for the United States, and a conviction that the proud country of Cervantes and Velásquez would never stoop to doing such a thing as blowing up the *Maine.* In the opinion of the French, English, and Germans, the Court of Inquiry has simply lied, although it reported no evidence of a conspiracy. Some see Spain as a tottering *grande dame* who needs to be defended, while others view her as a country still powerful enough to brush the Americans aside. Europeans think the American press is brash and silly; their own papers are full of contempt for the United States, as well as large quantities of misinformation.

These feelings of hostility abroad are not lost on Americans living there. In Paris, they are insulted on the streets every day, and they're beginning to leave the country in droves, to the dismay of their former landlords. Crane writes: "This war will be fought in English. I can at least swear in Spanish and it will be more comfortable all around. But I have not decided on going yet." He will, though.

Another observer, the French writer Charles Benoist, conveys the Spanish view of what's happening in an article titled *"L'Espagne, Cuba et les États-Unis."* He writes: "Cuba--it is the flesh of the flesh of Spain; it is part of the history, the glory, and the grandeur of Spain. If you pick up any Spanish newspaper Cuban affairs takes up the first, the second, the third page.

"Some soldiers pass by...along streets swept, in November, by the wind of the Guadarrama. You see them and point--'*soldades para Cuba.*' There are 20,000 about to go. That squadron that is going on maneuvers, this battery of artillery that returns to its barracks, they have but three young lieutenants and three old captains; lieutenants at eighteen, captains at fifty. Where are the rest? In Cuba. Thus, what you see and what you don't see--appearances, absences, departures--everywhere and every minute calls to mind Cuba."

Imperial Russia is taking note of the crisis, too, and some of the aristocracy, at least, are ready to advise. Prince Radolin, writing to Count von Bülow, reports: "Count Muraviev says...the dynasty can only be saved if the Queen puts herself in the forefront of a chauvinist agitation and, cost what it will, go to war, even if there is no chance whatever of a happy outcome. Count Muraviev employed these words: 'If the queen is wise, moderate, and truly patriotic, she will fall and be thrown out; if, on the other hand, she puts herself at the head of the column and is neither wise nor patriotic, who can save her crown?' This is cynical but so."

In Madrid, there is an American ultimatum to consider. Its terms are relatively harsh--an armistice until October 1, immediate revocation of the reconcentrado order, and if peace can't be achieved in Cuba by October 1, McKinley will be the final arbiter. Spain is willing to grant the armistice and the reconcentration, but permitting the Americans to settle matters in Cuba to suit themselves is another matter.

Desperate attempts to find a solution to the impasse are being made. Archbishop John Ireland comes to the White House, and after a conversation with the President, turns up at the French embassy to urge that the Great Powers unite in asking Spain to accept the American conditions. The powers aren't sympathetic.

The Queen Regent has been trying to avoid conflict. With the help of Segismundo Moret, an intense leader of the left wing, she has been trying to come to some kind of understanding with Washington. Their idea is to make Cuba a dominion, like Canada; Moret came by this solution naturally since he is in the Colonial Ministry. But the Queen herself is an obstacle to working out any kind of bargain. As historian Ernest May describes her, she's a "humorless, homely Hapsburg archduchess." Her sole concern is to preserve the throne for her twelve-year-old son.

In January, she asked for a secret visit from Ambassador Woodford, an appointment only Moret would know about, and when America's representative duly appeared, she took an imperial tone with him, talking about Weyler's recall and the promise of autonomy as though they were royal concessions. President Cleveland, she pointed out, had promised to denounce the rebels publicly if autonomy was granted, so why wouldn't McKinley follow his example? She would also like him to break up the Junta in New York.

When Woodford observed that there were considerable difficulties in bringing about such actions, the Queen interrupted him: "The President can do this and if he does it, the insurgents will know that they cannot get help; and their chief will accept autonomy and surrender, and this will stop the war and I shall have peace."

Woodford withdrew tactfully, leaving matters as unresolved as they were before; later the Queen sent Moret to him to try further persuasion, as well as to insist on absolute secrecy. Woodford could understand that much. He told McKinley: "Neither the Liberal Minister nor the Queen could hold their places if it were suspected that they had so far violated Spanish traditions and offended Spanish pride."

Since then, negotiations have gone no further. The Queen can't understand that America isn't able to negotiate a peace in Cuba on its own, and she now understands that Blanco isn't going to do what Weyler could not. That was confirmed for her by José Canalejas, the *Heraldo* editor, recipient of De Lome's indiscreet letter. At the end of his fact-finding mission, Canalejas had delivered a gloomy report to Segasta, and this was followed by a despairing private letter from Blanco: "The army, exhausted and anemic, filling the hospitals, without the force to fight or hardly even to hold up its weapons; more than three thousand concentrados dying or starving, perishing from hunger and misery around the cities; the people of the countryside terrified, prey to genuine horror, forced to abandon their farms or lands, suffering under the most hideous tyranny, with no recourse to escape their terrible situation except to go strengthen the rebel ranks."

As it turns out, Blanco has considerably exaggerated the military weakness of the Spanish Army, but nonetheless, as the crisis moves toward its climax, the Queen has to face the fact that everything has failed. Politically, it's impossible to abandon Cuba. Not only would her loyal Spanish subjects there be left high and dry, but the Army would feel that its notorious pride had been assaulted. Besides, the supporters of Weyler in Madrid, who opposed his recall, are saying that he would have put down the rebels if left alone, and a dangerous coalition is beginning to form around him--Carlists, republicans, Catalonian separatists, even a few anarchists, besides all the others who oppose the Regency for their own reasons.

Are there any options? One obvious choice is to appeal to the European powers and Britain to form a solid front against the United States. If it's solid enough, the Queen and her Cabinet reason, America will have to back off and the rebels will have to take whatever Spain wants to give them. If the other powers won't agree to a united front, such an impasse might possibly lead to arbitration, a process that could go on so long that either the rebels or America would give in.

It's worth a try to line up the powers, the government concludes, and diplomats begin working on them, especially England, Austria, France, and the Russians. They think they can count on Russia, since the St. Petersburg *Novosti* has already pronounced editorially what the Tsar's government is presumably thinking.

Says *Novosti*: "The Cuban government has an interest for Europe that is not only local but also general. The excessive enlargement of the Monroe Doctrine menaces all European states. It is necessary to recognize that the governments of Europe have contributed to the growth in the pretensions of the American republic by having done absolutely nothing to prevent a possible conflict. The Spanish government, for its part, has done all that it could to satisfy the Cuban populace. The insurrection would have halted long ago if it had not been artificially sustained. Have American politicians understood this situation as they should? Or do they suppose that the European powers will continue to stand by indifferently while events take their course?"

Well, yes, they will, and no doubt to *Novosti*'s surprise, Russia leads the parade of inaction, even though the Queen appeals to the Tsar through the Emperor of Austria. The Tsar eventually reverses himself after pressure from France and Britain, but by the time he does so, it's the British who decide this is not such a good idea after all. The Spanish Queen sends a personal appeal to Victoria, who doesn't bother to reply.

For a brief moment, however, in March, it seemed as though the Spanish might pull it off. The French reported that all the powers were prepared to give at least moral support to a plan that would call for an armistice, arbitration, and eventually continued Spanish control of Cuba. But then the British ambassador asserted that France had quite misinterpreted his country's position, which was that it seemed too soon to be talking about intervention.

Now more bad news. The Spanish ambassador in Berlin reports that Germany's getting cold feet and can't be counted on. This is followed by momentary *good* news; the Pope has stepped in and says he'll ask for an armistice if it will enable Spain to get out of this mess with its honor reasonably intact. The Cabinet can't make up its mind whether His Holiness is really being helpful, and every day its members are reading in the military press that war is inevitable. These journals would be annoyed to hear it, but they sound a lot like Hearst.

The Queen's last hope is Moret. She has less reason to fear the army than her Cabinet ministers, and maybe Moret, with her help, can make some sense out of this maddening situation. She instructs him to encourage the Pope, letting him know she'll accept his solution, and at the same time, she persuades the Cabinet to invite the Vatican to go ahead with a request for an armistice, which is done.

On April 6, the representatives of Britain, France, Germany, Austria-Hungary, Italy, and Russia appear at the White House with a note all of them have signed. The British ambassador reads it. Its language is diplomatic but the intention is plain. The powers call on the "feelings of humanity and moderation" which the President and the public are presumed to have, so that negotiations will be pressed toward a peaceful solution. The President, advised they were coming, has prepared a formal reply, which he reads. In equally diplomatic language, it tells the powers to go fly a kite. He speaks freely of America's "unselfish endeavors to fulfill a duty to humanity by ending a situation the indefinite prolongation of which has become insufferable."

Discouraged but persistent, the powers issue a *démarche* of a similar nature in Madrid. The Pope has already virtually pleaded with Spain to accept an armistice at once, if nothing else, but the Cabinet is as divided about what to do as the Republicans in Congress have been.

Our ambassador thinks an armistice is as good as peace, but it's quickly apparent that Spain has no intention of freeing Cuba, and so informs the Pope. That's been the sticking point all along. When this news reaches Washington, Congress will soon be called upon to pass a resolution demanding the end of Spanish sovereignty and authorizing the use of armed force to bring it about. McKinley will then have no choice but to sign it, even though he knows it's a declaration of war.

Time is running out. On April 6, Woodford sends a note that the Spanish regard as peremptory. In it, he says the United States had expected an armistice proclamation by noon of that day, and since none has appeared, he warns that unless one is announced by midnight, it will be too late to prevent Congress from passing the war message McKinley has already sent to it.

Woodford is not quite telling the truth--that is, he has told a diplomat's lie. He doesn't say that there's still a way to go in Congress before any actual war resolution is passed, but apparently the Queen and Moret understand, because it's three days before she responds, letting the midnight deadline go by. Then she tells Woodford that all the powers are agreed on an armistice.

There's only one more hurdle--her Cabinet. It meets that afternoon, confronting the bleak facts at last. It's clear that there is now no hope of avoiding war, and the armistice ploy is the only way Spain can gain enough time to pull its military socks up and prepare for conflict. Moreover, if they don't accept the armistice, they'll surely lose European support and find themselves alone in the world. Debate is short. An armistice proclamation is approved, dated April 10. Just in time. Already the British are saying they don't really want to offend the United States, and the Germans are shrugging their shoulders and murmuring that surely the Great Powers have more important things to think about.

No one has said anything about independence in this last-minute action, but the Spanish people interpret what's happened as a signal that Cuba is lost, and they swarm angrily into the streets of Madrid, Barcelona, and Valencia. The Weyler coalition has something to do with the intensity of these demonstrations. All the major newspapers, most notably *Heraldo* and *Imparcial*, are emitting Hearstian screams for war by this time, which means that the journals of independent opinion have joined the military sheets.

There are more last-minute attempts at Great Power intervention, torpedoed by British and German reluctance, and at last the Queen and her Cabinet understand there is no way out. The Spanish ambassador in Washington is recalled, and in Madrid, Woodford is given his passport. Moret sends the news to Blanco: "Consider war as declared. Hostilities will begin immediately."

Spain finds no consolation in the fact that few in Europe expect her to win the war. On the other hand, there's no sympathy for America. Most magazines and newspapers portray the United States as a bully picking a quarrel. They don't know that the Philippines are already secretly involved, and have no idea the war could extend so far. They simply can't believe America is qualified to be the seventh Great Power, but in another year they will.

Meanwhile, in Washington, the road to war, in spite of overwhelming pressure, has been just as torturous in its own way as the striving toward some kind of peace has been in Madrid. McKinley is willing enough to give the Spanish government more time to work out its problems, but since the *Maine* sank, he knows he can't restrain the Congress or the people much longer. It's down to a matter of days.

American ingenuity keeps stoking the fires to the last minute. Besides the lapel badges proclaiming "Remember the Maine!" and pictures of the doomed ship in shop windows and parlors all over the country, there is a brisk trade in chemically treated flimsies, sold on newsstands, depicting the *Maine* and a matador holding a torch. If you ignite the torch with a match, it explodes, sinking the ship. Cries for retribution are written on white peppermint lozenges, and mere children shriek for war. Cultural historians will someday puzzle over why the word "vengeance" is so seldom used, and instead, "atonement," "reparation," or "justice."

McKinley now stands virtually alone against the onslaught. He's pictured as weak and vacillating, a slave to Wall Street. Hearst charges, erroneously, that McKinley was the one who asked the Pope to mediate. His name is hissed in public places. Frantic Republican leaders beg him to wave the flag, but he stands on his principles, to the satisfaction of that minority which is still against intervention. No wonder McKinley can't sleep, and has to resort to drugs so he can get some rest. To those who see him daily, the terrible strain is visible in his haggard face and dark-circled eyes, and his obvious nervousness.

His friend Herman Kohlsaat, the Chicago publisher, knows what he's going through because, a little earlier, the President quietly guided him into the Red Parlor during a musicale in the

East Room and poured out his heart, with his head in his hands. Congress was driving the country into war, he complained bitterly, and we weren't even prepared for one. He was worried not only about his loss of sleep, but about his wife's health as well. At one point he burst into tears, although he couldn't afford a public breakdown.

In a last effort, he sends a message to Congress asking it to let him use whatever military means may be necessary to bring peace and stable government to the Cubans, but what he wants is a neutral intervention without recognizing Cuban independence. There's scarcely any mention of the *Maine* in this dry, matter-of-fact message, and no mention at all of vengeance.

This document is delivered on April 6, and Congress meets at noon to consider it, with 10,000 people jammed into the galleries and corridors of the Capitol. Everyone's expecting fireworks, and everyone's disappointed. At the last minute, the President asks for a few more days' time so that Americans can be evacuated from Cuba. He's had an urgent cable from Lee asking that this be done.

There's an even better reason. Like Spain, America can barely set its military machinery in motion and would like a little more time to organize. Also McKinley doesn't want to give the impression he's ignoring the Pope's last-minute efforts. And most of all, he doesn't want the world to think that America is rushing headlong into war, which is what it's really doing, while ignoring every effort to stop it.

McKinley is not only on the verge of war but very near a political disaster. The intransigents on the Hill, from both parties, are menacing him. Even the anti-interventionists are furious because he won't recognize the Republic. Theodore Roosevelt says McKinley has "all the backbone of a chocolate éclair," and Congressman Hugh A. Dinsmore, of Arkansas, thunders: "We talk about liberty. Then let us give the Cubans liberty. We talk about freedom. Let us give them the right to establish a government which they think will be a free government, and which does not reserve to us, the government of the United States, the right to say, after it is established, 'Ah, this is not a stable government.'"

In the face of these sentiments, Secretary of War Russell Alger warns: "Congress will declare war in spite of him. He'll get run over and the party with him." Navy Secretary Long is so frightened that he urges the President to delay his final war message no longer, but McKinley says, "I will not do such a thing if it will endanger the life of an American citizen in Cuba." He produces Lee's cable, asking for delay, and that afternoon a congressional delegation meets with him in the White House--leaders of the House and members of the Senate Foreign Relations Committee. A delay is granted, but the Capitol fairly seethes with unappeased rage. No one trusts the President, and some members are worried about midterm elections.

For three more days the suspense continues, while emotions reach a boiling point. One influential Republican senator bursts into the State Department, and shaking his fist at Day, yells ungrammatically: "Day, by God, don't your President know where the war declaring power is lodged? Tell him, by God, that if he doesn't do something, Congress will exercise the power."

Reporters gather about Speaker Reed while he's having breakfast in the Shoreham Hotel. They inquire about a message from ex-Governor Levi P. Morton of New York, asking Reed to use his influence to dissuade the warmongers. Reed, with a sarcastic smile, replies, "Dissuade them! Dissuade them! The Governor is too good. He might as well ask me to stand out in the middle of a Kansas waste and dissuade a cyclone."

In the end, however, Congress will not humiliate the President and raise a constitutional issue by taking matters into its own hands and declaring war. Nor will the President make a dramatic break with Congress and simply refuse to send a war resolution. His aides tell him that the public may share Congress's urge to make war, but it's uncomfortable about the runaway hysteria on the Hill. People liked the way McKinley stood up to the six foreign diplomats who tried to bring pressure to bear on him. When these men said, "We hope for humanity's sake you will not go to war," he answered, "We hope if we do, you will understand it *is* for humanity's sake."

While the politicians rage and maneuver in these last hours of peace, the machinery of war has already been set in motion. On April 9, the day before Easter, McKinley orders all Americans still in Havana to leave for Key West, meaning those few reporters and consular officials who are still lingering. Almost at the same time, Admiral Pascual Cervera y Topete gets his orders to move the Spanish fleet toward the Cape Verde Islands, then on to Cuba.

Cervera, whom the historian Ivan Musicant describes as "a kindly, generous man, also a fatal pessimist," is far from optimistic about his chances. He's written with foreboding to the Minister of Marine: "The conflict is fast coming upon us, and the *Colón* has not yet received her big guns; the *Carlos V* has not been delivered, and her artillery is not yet mounted; the *Pelayo* is not ready for want of finishing her redoubt...the *Vittoria* has no ordnance, and of the *Numancia* [the broadside ironclad] we had better not speak." The ships he's talking about constitute almost half of his battle fleet. Just the same, they're off to meet the United States Navy, which may not be in much better shape.

News of his departure reaches America and sets off wild alarm on the East Coast. Secretary Alger will recall: "They wanted guns everywhere, mines in all the rivers and harbors on the map." Several New England congressmen implore Roosevelt to send his best ships for the defense of Portland, Jekyll Island, Narragansett Bay, and other vital strategic strongholds. T.R. insults these special pleaders by sending them a Civil War monitor, manned by twenty-one members of the New Jersey Naval Militia. This craft, he confides to friends, is "useless against any war vessel more modern than one of Hamilcar's galleys." Naturally, that doesn't amuse the congressmen and they exert so much pressure that the Navy has to split up its North Atlantic Squadron temporarily.

All this alarm--if the East Coast citizens had only known-- over a Spanish fleet whose bottoms are so fouled from disuse that it can't travel at more than seven knots. Cervera has a variety of other problems, too. When he reaches Martinique after leaving Cape Verde, the French won't give him any coal and he has to go on to Dutch Curaçao where his ships get at least half of what they need. This means offensive operations are not immediately possible, and that's not all of Cervera's troubles. The fleet's engines and boilers are in sad shape, and he isn't sure just what part of Cuba he can reach safely.

In Europe, however, they're not worried about the admiral because they don't think the American fleet will be a problem for him. The London *Engineer*, for example, says it's "difficult to see where the usefulness of these heavily-armored floating citadels [meaning the American battleships] comes in except to capture and sink the *Pelayo*," the moth-eaten Spanish Navy's only real battleship. Of the American fleet's enlisted personnel, mostly immigrants, the *Engineer* has an even lower opinion: "Naval warfare is a grim and ghastly business," it observes portentously, "and no hirelings of an alien state are likely to come well out of such a terrible ordeal."

Ready or not, on the morning of April 22, with war still officially undeclared, the North Atlantic Squadron will slip out of Key West to blockade the Cuban coast. But are we any more ready to fight a naval war than the Spaniards? Some believe the United States isn't even a second-rate naval power. As for the Army, it's even less prepared, having been held to only 25,000 men; it hasn't fought a foreign power since the Mexican War in 1846.

Whatever the deficiencies on both sides, the clock is ticking toward midnight. On the day after Easter, McKinley sends his message to Congress, where it's greeted with violent protest two days later, after the committees have considered it. There are blows struck, or nearly struck, on the floor of the House before it finally passes, by a large majority--a joint resolution which more or less conforms with the President's wishes. Its principal feature is that it doesn't call for war, and doesn't give Congress any justification to pass a war resolution.

It's up to the Senate now, and there the war issue must be decided at last. The Senate Foreign Relations Committee is ready. The chairman, Senator Cushman K. Davis, gives the committee three resolutions amounting to a war declaration, since they declare Cuban independence, demand that Spain give up the island and withdraw its forces at once, and direct McKinley to use the armed forces to enforce these resolutions.

There's vehement dissent, led by Senator Joseph "Fire Alarm Joe" Foraker, who files a minority report signed by three other members. For the next four days they argue it out, noisily, while the President is freely defamed. But nothing can stop the war avalanche now. The Senate even adopts an amendment by David Turpin, an Indiana Democrat, which specifically recognizes the Republic. It's early in the morning of Sunday, April 17, when a joint resolution finally passes, leaving Republican control in tatters, since twenty-four Republicans have deserted the President in the belief that Congress has a right to recognize a foreign state. McKinley immediately challenges the Turpin amendment, asserting his constitutional rights. The Republicans rally their forces and in the early morning of April 19, the joint resolution finally clears both houses of Congress--without the Turpin amendment.

There's no great urge to acquire Cuba behind all the controversy, and even less enthusiasm for taking it into the Union. In this assemblage of primarily white Anglo-Saxon Protestants, Cuba is an alien land, filled with Catholics and black skins. We can have our crusade to free the Cubans, in short, and nearly everyone wants that much, but we aren't about to assume any further responsibilities. In the end, then, the President has a resolution he can endorse because it makes war on the moral grounds he's advocated from the beginning. Most of the important papers now support him in this final decision, and so do ninety percent of the letters that have poured into the White House during the crisis. McKinley finds consolation in this mail and reads some of it every day, but he asserts, "The people must not be unreasonable." They are, though, and the majority who don't write letters are more than eager for the Great Crusade, as they have been for some time.

Events move rapidly. McKinley signs the resolution on April 20 and sends the final ultimatum to Spain, while the press clamors in the corridors for more information.

When the ultimatum is brought in for McKinley's signature, several members of Congress are sitting in the Cabinet room, among them Senator William P. Frye, of Maine, whom Leech describes as "a vehement old fellow, who delighted his grandchildren by stamping around his house...shouting, 'Fe-fi-fo-fum! I smell the blood of an Englishmun.'" Frye asks how much time Spain is being given. Three days, the President tells him, and adds with one of his few attempts at humor, "Why, Judge, I suppose you would like to give them fifteen minutes." Frye just nods. He would.

A messenger from the Senate carries the ultimatum to De Lome's successor, Polo de Bérnabe, who asks for his passport a half hour later. In Madrid, Woodford gets these final terms by cable but he's already been told it's all over. On April 24, war is officially declared by Spain, and a day later, McKinley orders the blockade of Cuban ports. Two days after that, with the approval of Congress, he calls up 125,000 volunteers. There's one more unpleasant task. Poor old Sherman has had an extremely indiscreet conversation with the Austrian minister, caused by a loss of memory, and it's clear he has to go, to be replaced by Judge Day as Secretary of State.

In New York, on the day war is declared, the stock market falls by one percent, at that time enough of an event to merit a headline on the front page of the Brooklyn *Eagle*. But it's a momentary loss; the country is enthusiastically committed.

Everyone's happy but the President. He doesn't say much, at this juncture, but twelve years later, his decision is still a wound that won't go away. Only a year before the assassin's bullet reaches him, he will tell his former private secretary: "The declaration of war against Spain was an act which has been and will always be the greatest grief of my life. I never wanted to go to war with Spain. Had I been let alone, I could have prevented [it]. All I wanted was more time."

PART TWO

ONE HUNDRED DAYS OF HELL

1

FIRST REAL BLOOD: MANILA BAY

AFTER SO MUCH COMMOTION ABOUT CUBA, IT'S IRONIC THAT the first major blow of the Spanish-American War is struck on the other side of the world, in Manila Bay.

Since he took command of the Asiatic Squadron, Dewey has been waiting in Hong Kong for the war to start. Cables have kept him informed of what's going on, and even before Congress's joint resolution is signed by the President, he's unleashed. But how? The whole murky business of making war in the Philippines gets even murkier when the machinery becomes an object of inquiry.

Long has his own story. On the morning of April 25, the Secretary says, he went to the White House and sat beside the President on a sofa, waiting for him to approve a cable giving Dewey his sailing orders.

"Mr. President, I think this ought to go," Long said, according to his later recollection.

"All right, sign it," McKinley said.

Long swears he had nothing more to do with it, that the actual drafting must have been done by a clerk. That's his remembrance three years later. Captain Arent Crowninshield, head of the Bureau of Navigation, also in charge of Navy personnel and administration, has a different tale. On that historic morning, he says, he was playing golf at Arlington when he saw Long's carriage roll up and stop to talk briefly with him. The Secretary had his daughter in tow, and they were off for a day in the country. A little later, Crowninshield recalls, he went back to the Navy Department where he found a cable from Dewey, with the information that he'd been ordered to leave Hong Kong and proceed to Manila.

Who sent such an order, and wasn't it premature, since the United States hadn't yet actually declared war? Crowninshield couldn't ask Long, who was off somewhere in the countryside, so he hurried to the White House to see what the President knew. He found McKinley in his wife's sitting room, talking with Day, Attorney General John W. Griggs, and others. After a hurried consultation, it seemed that the President knew nothing about such an order, but he was ready to send one and asked Griggs to write it.

"Captain, you know how to write that better than I do," Griggs said to Crowninshield. "You go and write it. You'll find some blanks in the Cabinet Room." Webb Hayes, son of the former President, was in that room and he brought the blanks and a pencil. Crowninshield wrote out the order, the President read it aloud, and approved it with a single alteration. Then it was immediately translated to cipher at the Navy Department and sent off. It ordered Dewey to proceed at once to Manila and attack the Spanish fleet there. "You must capture vessels or destroy," the orders read, and they ended, "Use utmost endeavors."

So Dewey is told something he's already been ordered to do, if you believe Long, but who sent the original remains a mystery. Could it be T.R.? Logical enough, but this is another leak, if we can call it that, which will never be traced to its origins.

No matter. War is officially declared next day as McKinley signs the joint resolution in his bedroom, wrapped in his dressing gown (he's still having trouble sleeping), and now the United States is officially at war, a state the resolution records as having existed since April 21.

In Hong Kong, there's a problem. As soon as war became official, the British authorities in this Asian outpost declared neutrality, on orders from London, which means that the American fleet will have to move out of its comfortable berth. Just before the fleet leaves, the *Baltimore*, laden with ammunition and other ordnance, arrives from San Francisco and Dewey manages to delay long enough to have his ships painted gray over their everyday buff before he gives the order to up anchor and head for Manila, 600 miles away.

Of the fleet's departure, Colonel George A. Loud, of the revenue cutter *McCulloch*, the most modern ship in the lot, tells us: "The fleet was ordered to leave Hong-Kong harbor Sunday, April 24. The departure...made no little stir in Hong-Kong, the sympathy of the English there being with us. As the *Olympia* [Dewey's flagship] passed the English hospital ships, they gave us three hearty cheers. Three steam launches filled with enthusiastic Americans followed us down the harbor, waving flags and wishing us God-speed."

It's a last farewell, as far as the British are concerned. Before departing, Dewey writes: "It was not possible in the Hong Kong Club to get bets, even at heavy odds, that our expedition would be a success, and this in spite of a friendly predilection among the British in our favor. I was told, after our officers had been entertained at dinner by a British regiment, that the universal remark among the hosts was to this effect: 'A fine set of fellows, but unfortunately we shall never see them again.'"

The fleet sails in two sections, and it doesn't go far the first day. John T. McCutcheon, a reporter doing double duty as an artist-sketcher for the Chicago *Record*, is on a ship which sails (with others) a day later, and he writes: "About three o'clock the vessels dropped anchor in Mira Bay, which is a little land-locked harbor thirty-five miles north of Hong Kong. The four other warships, which had gone the day before, were at anchor, and the two cargo boats, the *Nanshan* and *Zafiro*, were lying off a short distance. The combined fleet seemed to be very formidable."

The halt is to wait for further orders as Dewey organizes his forces for battle. "The afternoon was spent distributing the *Baltimore*'s cargo of ammunition among the other ships," Lieutenant John M. Ellicott recalls. (The *Baltimore* had arrived from San Francisco, laden with ammunition and other ordnance, just before the fleet left Hong Kong.) "Next day many spars, chests, hatch covers and other articles of wood which could be splintered by shells were sent to the transports. Twenty-four hours later a tug arrived from Hong Kong bringing the *Raleigh*'s repaired machinery and the U.S. Consul [Oscar F.] Williams from Manila."

While they wait, Dewey assembles the crews and commanders and gives them something to arouse their fighting spirit, reading a proclamation issued by the Captain-General of the Philippines, Basilio Augustín Savila. "A squadron manned by foreigners," the captain-general proclaims, "possessing neither instruction nor discipline, is preparing to come to this archipelago with the ruffianly intention of robbing us of all that means life, honor, and liberty...to treat you as tribes refractory to civilization, to take possession of your riches. Vain designs! Ridiculous boastings!"

When they hear that, reports Joseph L. Stickney, of the New York *Herald*, who is also acting as Dewey's aide, "a roar of derisive laughter...[goes] up from the whole berth deck." But there's more. Savila declares that the American people "constitute all the social excrescences," and they have "exhausted our patience, and provoked war by their perfidious machinations. The struggle will be short and decisive. Spain will emerge triumphantly from this new test, humiliating and blasting the adventurers from those States which, without cohesion and without a history, offer to humanity only infamous traditions and the ungrateful spectacle of a Congress in which appear united insolence and defamation, cowardice and cynicism."

Savila adds a few more choice bits of bombast. He says the Americans think they can substitute Protestantism for Catholicism in the islands. He's partly right about that; some evangelical missionaries are already contemplating that possibility. If the invaders succeed, the captain-general goes on, they will force the inhabitants to man their ships and do hard labor. Savila has composed this inspiring message to be read to his soldiers in the belief that it will encourage their warlike spirit, just as Dewey is having it read for the same reason. Whatever the effect in Manila, for the men of the Asiatic Squadron, when they've stopped laughing, it moves them to a united wish to push the words down Savila's throat.

But what is Stickney, reporting all this for the *Herald*, doing as the commander's aide? A mere *correspondent* in such a responsible position? Dewey knows what he's doing. For one thing, Stickney is a former naval officer. For another, Dewey understands the power of the press and he's deliberately using the three reporters with the squadron to create a persona, a legend of a simple, selfless man who will shortly be a hero and after that, who knows?

The other two reporters have become correspondents by accident. Edward W. Harden, of the New York *World* and the Chicago *Tribune* (they're sharing), is the brother-in-law of Assistant Secretary of the Treasury Frank Vanderlip. He had been on a cruise to the Far East with his friend, John McCutcheon, on the revenue cutter *McCulloch*. When this ship was abruptly ordered to join the squadron, they found themselves instant correspondents.

The war is about to begin. Steaming ahead all night, the squadron arrives within sight of Luzon early on Saturday morning, April 30. No one is sure where exactly the Spanish fleet might be, but logically it should be lurking in Subic Bay. Logic, however, is not an attribute of the Spanish fleet commander, Admiral Patricio Montojo. With the laudable purpose of sparing civilians, he's moved his fleet of aging cruisers and shabby gunboats down Manila Bay, where the water is shallow. He figures, if his ships are sunk, the survivors will be able to climb up the masts and escape being drowned. So let's hear about logic. If he had stayed where he was, he could have doubled his firepower by getting the support of shore batteries. As it stands, the Americans are going to have three times his firepower, blasting from more modern guns with a superior range.

Off Luzon now, the *Baltimore* has all her four boilers going, and she's moving forward to link up with the *Boston* and *Concord*, fifteen miles ahead. The plan is to enter Subic Bay, about thirty miles north of Manila Bay, to see if the Spanish fleet is there.

"At 11:30 A.M.," McCutcheon writes, "the squadron is about eight miles from Manila Bay. The *Baltimore* has kept close to shore and is now below the horizon, only her smoke being visible. The flagship has signaled that a schooner overhauled by the *Zafiro* had no information to give. At 2 o'clock the distance to Subic Bay is ten miles, and to Corregidor, at the mouth of Manila Bay, about forty miles. The work of lowering the lifeboats of the *McCulloch* down halfway to the water is going on, with the object of getting them into water as expeditiously as possible if occasion arises.

"The *Baltimore*, *Concord* and *Boston* are supposed to have entered Subic Bay. They cannot be seen. At about 4 o'clock a faint column of smoke in the bay marks the position of one of our ships. The sail of another small schooner was seen about this time and bore down toward the squadron. As it reached the mouth of the bay the *Boston* and *Concord* were sighted coming out." The schooner is overtaken and boarded, but its captain says he didn't come from Manila and has no idea where the Spanish fleet is.

At least we know Subic Bay is empty. The Spanish fleet must be in Manila Bay, and the squadron moves toward it.

On board the *Baltimore*, Stickney is taking the notes that will continue his account: "Commodore Dewey stopped his flagship and made a signal for commanding officers to repair on board. When every gig had been called away, the captain of each ship was steering in solitary state toward the *Olympia*, no one needed to be told that we were on the eve of battle.

"The war council was of short duration. By seven o'clock the gigs were all hoisted at their davits, the flagship was again under way, and long before dark every vessel had taken her station, ready to run by the batteries at the mouth of the bay or to fight for passage, as circumstances might require. Aside from one light on the very stern of each ship, intended as a guide for the next in line, not a glimmer was to be seen aboard any craft in the fleet. As I looked astern from the *Olympia*'s taffrail, I could just see a faint suggestion of a ghostly shape where the *Baltimore* held her course on our port quarter.

"The moon had risen, and although it was occasionally obscured by light clouds, the night was not one in which a squadron ought to have been able to run through a well-defended channel without drawing upon herself a hot fire. Consequently, at a quarter to ten o'clock, the men were sent to their guns, not by the usual bugle call, but by stealthily whispered word of mouth."

About eleven-thirty, the entrance to Manila Bay rises on the horizon in the dim moonlight, with two dark headlands, one on each side. In between is a smaller mass: Corregidor, where the heaviest Spanish guns are reputed to be. Dewey has also been told that the entrance to the bay has been mined, and that torpedoes are waiting for the ships.

With something approaching nonchalance about these dangers, Dewey steers the *Olympia* directly toward the southern channel, which is the widest, with the *Baltimore* following him and the rest of the fleet in regular order. Not a sound from the forts. Can it be they don't know we're here?

But any hope of further secrecy is ended when the soot in the *McCulloch*'s funnel catches fire. Flames shoot up "like the fire of a rolling mill chimney," McCutcheon writes. "For a minute or two it burned and then settled down to the usual heavy black rolls of smoke." A breathless silence follows and then a light flickers on land, followed by a rocket streaking out of the darkness from Corregidor. Fire starts up again in the

McCulloch's funnel, burning so brightly it's making the ship a sitting duck for enemy shells. But no further response from shore.

How come? For reasons we still don't know, the Corregidor gunners have decided to let the fleet inside the harbor without firing. Shortly after midnight on Sunday morning, May 1, the Spaniards fire on the fleet for the first time, from a rock called El Fraile, and this salvo brings response--the first shots in the Battle of Manila Bay. As the ships creep along on the twenty-three-mile trip down the harbor, the only further action is the bizarre coincidence of Chief Engineer Randall, on the *McCulloch*, becoming the first Pacific casualty even before the fleets are engaged. He collapses and dies of heat prostration in the steaming tropical night.

At 4 A.M., coffee and hardtack are served to officers and men alike. They eat with an eye on the flickering lights of Manila, which they've been seeing on the horizon for some time. In another half hour, dawn breaks, revealing the city, only six miles away, the rising sun silhouetting its buildings. There's life in the harbor around them, but it's nearly five o'clock before it's possible to identify the ghostly shapes as merchant ships.

The fleet steams past the city--the flagship and the *Baltimore* followed by the *Raleigh*, the *Petrel*, the *Concord*, and the *Boston*, all in battle array. They're greeted with some desultory and ineffective fire from the shore batteries. Lieutenant Bradley A. Fiske, on the *Petrel*, recalls later: "I was roused from my sleep by a noise at my door and a voice saying, 'The Captain wants to see you on the bridge.' 'What about?' I asked sleepily. 'I don't know,' he said, 'but it is ten minutes to five, and they have begun to shoot at us.' Then I aroused my dormant senses and realized the fact that I was about to go into battle for the first time. When I reported to the Captain on the bridge, he simply smiled and said, 'All right.' I looked ahead in the dim morning light and saw the *Olympia*, *Baltimore*, and *Raleigh*. "The Spanish fleet is over there,' said the Captain, pointing over on our starboard side, and there could be discerned a few indistinct shapes that looked like ships."

In a few minutes, Fiske is perched on the foremast, measuring the distance between him and the enemy with a device he's invented called the stadimeter. What he sees, of course, is the waiting Spanish fleet, which he finds more awe-inspiring than it really is. The *Olympia* turns and heads for them, followed by the *Baltimore* and the *Raleigh*. At that moment, Fiske writes, "a shell, coming apparently from the direction of the city, struck the water close to the *Petrel* and exploded, throwing up an enormous quantity of water, which drenched us on the platform forty-five feet above." Fiske's assistant is a man noted for his perfect calm in any circumstance, and the lieutenant turns to see how he's taking the shelling. "That was pretty close, sir," the man says, unruffled.

The *Petrel*'s captain, E. P. Wood, "one of the most nervous men I have ever seen," in Fiske's view, is standing on the bridge, quite composed. He tells the lieutenant afterward that during the subsequent battle he didn't have the slightest physical sensation, although he had been on the bridge all night and most of the day before.

As soon as there's enough light, more shore batteries open up, and Dewey can see the seven ships of the Spanish fleet anchored under the batteries of Cavite. Dewey maneuvers his ships into firing range, about two and a half miles. One of the batteries on Sangley Point lobs a shell at the American fleet but it's short by a mile or so. Dewey is edging still closer, and at this point he gives the famous order, "You may fire when you are ready, Gridley," which Stickney, reporting it, abbreviates to the catchier, "You may fire when ready, Gridley," that becomes a part of the American vocabulary.

Stickney is on the bridge of the *Olympia* with Dewey when a shell bursts directly over them. The boatswain's mate at the after 5-inch gun emits a hoarse cry, "Remember the *Maine*!" and five hundred men at the guns echo him. At five forty-one, the *Olympia* lets go with its starboard 8-inch gun in the forward turret, at 5,500 yards. Soon the *Baltimore* and the *Boston* are adding their 2,500-pound missiles to the barrage, aiming at the *Castilla* and the *Reina Cristina*.

Stickney writes: "The Spaniards seemed encouraged to fire faster, knowing exactly our distance, while we had to guess theirs. Their ships and their guns were making things hot for us. The piercing scream of shot was varied often by the bursting of time fuse shells, fragments of which would lash the water like shrapnel or cut our hull and rigging. One large shell that was coming straight at the *Olympia*'s forward bridge fortunately fell within less than one hundred feet away. Another struck the

Rear Admiral George Dewey aboard the Olympia at Cavite

reproduced from the collections of the Library of Congress

bridge gratings in line with it. A third passed just under Commodore Dewey and gouged a hole in the deck."

Perched on the *Petrel*'s mast, Fiske has a splendid view of the action and recalls later: "As is well known, the American fleet paraded back and forth before the Spanish fleet, firing as rapidly as they could with proper aim. To me in my elevated perch the whole thing looked like a performance that had been carefully rehearsed. The ships went slowly and regularly, seldom or never getting out of their relative positions, and only ceased firing at intervals when the smoke got too thick.

"For a long while I could not form an opinion as to which way fortune was going to decide. I could see that the Spanish ships were hit a number of times, especially the *Cristina* and *Castilla*, but then it seemed to me that our ships were hit many times also, and from the way they cut away boats from the *Raleigh* and from other signs, I concluded the *Raleigh* was suffering severely. I could see projectiles falling in the water on all sides of our ship. Two of the ships in the Spanish column were evidently much larger than the others...and the Captain seemed naturally to direct fire at them. I saw also that the Spaniards directed their firing principally at the *Olympia* and *Baltimore*, which were our largest ships. I think everybody was disappointed at the great number of shots lost. Our practice was evidently much better than the Spaniards, but it did not seem to me that it was all that good.

"About the decks of the *Petrel* things were entirely different from what I expected. I had seen many pictures of battles and had expected great excitement. I did not see any excitement whatever. The men seemed to be laboring under an intense strain and to be keyed up to the highest pitch, but to be quiet, and under complete self-control, and to be doing the work of handling the guns and ammunition which is the result of what we all hope to get from drill."

That seems to be the situation on all the ships. Joel C. Evans, a gunner on the *Boston*, is directing twenty-five men carrying ammunition to the deck. He writes later: "Often I have been asked if we were afraid. My answer is that I never saw men as easy in mind as those below." Whenever they get a chance, they're watching the battle out of the portholes.

Heat and humidity are murderous. The gun crews are naked except for shoes and underpants. Some faint from the heat. Powder smoke settles down, choking everyone and half blinding the men. It's 116 degrees in the forward berth deck of the *Boston*, and in the engine room the men claim it's 200 degrees.

These latter feel close to hell. A stoker on the *Olympia*, Charles H. Twitchell, says, "The battle hatches were all battened down, and we were shut in this little hole. It was so hot our hair was singed. There were several leaks in the steam pipes, and the hissing hot steam made things worse. The clattering of the engines and the roaring of the furnaces made such a din it seemed one's head would burst. We could tell when our guns opened fire by the way the ship shook; we could scarcely stand on our feet, the vibration was so great. The ship shook so fearfully that the soot and cinders poured down on us in clouds. Now and then a big drop of scalding water would fall on our bare heads and the pain was intense.

"One by one three of our men were overcome by the terrible heat and were hoisted to the upper deck. Whenever a Spanish ship would make a move toward us some of the boys on the deck would shout down that they were coming for us full tilt. We knew it meant our death if [they] put a shot through her anywhere in our vicinity. I shall never forget those few hours. It seemed to me the longest day I ever lived. I'm not anxious to go through it again, and I don't think any of the others are."

Above this inferno, on the quarterdeck of the *Olympia*, stands the author of it all, Commodore Dewey, immaculate in starched whites, except for his uniform hat, which has somehow been lost, so he's wearing a checkered golf cap. Now he gives another famous order, after the fifth round of bombardment: "Draw off for breakfast." *Breakfast!* Is this a supreme example of American arrogance, as jubilant crowds at home will affirm later, or is there a more practical reason? Not until Dewey's autobiography emerges will we discover the need for breakfast was only secondary. The primary reason was that someone had reported there were only fifteen rounds of ammunition for the five-inch battery on the *Olympia*. He had worried about such a deficiency before the battle began, knowing his ammunition bunkers were only half full.

It's a false alarm, however. On the *Baltimore*, at least, there's enough ammunition, and the *Olympia* is in no imminent danger of running out. But Dewey has breakfast anyway because the air is so dense with smoke that it's no longer possible to fire accurately. When the air clears, the battle begins again, with the American ships operating in textbook fashion, steaming in a perfect column at six knots, then turning around and making another run for the benefit of the guns on the other side. Every run comes a little closer until there's only a mile separating the two fleets.

At that range it's possible to see for the first time, with the help of glasses, that the Spanish ships are in a bad way. Their battle strategy, if that's what it is, seems pitiful. Two of them are moored with springs on their cables, while others are steaming about aimlessly, sometimes getting in the way of each other's fire and having to retreat. Occasionally one will make a foray toward the American ships, but it's like an exhausted bull trying to charge the matador.

Dewey closes in for the kill. His ships are so close that the gun crews can see the devastating effort of their shots without glasses. Lieutenant Ellicott, on the *Baltimore*, writes of these crews: "Naked to the waist and grimy with the soot of powder, their heads bound up in water-soaked towels, sweat running in rivulets over their glistening bodies, these men who had fasted for sixteen hours now slung shell after shell and charge after charge, each weighing a hundred and fifty pounds, into their huge guns...under a tropical sun which melted the pitch in the decks."

As the fury reaches its climax, the Spanish *Cristina* turns away "like a steed bewildered in a storm," as Ellicott remembers. Fire spurts up from her forward decks, and a six-inch shell rips a jagged hole under her stern, causing another fire. A second shell bursts in this gaping wound, sending flame and smoke cascading from her ports and skylights. A jet of white steam rises from her smokestack high into the air. The *Cristina* is finished. She staggers toward Cavite until she runs aground under its walls.

The *Isla de Cuba*, now the Spanish admiral's flagship after the *Cristina*'s departure, is also under heavy fire, and so is the *Castilla*, where one shell after another bursts in her hull. Columns of black smoke rise in the humid air from the fires set inside. The *Duero* appears to be trying to escape and does so, but she's on fire too. All the other Spanish ships, except for the

Ulloa, are retiring, taking shelter at Cavite Arsenal, a spot from which there is no escape.

The *Baltimore* comes within 2,500 yards of the beach and exchanges salvos for ten minutes with the shore batteries--as Ellicott reports, "one of the most magnificent spectacles of the day. The big cruiser, slowing and creeping along at a snail's pace, seemed to be in a vortex of incessant explosions both from her own guns and the enemy's shells. At times she was completely shrouded in smoke and seemed to be on fire, while every shell she fired was placed in the earthworks as accurately as if she were at target practice.

"Canacan battery was the first to fall under the deadly fire. Its embankments of sand, backed by boiler iron, were torn up and flung into the faces of the gunners until panic took hold of them. Hauling down their flag, they tumbled into an ambulance and drove madly to the protection of Fort Sangley. The whole fire of the squadron was then concentrated on this fort. At last...the Spanish flag came down and a white flag was raised in its place."

Now the only survivor is the cruiser *Ulloa,* moored just inside Sangley Point. Almost torn apart by shells, all of her guns either dismantled or disabled, her crew jumps over the unengaged side and swims for shore. In a few minutes more, she turns over in a slow roll and sinks.

Meanwhile, the little *Petrel* steams on boldly, because of her light draught, right up to the arsenal. On the other ships, men are holding their breath, believing she'll come under heavy fire from hidden Spanish gunboats. But she tosses a few shots, unreturned, and the arsenal hauls down its flag, replaced by a white one, and the *Petrel* signals, "The enemy has surrendered."

So the Battle of Manila Bay ends, with a stunning victory for the Americans. Dewey's fleet has fired 6,000 rounds at the Spaniards, with only 142 hits; not an impressive average, but it's enough to have sunk seven of Admiral Montojo's ships and killed 161 men, with 210 more wounded. When the roll is called on the American craft, no one has been killed and only eight men are wounded. There's some splinter damage on the vessels, but not much else. All this is a tribute to the inaccuracy of the Spanish gunners and the incredible lack of tactics on the part of Spanish commanders.

NIGHT SPECIAL.

MONDAY'S [1,645,498] CIRCULATION.

NEW YORK EVENING JOURNAL

NO. 5,847—P. M.   NEW YORK, TUESDAY, MAY 3, 1898.   PRICE ONE CENT

MANILA SURRENDERS TO DEWEY!

AMERICANS AND INSURGENTS TO FORM A PROVISIONAL GOVERNMENT AND RULE THE PHILIPPINE ISLAND!

HONG KONG, MAY 3.—POSITIVE INFORMATION WAS RE
ADMIRAL DEWEY HAD CAPTURED MANILA. THE AMERICAN
WITH THE INSURGENTS ARE ORGANIZING A PROVISIONAL GO

New York Journal, May 3, 1898

courtesy, New York Public Library

The destruction of the enemy fleet is absolute. Dewey sends his chief of staff to the *Petrel*, where the surrender will be received, while he steams off to Manila, the others following a little later. His squadron anchors off the city, which displays no evidence at all that anything has been going on. People are gathering in the park to hear the usual evening concert as the sun goes down. But the Spanish disgrace is complete, as a few miles away the *Petrel*'s men burn seven war vessels right in the face of the military garrison in Cavite.

In both Washington and Madrid, no one will know exactly what's happened for an entire week. Most of this confusion is due to the Spanish governor-general, who mistakenly thought the Americans were beaten, and cabled a message of triumph to Madrid. Inevitably, this mistaken news was picked up by others and reached America, producing deep gloom momentarily. Even when the governor-general has discovered his error, he keeps on sending reassuring messages back home, afraid to admit the worst.

Dewey visits this official and suggests that, since the cable is Manila's only link to the outside world that either has at the moment, it ought to be considered neutral so everyone can use it. The governor-general refuses. Dewey has the cable fished up and cut. Americans are going to have to wait until he can send off a dispatch boat to Hong Kong.

The bearer of good tidings is to be the *McCulloch*, and on it are the Chicago *Tribune*'s Edward Harden and John McCutcheon, along with Joe Stickney, of the New York *Herald*. Both Harden and Stickney are fairly burning to file the first news of the great victory at Manila, each wondering how it will be possible to scoop the other. Before the ship left Manila, Dewey told them they could file any stories they liked about the battle or what led up to it--with two conditions. They mustn't speculate about what he intends to do next, and they must permit Flag Lieutenant Brumby, who's carrying the dispatches, to file them first.

On arrival in Hong Kong, the ship is met by Consul General Rounseville Wildman, who arrives in a steam launch to take them ashore. As they near the dock, Stickney gets ready to make a daring leap onto the pier and so does his rival. Both men jump, but Harden is younger and in better shape. He lands first. Both men run to waiting rickshaws and head for the cable office, but Harden outfoxes his rival by going down an alley and taking a shortcut. Still, they arrive at the cable office only minutes apart.

Harden immediately hands in his dispatch, but the Chinese clerk, who has never set eyes on such a lengthy message--3,000 words--says he can't accept it until he talks to the manager, in whose office Stickney is already making his own case. It's a verbal war. Harden says he was there first and ought to have precedence. The manager tells Harden he should have brought the dispatch to him first and that he doesn't have precedence. A shouting match begins. Harden stands on his rights and the manager stands on office protocol.

Seeing that he's not getting anywhere, Harden rushes back to the desk and files an urgent dispatch to the general manager of the cable lines in London, explaining the situation and recommending the manager's immediate dismissal. He sends the same message to the *World* in New York, but the manager refuses to transmit either of them, observing correctly that they aren't war dispatches. Then Harden produces his ultimate weapon. He tells the manager he'll pay for sending his war dispatches in cash, an ill-concealed bribe which the manager quickly accepts, agreeing that Harden can go first. Stickney will be second, and McCutcheon, who's in no particular hurry, will follow them. But Stickney has already left, believing his dispatch has gone first because he gave it directly to the manager. Consequently Harden is left alone to file his report of the battle, stamped "Urgent," and he pays for it at $9.90 a word, three times the commercial rate. The press charge is only $1.15.

At least Harden remembers to tell the manager that Dewey's dispatches have to go ahead of his. Brumby files them in code, with the specification that they must be repeated. This means that at each relay station the cable has to be repeated to the sender. As a result, Harden's dispatches pass Dewey's at the first relay station, and since there are six relays between Hong Kong and Washington, Harden gets a clean beat on everyone by six or seven hours.

His dispatch trickles into the *World* between 3 and 4 A.M., just in time to get fragments into at least part of the morning edition. But since the Chicago *Tribune* has a right to share the story, because of its contract with the *World*, there's an immediate conflict of interest. The *Tribune*'s man at the *World*, Farmer

Murphy, is its only protection. James Keeley, the remarkable managing editor of the *Tribune*, will write later:

"There was a poker game in the *World* office. Our correspondent, Murphy, was in it. When the cable operator called up to tell the *World* of this important message, all the others in the game had hands except Murphy. He answered the telephone. The operator read the message to him. He took it down, hopped to our leased wire, and we had it about five minutes later. I stopped the presses, yanked back about 30,000 copies of the city edition, locked the doors, and got out an extra which went to every subscriber." Only then did he call the President and Secretary Long to give them a detailed account of the victory.

Delirium sweeps America the next day. Dewey has the adulation he's longed for--in abundance. His picture appears on badges, banners, lithographs, transparencies--at last, he's the object of public adoration. "Dewey blue" becomes the national color. Babies are named for him, as are yachts, racehorses, cats, dogs, streets, hotels, recipes, a milk shake, phosphates, cocktails, and cigars. Wherever you look, there's a Dewey face, with its white mustache and calm blue eyes. It stares up at people from paperweights, pitchers, cups, plates, butter dishes, shaving mugs--even teething rings and rattles. Girls wear Dewey shirtwaists and Dewey sailor hats, while men put on Dewey neckties, scarfpins, cuff buttons, and watch chains. Some alert gum maker puts "Dewey chewies" on the market. A laxative producer makes a wild connection with an advertisement bearing "the 'Salt' of Salts" under Dewey's picture.

This is no overnight affair; it's going to keep on for eighteen months, long after the war in Cuba is over, when people will still be singing Victor Herbert's "The Fight Is Made and Won," as well as an even more popular ditty that first appears on the front page of the Topeka *Capital*. Written by Eugene Ware (a Kansas lawyer who produces poetry under the name of "Tranquil") at the request of the paper's city editor, it sweeps the country. "Sung to an air partly sentimental and partly triumphant," as Mark Sullivan puts it, the song begins:

Oh, dewy was the morning
Upon the first of May,
And Dewey was the admiral,
Down in Manila Bay.

And dewy were the Regent's eyes,
Them orbs of royal blue.
And dew we feel discouraged?
I dew not think we dew!

No matter that Dewey isn't yet an admiral. Congress makes amends at once by elevating him to Admiral of the Navy, a higher rank than anyone has yet held in the service. He's also told he won't have to retire when he reaches the proper age but can stay on at full pay. Princeton and the University of Pennsylvania give him honorary degrees. Inevitably a "Dewey for President" boom starts, ignited by "Marse Henry" Watterson, redoubtable editor of the Louisville *Courier-Journal*. Asked if he'll be a candidate, Dewey cables modestly: "I have no desire for any political office. I am unfitted for it, having neither the education nor the training. I have refused absolutely to consider any proposition whatever. This is final." How often have we heard these words? The idea has been planted and it will flower.

Meanwhile, Dewey is perfectly content for the moment to sit on the deck of the *Olympia* in Manila Harbor, meeting the correspondents who are converging on him by the boatload. In his gleaming white uniform, he holds court, fingering his mustache from time to time, alternately stroking his lucky rabbit's foot and his Chinese chow dog. Everyone is charmed by him.

Why this national outburst of euphoria? Not simply because it's the first battle and the first victory in the war, but because people believe Dewey has "taken" the Philippines. They don't understand that the Spaniards still control both Manila and the remaining islands. So the newspapers prattle on about how we must restore civil order in the Philippines and bring American law to the place. There's also a lively debate over whether we should simply avoid more trouble and sell the islands to Germany or Japan. The common belief is that we've planted the flag, and so we can dispose of the islands as we please, because we're invincible. It's the beginning of manifest destiny. The Republicans view the United States as a new Pacific power, businessmen lick their chops at the notion of a Far East trading foothold, churches see an opportunity to send missionaries and convert those sitting in the darkness of another religion.

Admiral Dewey and his faithful companion, Bob (Leslie's Weekly)

reproduced from the collections of the Library of Congress

But there are doubters, not only about manifest destiny but about Dewey himself, although it would be considered treason if any of this were voiced publicly. While Senator Lodge is comparing Dewey with Lord Nelson, Bradley A. Fiske, who was on the scene at Manila, is already beginning to have serious doubts. A lieutenant then, he'll be an admiral in time and will write to Sullivan: "If the Spaniards had put their fleet under the guns of Manila, not one American ship would ever have left the harbor. Dewey realized this situation at once and steamed directly at the Spanish fleet, ignoring the shore batteries. The Spaniards ought to have won the battle if they had fought it correctly. They had all the trumps."

There are critics abroad, too. They say everyone knows that the Spaniards have always been the victims of their own complacency. We've already seen the sorry condition of Cervera's fleet, as viewed by the commander himself, and now it's said that Montojo's ships were in even worse shape--the crews undisciplined, the vessels badly cared for, and a general inefficiency prevailing. The Toronto *Saturday Night*, safely over the border, has the nerve to say it out loud: it's absurd to put Dewey in the company of history's great sailors.

Nevertheless, there's much to be said on Dewey's behalf, as Sullivan summarizes it: "Dewey, with six fighting ships, operating 7,000 miles from a home base, boldly entered an unfamiliar harbor, sailing past modern, powerful, Krupp-equipped shore batteries, and destroyed an enemy fleet of ten fighting ships and two torpedo-boats fighting from anchorage (which overbalanced the American fleet's advantage of superior speed) at a place in the bay selected by the Spanish admiral as presumably giving him an advantage over the attacking fleet..."

Other naval powers are interested in how Dewey did it, and whether he's likely to do it again somewhere else. British, French, German, and Japanese warships enter the harbor after the battle and begin nosing about on the pretext that they're protecting the interests of their countries' nationals. They're all careful to respect the etiquette the situation calls for--except the Germans.

On May 6, the German cruiser *Irene* drops anchor in the harbor at a site of its own choosing without the formality of asking Dewey's permission, as protocol calls for. Three days later, another German cruiser, the *Kormoran*, arrives in the harbor in the middle of the night and drops anchor without a by-your-leave. Her lights are seen, however, and Dewey, apprehensive that this might be a Spanish ruse, using a German flag as disguise, sends a launch to board her. When she's hailed, the *Kormoran* ignores it, and the launch fires a warning shot across her bow. After that, there's no more trouble.

But the commander of the German ships, Rear Admiral von Diederichs, seems to be embarking on a campaign of petty annoyance. On the pretext that he's protecting his country's interests, he has five German vessels in the harbor at one time, although the only interest he's protecting is that of a German importing firm. Dewey even believes the Germans might be planning to give the Spaniards armed help.

Even in this mini-crisis, without any substance to it, Dewey manages to come off smelling even more like the proverbial rose. At the battle, one of his captains was Joseph Bullock Coghlan, commander of the *Raleigh*, whose ship had been first to return the fire of the land batteries. Coghlan is also the first of Dewey's officers to return home, and nearly a year later, he's given a dinner at the Union League Club, where he relates some grandiose tales about Dewey, including how the admiral faced down the Germans after the battle was over. Then he recites a piece of atrocious doggerel called "Hoch! Der Kaiser," beginning:

> *Der Kaiser of dis fatherland*
> *Und Gott on high all dings command.*
> *Ve two--ach! Don't you understand?*
> *Myself--und Gott.*

Next day, New York's German-language paper, the *Staats-Zeitung*, is full of outrage. Under a sarcastic headline, "OUR AMERICAN COUSINS," it describes Coghlan's speech and how the boys at the Union League Club whooped it up with "Der Kaiser" in song. This again "reflects the hatred of the Germans," says the *Staats-Zeitung*, adding that the offensive poem was written by "a Bowery bard."

Herr von Holleben, the German ambassador, files a protest with the State Department, which State doesn't take seriously. Secretary Hay politely deplores the lack of good taste, but asserts it's the Navy Department's problem, not his, and since the incident occurred in a private club, maybe no one can be reprimanded. However, as a sop to international relations, the Navy slaps Coghlan's wrist with a reprimand.

This incident has an unanticipated effect. It travels all over the country and fuels further the adulation of Dewey. Americans will continue to be convinced that the Philippines phase of the war was over with a single battle, as they were when they first read the glad Maytime news. No one foresees the long, bitter road that lies ahead.

2

GOING OFF TO WAR

WHEN PEOPLE AREN'T TALKING ABOUT DEWEY IN MAY 1898, they're exhorting the government to get on with it. Destroy Cuba and anything else Spanish in sight is the popular will. The euphoric feeling is that it won't take long and will be relatively easy.

The armed services are more than ready to oblige. On the day after Manila Bay, before the outcome is known, Army and Navy hold a joint meeting and decide to fight a land war in both Cuba and the Philippines. For the next three months, however, it's going to be extremely difficult to plan anything with Dewey, who's sitting on the far end of a cut cable, 10,000 miles away.

Meanwhile, there's plenty to do in the Caribbean. As the first wave of hysteria sweeps over the country, the naval blockade of Cuba put in place a month ago produces the war's first casualties in this theater. Patrolling the Cuban coast, the torpedo boat *Winslow* slides a little too close into the harbor of Cárdenas, comes under heavy fire from masked shore batteries, and is disabled. The *Wilmington*, standing off nearby, comes to her rescue and her men frantically try to cast a tow line onto the *Winslow* under a rain of shells.

It's almost impossible to get the line fastened until Elijah J. Tunnell, a black cabin cook from Accomac County, Virginia, comes up from his galley, ready to help. He and Ensign Worth Bagley no sooner succeed in fastening the line than a shell kills both men and three others besides. But was it a shell from the Spanish batteries? Some papers report later that it may well have been our old acquaintance "friendly fire," coming from the *Wilmington*. Tunnell and Bagley fall within seconds of each other (black historians will insist later that Tunnell fell first).

Both Tunnell's legs are blown off, and he's otherwise gruesomely mutilated, but he's conscious enough when the *Winslow* is pulled free to inquire, "Did we win the fight, boys?"

Someone says, "We sure did," and this cabin cook who may be the Cuban War's first casualty replies, "Then I die happy." Also unrecognized. In accounts of the battle, it's the white Ensign Bagley who's hailed as a hero, the only naval officer to die in the war. Tunnell is just another name on the casualty list.

For the time being, it's going to be a naval war, so the Navy Department believes, and Cuba will get first priority. Not to be outdone, the Army is stirring itself for an invasion, even though the rebels haven't asked for one. In fact, Gómez is opposed to having American troops on Cuban soil. All he wants from the Americans, he keeps saying, is ammunition, food, a continued blockade, and moral support. He and his ragged army will defeat the Spanish themselves, which no one in Washington believes.

The Navy is rapidly beefing up its resources. Hasty orders are sent to Captain Charles Clark, of the battleship *Oregon*, which had just come out of drydock at Bremerton, Washington, when the *Maine* sank, to fuel and come as fast as possible from the Pacific to Cuba, an 11,000-mile trip around South America, through the treacherous Straits of Magellan. European naval experts, who have been wrong about everything thus far, are wrong again. They predict the *Oregon* will founder in the heavy seas of the South Atlantic.

For a perilous moment, Captain Clark has reason to believe they might be right after all. As he approaches the reefs at the western side of the straits, night has fallen and a furious gale is rolling up mountainous waves. Lieutenant E. W. Eberle will recall later that it was "a night of great anxiety for those on watch, but with two anchors down, and engines ready for instant use, we rode out one of the most severe gales that had been experienced along that stormswept coast for many a month." The *Oregon* sailed on March 19; she arrives in Key West on May 26, an unprecedented voyage of sixty-eight days.

This triumph elicits another salvo of national praise, especially in Captain Clark's native Vermont, already delirious about Dewey. The Rutland *Herald* says editorially: "Commodore Dewey is a Vermonter, has with him a commander who is a Vermonter. The commander of the *Oregon* is a Vermonter, and the first man to give the United States Senate and through it the country a clear statement of Spanish barbarities is a Vermonter. It is difficult to say just how long the war between Spain and Vermont will continue."

With or without Vermonters, the Navy dreams of catching Cervera's fleet somewhere and destroying it, thus ending the war and getting all the credit. The question is, where's Cervera? Admiral William Sampson's North Atlantic Squadron has been searching the waters around Cuba with no success. In fact, the press is doing a better job of tracking the elusive Spaniards. When Cervera paused in the Cape Verde Islands before setting off for Cuba, an enterprising *Herald* correspondent chartered a boat and followed him for twelve hours after the fleet left. Another *Herald* stringer, on Martinique, was first to report Cervera's arrival in the Western Hemisphere when he stopped there.

Since then, however, the admiral seems to have vanished. Getting a little frantic about it, the Navy orders Winfield Scott Schley's Flying Squadron to leave Norfolk, where it had been sent to protect coastal cities, and join the hunt for Cervera. Schley, whom Joyce Milton describes as "a stubborn befuddled old commodore," is absolutely convinced Cervera is inside Cienfuegos Harbor and sets up a cordon outside it, although the harbor itself is empty of Spanish warships.

Harry Scovel has his own theory of how to find Cervera. Simple, he says, just circle Cuba in a fast boat. He's so convinced that he even spends several thousand dollars of his own money to make a deal with the *Herald* for a joint *World-Herald* expedition, chartering the modest little yacht, the *Sommers N. Smith*, for the purpose. The subsequent voyage is hair-raising--storms, fifty-mile-an-hour winds, among other perils--but the ship actually circumnavigates Cuba in just seven days, a journey of 1,586 miles.

For Scovel, at least, it's an exhilarating trip, full of incident. Several American ships fire on the *Sommers N. Smith*, mistaking the yacht for a Spanish vessel, and one of them, the *Dolphin*, lobs a shell from three miles away, the shot passing between the yacht's masts, only fifteen feet above the deck. Off Santiago, she's halted by a scout ship, the *St. Paul*, commanded by Captain Sigsbee, formerly of the *Maine*. He tells the reporters that Cervera isn't at Santiago, and adds that it will be in their best interests, as well as the Navy's, if they get the hell out of the area immediately. They take the hint and return to Key West. As the ship docks there on June 1, a newsboy appears hawking papers and they see the headline: "SPANISH FLEET BOTTLED UP AT SANTIAGO." Foiled again.

It takes awhile for them to find out what happened. It appears that Cervera saw no hope of slipping into Havana or any other port on the Atlantic side. The only possible place remaining was Santiago, and on May 19, he brought his moth-eaten fleet into the city's harbor, amid the glad cries of the populace. He had never once sighted a hostile ship although whole squadrons had been looking for him.

That's where Schley finds him at last, after committing so many blunders in the search that he'll eventually be called up before a Navy Court of Inquiry. Apprised of the great discovery, Sampson turns his own squadron toward Santiago, and on the way he concocts a daring plan with a young engineering graduate, Ensign Richmond Hobson, designed to block the harbor.

Reaching Santiago, Hobson and seven volunteers carry out the plan. They take a disabled collier, the *Merrimac*, and make it into a floating bomb. Ten watertight cans, each loaded with seventy-eight pounds of dynamite, are fastened to the hull. Aboard this deadly craft, they sneak up just before dawn into the harbor's mouth and Hobson presses the switch. Only he has confidence that anyone will survive; the others are prepared for suicide. Nevertheless, everyone escapes in a small catamaran brought along for the possibility of survival. The amazed Spaniards haul them ashore--one story says Cervera himself assisted in the rescue--where the crew is even more amazed to be alive. They're taken prisoner and the plot itself is a failure because, as it turns out, the sunken *Merrimac* hasn't really blocked the harbor. But when news of this exploit reaches America, it's seen as so daring that no one cares whether it succeeded, and Hobson becomes the war's first authentic hero.

He isn't the first one to think of such an idea, however. At the start of the war, Hearst instructed Creelman, then in London, to buy "some big English steamer" and arrange to have it sunk in the Suez Canal so that the Spanish fleet couldn't be sent to the Philippines. Creelman actually tried to find a suitable ship, but when it became clear that Cervera was going to sail for Cuba instead, Hearst scrubbed the plot, no doubt to Creelman's relief.

At Santiago, whether the harbor is blocked or not, Cervera and his fleet are safely inside it. When news of his arrival reaches the Navy, Admiral Schley is already on his way to Santiago,

The Washington Post.

WASHINGTON. SUNDAY. MAY 29, 1898—TWENTY-EIGHT PAGES.

SCHLEY'S BLOCKADE

Twelve American Warships Are Now Off Santiago.

CERVERA IS SECURE WITHIN

Harvard Arrives at Kingston with Dispatches from the Commodore.

FEARS FOR SAFETY OF THE EAGLE

Three Alleged Spanish Warships Sighted Off Jamaica, and the Dispatch-boat Was Compelled to Leave Port Under the Neutrality Regulations—Commodore Schley Was Off Cienfuegos on Monday Last with His Fleet—A Close Watch Has Been Kept on Santiago Harbor Since the Arrival at that Point of the Spanish Fleet—The Conditions at Cienfuegos Have Not Changed.

PORT OF SANTIAGO DE CUBA

VIEW OF ENTRANCE

NOW FOR INVASION.

Nothing in the Way of a Strong Movement Upon Cuba.

Washington Post, May 3, 1898

having eliminated all the other possibilities, but he's running low on coal. A collier is standing by, but the seas are too heavy for refueling, so he's compelled to return to Key West.

Again heading for Cervera's hideaway, Schley is now having engine troubles, and he's also intercepted by an auxiliary cruiser bearing orders from Washington: "All Department's information indicates Spanish division is still at Santiago...and that the enemy, if therein, does not leave without decisive action." At that moment, Schley is nearly out of coal again and he replies: "Much to be regretted...forced to proceed for coal to Key West."

The delay is brief, however. Schley gets refueled and on May 28 the Flying Squadron, joined four days later by the North Atlantic Squadron, sets up a blockade of Santiago in a semicircle about five miles off the harbor. Cervera's natural pessimism must plummet his spirits to new depths when he learns what's surrounding him: five battleships (the *Iowa*, *Indiana*, *Massachusetts*, *Oregon*, and *Texas*), two armored cruiser flagships (Sampson's *New York* and Schley's *Brooklyn*) on the flanks, and smaller craft, including cruisers, torpedo boats, and armed yachts, patrolling the shore inside the blockade line.

All this naval firepower requires large quantities of coal, and Key West, 900 miles away, is too far off to provide a daily supply, so on June 10, a fueling base is established about forty miles east at Guantánamo, which a force of 850 Marines secures.

If the Navy is now ready for war, so are the correspondents about to cover it. Their fleet is without any firepower to speak of, but it's numerous. The *Journal* has two yachts, the *Buccaneer* and the *Anita* (Hearst's newest), and in time it will have eight craft of various sizes and shapes on the firing line. The *Herald* has chartered Sommers N. Smith's magnificent yacht, described by Davis as "big as [Commodore] Benedict's." The *World* rises above hiring yachts, although Joseph Pulitzer owns one of the largest, but it does acquire two tugboats, the *Triton* and the *Confidence*, as well as the old reliable *Three Friends*, whose filibustering crew know Cuban waters as well as anyone.

Meanwhile, the correspondents have been gathering at Key West since March. When Harry Scovel arrives there from Havana, he finds the Key West Hotel overflowing with reporters, some of whom are paying $5.00 a night just to sleep on a hallway cot. Everyone is melting in 100-degree heat, and there's such a shortage of water that vendors are selling it in the streets for fifty cents a gallon. Reading matter is scarce, since the newspapers and magazines that do arrive are gone within minutes. There's not much else to do. Eating is no pleasure because the hotel's dining-room food is memorable in the wrong way. Yet no one's complaining. Frances Scovel writes home: "The correspondents are kicking up their heels." They can't wait for the war to begin.

Among those present is Stephen Crane, who tried first to enlist in the Navy but had to settle for a correspondent's job on the *World*. Crane isn't impressed by Key West, which he calls a "mangy little city filled with journalists, harlots, and mosquitoes, who all found a nightly meeting-place in the gambling-hell." His fellow reporters don't think much of *him* at this point. Some actively dislike this eccentric, twenty-six-year-old who isn't interested in idle conversation, and doesn't want to talk about what he saw in England, or much else. A diplomat he's not.

This is even more apparent when he comes up to Tampa to examine a sandy camping place where troops are gathering. The eager volunteers arriving there are insulted when he asks, "Don't the militia take an oath to defend the country anyhow?" But the real Crane emerges when he gives a Wisconsin boy, discharged because of heart trouble, $50 so he can get home.

In his most negative mood, however, Crane spends some time in Tampa observing and belaboring his fellow journalists. He writes on June 2: "The sailor men of Sampson's big canoe ought to make us all ashamed of our trade. The papers come aboard the flagship, and who, I ask, wants to see this goulash of legendary lies and solemn rumors? We do, we the cynics of Fleet Street and Park Row, the Rudyards, the lords of the popular mind. The Jackies just look at all this manure and say, Well--and go on polishing brass. Davis and I tried to make them excited by donations of headlines and they said, Well--and peeled more onions. It is now the fashion of all hotel porches at Tampa and Key West to run Davis down because he has declined a captaincy in the army in order to keep his contract with his paper. The tea party has to have a topic."

At least, and at last, Crane gets to see something of the war. He's with three other reporters on the old reliable *Three Friends* when the Marines land from their gunboats on Guantánamo, preparing the way for a coaling station to serve the blockade fleet. Crane describes the landing: "It was at nightfall, and on the outward point a small village was burning, and it happened that a fiery light was thrown upon some palm-trees so that it made them into enormous crimson feathers. The water was the color of blue steel; the Cuban sands were sombre."

The Marines camp on a hill and begin digging trenches. An alarm sounds during the night, but Crane, restless, wanders off, as he says, "in search of some other man who had no occupation." He can't fight, and he can't help the men down at the shoreline who are unloading three-inch fieldpieces, singing as they work, "There'll be a hot time in the old town tonight," which is going to be the unofficial anthem of this campaign.

Crane finds his unoccupied man, a young assistant surgeon, John Blair Gibbs, thirty-nine, a Rutgers graduate with his medical degree from the University of Virginia. A bachelor, Gibbs had volunteered early on, the first doctor to offer himself, and was assigned to the USS *Panther*. Gibbs knows something about war: his father, a major, was one of the last men to fall at Little Big Horn. He and Crane talk about consumption (one of Crane's medical problems) and become instant friends through the long night. Everyone tries to get a little sleep before dawn, but it's difficult with Cuba's ever present land crabs scuttling over them.

When morning comes, firing begins abruptly. Cuban scouts inform the Marines that they're surrounded by guerrilla sharpshooters. Actually, about 3,000 Spanish soldiers are in the neighborhood and toward the middle of the afternoon the next day, they start shooting. Some of the men are swimming in the bay when the firing starts, and they run to their posts stark naked. Some even charge (on orders) into the jungle where the snipers appear to be. Surely the Spaniards have the advantage here, but they simply disappear for the time being, although they keep up a desultory fire right into the second night, until midnight, when they open up in earnest.

In the darkness, Crane takes the men's canteens and goes down to the supply base at the shore to get them refilled, lugging them back up the hill on his shivering shoulders. Gibbs notices the shivers, gives him quinine, and tells him he should leave as soon as possible, or at least take shelter on the *Marblehead* or one of the other gunboats, but Crane refuses. He wants to see the war.

    Through the hot, humid night, Crane sticks it out beside the signalmen who are flashing messages to the *Marblehead*, an activity that soon draws fire from the brush. Crane hears a man dying, not more than several feet away from him, but it's so dark he doesn't know it's Gibbs. Crane writes later: "He was dying hard. Hard. It took him a long time to die. He breathed as all noble machinery breathes when it is making the gallant strife against breaking, breaking. But he was going to break. Every wave, vibration, of his anguish beat upon my senses. He was long past groaning. There was only the bitter strife for air which pulsed out into the night in a clear penetrating whistle with intervals of terrible silence in which I held my own breath. I thought this man would never die. I wanted him to die. Ultimately he died.

    "At the moment the adjutant came bustling along erect amid the spitting bullets. I knew him by his voice. 'Where's the doctor?' A man answered briskly: 'Just died this minute, sir.' It was as if he had said: 'Just gone around the corner this minute, sir.'"

    Crane realizes now that his new friend Gibbs--the volunteer surgeon, noted yachtsman and socialite--solicitous for him only a few hours before, is the man who died so hard in the pitch-blackness of the night.

    The day dawns, "by inches, with an obvious and maddening reluctance, and Crane wants to believe that he must be mistaken about his friend's death. Then he sees a clump of men near him and thinks they're all dead. In fact, they're exhausted Marines who slumped into sleep around Gibbs's body "in such abandoned attitudes that one's eye could not pick the living from the dead until one saw that a certain head had beneath it a great dark pool." Gibbs's simple burial service, along with others, is interrupted by sporadic fire, and the whole episode will appear fourteen years later in Crane's vivid short story, "The Upturned Face," in *Ainslee's* magazine.

    Shivering though he is with fever, Crane sticks it out the next night, when the Spanish close in on the camp, so near they're no more than a pistol shot away. At night, he finds himself lying beside the signalmen again, watching their cool conduct while the bullets fall around them. He writes: "I could lie near and watch the face of the signalman, illumined as it was by the yellow shine of lantern light, and the absence of excitement, fright, or any emotion at all upon his countenance, was something to astonish all theories out of one's mind."

In his dispatches, Crane writes frankly about his own emotions, disclosing how he lies awake at night, hoping the illness gnawing at him will spare him from further shooting. But he conceals his feelings from everyone. When Captain George Elliott invites him to go with two companies of Marines on a mission inland to destroy the Spaniards' water supply, he doesn't hesitate. A skirmish begins, and Crane makes himself useful by carrying messages between company commanders. The captain commends him in dispatches, and Major Charles McCawley writes to him later: "...You were the only outsider who saw it all and we regard you as an honorary member of the Corps."

After this episode, Crane has to give up; he's half delirious with fever. The *Three Friends* takes him back to Fort Antonio.

Eventually the Marines take charge on Guantánamo. They advance into the jungle and quickly sweep out the sharpshooters who've been tormenting them. They get help from one of the landing fleet, the *Dolphin*, which lays down a barrage in front of their advancing column. The Spaniards retreat and virtually disappear. Guantánamo will be ready for the colliers soon.

Back home in patriotic America, the troops are gathering for the grand assault. William Allen White writes exuberantly in his Emporia *Gazette*: "...Everywhere in this good, fair land, flags were flying. Trains carrying soldiers were hurrying to the Southland...and little children on fences greeted the soldiers with flapping scarfs and handkerchiefs and flags; at the stations, crowds gathered to hurrah for the soldiers, and to throw hats into the air, and to unfurl flags. The fluttering of the flags drowns the voice of cheers that may be in the air.

"The cheering crowds, the women bearing boughs of lilacs and garden flowers of the new spring to the car windows helped the youths' spirits, and when they filed down the asphalt streets of the capital and had halted in front of the State House to hear the Governor make a speech, they were sure that it would be all up with Spain from that hour."

Even William Jennings Bryan becomes a colonel in a Nebraska "silver" regiment. The Administration makes certain it will never get any farther south than Florida.

A dimmer view of war preparations is taken, quite naturally, by Ambrose Bierce, the acid satirist of his time, who quite inexplicably is writing a column for the Hearst newspapers, with whose policies he is in nearly total disagreement. Why does Hearst keep printing the subversive stuff he turns out? Not even Hearst seems to know. Probably he thinks it sells papers.

In any case, Bierce, who at the moment is based in San Francisco (he'll move to Washington later), observes the boys going to war, and writes: "Marching through the streets of San Francisco in the cool of the morning on Monday last, the budding heroes of the First California Volunteers, each bearing the handicap of sixty or seventy pounds of arms and outfit, were visibly distressed by the warmth of their habiliments." He means that the Army, as it so often does, has clothed its recruits in uniforms designed for the wrong climate.

Troops are gathered in five different encampments: Camp Thomas, at Chickamauga Park, Georgia; Camp Alger, in Falls Church, Virginia; and others in Mobile, Alabama; Tampa, and San Francisco. Regulars are concentrated at Chickamauga, New Orleans, Mobile, and Tampa.

One of these regulars, M. B. Stewart, describes the assembling process: "Sudden orders sent regiment after regiment speeding toward southern concentration camps. A brief order, a period of frenzied packing, a moment in which each donned a blue flannel shirt, exchanged cap for campaign hat, wrapped his trousers around his calves and encased them in canvas leggings, strapped on a revolver, kissed his wife, if he had one, and was ready. Unprepared in every sense for war, we went about our job with a cheerfulness, activity and zeal born of our own vast ignorance."

Once in camp, life is certainly different. A Kansas boy who finds himself in the 1st Illinois Cavalry, writes home from Chattanooga: "There is one thing distinctly noticeable about army life that the 'young patriot' soon discovers and that is its lack of romance and the extremely practical turn given to everything."

Families left behind have something else to worry about if they're reading Ambrose Bierce. He writes on June 12: "A good deal of pother is making anent the moral atmosphere of Camp Merritt, the provocation lying in the fact that it hasn't any. The young female patriot, it appears, pervades the camp in super-adequate quantity, intent upon debuttoning the soldier boy for adornment of her own comely person; upon endowing him with objects and substances more or less comfortable to his tooth, but unrestful to his insides, upon inspection of his bed and board, which are identical; upon interchange of indiscretions." Bierce quotes with mock approval a statement from Captain Sarah Fry, of the Salvation Army, whose "solemn judgment on the needs of the situation is very other-worldly: 'What we want in this camp every night are lectures on social purity by the leading ministers of the city.'"

Describing those patriot women left at home, Bierce rises to new heights of misogyny: "It cheers to note the lively female of our species coming gallantly to the front and throwing herself into the imminent deadly breach for God and Country! She means well, the good girl, and has never a doubt of the importance and efficacy of her services to the Cause. With her deft and willing fingers, she fashions pin-cushions and needlebooks and button-bags for the soldier's knapsack, supplies his need with an abundant bordery of perfumes and proprietary medicines, presses upon him cases of assorted flat-irons to burnish his shirts withal. It is now proposed to outfit him with pajamas, which he will find very useful in the tropics for dealing with the natives."

The officers who are going to command all these volunteers and regulars are also gathering, most of them in the Moorish splendors of the Tampa Bay Hotel, which is Fifth Corps headquarters. On its spacious verandas are rows of rocking chairs, almost always filled to capacity. Surveying them, the intrepid Davis writes: "During the early part of May, the myriads of rocking-chairs on the long porches were filled with men. This was the rocking-chair period of the war. Officers who hadn't met in years, men who had been classmates at West Point, men who had fought together and against each other in the last war...were gathered together. Their talk was only of an immediate advance. It was to be 'as soon as Sampson smashes the Cape Verde fleet.'"

No one has grasped the sorry condition of Cervera's ships, now bottled up in Santiago Harbor. Even Frederick Jane, originator of that naval Bible, *Jane's Fighting Ships*, has made spectacular wrong guesses about the Spanish vessels. While he talks solemnly about the possibility that this powerful fleet might be able to attack the East Coast of America, poor Cervera has seen nothing to alter his prewar prediction that the conflict will "mean a terrible catastrophe for poor Spain."

If Cervera could see Key West, he might be ready to throw in the sponge at once. This little naval station has become a major base. You can hardly see through a forest of masts. Droves of press boats come and go. Vessels from the blockade arrive for fuel and repairs. Inspecting it on the day war was declared, Davis wrote: "At the water's edge one could see launches, gigs, and cutters streaking the blue waters of the bay with flashes of white and brass; signal flags of brilliant reds and yellows were spreading and fluttering at the signal halyards; wig-waggers beat the air from the bridges, and across the water, from the decks of the monitors, came the voices of men answering the roll: 'one, two, three, FOUR! one, two, three, FOUR!'"

Davis had attached himself to the *New York* when it sailed to blockade Havana, and wrote of his departure: "The leaden-painted warships moved heavily in two great columns, the battleships and the monitors leading on the left, the cruisers moving abreast to starboard, while in their wake and on either flank the torpedo-boats rolled and tossed like porpoises at play."

For ten days, until he caught a returning ship to Key West, Davis observed this early blockade (before Cervera's fleet was located) and found it a fascinating scene. There were, he reports later, "some exciting races after blockade-runners, some heavy firing, some wonderful effects of land and sea and sky, some instances of coolness and courage and of kindness and courtesy; but what was more impressive than all else besides, was the discipline of the ship's company and the perfection of her organization."

Civility in war? Davis finds it again, not when the *New York* bombards the Matanzas earthworks--first land combat engagement since the Civil War--but in what seems a rather peculiar way one evening when the ship lets go at some Spanish soldiers who have been firing their rifles harmlessly at the vessel. Sailors come on deck to watch the fun, and Davis writes: "As each shell struck home they whispered and chuckled. Meanwhile from below the sounds of the string band playing for the officers' mess. This is not a touch of fiction, but the reporting of cold coincidence, for war as it is conducted at this end of the century is civilized." Not for long, however, if this is in fact civility.

But he's right about the discipline. There's a traffic in spies and agents between ship and shore. One of them, Lieutenant A. S. Rowan, struggles all the way across Cuba to deliver a message to Garcia (which no doubt would have been accomplished more easily if they'd sent Harry Scovel instead). Rowan's journey is immortalized by Elbert Hubbard's essay, "A Message to Garcia," which will be recited in schools for a generation and sell in print by the millions. What is this message being sent wholesale to schoolchildren and the populace? Blind obedience to orders.

A much more daring but uncelebrated probing of Spanish territory is Ensign Henry H. Ward's foray with a commandeered yacht, which he sails in and out of the harbors of Cádiz, the Canaries, and San Juan, Puerto Rico, figuratively thumbing his nose at the enemy while he's conducting this reconnoitering under sail.

At home, the American expeditionary force is gathering itself. Never in its history has America fielded such a nondescript army, not even in the Revolution, nor one so ill equipped. That is because the War Department permitted no buying or ordering of anything until the war was actually declared. Consequently, the soldiers will be carrying old Springfield carbines left over from the Civil War, as opposed to the enemy's modern Mausers using smokeless powder. Medical and hospital supplies are on the way, but slowly. The volunteers get heavy blue uniforms--ideal for tropical heat, as Bierce notes.

The only thing this army will have in abundant quantities is enthusiasm for war itself, and against the Spaniards in particular. Everyone wants to kill somebody, it seems, and when they get to the scene of action, it will appear that this is more important than liberating Cuba. At the beginning, the country had from 28,000 to 50,000 regulars on hand, but after war is declared, McKinley makes a grand gesture and offers to raise and equip 216,500 volunteers, although less than half that number are needed. Volunteer militia have supplanted the common militia, and in most states are called "the National Guard," even though their legal status is uncertain. But the Guard, with its roots deep in local and state politics, is so thoroughly politicized that the President and Secretary of War Alger, an old brigade commander of cavalry under George Custer, can hardly ignore it.

Some of these young Guardsmen, however, lose their enthusiasm for war under the stress and strain of camp life. They begin to mutter about their responsibilities at home and refuse to transfer to the federal service. Company C, from Galesburg, Illinois, finally chooses to go home and, as Linderman tells us, "were jeered unmercifully...and were ordered to remove their uniforms and get out of camp." As they scuttle off, they're followed by cries of "traitor," "Spaniard," and "Go home to momma." They are said to lack "sand."

Seven of the men from Company I, out of Clyde, Ohio, are stretched around trees by their comrades and have their buttocks beaten, while their officers look on, before they're allowed to leave. Company B, from Fremont, Ohio, has only one defector, but he has all his hair clipped off and is ridden out of camp on a rail. All those returning home will be subjected to virtual isolation by former friends and the community when they get there.

On the Fourth of July, with the war raging, 600 Pennsylvanians at Camp Alger decide to go home and celebrate. They're pursued by cavalry detachments when they leave camp, and are brought back. Desertions are an almost daily occurrence, but often these defectors plead that they only want to go home for a few days "and have a good time."

There's no question about who are the most eager volunteers. T.R. has left his Navy post and, as a colonel, has organized his Rough Riders, a motley lot recruited in every corner of the country, from under the elms of Yale's campus to the plains of the West, all of them dedicated warriors constantly inspired by their belligerent commander. Of his men, the colonel says later, they "all earnestly wished for a chance to distinguish themselves, and fully appreciated that they ran the risk not merely of death, but of what was definitely worse--namely, failure at the crisis to perform duty well."

There is a "malaise" in America, Roosevelt believes--certainly not the last politician to make this accusation. Individual standards have deteriorated, he warns, but all this can be cured by the transforming power of war. Various well-known Americans agree with him. Owen Wister, the novelist, thinks people are making too much money and it will do them good to endure the casualties of war and restore them to fundamentals. William Allen White says war's sorrow will "chasten a nation deserving of punishment," a biblical view from the heart of

Kansas. Senator William Allen, of Nebraska, hopes war will do away with America's "dry rot." In his customary inclusive way, Ambrose Bierce welcomes "war, famine, pestilence, anything that will stop people from cheating."

Doesn't anyone want to give peace a chance? T.R. calls peace "a condition of blubber-like and swollen ignobility, fit only for huckstering weaklings, dwelling in gray twilight and heedless of the higher life." William James doesn't quite agree with him, but says he does think the American character is in danger of disintegration. The vitality released by war, he hopes, "might hammer us into decency." His brother Henry sarcastically identifies himself as a "poor worm of peace" compared with the "brilliant men of action." He's been studying military history, especially the career of Napoleon, so he is no doubt biased.

Few of the volunteers understand, or even know about, any of this; they're ready to demonstrate their individual worth against the enemy, no matter what it costs. They don't think the war will take long, and they're even afraid it will end before they can get to it. They believe ardently that combat experience is the essence of war.

Observing the organization of Roosevelt's Rough Riders, others conclude that this must be the best way to get to the front; consequently the redoubtable colonel soon has two rivals, "Grigsby's Cowboys," commanded by Melvin Grigsby, and "Torrey's Rocky Mountain Riders," under Jay L. Torrey. But the Cowboys never get any nearer Cuba than Camp Thomas, and the Rocky Mountain Riders are lost somewhere in the Florida miasma.

While the expeditionary force is gathering itself, the officers who will command them are still plotting the war's conduct, in an extremely limited way, in that most unlikely of surroundings, the five-story, Spanish-Moorish-Victorian Tampa Bay Hotel, which Davis has already written of so disdainfully. He finds it bizarre that such serious business is being carried out by this collection of old Union and Confederate veterans on broad verandas attached to the hotel's red brick facade, with its thirteen silver minarets--for the months of the Moslem calendar, it's said.

Among the lawn's luxuriant oleanders, peacocks strut, drinks are served in the shelter of the lobby's potted palms, and the hostelry's 500 rooms are filled. When war and destruction are not being plotted, the officers and at least some of the correspondents mingle on the hotel's golf course, or walk in its formal gardens, or try their luck in a casino known as the Oriental Annex, which has its own swimming pool and dance hall. At night, colorful electric lights illuminate the casino and the verandas. "A Turkish harem without women," one correspondent calls the place.

This hotel is the creation of the man who virtually invented Tampa, Henry Plant, owner of the Plant Line steamers that run to Key West and Cuba, who brought the town's first rail line to its sandy wastes in 1884--a move that created a boom city by 1890.

Only yesterday the Tampa Bay Hotel had been a winter playground for the often idle rich. Now the strains of waltz music drift in form the regimental band's concert at the nearby pavilion, while in their white wicker chairs formerly deadly enemies refight the Civil War and plan the next one.

General William Rufus Shafter, who's going to command the land forces, thrusts his three hundred pounds into one of the veranda chairs, which can hardly contain him, and this former Union officer happily discusses tactics with our old friend from Havana, Fitzhugh Lee, a former Confederate officer, transferred from his consular post to be a major general.

McKinley thinks it's a nice thing to have all these old enemies sharing the command. It sends a message, he believes, that the Civil War is really over. That's a notion easy to accept when we contemplate the figure of Joseph "Fightin' Joe" Wheeler, the man whose Confederate cavalry once gave General Sherman's troops so much trouble, now a prematurely old man at sixty-two, thin and stoop-shouldered, wearing a linen duster over his uniform in temperatures above 100 degrees.

There are also 128 correspondents in Tampa, including two women. One is Anna Benjamin, of *Leslie*'s magazine, and the other is a Canadian freelance reporter, Kathleen Blake Watkins. When a male reporter strikes up a conversation with Benjamin, she says defensively: "I know what you think. You think it's ridiculous my being here; you're laughing at me wanting to go, that's the worst of being a woman. But just let me tell you, I'm going through to Cuba and not all the old generals in the world are going to stop me."

She's right. The old generals will try to derail her, but she will go to Cuba, although she doesn't have a prayer of leaving with the other reporters and the Army when the invasion begins. Like Scovel, she's resourceful. She hurries down to Key West and hooks a ride to the war zone on a collier. Later on, when the affair in Cuba is over, she will manage to get as far as Manila and cover the Insurrection, go on to report events in China and Japan, and just keep on going around the world, coming back to Europe on the Trans-Siberian Railroad. Her career as an author and lecturer will be assured.

Kathleen Watkins is a different type. She will not get to Cuba, but she will be given some respect as "just one of the boys," wasting no time on the verandas but spending hours in the camp on Picnic Island, talking to soldiers and getting their stories as a kind of early Ernie Pyle.

Of course Davis overshadows all the rest of the press corps. "I expect to get rich off the war," he writes home confidently, as well he might, since he's covering for the *Herald*, *Scribner's* magazine, and the London *Times* while he's taking notes for a book he intends to write when it's over. Practicing to be rich, he has no sooner arrived in Tampa than he buys himself a Kentucky filly called Gaiety Girl, who he thinks will achieve immortality as the horse who "carried the news of the fall of Havana to Matanzas, fifty miles under fire," with guess who aboard.

It had been a hard decision when McKinley offered to commission him an Army captain. Davis was afraid that if the war went on longer than a year, "it would bore me to death." But on the other hand--with Frederic Remington and Colonel Arthur Lee, a British miliary attaché, for counsel--he shut himself up in his hotel room for hours and rehearsed all the various scenarios pro and con, before he turned down the President, after which, for a while, he was sorry he had.

As Tampa gears up for the invasion, Davis is infuriated to discover that he's going to be sharing the *Herald*'s pages with another correspondent, Poultney Bigelow, who is almost as arrogant as he is. Instant hate between the two men. Bigelow can't stand to walk into the hotel dining room and see Davis holding court with the other reporters, a row of medals across his jacket. It's a double-dipped satisfaction when Bigelow is able to scoop his eminent rival.

That happens when he encounters a man he's known for years, Captain H. J. Dorst, master of one of the most unusual craft the Navy has assembled in a fleet drawn from every port on the East Coast and elsewhere. She's the *Gussie*, a sidewheel double-decked river steamer at least forty years old if she's a day. She's certainly the most colorful craft in the fleet--bright red with green shutters, her interior full of mahogany and mirrors. Just the thing for invading Cuba.

That's what the *Gussie* is about to do, Dorst tells Bigelow. The Army is officially sponsoring what amounts to a filibustering expedition, intending to supply the insurgents with fresh arms, and she's sailing that night. Naturally, Bigelow wants to sign on, but Dorst says he's promised Davis (of all people!) an exclusive.

This situation calls for extraordinary measures, and Bigelow doesn't hesitate. He beards Davis directly in the hotel lobby and somehow convinces him to give up his berth. Only one thing could have persuaded him. Roosevelt and his Rough Riders are expected any day and, scenting reams of lucrative copy, Davis intends to meet him.

Bigelow apprises the captain of the switch, and Dorst promises that he and Rufus Zogbaum, a *Harper's Weekly* illustrator, will be the only members of the press aboard. That's before he meets Kathleen Watkins, who pries the whole story out of him. She knows he'll never let her aboard, but she has her revenge by spreading the story of this supposedly secret expedition among her fellow correspondents. Consequently when Bigelow shows up at the pier, with his typewriter in a sailor's bag on his shoulder, he finds he's going to share the story with four other reporters, including the ubiquitous Ralph Paine, who's now back in the competition.

By this time, everybody in Tampa knows about the secret expedition, so that when the *Gussie* prepares to stagger out to sea at midnight, the pier is crowded with reporters and other well-wishers. Next morning every paper in the country has the news, and the Atlanta *Constitution* headlines whether deadpan or seriously no one can be sure, "CUBAN INVASION BEGINS TODAY." "Today" is not quite correct. Captain Dorst has decided that, since secrecy is no longer possible, he'll sail at noon on the following day. But then there's another postponement. The Navy has promised an escort vessel, the revenue cutter *Manning*, but the wigwaggers get their signals mixed and a lighthouse tender, the *Mangrove*, appears instead. At last they sort it out, the *Gussie* is towed to sea and, accompanied by the

Manning, thrashes her way into open water, where a heavy squall quickly separates the two ships.

As it turns out, this is a serious mistake because the delay of nearly two days has brought a sudden disaster to the insurgents waiting for the *Gussie*'s cargo. A Spanish patrol caught up with them, and after a brief fight, the Cubans scattered into the jungle. So the *Gussie* steams on into what may be an ambush, her lights blazing from each porthole in violation of every known rule. There may even be "friendly fire" from the American blockade line ships because no one has told them of this expedition. It's not surprising, then, that the *Gussie* is the target of seven different ships in less than four hours.

Waiting for her arrival near Baracoa is none other than Harry Scovel, by prearrangement with Captain Dorst, an old friend from Greco-Turkish War days. Scovel has just put two spies ashore and is waiting on the *World*'s tug, the *Triton*. The sun is scarcely up when Scovel sees--and can't believe what he's seeing--the laggard *Gussie*, running too close to shore, all her lights on, and heading in the direction of Cabañas, a fort with a garrison of some 2,000 Spanish soldiers.

No one knows, least of all Scovel, why Dorst has chosen to make a landing on Arbolitas Point, near the harbor's western entrance. The *Gussie* launches some boats toward shore and they're immediately bogged down on a sandbar while still 200 yards from land. As they're trying to free the boats, a Spanish mounted patrol appears and begins shooting. The reporters are involved in the struggle too. Paine tries to save one of the horses and is almost trampled. James Archibald, of the San Francisco *Post*, has the distinction of being the war's second civilian land casualty by getting himself shot in the arm.

It's a fiasco. Scovel, unable to pick up the spies he's put on shore, disgustedly sets a course for Key West. Against everyone's advice, Dorst stubbornly tries another landing near Matanzas, but he can't find any rebels in sight to take his cargo, so after a day of indecision he give up and returns to Tampa, where he learns that, while he was gone, he's been made a lieutenant colonel.

At least Bigelow gets his scoop, such as it is. Writing on board the *Gussie* during the return trip, he reports: "That the failure was unattended by any loss of life on our part seems more due to good luck than to good judgment. When the war is over, some comic opera librettist can find inspiration in the adventures of the *Gussie*, whose movements from the time she left Key West until she returned were as frivolous and flighty as her name."

Bigelow sneaks this story past the military censorship that's been installed by giving it to a Pullman porter on a New York–bound train, with instructions for delivering it. The immediate result is a shakeup in the censorship office and a strict tightening of the rules. The first major battle between the Army and the press over censorship also breaks out. Editors and publishers are irate, but some in Congress think the Army's still too lenient. They're told that anyone who gets out of line will never see Cuba.

One of the stories Bigelow can't write is what's going on at the training camp near Lakeland, Florida, where his brother, Captain John, is stationed as a white officer with the famous 10th Cavalry (colored), of whom we're soon going to see a lot more. They're the "buffalo soldiers," brought in from the Western wilds of Fort Custer and Assiniboine, in Montana, where they've been hunting down Indians since the Civil War ended. John Bigelow admires these men and he's indignant at the way they're being treated in camp. Shopkeepers in the town won't serve them. Worse, an officer in the New York 71st, a National Guard unit known as the "Gallant Seventy-first," complains that it's humiliating to his men, who are mostly from the upper social strata of New York, to have black troops in the same camp with them.

If Bigelow can't get that story through the censors, he finds something else, at nearby Picnic Island, where the troops are being trained for Cuba. He begins to lay about him with story after story exposing the incredible blundering that infests this invasion. He's the first to report on the issuing of winter-weight uniforms to soldiers headed for the tropics, as well as shoes that simply fall apart in wet weather. He notes that many have hats that don't fit, and rifles but no ammunition. Whole regiments are running to the latrines and the medics after eating tinned pork.

Bigelow is also first to point out the unbelievable difficulties the Army is going to face when it tries to get this expedition on the transports that will carry them to Cuba. He even charges that Tampa was chosen as the embarkation point only because of Henry Plant's political influence. Bigelow also exposes how political patronage has dictated the granting of commissions to volunteers, sometimes to men whose knowledge of the military is primitive; for example, the major who didn't know he ranked higher than a captain. "Nobody dares complain for fear of appearing unpatriotic," Bigelow writes. "Still it will do no harm to hear a little of the truth."

It does do plenty of harm, though, as far as Bigelow is concerned. The truth, as always, is too uncomfortable for those in authority. Not only are his press credentials revoked, but he's attacked in the *Herald* as a man whose stories are "un-American...and calculated to give courage to the enemy."

But even Davis, who has no use for Bigelow, knows he's right. The "readiness of the volunteers to be sacrificed" is "a pathetic spectacle," he writes home to his brother. But it's dangerous to print the truth because families all over America are going to be much disturbed by it.

Scovel is going to be in trouble, too, accused of having stowed away on the Navy's armed tug, the *Uncas*, an affair which causes another outburst of indignation toward the yellow press. Back in Key West after the *Gussie* affair, he has discovered that Captain Dorst's incompetence has nearly cost the lives of the two spies he put ashore, whose information was to be used by military intelligence besides providing material for stories he might write. The two men are prisoners in Morro Castle, Scovel learns from the chief Spanish censor in Cuba, Ramón Mendez, who is his friend and a rebel sympathizer.

Since two Spanish naval officers are being held in Fort Thomas as prisoners of war, it's proposed that an exchange be made. The *Uncas* will go down to Havana to negotiate the details, and Commodore John C. Watson, who's running the espionage ring, suggests that Scovel follow in the *Triton* to help if needed.

All this, of course, must be kept a deep secret from Harry's fellow reporters. The *Triton* is to slip out of Key West in the dead of night and rendezvous with the *Uncas* at sea. However, Scovel is told by the harbormaster that his permission to depart during curfew hours (8 P.M. to 4 A.M.) has been revoked because of a private war going on between Navy officers over the goings and comings of the press boats. By the time Scovel gets the *Triton*'s crewmen scooped out of the local bars, it's too late to sail.

Lieutenant Brainard, commander of the *Uncas*, invites Scovel to go with him. He already has one journalist on board, E. F. Knight, a British reporter who has credentials from the Spanish government. The trip to Havana is without incident, the negotiations are carried out successfully, and the *Uncas* returns to Key West. As the ship touches the dock, Scovel is off and running to the cable office, while other reporters on shore are trying to get something out of Brainard, who isn't saying anything. Someone, identity unknown, rushes off to file a complaint with Commodore George C. Remey, who's waiting for Scovel when he comes out of the cable office.

Was he aboard the *Uncas?* Remey asks him. Scovel admits it. That's enough for the commodore, who vows to strip Brainard of his command, but Scovel, thinking fast, saves the lieutenant's career. "It wasn't Brainard's fault," he says. "I thought they might need an interpreter, so I stowed away and he couldn't very well throw me overboard." To make sure, Scovel sends a wire to the Navy Department, repeating his story. This proves to be a mistake. Brainard is saved, but Secretary Long wants no more journalistic stowaways and he issues an order permanently barring Scovel from going aboard any Navy ship or even entering a Navy installation. Long goes even further. All naval personnel, he decrees, are forbidden to have "any conversation whatever concerning the subject in any way pertaining to the Navy with representatives of the press." Dreadful syntax, but the meaning is clear, except for a hidden agenda. It's an indirect slap at Admiral Sampson, who's been relying on the reporters for much of his intelligence, since what he has to work with otherwise is inadequate. Long doesn't understand this; he just wants Sampson to stop accommodating the reporters.

But the secretary has underestimated Sampson. After the *World* protests vociferously that press freedom has been violated, the admiral coolly decides to ignore Long's order, on the ground that no civilian, not even a Cabinet member, can tell him who's allowed on his ships. So Scovel continues to be welcomed on the *New York*, and he uses the Navy's armed tug, the *Tecumseh*, to plant more spies on the Cuban coast and obtain intelligence information from the rebels. Long's order simply gets lost in the vast trash bin of Navy paper.

Some kind of liaison with the rebels is certainly in order. The Junta has signed an agreement with the United States putting Gómez's army under command of the invasion forces, but no one has told the general he has to take orders from Americans. Washington can't understand why Gómez thinks this is insulting, but in Havana, Blanco sees a possible opening. He sends a letter to Gómez, recommending that he join forces with the Spaniards against the common American enemy. If he does so, Blanco promises, Cuba will get her independence, and after the war, "Spain as a loving mother will open her arms to a new daughter of the Nations of the New World, which speaks her language."

Gómez doesn't like this any better than the Junta's order. "We are fighting for an American principle," he writes back to Blanco, "the principle of Bolívar and Washington. You say that we belong to the same race and invite me to fight against a foreign invader, but you are again mistaken because there are no differences of blood or of race. I believe in only one race, humanity." The general's problem, it seems, is that he's well ahead of his time.

Sampson makes another try at placating Gómez. He sends a party of five journalist volunteers (not including Scovel), who come to be known as the Gómez Commission, to establish communications with the general. Major W. D. Smith is to be their guide. Among the commissioners is H. J. Whigham, the noted Scottish amateur golfer, now working for the Chicago *Tribune*. Sampson selects the *Triton* for their transportation, and equips it with a Navy howitzer. Before the commission members leave, Sampson shakes their hands, wishes them well, and gives each one a brace of pistols.

The *Triton* arrives off Punta de Gaguanes, but the crew is not about to brave the submerged reefs again, so Smith commandeers a passing fishing boat to take his charges ashore. They have no trouble finding Gómez, but they're shocked to discover that he isn't at all happy about America's declaration of war and its plans to invade. He reiterates that he doesn't want even one American soldier on the island. All he wants is supplies and munitions, as he's insisted from the beginning, and he'll do the job himself.

Whigham asks the general what would happen in that case when (and if) the Spanish surrender. Gómez gives him a tough answer: "The [cease-fire] would be granted, because the Americans have been so humane," Whigham reports to his paper. "This he said with an air of contempt for so foolish a quality--and that was exactly what the Cubans did not want. They desired an eye for an eye and a tooth for a tooth. Theirs was not a civilized war--these his very words--but a war of extermination, and no Cuban would be satisfied until every Spaniard was killed or driven from the island."

With the failure of the Gómez Commission, the invasion is now a certainty, which it always has been, whether the general likes it or not. Scovel denounces it as "criminal" on the front page of the *World*, and that doesn't endear him to the authorities. He predicts (erroneously) that American volunteers will just bog down in Cuba's hostile climate and won't find the war any more winnable than the Spaniards have. "Ask Gómez what he wants and let him have it," is Harry's prescription, under a headline, "GOMEZ WILL HAMMER AT HAVANA'S GATES."

But Sampson, a determined old sea dog, wants to make one last try. He writes Gómez a personal letter, saying, "I have the honor to inform you of the presence of the Squadron under my command off the coast of Cuba. Desiring information for my government, I would be very much pleased to have you inform us as to your ideas concerning cooperation, and your needs as to arms, munitions, and supplies in general. The bearer, Mr. Sylvester Scovel [!] is empowered to treat with you in my name."

Ambassador Scovel speeds to Cuba on the torpedo boat *Porter*, which arrives off Caibarién. The crew contemplates how to get through the shallows under the nose of a Spanish garrison only a half mile away. Scovel thinks it's too dangerous to attempt a landing and persuades Lieutenant Fremont, the *Porter*'s commander, to put him and another man ashore several miles away. From there he believes he can meet Major Smith and the commissioners at some rendezvous point and also deliver Sampson's letter. Fremont says he'll come back in a week and pick them up.

But the *Porter* is no sooner out of sight than Scovel realizes he's picked the wrong place to land. He's on a promontory, separated from the mainland by a marsh several miles wide. There's no help for it. He and his companion have to wade through muck three feet deep, with the stench of stagnant water in their noses, until they get to dry land. Two surprises await them. Smith's party is quite near, and offshore can be seen five Spanish gunboats, heavily armed, obviously lying in wait for the *Porter*'s return.

Scovel knows Sampson sets considerable store by this craft--"You be sure and take good care of that ship," were his parting words--and he figures his first priority is to save the *Porter* somehow, but he can't do that and also get the letter to Gómez. One of the reporters who joins them with the returning commissioners is Frederick Somerford, another *Herald* correspondent, and he volunteers to deliver the letter, even though, after being with the general for several months, he's nearly starving when he joins Scovel.

Somerford takes off, and a few hours later two Cuban fishing boats show up, nosing in through a channel. Their crews come ashore a hundred yards or so from where Scovel and the commissioners are camped. "We're going to take those boats," Smith declares, and they do. He deploys the correspondents in the bush, and at his signal, they storm out, yelling and shooting their pistols. The startled fishermen are no match for this impromptu army, but what they fail to understand is that they're prisoners of the New York *World* and the Chicago *Tribune*.

Just as the triumphant correspondents are about to take off, Somerford comes running down the beach. He's encountered Gómez unexpectedly in the process of moving his headquarters, so he not only delivered the letter but was carrying the general's reply as well as a note of greeting to McKinley. The fishing boat slips out to sea, the men stripped to the waist, trying to look like native fishermen, and sail away right under the noses of the Spanish gunboats. Three days later, they're in Key West--just in time. The torpedo boat *Ericsson*, substituting for the *Porter*, had been just about to set out on the rescue trip.

Gómez has merely repeated his position in his letter to the President, but it doesn't matter because the launching of the expeditionary force is beginning to get under way in what must be the most fouled-up operation in American military history.

General Nelson Miles, the old Indian fighter who achieved fame by pursuing Chief Joseph and his Nez Perce tribe across half the continent, had been given command of 70,000 troops a week after Dewey's victory, with orders to seize Havana. Miles was profoundly irritated by these orders. Didn't anyone in Washington know that such an expedition wasn't possible just yet? No one did. Certainly not Secretary Alger, who was already breaking down, physically and mentally, under the strain. Nor the President, who has no talent for these matters.

Miles informs them that one reason alone would be enough to delay any such venture. He doesn't have enough ammunition, and almost everything else he needs is also lacking. All right, says Alger, we'll pour all we've got into Tampa, the embarkation point, and soon railroad cars are moving--not the guns and ammunition which are really needed--but mountains of food and quartermasters' supplies. There are enough rations for 70,000 men who aren't there yet, including enough bacon to last everyone for ninety days.

Unfortunately, the government doesn't have any storage space for this immense quantity of supplies, and so, in short, thousands of loaded railway cars are jammed into sidings all the way from Tampa to Columbia, South Carolina. The War Department has known of this shortage of storehouse space for weeks, and it has also known that few provisions have been made for the volunteers' camps. The quartermaster reports that all he's got left in his main warehouse is a quantity of blankets and "a pretty good stack of mess pans," which have been there since the Civil War.

Near paralysis settles on Washington at this crucial juncture. Alger seems out of it, or at least highly confused, but McKinley, who thinks the expedition is a minor affair in any case, won't remove him because, after all, the old man is patriotic and presumably loyal. The War Department would just as soon postpone the whole thing anyway until fall, when the threat of yellow fever will be much diminished. No wonder that the historian Frank Freidel, in retrospect, wrote of this expedition: "Even by the standards of nineteenth-century warfare it was bizarre and risky almost beyond belief."

It's also almost beyond comprehension why Tampa was chosen as the embarkation point in the first place. Plant, the promoter who lifted the place out of the sand into eminence as a tourist resort, never intended Port Tampa, its link to the sea, as anything more than a place for small steamers to dock on their way to Key West or Cuba. He had a narrow channel dredged so that a tongue of land could be used as a pier. Only two ships at a time can be tied up there; all the others will have to stand by in the channel and wait their turn to load. The Army has laid down some new railroad tracks on this makeshift pier, but they're not nearly adequate, and stevedores are going to be doing most of the loading, as Freidel tells us, carrying "provisions on their backs across fifty feet of sand and up a steep ramp into vessels." This is such exhausting work that, as it turns out, when their shifts end, the men fall down on the pier to sleep, further impeding traffic.

It's nine miles back to Tampa itself from the pier, and the only connection is a single-track railroad, already cluttered because Plant has insisted on blithely running excursion trains of tourists to see the show, besides his regular train-boat service.

This is the situation that confronts General Shafter when he gets what he believes are his final orders on May 30. The War Department's message in cipher reads: "You are directed to take your command on transports, proceed under convoy of the Navy to the vicinity of Santiago de Cuba, land your force at such places east or west of that point as your judgment may dictate, under protection of the Navy, to capture or destroy the garrison there, and...with the aid of the Navy capture or destroy the Spanish fleet now reported to be in Santiago harbor. On completion of this enterprise, unless you receive other orders or deem it advisable to remain in the harbor of Santiago de Cuba, re-embark your troops and proceed to the harbor of Port de Banes....When will you sail?"

When indeed? Shafter, a no-nonsense old soldier, is willing enough, but he's hardly up to *this* job. He doesn't have much aptitude for logistics, to begin with, and he's had no experience at all in transporting and supplying an army. Consequently he makes the initial mistake of failing to visualize what he's up against. He doesn't begin to understand what he's facing until he gives the order to embark.

Then he finds out that all those railroad cars loaded with provisions, stacked up between Tampa and Columbia, have not been invoiced and the cars are unmarked, so there's no way of telling what's inside them until someone sorts out their contents. When that's done, he has to load whatever provisions he can manage, and his army as well, onto a weird collection of ships chartered by the War Department. They're being refitted with bunks, and stalls for horses and mules, so it's June 1 before they're ready to take on any cargo. On May 31, he's reported optimistically that he could sail in three days, but the date arrives and the situation, as they'll say in a later war, is snafu.

General William Rufus Shafter

reproduced from the collections of the Library of Congress

General Miles comes down to find out what's holding things up and reports back: "There are over 300 cars loaded with war materials along the roads about Tampa. Stores are sent to the quartermaster at Tampa, but the invoices and bills of lading have not been received, so that officers are obliged to break open seals and hunt from car to car to ascertain whether they contain clothing, grain, balloon material, horse equipment, ammunition, siege guns, commissary stores, etc." To this, Alger replies petulantly: "Twenty thousand men ought to unload any number of cars and assort contents. There is much criticism about delay of expedition...."

Obviously, Shafter isn't going to get sympathy, much less any help, from Washington. Gamely, he takes charge himself, first from a post on the Tampa Bay Hotel's piazza, but soon moving right down to the pier, sitting on two cracker boxes strong enough to support his great weight and using a packing case as his desk. He continues to get nothing but bad news. On June 6, when the ships are reported ready for embarkation, he learns that these craft are able to take only 18,000 men, or 20,000 at most, not the 25,000 he's counted on. Every regiment wants to get on board, and already they're preparing for a frantic race to embark.

Next morning, trainloads of soldiers are converging toward the pier, only to be stopped cold by, as Leech describes it, a "solid mass of boxcars and flatcars, spilling out crates, bales, baggage, vehicles, and mules." The single track to the pier is completely blocked and everything's at a standstill, but Shafter calmly announces that the transports will sail at dawn. There's a free-for-all, and possibly by the divine intervention that protects America and drunks, the tracks get cleared, the trains to the pier begin to move, and the embarkation is under way at last.

Trooper Arthur Fortunatus Cosby, of the Rough Riders, describes his part in it: "At six o'clock [in the evening] we lined up, the whole regiment, and took the sandy, dirty, hot walk to the Tampa Bay Hotel to be paid. It was ten by the time we returned, all this for $2.10, my pay. Then we were ordered to prepare at once to leave. We rolled up a sleeping blanket, half of a shelter tent, and poncho with such clothes and comforts as we could, together; threw this over our shoulder, put on our cartridge belts with 125 rounds, took our canteen and eating things, then added a haver-sack [two canvas bags] with some rations issued to us, and with our carbines we were ready."

Cosby and his comrades were in for a bad night. T.R. writes indignantly in his diary: "Worst confusion yet. R.R. system is utterly mismanaged. No military head. No allotment of transports. No plans." All the trains, it seems, are trying to move to Port Tampa at the same time on the single track.

It's past 5 A.M., after marching first one place then the other, before the Rough Riders are able to get on some coal freight cars. In only an hour, they're at dockside. And they're the lucky ones.

William Dinwiddie, surveying the scene for the Washington *Star*, writes: "One regiment--the 6th U.S. Infantry--struck its tents at 9 o'clock Tuesday night and waited until 2 o'clock Wednesday at Tampa until it was moved. The experience of these men was particularly discouraging since they traveled in a stock train, standing for four hours in soft filth, while the cars were sidetracked and jostled about in scalding midday sun. Hardly a murmur came from the men when they were put aboard this ill-smelling train, so great was the desire of every man to go to the front."

On the pier itself, thousands of soldiers, tired and hungry, have stood for hours before they could get on a transport. Others, like the black troops of the 10th Cavalry, under Captain John Bigelow, Jr., have had an easy trip to the pier, riding on coaches equipped with water coolers, but after they arrive, they get nothing to eat after a breakfast of coffee and hardtack at 3 A.M.

The correspondents are also part of this insane rush. At night on June 7, they're informed that eighty-nine of them will be taken aboard Shafter's headquarters ship, the *Segurança*, or if not that ship, some other vessel. They must be on the pier at 2 A.M., they're told. As Dinwiddie reports: "For the next few hours, the corridors and lobbies were jammed with men and baggage. It was a motley assembly which scurried through the hotel, in canvas hunting suits, in white duck, in the brown fatigue clothes of the army, and even in immaculate white shirt fronts and patent leathers. Six-shooters, machetes, and belts full of ammunition circulated through the halls, while broad shoulders were strung with shoulder straps from which dangled canteens, rolls of blankets, binoculars, Kodaks, and purses filled with notebooks. Two o'clock came, and then 3, and 4, and 5, bringing the first glimmer of a beautiful dawn, before the train was loaded with headquarters' and correspondents' luggage and pulled slowly away from the great hostelry, where, so far as outsiders could see, had been enacted one long comedy of gaiety and pleasure for seven weeks."

Meanwhile, early in the morning, the Rough Riders have reached Port Tampa, where T.R. sees with dismay that there are already 10,000 men on the pier. The quartermaster is there, allotting space, and he tells Roosevelt that the Rough Riders will be on the *Yucatan*. Of what followed, T.R. wrote later: "Colonel Wood jumped in a boat and went out in midstream [to commandeer the ship]. I happened to find out by accident that the transport *Yucatan* had also been allotted to the Second Infantry and the Seventy-first New York, and I ran down to my men and left a guard and took the rest and rushed them down to the dock and got on the *Yucatan*, holding the gangplank against the Second Infantry and Seventy-first New York."

Captain Anthony J. Bleecker, of the 71st, appears with his troops and finds Roosevelt's substantial bulk blocking the gangplank.

"Hello," T.R. greets him. "What can I do for you?"

"That's our ship," Bleecker says.

"Well, we seem to have it," Roosevelt replies coolly.

Telling the story later, T.R. likes to embellish it a little and says the 71st had to spend the next two nights on their train, but in fact this regiment had to wait only a few hours before they embarked on a newer and much more comfortable craft, the *Vigilancia*.

At last they're all on board, the largest military expedition ever to leave the United States up to that time. On the transports are 819 officers and 15,058 enlisted men, besides 30 civilian clerks, 272 teamsters and packers, and 107 stevedores. The livestock includes 2,295 horses and mules, with their harness, plus 114 six-mule army wagons, and 81 escort wagons. Someone has decided that wagons are just as good as ambulances, so only seven of the latter are boarded.

The artillery doesn't begin to measure up to what these men are supposed to accomplish. There are sixteen light guns, four 7-inch howitzers, four 5-inch siege guns, a Hotchkiss revolving cannon, an automatic dynamite gun, eight 3.6-inch field mortars, and four Gatling machine guns. Do they call this firepower? Only the Rough Riders and a few others have modern rifles and smokeless powder.

Some of the fleet has already started down the bay and Shafter is just about to board his headquarters ship when he gets a frantic wire from Alger: "Wait until you get further orders before you sail." Washington has had a fit of panic because the yacht *Eagle* reported the day before that it had seen a Spanish armored cruiser second class steaming along in the San Nicolás Channel. Alger gets confirmation of the sighting from another Navy ship, the *Resolute*.

So the transports that have already departed have to be called back, but since it's beyond reason to even contemplate unloading and loading again, there's nothing to do but wait until the Navy checks out the sighting. Dinwiddie describes the resulting misery: "For nearly five whole days the army lay idly at rest, waiting patiently. It was a frightful ordeal for the army...one in which the men suffered mental depression and physical devitalization, largely shared by the ranking officers, who feared that under the torrid sun and in the superheated and illy-ventilated holds, where the masses of the army lay gasping...an outbreak of fever was imminent. Fevers did appear, but fortunately they were all malarial, and the dread typhus did not make its appearance."

Shafter uses the delay to sort out and load more essential equipment that would otherwise have been left behind. In fact, when Alger sends him orders on June 12 that it's safe to sail now (if there was a Spanish cruiser, it's disappeared), badly needed medical supplies have only just arrived. At that, it takes two days more to reload the animals, who had to be taken off, and to put fresh water on the transports.

As the flotilla casts off for the second time, Davis reports that on board the ships a portentous quiet prevails, a mood reflected on the pier, where no one is waving or calling goodbye. Even the omnipresent band is silent. All that remains on the dock, Davis reports, are "three colored women and a pathetic group of perspiring stevedores and three soldiers."

The flotilla moves into the open sea toward Cuba in three long lines of thirty-two transports, a towing barge, and a schooner with a cargo of extra water. Three lighters are also in attendance, but one sinks en route. The Navy escort surrounding them is spread over thirty or forty miles. Davis writes: "Sometimes we moved at the rate of four miles an hour, and frequently we did not move at all," consequently it will take two and a half days to make the passage.

Davis approves of the escort, but with reservations: "The war-ships treated us with the most punctilious courtesy and concealed contempt. And we certainly deserved it. We could not keep in line and we lost ourselves and each other, and the gun-boats and torpedo-boats were busy rounding us up, and giving us sharp, precise orders in passing, through a megaphone, to which either nobody on board made any reply, or everyone did. The gun-boats were like swift, keen-eyed, intelligent collies rounding up a herd of bungling sheep."

For the sheep left behind, there is only gloom over missing the boat, except for those who lost their enthusiasm in camp before the embarkation, and some of the older Guardsmen who find themselves, as Linderman tell us, "no longer interested in anything beyond what a later War Department study would castigate as 'the club features of militia organizations'"--a complaint dating back to the Revolution and Washington's militia problems. Some of the militiamen, in fact, say they've decided not to serve, at the last moment, and go home.

Alger had asserted early on that there was "going to be more trouble to satisfy those who are not going than to find those who are willing to go." What he didn't understand was that volunteers want combat, not service, and when they found out that some of them were going to be denied fighting at the front, they lost interest in the war.

Among these are Grisby's Cowboys, who make a violent protest by trying to break into the Camp Thomas theater, and have to be restrained by provost guards, who charge them with bayonets and hurt a dozen or so men. But there are more who, having been left behind, want no part of the conflict. As Alger laments, "The increased army had already been organized before the clamor for discharge from the service began."

Nevertheless, after the ships sail away, some of those left behind find their lives unbearable. An officer on General James H. Wilson's staff, Captain Augustus Gardner, writes home to his wife: "Santiago will fall before we can get there. Everyone here is frightfully dispirited at the sudden change in orders. You can't find a man who cares a damn whether there is yellow fever in Santiago or not, or who experienced any pleasure at the news of [that city's] surrender." Later when he's part of the quiet occupation of Puerto Rico, he writes again: "The rumors of peace are thick and everyone is more disgusted than ever. I am not bloodthirsty, but I should like to see a little real fighting after all the farce." Still others complain they've had "no fair chance at the enemy."

They should count their blessings. Those men on the transports are soon going to do "a little real fighting" and it won't be pretty.

3

ON THE BEACH AT DAIQUIRI
AND SIBONEY

As the invasion fleet circles the north coast of Cuba, it moves along the shore for days at a pace so slow it would make the convoy an ideal target for shore batteries, if any, but they don't speak. The Spaniards know the Americans are there, however. They extinguish the lighthouses at night, so that no aid will be given the enemy. Peering through the darkness at the convoy's running lights, Charles M. Pepper, of the Washington *Star*, thinks they look "like the struggling street of a floating city. The signals were flashed at a lively rate for a time like a string of colored lanterns swinging from the masts."

Nothing, apparently, has been learned from the *Gussie*'s expedition because the rules of warfare are once more casually flouted on Shafter's headquarters ship. While the other transports in the convoy are dark except for their running lights, the *Segurança* is lit up as brightly as though she were lying in port on a gala night; her band is playing ragtime. Davis reports, with unconcealed disbelief, that this flotilla is as conspicuous as "Brooklyn or New York with the lights of the bridge included."

This makes the foreign military attachés on board the *Segurança* more than a little uneasy. They wonder why God is keeping the Spanish torpedo boats from picking off these sitting American ducks, one by one. Commenting on the Nervous Nellies, Davis explodes in a most uncharacteristic tribute to the whole expedition. "The foreign attachés," he writes, "regarded the fair weather that accompanied us, the brutal good health of the men, the small loss of horses and mules, and the entire freedom from interference on the part of the enemy with the same grudging envy that one watches a successful novice winning continuously at roulette. It was a most happy-go-lucky expedition, run with real American optimism and readiness to take big chances, and with the spirit of a people who recklessly trust that it will come out all right in the end, and that the barely possible may not happen. As one of the generals on board said, 'This is God Almighty's war, and we are only His agents."

Nothing is said about the terrible overcrowding, or the sheer misery in the holds, or the abominable cold food, or the warm water that produces nausea if the ship hasn't already done so. These foul ships were originally intended only for animals and cargo. Now they're launching pads for disease--with almost no provision for medical care. Nevertheless, the spirit Davis writes about is certainly there in abundance. A private writes home: "No one could be really mad--hell, we were off to Cuba, weren't we?"

But what's come over Davis, this reporter who has been saying so many unkind things about the Army? It stems from something that happened just before the embarkation, part of his long-running feud with Bigelow. On June 5, a story by Davis had appeared in the *Herald*, repeating publicly what he had been saying privately for some time--namely, that ignorant politicians were serving as officers in the volunteers, and that consequently training the men was endangering their health.

On the heels of these charges came a much more devastating blast from Bigelow, who denounced profiteering, political promotions, general unreadiness in the Army, and Alger's failure (until then) to appoint a single commander-in-chief. It was more than Davis could stomach. That scoundrel Bigelow had gone too far, he said, and performed a 180-degree right turn, denouncing his rival's statements as both untrue and un-American, as well as treasonous and seditious. Replying, Bigelow called Davis an "amateur war correspondent" (unkindest cut of all!) and repeated his charges. Davis didn't respond publicly, but privately he declared, "The trouble with Bigelow is that the man is crazy. He is also right in many things he says, only it is no use saying them now."

For a little while after this exchange, Davis is the fair-haired boy with Miles and Shafter, who look upon him as "the champion of the Army," and that's why Davis is painting such a rosy picture of the invading army which is only partly, though substantially, true. What a meeting of great minds--Davis's and the generals'. Unfortunately this new relationship will soon come to a crashing halt, and Davis is going to be in big trouble.

As the convoy nears its chosen landing place at Daiquiri, it looks as though Bigelow might have overestimated the Army's capabilities. This landing, in Freidel's words, "could have been one of the worst military disasters in United States history if the Spanish had shown more initiative." For one thing, Lieutenant General Arsenio Linares Pombo knows exactly where the Americans are going to land. For another, the beach at Daiquiri is easily defensible.

The obstacles to a successful landing seem almost insurmountable. Ships are going to have to anchor in an unprotected open roadstead, with heavy surf between them and the land. Once ashore, from there to Santiago, a limestone bluff, 200 to 250 feet high, runs most of the way. Along this ridge, placed on strategic hilltops, are blockhouses. So, besides the rugged terrain, Shafter is planning to throw 17,000 men against forts supposedly manned by 12,000 seasoned Spanish troops.

The reason this doesn't become a tragic error is because General Linares does something inexplicable. He chooses not to deploy any more than a small portion of his army in those blockhouses overlooking Daiquiri, Siboney, and the beaches west of Santiago, from which they could have devastated the Americans, as the foreign attachés gloomily forecast. Instead, he's drawn his men back so that they're mostly defending the area around Santiago. Not much more than a corporal's guard is protecting Daiquiri, and a somewhat larger number are near Siboney, just down the beach, where Shafter plans to land the remainder of his forces next day.

The general has his reasons for what he's doing. He fears yellow fever more than he does the Spaniards, and the less time the Army has to spend here the better, he thinks. He's also afraid of heavy losses, remarking to his adjutant general, E. J. McClernand, that times have changed since the Civil War, when people at home became accustomed to hearing of staggering casualties. His idea is to minimize that possibility and avoid the fever too by simply throwing his army in lines around Santiago and demanding its surrender. Sampson can then take care of Cervera any way he likes and the war will be over.

This kind of thinking in the expedition's high command, and particularly Shafter's thinking, is the primary cause of the constant feeling among some officers and correspondents that rescuing Cuba from the Spaniards could be an American disaster at almost any time. They don't have much confidence in

Shafter, this sixty-three-year-old former cavalry officer, in spite of his Medal of Honor. Certainly no one can miss his presence. Mounted on his bay stallion, reputed to be the largest horse in the Army, Shafter is legendary for his parade appearances. Personally, he's outspoken, gruff, given to quick bursts of anger, not easy to get along with, although his aide, Lieutenant John Miley, is loyal and unquestioning.

At least he understands that most of his army isn't combat ready, but it doesn't seem to bother him. His best units are the black 9th and 10th Regiments, the so-called "buffalo soldiers," brought in from the Western prairies, and now dismounted, like all the other cavalry, because the terrain in this part of Cuba, we discover a little late, is not designed for cavalry charges. Shafter would have brought the horses anyway, but they had to be left behind in Tampa because there was no room.

Even the faithful Miley has to admit his commander has only a rudimentary knowledge of logistics and knows virtually nothing about amphibious landings. Miley admits later that Shafter really meant to push on to Santiago at once, and at first "did not realize it would take a week to completely disembark the command and supplies."

So the expedition is close to its first moment of truth when the transports approach Cuba at daybreak on June 20, and those on board see the rugged Sierra Maestra mountains rising out of a blue mist. Before anything else happens, Sampson comes up from the blockade line to discuss plans with Shafter, and the two of them, with their aides and a few reporters, go off in a Navy gig to a point eighteen miles west of Santiago so they can confer with General Calixto García, the Cuban regional commander.

Unexpectedly, this conference turns into a humiliating experience for Shafter. To reach the general's temporary headquarters, high up in the cliffs overlooking Aserradores beach, it will be necessary to ascend along a steep switchback trail, a journey nearly impossible for Shafter in ordinary circumstances but now he's developed a gouty foot, which means there's no chance. If they can find a horse strong and large enough to carry him up, he might make it, but there are no horses of any dimension about. After a frustrating, irritable delay, someone does find a white mule, and this superior animal manages to get the general to the top of the cliff.

Up to now, at least, the Cubans have been extremely welcoming. When the gig landed, a group of rebels, stripped to the waist, came to meet them, shouting a welcome, and wading out to pull the gig ashore. They even carry some of the officers and a few correspondents on their shoulders to dry land.

García is waiting for them, and since it's the first time the Americans have met this commander of the Second Department, they are naturally curious and look him over carefully. What they see is a tall man with sharp eyes whose trailing white mustaches loop gently off his face. Above the bridge of his nose is a noticeably large, hollow scar, the souvenir of a suicide attempt during the Ten Years' War. Thinking he was about to be captured, and preferring death to captivity, García had shot himself under the jaw. The bullet came out through his forehead just above his nose, but miraculously, he was neither captured nor killed.

The Americans already have very little expectation that the Cubans will be useful, and García is beginning to think that these invaders are going to relegate him and his men to a back seat. Nevertheless, all hands get down to business. Sampson opens by declaring he believes the Army should land on both sides of the harbor, then charge up the hill and take Morro Castle, along with the batteries at Socapa. After the Army has accomplished this little trick, the Navy will sweep away the mines at the harbor's entrance and attack Cervera's fleet.

Shafter is aghast at the plan. This admiral, whom he doesn't like much anyway, wants his men to climb a 230-foot cliff and seize a stone fort full of defenders. "It would have been the height of folly," he writes later. He insists on his original plan--landing at Daiquiri--and García agrees with him. It's only fifteen miles from there to Santiago, and the Cubans say the little town selected for the landing is defended by only 300 soldiers, whom they promise to drive away, or at least keep them so occupied that the Americans can easily come ashore. The agreement satisfies everyone but Sampson, and on this somewhat uncertain note, the conference breaks up.

Shafter returns to his command ship in a bad mood. The humiliation of that cliffside climb still lingers, and he's resolved to stay on the ship as long as possible. As far as he's concerned, he's in Cuba to make history and advance his reputation, and he knows that if General Miles, back in Washington, finds out what his physical condition really is, a recall is quite possible and he'll miss his great opportunity.

The landing is scheduled for June 22, and before dawn on that day, Trooper Cosby is writing home to his mother: "I do not think we shall have any fighting where we are going to land but there is always the chance. The sun is rising and we are drawing nearer shore so goodbye."

At nine-thirty, the *Segurança* begins a preparatory shelling of the beach with its limited armament and before long General Demetrio Castillo, the regional Cuban commander, is visible on a ridge above the town, surrounded by a mounted escort who are waving a large Cuban flag, mistaken by the Americans for the Spanish emblem. They open fire on it before this mistake gets sorted out.

Fires can be seen beyond the beach. There's a high iron pier which looks like a formidable obstacle instead of a help. Ironically, this pier is the remnant of a collaboration between the two warring countries. It was built by the Spanish-American Iron Company, rising more than forty feet above the water, and in happier days was used to load ore. Now one of the old ore cars is on fire, and the company's machine shop on shore is blazing too. A blockhouse looks down on Daiquiri from a steep hill, but no defenders are visible.

Sampson may not approve of Shafter's plan of operation, but the Navy is ready to support him. As the landing boats move toward the shore, six of the blockade ships come up and lay down a barrage behind Daiquiri to discourage opposition. Observing it, Malcolm McDowell, of the Chicago *Record*, writes, "For twenty minutes, the rapid firing and machine guns beat the long roll with the heavy ones coming in with booms and thumps like a great bass drum. The shells ripped through the trees, smashed the cliffs, uprooted great palms and tore up the earth with a vindictive vigor which delighted the soldiers."

Everyone's watching the blockhouse, but no return fire comes from it, nor do the Navy's gunners manage a hit. But enough is enough. This heavy fire is virtually destroying the hillside and endangering the waiting rebels. One of them runs out to the end of the pier waving a white cloth. He's signaling that the Spaniards have gone, but some think he's surrendering.

Now Shafter has another problem. The chartered transports are commanded by civilians--insolent and cowardly, in

Crane's opinion--some of whom pay no attention to the general's disembarkation orders and pull back their ships to the safety of open water, with medicines and other essential equipment still in the holds. It takes the Navy to herd back these captains whose craft were leased to the government for exorbitant, profiteering sums.

As usual, T.R. is lucky. While he's fuming because the *Yucatan* can't get close enough to shore so that his troops can disembark, the converted yacht *Vixen* moves alongside, and Lieutenant Sharp, in command of her, hails Roosevelt, who's delighted to see his former Assistant Secretary of the Navy. Roosevelt boards the *Vixen* with Colonel Leonard Wood, his superior (T.R. is actually a lieutenant colonel, although he behaves as though he's the commander). The Cuban pilot tells them he can take the *Yucatan* within a few hundred yards of the beach, and after that it's up to them. He does it so skillfully, other transports follow, but there are still holdout civilian captains who won't take the chance. One waits for two days until he makes up his mind to try it.

Davis writes: "Under the cover of the smoke [from the bombardment], the long-boats and launches began to scurry toward the shore. The men in the boats pulled harder at the oars, the steam-launches rolled and pitched, tugging at the weight behind them [as they towed the lines of boats], and the first convoy of five hundred men were soon bunched together, racing bow by bow for the shore. A launch turned suddenly and steered for a long pier under the ore-docks, the waves lifted it to the level of the pier, and a half-dozen men leaped through the air and landed on the pier-head, waving their muskets above them.

"At the same moment two of the other boats were driven through the surf to the beach itself, and the men scrambled out to their feet on the shore of Cuba. In an instant a cheer came faintly from the shore, and more loudly from the war-ships. It was caught up by every ship in the transport fleet, and was carried for miles over the ocean. Men waved their hats, and jumped up and down, and shrieked as though they themselves had been the first to land."

There's anxiety on the headquarters ship, where the foreign attachés and reporters watch the landing operation. "We held our breath," Remington writes later. "We expected a most desperate fight for the landing." It's soon established that this is not going to be the case, but Shafter orders the reporters to stay on the *Seguança* until all the troops have been landed.

Davis walks up to the general and observes, "I see the order for disembarkation...will keep back reporters."

"That's true," Shafter tells him, and explains that he wants the troops to be ready if any fire from the jungle develops.

"But I'm not an ordinary reporter," Davis tells him, with his usual sublime confidence. "I'm a descriptive writer."

"I don't give a damn *what* you are," Shafter replies crisply. "I'll treat all of you alike."

End of the brief affair between Davis and the Army command, especially Shafter, about whom he never writes a kind word again.

The other correspondents don't understand Shafter's reasoning and they're offended too. One of them writes months later: "From the moment of the issuing of that order...pencils began to be sharpened for General Shafter--and they have not yet lost their point."

Meanwhile, the reporters have to figure out, if they can, how to disobey Shafter's orders and get ashore. One solves the problem by wrapping his camera in some clothing and persuading an orderly to take it on a landing boat, after which he fearlessly jumps over the side into a strong riptide and starts swimming for shore, clinging to one of the towlines pulling the boats. By the time most of this contingent reaches Daiquiri beach, he's taking their pictures.

As it goes on, the landing becomes increasingly hazardous. Sometimes it seems as though the incoming craft are going to be picked up by the crashing surf and dashed against the piles. During the afternoon, there's a heroic incident when two black soldiers of the 10th Cavalry slip as they try to climb onto the pier and fall into the water. Captain Bucky O'Neill, a Rough Rider who will one day be the mayor of Prescott, Arizona, jumps in after them but can't save their lives as the waves dash them against the piles. There are no more human casualties, only the smashing of several boats and one launch.

Getting the artillery on shore is an even more difficult job and it takes the next two days. Guns and ammunition reach the dock on lighters, but it's necessary to throw the horses overboard, to be caught up by landing boats and led through the breakers. Sometimes they're simply washed ashore. Not many are lost, yet it's an ordeal for these animals and it's some time before they're ready for service again. The landing is bad enough, but they need to recover from their hot, dark confinement on the transports. These horses are "the picture of dejection and weariness," an artillery officer notes. Everyone agrees it's amazing that only fifty or so horses died during the trip, and only five or six others were lost getting ashore.

These cavalry horses are as disciplined as their riders. When some of them floundered in the water, lost their sense of direction, and started swimming back to the transports, an alert bugler on shore sounded the correct call and they responded instantly, turning around and swimming toward him.

Somehow this disorderly disembarkation is accomplished, with 6,000 men making the trip on the first day. But some officers are dismayed by what's happening. Captain John Bigelow has a feeling that no one is in control, and he writes: "I was looking at this time for a general order congratulating the troops on the success of the expedition thus far, commending them for their behavior on the transports, giving them some information about the enemy, and perhaps a hint of the plan of operation, and appealing to their pride and ambition to answer the extraordinary demands to be made upon them. As many of the officers had never been in the presence of their commanding General, I thought there would be a review, or that the General would take occasion to ride with the staff along the front of the troops drawn up in line, so that he could see them, and they him. But there was no inspiring or congratulatory order, and I, for one, never saw General Shafter during the campaign."

It's the junior officers, then, who are in charge. They quickly deploy a squad to examine the empty house where the Spanish commandant lived. They find an unfinished letter on his desk--apparently he left in a hurry--in which he assures General Linares not to worry, he's capable of resisting any American attack. He was surely in a position to cause the invaders a great deal of trouble, but before he could finish his letter, the general ordered him back toward Santiago.

Just the same, the freshly landed soldiers are nervous, and so, when the Rough Riders run up the American flag over the now empty blockhouse, they break out in cheers and general pandemonium prevails, as Malcolm McDowell tells his readers: "A quarter of an hour of whistles, shrieks, cheers, yells, drum flares, bugle calls and patriotic songs were sent up...Then the noise ceased, and out of it came the strains of the Star Spangled Banner from a regimental band on the *Matteawan*. The soldiers ashore and the soldiers afloat were quiet until the brasses became silent, and then three full-lunged hurrahs crashed against the hills, and the salute to the flag was complete."

Here we are on the beach, then, at last. Cuba has been invaded. Shafter seems to have disappeared somewhere, and his subordinates take over. The troops are sweating and uncomfortable in their thick wool, the dismounted cavalrymen and the infantrymen (they're being called "doughboys" for the first time) mingle and bathe their mosquito bites with salt water. T.R.'s 1st Volunteer Cavalry (to give them their official name) are camped by themselves, and from time to time T.R.'s stentorian voice can be heard demanding food and clean water for his collection of "tramps, actors, cowboys, expert bartenders, millionaires, and football players," as author Thomas Beer describes them.

The retreating Spaniards have left a trail of destruction behind them. A roundhouse on the hill contains only a destroyed locomotive and some ammunition. As troops move into Siboney on the second day, they find another roundhouse with a half dozen locomotives the Spaniards didn't have time to wreck but tried to take out of action by removing vital parts. This is no problem for the former railroad men in the expeditionary force, who quickly repair them. They can't be used to move troops and supplies toward Santiago, however, because the tracks have been ripped up. Only a narrow, nearly impossible road remains for the advance.

Siboney has also been abandoned by the Spaniards, as well as being a victim of the Navy's bombardment as Major General H. W. Lawton's troops take it over. (Six-foot-four Lawton is the man who captured Geronimo after a 1,300-mile chase.) These men can't believe the Spaniards aren't still waiting for them in the brush just outside town, so uneasy sentries fire occasional shots at every suspicious noise. Most of the noise is caused by land crabs. Not even war stops them. A soldier in the 6th Infantry writes home: "To be awakened from a doze of exhaustion by soaking rain, with land crabs clinging to one's ears, nose and hands and creeping all over the body, is not soothing to the nerves of those not accustomed to the ways of the scavenger."

Soldiers don't know it, but it's the mosquitoes, those deadly carriers of yellow fever, that they should be worrying about.

Siboney is to be the base for assaulting Santiago. Once it was a quiet, shabby little place of about a thousand inhabitants. Now it swarms with the vast apparatus of the Army. What no one seems to understand is that it's also a death trap. A not so innocent little creek purls along behind the village, flowing into a stagnant pond, the centerpiece of a slimy swamp, an absolutely ideal place for hatching malaria and yellow fever carriers. People had already been dying in Siboney before the Americans got there. The town is filled with those too weak to leave it, as well as with refugees from the interior.

Americans are now meeting Cubans, most of them for the first time, and even those who arrived with noble thoughts of freeing an oppressed people quickly discover they really don't like them much. General Castilla's insurgent regiment passes through Daiquiri on its way to join up with the American advance, and Charles M. Potter, of the Washington *Star*, reports: "The strings of cloth which answered for shirts and other garments could hardly be said to clothe the nakedness of the men. Some were barefoot, while others had a kind of straw sandal, which protected the sole of the foot. A few had machetes along, but the majority had guns as well. These were the old style Remingtons or discarded Springfields."

If they had known their own history, these patriotic American invaders would have understood that the ragged rebels aren't so much different, except in color, from that other ragged set of insurgents who fought the American Revolution. As it is, an enormous cultural gulf begins to open up.

At first the soldiers share their rations with these obviously hungry Cubans, both military and civilian, who gather around them, but charity and comradeship give way to annoyance, then to simple disgust. John Black Atkins, of the Manchester *Guardian*, informs his British readers: "Whenever one lighted a fire a Cuban presented himself, at the sign of the smoke, quietly and inexplicably like a genie, and asked for food." It seems that these insolent freedom fighters believe what they've heard about Americans--that they're rich and generous. Their approach is simplicity itself. They walk up to a soldier and point to his shirt, or his coat, or his trousers, or anything at all, and then point the finger at themselves, evidently believing that all they have to do is ask and it will be given, because there's so much more where that came from.

Little incidents keep pointing up the gap between different peoples. The Americans liberate a bull from some householder's stable and propose to kill it for a feast that will extinguish momentarily the memory of hardtack. They plan to shoot the animal, but the Cubans protest and take over, stabbing it to death with knives, while the Americans look on with unconcealed distaste, which is a bit hard to understand since slaughtered food animals are not shot to death at home. But the soldiers begin to ask, "Why should we fight for these unlettered, dirty savages?"

As the occupiers spend their second night in Siboney, many of them are conscious that the Spanish outposts are no more than three miles away. Davis writes: "No one slept that night, for until two o'clock in the morning troops were still being disembarked in the surf, and two ships of war had their searchlights turned on the landing place, and made Siboney as light as a ball-room. Below the former home of the Spanish commandante...lay the camp of the Rough Riders, and through it Cuban officers were riding their half-starved ponies, scattering the ashes of the camp-fires, and galloping over the tired bodies of the men with that courtly grace and consideration for Americans which invariably marks the Cuban gentleman.

"Below them was the beach and the roaring surf, in which a thousand or so naked men were assisting and impeding the progress shoreward of their comrades, in pontoons and shore-boats, which were being hurled at the beach like sleds down a water chute. It was one of the most weird and remarkable scenes of the war, probably of any war. It was a pandemonium of noises. The men still to be landed were singing in chorus, the men already on shore were dancing naked around the camp-fires on the beach, or shouting with delight as they plunged into the first bath that had been offered in seven days, and those in the launches as they were pitched head first at the soil of Cuba, signalized their arrival by shouts of triumph."

Are these the proper actions of an army whose enemy is only three miles away? They're lucky the Spanish commanders are so old-worldly in their tactics that they never think of striking a hard blow at this scene of wild confusion and choke off the invasion before it can get organized. Instead, they're working all night and the following days to strengthen their fortifications at nearby Las Guásimas, the first obstacle for the Americans to surmount on their way to Santiago.

4

LAS GUÁSIMAS: THE FIRST LAND BATTLE

AT 5:40 A.M. ON THE MORNING OF JUNE 24, "FIGHTIN' JOE" Wheeler gives the command to throw his men at Las Guásimas, in the war's first land battle. The Rough Riders, along with the 1st and 10th Cavalry regulars, all hands dismounted, are to move westward and knock out Spanish emplacements so that a general advance can follow.

But why Joe Wheeler, not Shafter? The commander is nowhere to be seen. He's still on the *Segurança*, suffering from gout, the heat, a touch of fever, and memories of humiliation. When, if ever, he intends to take charge, no one knows.

The commander has issued one order, however. He wants the dismounted cavalry to be held back as a rear guard for Daiquiri, a command that, if carried out, would have surely inspired a mutiny and caused T.R.'s death from apoplexy. Wheeler claims with a straight face that he never got the order, and acts accordingly. He's ready to assault the Spanish with everything he's got. So instead of serving as a rear guard, the cavalry has become an advance force.

Wheeler's old friends from Civil War days aren't surprised by his enterprise. They remember him as a fearless Confederate cavalry officer who took so many chances he found himself in a federal prison at the end of the war, sharing confinement with Jefferson Davis himself, both of them in the custody of General Miles, who of course is now the supreme commander of this expeditionary force. Fortunes of war, and all that.

After he got out of prison, Wheeler found himself so famous he was elected to Congress, where he spent the next twenty years. One of the former Civil War officers who reminisced with him on the shady verandas of the Tampa Bay Hotel had inquired jovially, "Well, General, how does it feel to wear the blue again?" And the old West Pointer, an incurable Army man, had answered honestly: "I feel as though I had been away on a three weeks' furlough and had just come back to my own colors."

As he advances, Wheeler knows something of what confronts him, but not much. General Castillo's rebel Cubans had fought these same enemy troops the day before, a minor affair demonstrating that the Spaniards were few in number but tough. To get to them, the Americans must traverse narrow jungle roads and trails. As the march begins, Wheeler learns he can't count on Castillo today. When the Americans went to call him into action, guards outside his quarters were told that the general and his soldiers were tired from yesterday's exertion. They were sound asleep.

What Wheeler doesn't know is that Las Guásimas is not only going to be a hotly debated affair, but should have been the decisive battle of the war, ending in an American defeat. From their trenches at the crest of a 250-foot ridge, the Spaniards look out over rugged terrain, the jungle stretching away below to the beach. Nor is there any way to bypass them. As Freidel puts it, "If Linares' main army had fought there with the skill and courage it displayed later, it could have blocked the Americans on a miasmic coastal strip, until yellow fever ruined them." But the main army isn't in those trenches on the hillcrest. There are only about 1,500 of them--Crane swears no more than 500--and they seem to regard themselves as a picket line, designed to hold the Americans at bay while the main forces are concentrating for the defense of Santiago.

Nevertheless, this meager Spanish line is going to be a test for some notable American officers, and for their men who were so anxious to go to Cuba and fight for the nation's honor and their own, never mind liberating the bloody Cubans.

As Wheeler's advance force moves out, five of the correspondents, including Davis and Crane, have attached themselves to the Rough Riders, those showpieces of the Army, whose validity is about to be tested. Is it possible that this motley crew can live up to the reputation it's already acquired? One writer describes them as "lean, slit-eyed plainsmen with names like Cherokee Bill and Rattlesnake Pete," who "served beside men from Boston's Somerset Club and the Knickerbocker Club of New York, crack polo players, tennis champions, steeplechase riders, Princeton linemen, Yale's finest high-jumper and a whole contingent from Teddy's Harvard, led by two ace quarterbacks."

Not much more is known about the true leadership qualities of their commanders, Roosevelt and Leonard Wood.
Everyone is familiar with T.R. as a public servant, but does this
man who barks more than anyone else have a bite to match?
We'll see.

At least everyone knows T.R., but Wood is just about to
emerge from relative obscurity. He's a colonel in the volunteers,
whose permanent rank is assistant surgeon, a captain. After
Harvard Medical School, he went immediately into the Army
and helped chase Geronimo before General Lawton caught the
elusive Apache. For these and other services, he was given the
Congressional Medal of Honor. He and T.R. have been friends
for only a year. They organized their cavalry unit together soon
after war was declared. Wood is at the threshold of a distinguished career which will make him the Army's chief of staff in
1910, and ten years later an unsuccessful bidder for the
Republican presidential nomination.

Correspondents joke about them and their troops--
"Teddie's Terrors," or "Wood's Weary Walkers," they sometimes
like to call them--but after Las Guásimas, Crane will speak for
most of his fellow correspondents when he says that "no man
can ever question the gallantry of this regiment."

At the moment, however, the Rough Riders and Wheeler's
other cavalry units are shortly to discover that the Spanish regulars have learned something about tactics from fighting the
rebels. They've abandoned the conventional European style of
combat and adopted the tactics of the guerrillas, as the Marines
at Guantánamo have already learned.

Approaching the Spanish outposts, the Americans are
marching along "this narrow winding path," Crane tell us, "bab-
bling joyously, arguing, recounting, laughing, making more
noise than a train going through a tunnel." He can't help comparing these picnicking troops with the professionalism of the
Marines he saw at Guantánamo.

As they move along, Crane hears the coo of the Cuban
wood dove, passing from hillock to hillock, and remembers
that it was this signal, used by the Spanish sharpshooters, that
presaged the deaths of those Marines. But when he mentions
this, he's told authoritatively that the Spaniards don't use this
signal. Crane is already frightened before a shot is fired
because, as he writes later, he was afraid "this silly brave force

was wandering placidly into a great deal of trouble."

T.R., Wood, and the Rough Riders are well ahead of the others, along with the correspondents, and they've stopped in a glade to rest for a moment. Davis is instructing Wood about the Cuban flora and fauna, while T.R. is relating an amusing story about a luncheon meeting he had with Hearst at the Astor House--until he picks up a few strands of barbed wire lying beside him. Breaking off, he holds up the wire and examines it. "My God!" he shouts. "These wires have been cut today!"

Everyone jumps up and looks around warily. There's a movement in the brush but it's Wood and Captain Allyn Capron, Jr., who've been quietly conferring. Quickly, they deploy troops on both sides of the trail, but before they're finished, firing breaks out. The skirmish that follows takes only an hour and five minutes, but to the men involved it will seem like all afternoon. Sharpshooters in the trees are the invisible enemy, and the deadly "pop" of their Mausers is like "a soda-water bottle being opened close to the ear," as Crane puts it. Men fall without even glimpsing the enemy.

Edward Marshall, of Hearst's *Journal*, writes: "The man lives, he is strong, he is vital...when suddenly, 'chug,' he is dead." Those who are hit regard themselves "with astonishment rather than with despair," Marshall observes, "shocked that decisions have been rendered with none of that moral involvement they were determined to invest."

It's the invisibility of the enemy that daunts these troops at first. "How helpless, oh, how helpless we feel," a soldier writes home. Even T.R. is bewildered. He recalls later: "It was very hard trying to stand, or advance slowly, while the men fell or were wounded, shot down from we knew not whence, for smokeless powder renders it almost impossible to place a hidden foe."

John Black Atkins, reporting the scene for the Manchester *Guardian*, writes: "To the private soldier the whole thing was mysterious, unnerving, baffling. Where was the fire coming from?" A trooper tries to convey this strange sensation: "It is almost impossible to realize that it is you they are firing at. You feel like saying, 'You damn fools, don't point your confounded guns this way.'"

Yet they persist, these volunteers and regulars fighting together. Crane reports: "Our people advanced, deployed, reinforced, fought, fell--in the bushes, in the tall grass under the lone palms--before a foe not even half seen. Mauser bullets came from three sides. These troops went forward in skirmish order and in five minutes they called for reinforcements. They were under a cruel fire but their conduct, by any soldierly standard, was magnificent."

At the head of the Rough Riders, T.R. and Wood are demonstrating fearlessness in their first test. Neither will take advantage of any shelter as long as their men are exposed. A bullet sears Wood's wrist, taking away his gold cufflinks. Another strikes a palm tree so near T.R.'s head that splinters hit his ear and eye, with no serious damage. Davis, who's testing himself too, is at the side of these leaders, acting almost as if he were a third commander. He's the first to locate the Spanish troops for Wood, and at one point finds a rifle and takes a few shots at the enemy himself. Wood is so impressed with this correspondent's daring that he cites him for bravery in combat under fire, and Davis returns the compliment by giving most of the credit for the subsequent victory to the Rough Riders, who in any case deserve it.

Crane sees the Rough Riders advancing "steadily and confidently under the Mauser bullets. They spread across some open ground--tall grass and palms--and they began to fall, smothering and thrashing down in the grass, marking man-shaped places among those luxuriant blades. Then the Spaniards fled. They had never had men fight them in this manner and they fled. The business was too serious."

Serious--and lucky. "Wood's bluff," they're going to call this final charge of the Rough Riders against the entrenched Spanish troops. It's a bluff because the charge has nothing behind it. It's only a thin skirmish line advancing as though an entire regiment is close behind it, the men breaking out of the bushes and from behind trees, cheering as they come, moving into the sunlight. The Spaniards can't believe that this is most of the available American fighting force; they're sure there must be thousands of men following. Consequently they fire a few volleys, then break and run toward their next line of defense, the hills around Santiago. This improbable battle is over.

A few minutes later, John Bigelow's black 9th Cavalry comes up to reinforce the Rough Riders. A correspondent for the Chicago *Record* writes: "As they came along the trail, they had met the wounded making their way back to Siboney--either hobbling along with the poor assistance of a stick picked up on the wayside or mounted on one of the few mules that had been taken to the front--and the sight of the white pain-distorted faces and the bloodstained garments stirred them to a veritable battle fury." It's all Bigelow can do to restrain them from rushing after the vanishing Spaniards. They're frustrated now, but their turn is coming soon enough.

Some of the correspondents, seeing battle scenes for the first time, are shocked by the way soldiers talk about the dead, in a joking manner that tries to disguise the reality. One of the reporters, Burr McIntosh, encounters an officer who tells him that Hamilton Fish, Jr., grandson and namesake of Grant's Secretary of State and former captain of the Columbia rowing team, is one of the day's victims, along with Captain Capron, a highly popular officer and a well-known amateur boxer. After hearing this news, McIntosh writes, "It was several minutes before I felt like standing to resume the march." A soldier, seeing someone he knew among the dead, tells McIntosh: "He said they couldn't ketch *him*, and they got him the first time," at which several of his comrades laugh.

McIntosh finds Fish's body and lifts a blanket to look down at his face. While he's taking a picture of Fish and the dead soldier lying beside him, he hears troops standing nearby laughing and joking, and writes: "I felt a resentment toward certain of these men who were joking with that boy's body lying within a few feet of them--a resentment which I never expect to be able to overcome. This feeling is shared in at least some degree by many other correspondents, and by some officers as well."

Coming toward the front line, where the Rough Riders are pulling themselves together, Crane encounters a soldier who tells him, "There's a correspondent up there all shot to hell," and then guides him to the spot. The wounded man is Crane's friend, Edward Marshall, who's encouraged and helped him from the start of his career.

"Hello, Crane," Marshall greets him.

"Hello, Marshall. In hard luck, old man?"

"Yes, I'm done for."

"Nonsense! You're all right, old boy. What can I do for you?"

"Well, you might file my dispatches. I don't mean file 'em ahead of your own, old man--but just file 'em if you find it handy."

Crane writes later: "I immediately decided he was doomed. No man could be so sublime in detail concerning the trade of journalism and not die."

The surgeons have established a small field hospital in the middle of the trail, a short distance back, and Marshall is carried there by six soldiers, who wrap him up in a tent. Wounded troops are filling up the makeshift hospital as they crawl, walk, or are carried to it. Crane listens to them talking, admiring their bravery, noticing the variety in these volunteers.

"'Say, doctor, this ain't much of a wound. I reckon I can go on back to my troops,' said Arizona.

"'Thanks, awfully, doctor, awfully kind of you. I dare say I shall be all right in a moment,' said New York." While they're working on Marshall, Crane observes the doctors, "gentle and calm," moving about "without the common senseless bullying of the ordinary ward. It was a sort of fraternity game. They were all in it, and of it, helping each other."

Four years later, Marshall described in "Stories of Stephen Crane," printed in *Literary Life*, what happened in that field hospital where he lay with a bullet in his spine. "The thermometer...would have shown a temperature of something like 100 degrees. Yet Stephen Crane--and mind you, he was there in the interest of a rival newspaper--took the dispatch which I managed to write five or six miles to the coast and cabled it for me. He had to walk, for he could get no horse or mule. Then he rushed about in the heat and arranged with a number of men to bring a stretcher up from the coast and carry me back in it. He was probably as tired as a man could be and still walk. But he trudged back from the coast to the field hospital where I was lying and saw to it that I was properly conveyed to the coast."

They carry Marshall into the base hospital at Siboney, half delirious, singing snatches of "On the Banks of the Wabash." In the dispatch that Crane files for him, he writes: "I saw many men shot. Every one went down in a lump without cries, without jumping in the air, without throwing up hands. They just went down like clods in the grass. I did not hear the bullet shriek that killed Hamilton Fish. I did not hear the bullet shriek which hit me. The surgeon told me I was about to die. The news was not pleasant, but it did not interest me particularly."

Marshall survives, but he loses a leg and spends months in hospitals, lucky not to join those seven Rough Riders buried after the battle. In this deadly skirmish, the Americans get off with only sixteen dead and fifty-two wounded, while the Spanish, who outnumbered them, lose ten killed and twenty-five wounded.

Crane is also a heavy loser in this battle. By taking care of Marshall, he is unable to file his own stories for a while, and in fact misses large parts of the action. For his pains, he's sacked by the *World* for aiding a rival paper, and it's nearly two months later before the *Journal* rewards him by taking him on. By that time the war in Cuba is virtually over. But before the sun sets on Las Guásimas, he writes an apt and durable summary of this testing ground: "...The day was done. The Rough Riders had bitten it off and chewed it up, splendidly."

Or had they? No sooner are the guns silent than the recriminations begin. Crane calls the action "an ambush" and "a gallant blunder." But in their first reports, most of the correspondents agree that the Rough Riders moved too rapidly, paying no attention to the advice of their Cuban scouts and so getting too far ahead of the regulars.

Naturally, T.R. and Wood are outraged by the implication that their enthusiastic advance was in part responsible for the death of good men. It takes them just twenty-four hours to put out their own version of the event. They place the blame entirely on the Cuban scouts, whom they accuse of telling them the Spanish gun emplacements were farther down the road than they actually were.

Davis joins in the argument. He admits that "none of us believed that there were any Spaniards this side of Santiago," but he's certainly not ready to blame the Rough Riders or their commanders. The accusation about the scouts, with its implications of either treachery or dereliction of duty, gets around and causes a great disturbance, destroying most of what's left of good relations between American troops and Cubans.

As Joyce Milton tells us, "Influenced by romantic stories like Evangelina's, Americans had expected to be welcomed as liberators by grateful dark-eyed señoritas and cheering crowds of patriots." This attitude was not confined to the soldiers. George F. Kennan, then the *Outlook* magazine's correspondent, wrote: "The Cubans disappointed me, I suppose, because I had pictured them to myself as a better dressed and better disciplined body of men, and had not made allowance enough for the hardships and privations of an insurgent's life."

Soldiers make no such allowances. They're now calling the Cubans "half-breed mongrels," "villains," and "mango-bellied degenerates." A lieutenant writes home, disdainfully: "The valiant Cuban! He strikes you first by his color. It ranges from chocolate yellow through all the shades of deepest black with kinky hair. The next thing you notice is the furtive look of the thief. Next you notice that he is dirty. He is infested with things that crawl and creep, often visibly, over his half-naked body."

Nobody is recording what the Cuban soldiers think of Americans, but Gómez puts himself plainly and indignantly on record. He believes the invaders want to use his men only as porters or trench diggers. "My men are soldiers, not laborers," he growls. Few of the Americans know that the general never wanted them at all, and they continue to complain. While they dug trenches in the sweltering heat, they charge, the Cubans sat by and ate the rations distributed by American commanders. Some of these slackers may have been the petty thieves, scroungers, and hungry men known to be part of Gómez's army, but surely not all were, by any means. Some of them must have been those so desperate to feed their families hiding back in the brush that they would steal anything in sight.

Crane foresees that no good can come to the Cubans because of this bitter division. "If [the Cuban soldier] stupidly, drowsily remains out of the fights," he wonders, "what weight is his voice to have later in the final adjustment? The officers and men of the army, if their feeling remains the same, will not be happy to see him have any at all."

As the argument over the Cuban scouts continues to rage, and more fingers are pointed, a voice we haven't heard for a while enters the argument. George Rea charges that Wood was in such a hurry to keep ahead of the regulars that he had no time to listen to his scouts, who had a plan, Rea says, that would have trapped the Spaniards and annihilated them. This story doesn't do much for press relations.

The other unanswered question after Las Guásimas is, where was Shafter while the first battle of the war was going on? Hearst has arrived on the scene by this time in person--or at least, he's cruising off Siboney on his luxury yacht, the *Sylvia*, complete with ice, fruit, and material supplies, accompanied by reporters and photographers, notably John Hemment. Hearst intends to unravel the mystery of the missing commander by interviewing him. He locates the *Segurança*, where he's told Shafter is, and comes alongside with a reporter, Jack Follansbee, Hemment, and two men carrying the photographer's equipment. The general is not happy to see them coming, but after all, it *is* Hearst, a powerful maker of public opinion, and he permits them to climb aboard.

Shafter may hate correspondents like Davis, and he's still steaming inwardly about the *Gussie* incident, but his general dislike of the press doesn't extend to Hearst. They've known each other since Shafter was a colonel at Ford Ord, where the San Francisco *Examiner*, Hearst's first paper, was generous in its publicity coverage. Consequently he's now disposed to grant the publisher an exclusive interview.

Hearst finds the general suffering from the heat, stripped down to flannel shirt and trousers, sitting in the main salon on the *Segurança*, which had been a passenger liner in happier days. He conducts the interview, which is polite but unproductive, possibly because Shafter has just read the casualty report from Las Guásimas and he's depressed. Nothing much of what he says can be printed, but that's no obstacle to Hearst journalism.

Although the general's visitors are shocked by his obvious physical collapse and gloomy posture, and Hearst gets the idea that Shafter means to run this campaign without getting off the boat, the story he writes afterward for the readers who would question his patriotism if he wrote anything else is full of cheery observations of Shafter as a "bold, lion-hearted hero...a sort of human fortress."

Caught off base by this exclusive, Pulitzer's *World* counters a few days later with a profile pieced together from interviews with men who had served with Shafter in the 1st Infantry command. In this story, the gouty, moody, sweltering commander is seen as "jumping about lively as a cricket...the sort of officer who always has his coat off when anything is doing."

Later on, the press won't be nearly so kind, and as Milton says, Shafter's "bloated, misshapen body," will be seen as "a metaphor for the whole campaign."

Meanwhile, it's on to Santiago.

5

THE HILLS OF SANTIAGO: KETTLE AND SAN JUAN

SO FAR IT'S BEEN ONE BLUNDER AFTER ANOTHER, THIS invasion. While they're fighting at Las Guásimas, unloaded ships are still lying off Daiquiri and Siboney, full of necessary cargo. In Washington, they're saying that the landing has been as fouled up as the embarkation, if that's possible.

What happens next? The War and Navy departments are taking different views. Secretary Long and Sampson believe Shafter is going to attack the fortifications at the entrance of Santiago Harbor, in which case the war will be over soon, and plans are already being made to send at least part, if not all, of Sampson's fleet to reinforce Dewey at Manila. Secretary Alger and Shafter believe Santiago's fortifications, four miles from the harbor, should be attacked first. These fundamental differences aren't about to be reconciled and, oddly enough, aren't even discussed. Shafter simply means to carry out his plan, so incapable of understanding the meaning of "cooperation" that he won't even talk about strategy with the Navy after the first impasse with Sampson.

If anyone had asked him, Shafter would undoubtedly have said, "They've got all those ships blockading the harbor, why don't they just go in and capture the Spanish fleet?" But since nobody's asked, Sampson assumes that, in spite of what Shafter told him after the landing, he's going to attack the heights around the harbor. The admiral finds it both astonishing and irritating when this stubborn old fool of a general makes it clear that he has no intention of doing what the Navy wants him to do.

Shafter describes himself as "committed," meaning, "Don't bother me." His plan is to approach Santiago along a narrow coast road from Daiquiri to Siboney, which he's already done, and then strike off inland toward the village of Sevilla, about a half-dozen miles from the capital, after which he will follow the jungle trail and atrocious road toward the heights around Santiago, where the entrenched Spaniards are waiting for him.

Sampson still holds a forlorn hope of persuading him to send 2,000 men, aided by the insurgents and Marines from Guantánamo, to attack the batteries on the harbor heights. But Shafter won't even consider any kind of compromise, and Sampson retreats into brooding silence, like an unrequited lover. After all, he's given Shafter fifty cutters and other small craft to get his army disembarked, a task the Navy men performed with professional skill, and Shafter has acknowledged this help in a cable to the War Department, saying the job couldn't have been done otherwise. As Leech remarks, "Shafter had no objection to cooperation if he didn't have to do it."

Now, after Las Guásimas, its lessons unlearned, the jubilant troops (minus Shafter for the time being) are ready to run right over the Spaniards, whom they characterize with confused geographical bigotry as "dagos." Confusion, in fact, seems to permeate the whole operation. The men put up their tents around Sevilla and shed most of their equipment because it's so oppressively hot.

Shafter, still maintaining his headquarters on the *Segurança*, comes ashore and shuttles heavily between Daiquiri and Siboney, riding a large horse someone's found. They've built him a platform so he can mount. Riding to the front one day, he trots past the beaches, which are littered with forage bales, but he doesn't seem to see this, or to realize that only the essentials have been unloaded. All he's interested in at the moment is making a squalid military base out of Siboney, with quartermasters' huts, and service offices for telegraph, postal, and other essential services. The Medical Corps takes over a building put up by the now departed American mining company and makes a hospital out of it.

Shafter isn't the only mounted commander. Davis, who acts like one, finds his horse after it's unloaded, and even though he has a touch of sciatica and is painfully sunburned, rides with General Adna Chaffee to a conical hill called El Pozo, seven miles from Siboney, and examines the forward picket line the Americans have established. Through their glasses, these two commanders can see that the trail (it would be overly generous to call it a road) forks after it leaves El Pozo, one branch climbing up the Sierra Maestra foothills to the village of

El Caney, the left going off toward Santiago, looping down into the valley of the Aguadores River and disappearing into dense jungle. The San Juan Heights are on the far side of this valley; they constitute the chief barrier to approaching Santiago. On the side of San Juan Hill itself, Davis can see the forms of red and blue farmhouses shimmering in the tropic heat. At the top of the hill is a blockhouse, resembling a Chinese pagoda, as Davis writes romantically.

Through his glasses, he observes "a long, yellow pit" on the hillside of San Juan, "and in it we could see straw sombreros bobbing up and down, and under the shade of the blockhouse blue-coated Spaniards strolling leisurely about or riding forth on little white ponies to scamper over the hills. Rifle-pits were growing in length and in number, and...in plain sight from the hill of El Pozo, the enemy was intrenching himself at San Juan and at the little village of El Caney on the right, where he was marching through the streets. But no artillery was sent to El Pozo hill to drop a shell among the busy men at work among the trenches, or to interrupt the street parades in El Caney."

What Davis is seeing represents a considerable feat by the Spanish defenders of Santiago. They've dug more than 4,000 yards of trenches and ditches, some with blockhouses support-ing them, and a stone fort at El Caney. Yet they're also having their own problems. Supplies are perilously short. Last spring merchants were afraid the army was going to confiscate all their supplies so they sold the lot and didn't replace them. Before the Americans blockaded the harbor, a German ship had unloaded 14,000 sacks of rice, but otherwise there's hardly enough food to last the troops and the citizens of Santiago for a month.

Examining the blockhouse through their glasses, the two men can see soldiers streaming out of it to dig trenches. Perusing his trail map, Chaffee notes that the Santiago road divides again somewhere in the jungle but they can't see the division. An excellent tactician, Chaffee envisions the trouble lying ahead: "Of course the enemy knows where those two trails leave the woods," he says. "They have their guns trained on the openings. If our men leave the cover and reach the plain from those trails alone they will be piled up so high that they will block the road."

Davis believes the maps are so inaccurate that, as he says, they rank with "the best efforts of American fiction," but when

Lieutenant Miley is informed of this looming danger, he isn't interested enough even to send out scouts who would assess it. The prospect lying before this expeditionary force would be enough to discourage any but hopelessly enthusiastic volunteers, and toughened regulars to whom one war is as good as another. On the east side of Santiago, the only approach to the city except by way of the landlocked harbor on its west, lie the high, barren ridges of the San Juan Hills, their crests dented with earthworks and protected by barbed wire. The road to the hills from Sevilla twists through the jungle of a valley in between, as Chaffee has confirmed, with the town and heights of El Caney on the north, and comes out at last between the outer defenses, at that point only a mile from Santiago.

This is all Shafter knows about the tactical problem ahead of him, and all he's going to learn. Wheeler undertakes a reconnaissance and engineers try to fashion topographical maps, but no one, including the regional Cuban commander, General García, can give him any reliable information about the Spanish positions, or how they're distributed. García does tell him the Santiago garrison consists of 12,000 men, half of the forces in Cuba, but in fact there aren't nearly that many.

Even the place names aren't entirely clear to the Americans. The outer ridges ahead of them are known collectively as the San Juan Hills, but there *is* one San Juan Hill on the highest elevation, where a large blockhouse crowns the summit. Shafter sends a note to Sampson saying he wants to "get the enemy in my front and the city at my back," a laudable idea if he can do it. Once past this hill, Shafter thinks, the Spaniards will either surrender or retreat within range of the blockading fleet. To protect the advance on San Juan Hill, it will be necessary to capture El Caney. Lawton and Chaffee have already reconnoitered that strong point and they've told Shafter it has to be a major goal in the main assault.

The general has now left Siboney and established headquarters at Sevilla, but he's far from being in condition to direct the battle. He's dizzy with fever, and when he painfully rides out to examine the terrain, the survey is perfunctory. Nevertheless, he summons his divisional commanders and tells them that the push toward Santiago will begin next morning at daybreak (he expects to capture the capital that day), with El Caney an essential objective. He designates Lawton's division, supported by another brigade of regulars--7,000 men all told--to seize it.

After Lawton is engaged, the 8,000 troops remaining are to advance on San Juan Hill, led by the cavalry and guided from aloft by an observation balloon as they pass through the jungle. Coming out in the open again, these men are to deploy themselves, cavalry on the right, infantry on the left, and to fill a gap in the north, Lawton's force is supposed to come down from El Caney after it's taken and join in the attack, since Shafter assumes this village will be no problem. García's Cubans are also to occupy the gap, instructed to prevent the arrival of a Spanish relief column, reported to be on its way from Manzanilla, 8,000 men strong. The idea, says Shafter from his fevered brain, is to take San Juan Heights before the relief column (less than half of what he thinks it is) can get there.

Apparently Shafter doesn't really put much stock in his own plan of attack. Writing about it later, he says: "There was no strategy at all, and no attempt at turning their flanks. It was simply going straight at them."

He wants no help, or very little of it, from the Navy, so he refuses to employ the veteran Marines from Guantánamo, and he doesn't bother to tell Sampson where the Spanish emplacements are on the San Juan Hills, although they're well within range of the blockade ships outside the harbor. Shafter doesn't have much confidence in naval bombardments, and he particularly doesn't want to share any possible glory with the Navy. All the artillery support his men are going to get is from four light field pieces. Against the contrary evidence, he will insist long afterward that more guns would not have been useful. He's even sparing with those he possesses. One is sent with Lawton for the assault on El Caney, another is mounted on a hill at El Pozo, instructed to soften up San Juan before the assault, and the others are kept back in reserve.

Why such weak artillery support? Because Shafter thinks he's going to have no difficulty blasting his way into Santiago, even though he's throwing infantry against entrenched positions. He rationalizes all this later on by asserting that artillery wouldn't have much effect on stone blockhouses or on Spaniards "in little narrow trenches with dirt thrown up."

What seems inexplicable is why his generals, all professional soldiers and most of them Civil War veterans, accepted

his plan and never even questioned the worst omission in it--
dividing his forces at the beginning of a major battle. Doesn't
anyone remember the Civil War? Only Chaffee objects to this
hasty assault. He points out that there's only one trail and a
small road leading through the jungle to open ground before
San Juan Hill so the Spaniards will know exactly where the
troops are going to emerge from cover, which will inevitably
mean heavy casualties. Chaffee wants to clear a parallel trail,
with small paths leading from it to open ground, so the whole
force can emerge more or less simultaneously. Whether Shafter
ever heard of this idea is unknown; if he did, he ignored it.

Nor is this the end of the general's mistakes. What are the
divisional commanders supposed to do when they get out in the
open? Shafter doesn't tell them, and fails to give them the
authority to decide for themselves. In the end, what he's doing
is to send 8,000 men down through a narrow funnel bisected by
a small river they'll have to cross. He expects to direct this
attack from his headquarters, three miles away, and never imag-
ines that his communications will be interrupted. If he wants
only to "do it quick," as he says later, what he's done instead is
to write himself a prescription for possible disaster.

On the day before the assault, June 30, Shafter meets
with his general officers in his tent to draw up the orders, but
by the time messengers can deliver them, it's 3 P.M., which
means that the whole army has to strike camp in a hurry and
crowd down the narrow, muddy road. The resulting confusion
is unbelievable. They have only three miles to travel to their
forward positions, but it takes some of them more than eight
hours. Long after midnight, they're still slipping and sliding
along the jungle trail.

"It was as though," Davis writes, "fifteen regiments were
encamped along the sidewalks of Fifth Avenue and were all
ordered at the same moment to move into it and march down-
town. If Fifth Avenue were ten feet wide, one can imagine the
confusion. Twelve thousand men...treading on each other's toes
in three inches of mud move slowly, and after three hours, it
seemed as though every man in the United States was under
arms and stumbling and slipping on that trail. There were cavalry, mounted and dismounted, artillery with cracking whips
and cursing drivers, Rough Riders in brown, and regulars, both
black and white. Three miles away across the basin of mist, we

could see the street-lamps of Santiago shining over the San Juan Hills. Above us, the tropical moon hung white and clear in the dark purple sky. Before the moon rose again, every sixth man who had slept in the mist that night was either killed or wounded."

Davis, who's with the Rough Riders, is fascinated by the Signal Corps's reconnaissance balloon, floating a thousand feet above the men struggling along the trail. Two of Shafter's aides, Lieutenant Maxwell and Lieutenant Colonel Derby, are in command up there, their globe tethered to the ground by means of a cable unrolling slowly from a wooden reel on the flatbed of a wagon. These officers can communicate what they see through a field telephone. At sunset, the balloon is still floating.

Of all these advancing men, T.R. is no doubt the happiest. Two generals, Wheeler and Young, have fallen ill with fever and Wood has been ordered to replace the latter, being commissioned a brigadier general on the spot, leaving T.R. in sole command of the Rough Riders.

At 8 A.M., on the morning of July 1, Captain George S. Grimes, of Battery A, 2nd Artillery, opens the battle from his position on the left of the road from El Pozo to Santiago, only 2,500 yards from San Juan Hill. The subsequent artillery duel with the Spanish gunners that goes on for forty-five minutes is "of the fiercest character," as Crane terms it.

T.R. writes of the barrage later: "For a minute or two there was no response. There was a peculiar whistling, singing sound in the air, and immediately afterward the noise of something exploding over our heads. It was shrapnel from the Spanish batteries. We sprang to our feet and leaped on our horses." Roosevelt suffers a wound when a piece of shrapnel falls on his hand, "raising a bump about as big as a hickory nut." But that shell also wounds four of his men, as well as two or three regulars. Another explodes in the midst of the Cubans, killing and wounding many of them. The remainder, says T.R. with remarkable insensitivity, "scattered like guinea-hens."

Another observer of this scene is Frederic Remington, who's been sketching horses dragging artillery up the hill. When the duel begins, however, he and everyone else in the vicinity scramble for safety. "Some gallant soldiers," Remington reports, "and some as daring correspondents as it is my pleasure to know did their legs proud there. The tall form of Major John Jacob

Astor moved in my front in jack-rabbit bounds. Prussian, English, and Japanese correspondents, artists, all the news, and much high-class art and literature were flushed and went straddling down the hill."

As the Spaniards open up, hell, or something very near it, breaks out on the jungle trail, and the villain is the observation balloon, which Shafter considers the only reconnaissance he needs. What it does, however, is to mark clearly where the troops are advancing. Davis writes: "It came blundering down the trail, and stopped the advance of the First and Tenth Cavalry, and was sent up directly over the heads of our men to observe what should have been observed a week before by scouts and reconnoitering parties. A balloon, two miles to the rear, and high enough in the air to be out of range of the enemy's fire, may some day prove to be of use and value. But a balloon on the advance line, and only fifty feet above the tops of the trees, was surely an invitation to the enemy to kill everything beneath it. And the enemy responded to the invitation.

"A Spaniard might question if he could hit a man, or a number of men, hidden in the bushes, but had no doubt at all as to his ability to hit a mammoth glistering ball only six hundred yards distant, and so all the trenches fired at it at once, and the men of the First and Tenth, packed together directly beneath it, received the full force of the bullets. The men lying directly below it received the shrapnel which was timed to hit it, and which at last, fortunately, did hit it.

"This was endured for an hour, an hour of such hell of fire and heat, that the heat in itself, had there been no bullets, would have been remembered for its cruelty. Men gasped on their backs, like fishes in the bottom of a boat, their heads burning inside and out, their limbs too heavy to move. They had been rushed here and rushed there wet with sweat and wet with fording the streams, under a sun that would have made moving a fan an effort, and they lay prostrate, gasping at the hot air with faces aflame, and their tongues sticking out, and their eyes rolling. All through this the volleys from the rifle-pits sputtered and rattled, and the bullets sang continuously like the wind through the rigging in a gale, shrapnel whined and broke, and still no order came from General Shafter."

A terrible confusion develops. General Kent's division is now blocking the trail completely and troops can't even retreat because for two miles behind them there's a solid mass of men. On the other hand, if they stay where they are, they'll be slaughtered. The single alternative is to plunge ahead somehow and assault the San Juan Hills. "A series of military blunders," Davis reports, "brought seven thousand American soldiers into a chute of death, from which there was no escape except by taking the enemy who held it by the throat and driving him out and beating him down. So the generals of the division and brigades stepped back and relinquished their command to the regimental officers and the enlisted men."

Crane is there, too, and witnesses the death of the deadly balloon, "dying, dying a gigantic and public death before the eyes of two armies. It quivered, sank, faded into the trees amid the flurry of a battle that was suddenly and tremendously like a storm. The American battery thundered behind the men with a shock that seemed likely to tear the backs of their heads off. The Spanish shrapnel fled on a line to their left, swirling and swishing in supernatural velocity. The noise of the rifle bullets broke in their faces like the noise of so many lamp-chimneys or sped overhead in swift cruel spitting. And at the front the battle-sound, as if it were simply music, was beginning to swell and swell until the volleys rolled like a surf."

Captain Howes comes back down the trail to find out what's happened to the 1st and 10th, and encounters Colonel Derby, who's just climbing out from what's left of the balloon. "I saw men up there on those hills and they're firing at our troops," the colonel tells him. The captain's reply is "lost in history," Davis says, but it can be easily imagined. However, Derby had made one far more significant observation before the balloon collapsed. He had seen a road running off left from the main road, crossing the Aguadores River about 500 yards downstream. General Kent turns his division into this road to escape the congestion and the devastating fire demoralizing his troops.

Meanwhile, the bottleneck continues. First Lieutenant John J. Pershing, of the black 10th Cavalry, less than two decades away from the supreme command of a far larger expeditionary force, describes it: "The road...follows tortuous and narrow, along the river through the swampy jungle, then crosses the river and passes toward and between the San Juan Hills. The regiment moved slowly along this road under the scorching sun and sweltered; a few men were overcome with heat; already, an occasional bullet nipped a leaf above our heads. Impatient at delay the regiment and brigade finally swung past the waiting infantry and moved further down the road.

"When the Tenth Cavalry arrived at the crossing of the San Juan River, the balloon had become lodged in the treetops above and the enemy had just begun to make a target of it, no doubt correctly supposing that our troops were moving along this road and were near at hand. A converging fire from all the works within range opened upon us that was terrible in its effect; the Seventy-first New York, which lay in a sunken road near the ford, became demoralized and well-nigh stampeded; our mounted officers dismounted, the men stripped off at the roadside everything possible, and prepared for business.

"We were posted for a time in the bed of the stream to the right, directly under the balloon, and stood in water to our waists waiting orders to deploy. Remaining there under the galling fire of exploding shrapnel and deadly Mauser volleys, the minutes seemed like hours. General Wheeler and his staff stood mounted a few moments in the middle of the stream. Just as I raised my hat to salute...a piece of bursting shell struck between us and covered us both with water."

Pershing's remarks about the 71st New York Volunteers are the beginning of a scandal. As the only militia present in this battle, they have something to prove, but they're taking heavy fire and they're badly officered, so it should be no surprise in the circumstances that they break ranks and flee in panic. The rest of the brigade pushes them aside into the thickets and steps over the legs of the fallen in order to advance.

General Kent, meanwhile, is surveying the river crossing, having gotten out of the deadly road funnel, and after consulting with Lieutenant Miley, he decides that he must move on to assault San Juan Hill, directly in front. Old General Hawkins, his white hair making him conspicuous as it flows from beneath his cap, is assigned to lead the charge, and begins to deploy troops, under heavy fire. Wheeler's cavalry bloodies the shallow ford waters of the Aguadores (known to the troops as San Juan River) and takes a position on the right, in front of Kettle Hill, which is the Spaniards' advanced position. Colonel Charles A. Wikoff moves his men across the river into an open meadow at the far end of which are the San Juan fortifications, no more than 500 yards away. While he's directing his infantrymen to their positions, Wikoff is struck by a Spanish bullet and dies a few minutes later. Hawkins's 6th Infantry are under such devastating fire that they lose a quarter of their men in ten minutes and have to retreat.

Watching this scene, Malcolm McDowell, of the Chicago *Record*, reports: "Our men continually cried, 'Show us those ---. For God's sake don't keep us here to be shot without giving us a show.'" They're raving mad because they can't see anything to shoot at, and meanwhile they're approaching annihilation. George L. Newgarden, regimental surgeon of the 3rd Cavalry, observes later: "It is a marvel that every living thing thereabout was not either killed or wounded. The wounded came pouring in from over the bank in a steady stream, some limping, some hopping, others holding their arms to their sides or abdomen, many using the rifle as a crutch or support, and a number carried in by their comrades."

Remington chooses a single example of the awful scene: "One beautiful boy was brought in by two tough, stringy, hairy old soldiers, his head hanging down behind. His shirt was off, and a big red spot shone brilliantly against the marble-like skin. They laid him tenderly down, and the surgeon stooped over him. His breath came in gasps. The doctor laid his arms across his breast, and shaking his head, turned to a man who held a wounded foot up to him, dumbly imploring aid, as a dog might. It made my nerves jump, looking at that grewsome [sic] hospital, sand covered with bleeding men."

Stephen Crane passes by the crimsoned river crossing and writes: "I looked down into a miserable huddle at Bloody Bend, a huddle of hurt men, dying men, dead men. And there I saw Reuben McNab, a corporal in the 71st New York Volunteers, and with a hole through his lung. Also, several holes through his clothing. 'Well, they got me,' he said in greeting. Usually they said that....I had looked upon five hundred men with stolidity, or with a conscious indifference which filled me with amazement. But the apparition of Reuben McNab, the schoolmate, lying there in the mud, with a hole through his lung, awed me into stuttering, set me trembling with a sense of terrible intimacy with this war which theretofore I could have believed was a dream--almost."

The worst of the day's ordeal is the long wait under fire. Frank Knox, who left studying for the ministry to join the

Rough Riders, and who will one day publish the Chicago *Daily News* and run for the vice-presidency on Alf Landon's ticket, writes home: "Now it is hard enough to face those ugly bullets with your own carbine smoking in your hand, but it becomes doubly hard when you lay under a hell of fire and can't fire a shot in reply. Such was our situation all the morning."

In spite of the horror, and notwithstanding the casualties, troops emerge from the funnel and get across the crimson river, arriving at the meadow's edge, where there's no choice but to advance or retreat. They advance. Roosevelt, now mounted, is one of the first to break from cover, released as though from a catapult. He's waited hours for orders to advance, but communications have broken down between Shafter's headquarters and the front, so Lieutenant Miley has to run back and forth with the messages. None too soon for T.R. He's been sitting out there in the hot sun, watching men get picked off by snipers.

As the Rough Riders rush forward, they overtake a rear platoon of the black 9th Cavalry, holding their position under heavy fire, having not yet received any orders. T.R. gallops toward them, and they see an apparition, polka-dot bandanna flying out from under his hat. "If you don't wish to go forward," he shouts at them, "let my men pass, please." Some troopers, carried away, get up and follow him, others stay put, disciplined men waiting for orders.

Someone on El Pozo shouts, "By God! There go our boys up the hill!" Crane feels "the thrill of patriotic insanity. Yes, yes, they are going up the hill, up the hill. It was the best moment of anyone's life." But Davis writes: "It seemed as if someone had made an awful and terrible mistake. You felt that someone had blundered and that these few men were blindly following out some madman's mad order. It was not heroic then, it was merely pathetic. The pity of it, the folly of such a sacrifice was what held you."

This is the Rough Riders' famous charge up Kettle Hill, not nearby San Juan, as it will be remembered, when the illustrators perpetuate this assault with pictures of bayonets glinting in the sun, swords raised to strike, many on horseback. But there were no bayonets, no swords, nothing but out-of-date rifles and will power. The artists had to paint in horses because no one would believe the Rough Riders weren't riding.

Recalling it all in his memoirs, Davis writes: "I have seen many illustrations and pictures of the charge on the San Juan Hills, but none of them seem to show it just as I remember it. In the picture-papers the men are running up the hill swiftly and gallantly, in regular formation, rank after rank, with flags flying, their eyes aflame, and their hair streaming, their bayonets fixed, in long, brilliant lines, an invincible, overpowering weight of numbers. Instead of which I think the thing which impressed me the most, when our men started from cover, was that they were so few."

Kettle Hill is only a small outcropping at the right of the main Spanish fortifications on the San Juan ridge, but under the circumstances, it takes incredible courage to climb it. One of the troopers, Edgar A. Knapp, remembers: "We made our charge up the Hill...and it was a daisy, except for our terrible losses as men fell on all sides of us as we rushed up. A charge of this kind is a wonderful thing, as when you see a man leading you, and all are rushing and cheering, the biggest coward in the world could not resist rushing forward, even though he knew for a certainty that he would be shot."

As they near the summit, T.R., pistol in hand, shoots a Spanish officer, and writes home about it: "Did I tell you I killed a Spaniard with my own hand?" Other Riders feel the same sense of fulfillment. A wounded man exults: "Damn near stepped on the [Spanish] son-of-a-bitch--then he got me. But I got him...I got mine. Now you go and git yours."

This is the kind of fighting the Spaniards don't understand and are highly critical of when they talk about it later. They complain that the black 10th Cavalry doesn't return their fire or retreat but "just keeps coming on up the hill." A prisoner of war charges that Americans don't observe the rules and tried to catch Spanish soldiers with their hands.

A Spanish officer confesses: "What especially terrified our men was the huge American Negroes. We saw their big, black faces through the underbrush, and they looked like devils. They came forward under our fire as if they didn't the least care about it."

On the American side, there are a number of conversions from traditional bigotry. A white lieutenant in the 9th Infantry writes: "I am from Virginia and have always had the usual feelings about commanding colored troops. But after seeing that charge of the Twenty-fourth up San Juan Hill, I should like the best in the world to have a Negro company. They went up that incline yelling and shouting just as I used to hear when they were hunting rabbits in Virginia. The Spanish bullets only made them wilder to reach the trenches."

T.R.'s charge with the Rough Riders makes him a popular hero that day, but among the regulars and some of the correspondents, it's a different story. The regulars say he exceeded orders and took the Rough Riders out ahead of the regular cavalry. His reputation isn't helped later in the afternoon when he accosts some black troopers of the 10th, under orders to go to the rear and bring up some entrenching tools. He thinks they're running away and calls them cowards.

The colonel's own troopers tell him, "You won't have to shoot these men, Colonel. We know those boys." Other men from the 10th shout, "We'll stay with you, Colonel." Clearly, T.R. is wrong and realizes it because the next day he virtually apologizes to the 10th. Yet after the war, in an article written for *Scribner's*, he declares that black officers were of no help without their white officers, and without these leaders, non-commissioned officers couldn't be depended on. In fact, black troops and regulars made several charges along the front that blistering day, and did so after nearly all their officers were killed or wounded, according to white eyewitnesses. Sergeants often led the charge when no white superior officers were available, as they had done earlier at Las Guásimas.

Regulars also say the Riders were so undisciplined and so hot to fight that they shot at Americans as well as Spaniards. Poultney Bigelow hates T.R. so much that after the war he makes a virtual career of denouncing "our cowboy Napoleon." Bigelow does his best to expose the "myth of San Juan Hill," but it's too late. Whether Kettle or San Juan, it's already entrenched in American mythology.

Black revisionist historians will later give us another view of what went on at Kettle Hill. In this version, it was the 9th and 10th Cavalry that reached and destroyed the Spanish defenders while T.R. and the Riders were caught between a barbed-wire fence and a precipice, and would otherwise have been annihilated.

Yet it's the heroic figure of Roosevelt that lingers in the memory, even for skeptics like Davis, who describes him "mounted high on horseback, and charging the rifle-pits at a gallop and quite alone, made you feel that you would like to cheer. He wore on his sombrero a blue polka-dot handkerchief...which, as he advanced, floated out straight behind his head, like a guidon. Afterward, the men on his regiment who followed his flag, adopted a polka-dot handkerchief as the badge of the Rough Riders."

Not everyone knows that T.R. has a small half-secret. He's so worried about losing the eyeglasses which protect his poor eyesight that he carries a half-dozen spare sets sewn into his uniform, even one inside his hat.

In any case, controversy or not, there's T.R. on top of Kettle Hill at last, and he writes: "When I got abreast of the ranch buildings on top, I turned and went up the slope. Being on horseback I was, of course, able to get ahead of the men on foot, excepting my orderly, Henry Bradshar, who had run ahead very fast in order to get better shots at the Spaniards, who were running out of the ranch buildings. Some forty yards from the top I ran into a wire fence and jumped off Little Texas, turning him loose. He had been scraped by a couple of bullets, one of which nicked my elbow, and I never expected to see him again.

"As I ran up the hill, Bradshar stopped to shoot and two Spaniards fell as he emptied his magazine. These were the only Spaniards I actually saw fall to aimed shots by any one of my men, with the exception of two guerrillas in trees. Almost immediately afterward the hill was covered by the troops, both Rough Riders and the colored troops of the Ninth, and some men of the First. No sooner were we on the crest than the Spaniards from the line of hills in our front, where they were strongly entrenched, opened a very heavy fire upon us with their rifles. They also opened upon us with one or two pieces of artillery, using time fuses which burned very accurately, the shells exploding right over our heads.

"On top of the hill was a huge iron kettle, or something of the kind, probably used for sugar refining. Several of our men took shelter behind this. We had a splendid view of the charge on the San Juan Hill block-house on our left..."

Now the historic charge up San Juan begins. The way is prepared by Lieutenant John H. Park's detachment of Gatling machine guns. Until now, these weapons have been disparaged because their short range had made them virtually useless in the Indian wars. Soldiers called them "coffee grinders." Now, however, they're coming into their own. Just how successful they are is testified to by a Spanish officer who tells Park later: "It was terrible when your guns opened--always. They went br-r-r, like a lawn mower cutting the grass

Teddy Roosevelt and the Rough Riders atop Kettle Hill

reproduced from the collections of the Library of Congress

over our trenches. We could not stick a finger up when you fired without getting it cut off." By the time the troops start climbing the hill, some Spaniards are already running from this destructive barrage of bullets.

The 6th and 10th Infantry lead the charge. Watching them, Crane reports: "Up went the regiments with no music save that fierce crashing of rifles. The foreign attachés were shocked. 'It is very gallant, but very foolish,' said one sternly. 'Why, they can't take it, you know!' 'Never in the world,' cried another. 'It is slaughter!'"

Davis is there, too, of course, and gives us one of his best battle reports: "They had no glittering bayonets, they were not massed in regular array. There were a few men in advance, bunched together, and creeping up a steep, sunny hill, the top of which roared and flashed with flame. The men held their guns pressed across their breasts and stepped heavily as they climbed. Behind these first few, spreading out like a fan, were single lines of men, slipping and scrambling in the smooth grass, moving forward with difficulty, as though they were wading waist high through water, moving slowly, carefully, with strenuous effort. It was much more wonderful than any swinging charge could have been.

"They walked to greet death at every step, many of them, as they advanced, sinking suddenly or pitching forward and disappearing in the high grass, but the others waded on, stubbornly, forming a thin blue line that kept creeping higher and higher up the hill. It was inevitable as the rising tide. It was a miracle of self-sacrifice, a triumph of bull-dog courage, which one watched breathless with wonder.

"The fire of the Spanish riflemen, who still stuck bravely to their posts, doubled and trebled in fierceness, the crests of the hills crackled and burst in amazed roars, and rippled with waves of tiny flame. But the blue line crept steadily up and on, and then, near the top, the broken fragments gathered together with a sudden burst of speed, the Spaniards appeared for a moment outlined against the sky and, poised for instant flight, fired a last volley and fled before the swift-moving wave that leaped and sprang up after them."

Surprisingly, as Freidel points out, the casualties are relatively light in spite of the intense Spanish fire because most of the bullets are going over the Americans' heads. However, when the men make their final rush to the top, T.R., on Kettle Hill, orders his troops to charge the Spanish entrenchments just ahead.

This turns out to be a little premature. Roosevelt recalls later: "Thinking that the men would all come, I jumped over the wire fence in front of us and started at the double, but, as a matter of fact, the troopers were so excited, what with shooting and being shot, and shouting and cheering, that they did not hear, or did not heed me; and after running about a hundred yards I found I had only five men along with me." Of these, two are wounded.

Turning back, T.R. rallies his men, who explain they haven't heard his command, and takes along with him men from other regiments who are milling around at the crest. Other troops on the hill join him and they all charge with a rush against the next line of entrenchments. Most of the defenders run before this mixed bag of men can get to them, except for a few who either surrender or are shot down. The triumphant Americans jump into the trenches and find them filled with dead men wearing the light blue and white uniform of the Regular Army. T.R. and Bradshar, running up, have a narrow escape when two last survivors leap up and fire at them from no more than ten yards away. They miss and turn to run. T.R. fires twice and kills one of them; he thinks there's some justice in this because the revolver once belonged to one of the men on the *Maine*.

By this time, San Juan Hill is a scene of further confusion. Regiments have been broken up in the charge and they're all mixed in together, white and black regulars with Rough Riders and what remains of the militia. They're still under fire from entrenchments a little farther on, and T.R., getting together what he calls "a mixed lot of men," pushes on against these defenders and drives them through a line of palm trees and over the crest of a chain of hills toward the defenses of Santiago, which the Americans can now see as they reach these crests.

Firing is still intense from the entrenchments remaining. Remington and other correspondents are climbing the hill behind the advance for a better view, and the intrepid illustrator reports: "The shrapnel came screaming over. A ball struck in front of me, and filled my face and hair with sand, some of which I did not get out for days. It jolted my glass and my nerves, and I beat a masterly retreat, crawling rapidly backwards."

Crane is bolder, and in fact is exhibiting a kind of peculiar recklessness, seeming to invite death and talking about which part of his body might be hit. At one point, he's walking back and forth at a place where Wood, Davis, and several units are lying on the ground resting. In spite of the intolerable heat, he's wearing a gray English waterproof, which makes him doubly conspicuous. Some of the cavalrymen call to him, suggesting he wear furs if it isn't hot enough. Davis notices, too, and he's afraid the pale coat will draw fire. Some of the soldiers yell at Crane, swearing. Even a Spanish officer walking along the trenches a few hundred yards away can see him, and aims his walking stick playfully at this foolish American. Crane seems pleased by all the attention.

Davis yells at him, and writes of the effect: "Crane jumped as if he was waking from a nap and looked at me, astonished by my voice, perhaps. He flattened out on the grass and crawled back behind a small hillock. But pretty soon he rose on his knees and then stood up once more, absorbed in watching. I called out as sarcastically as I could that Colonel Wood and I were not impressed by his courage and he blushed scarlet before he lay down. He did not stay long after that but helped a wounded man back to the battery at El Pozo."

Soon, however, he's returned and moving around again. Davis gets up, steps over a few soldiers, and catches Crane by the shoulders, making him lie down. A bullet knocks off his hat and the leather on his field glasses is chipped by another shot.

Remington, having previously retreated, returns to the fray: "I again started out to the hill, along with a pack-train loaded with ammunition. A mule went down, and bullets and shell were coming over the hill aplenty. The wounded going to the rear cheered the ammunition, and when it was unpacked at the front, the soldiers seized it like gold. They lifted a box in the air and dropped it on one corner, which smashed it open. 'Now we can hold San Juan Hill against them garlics--hey, son!' yelled a happy cavalryman to a doughboy."

With the mix of white and black troops in the battle, individual epiphanies occur. Separated from the other Rough Riders, Frank Knox recalls: "I joined a troop of the Tenth Cavalry, colored, and for a time fought with them shoulder to shoulder, and in justice to the colored race I must say that I never saw braver men anywhere." Jack Pershing also feels this sense of unity: "White regiments, black regiments, regulars and Rough Riders, representing the young manhood of the North and the South, fought shoulder to shoulder, unmindful of race or color, unmindful of whether commanded by an ex-Confederate or not, and mindful only of their common duty as Americans."

In the late afternoon, after four o'clock, the fighting on the San Juan Heights subsides and an uneasy semi-quiet prevails. Crane, Davis, and some of the other correspondents come back down the hill to see the battle's late stage from a different perspective. They discover Harry Scovel, busy writing his story while a servant holds a horse ready to take the copy back to Siboney for filing. Harry's story is patriotically (and truthfully) upbeat, like those of others, but inside he's boiling. At Bloody Bend, he'd seen the fateful balloon and the frightful bloodshed that followed. Men had told him horror stories such as finding a soldier's penis lying in the dirt of the trail. He's furious at Shafter for the series of blunders that led to such carnage, and he's also upset by what happened to the 71st New York Volunteers. The story of their panic has spread among the other soldiers, and they're writhing under taunts, even threats of violence by men who think they're cowards.

Scovel might have been even more disturbed if he had seen J. C. Hemment, Hearst's noted photographer, having his lunch earlier that day farther to the rear on the jungle trail, in a clearing. Hemment had brought with him from the *Sylvia* a supply of excellent food from the yacht's pantry; it was served with linen napkins and real china, with a servant standing by, shielding him from the sun with an umbrella while he ate a chicken sandwich.

Hearst, his boss, is elsewhere, at the assault on El Caney, the day's longest and fiercest battle. W.R. is making history himself, the first publisher since the Civil War to cover a war in person, on the battlefield, in living color.

6

EL CANEY: THE LONGEST BATTLE

WHAT IN THE WORLD IS EL CANEY THAT IT TAKES NINE HOURS of bitter fighting before the Americans capture it? Nothing much more than a little town whose palm-thatched and tile-roofed buildings rest on a hill that's not particularly steep. The village is dominated by a stone church. Local legend asserts that Cortez prayed there before departing to slaughter a large number of Mexicans on behalf of his faith and his Queen. Something of his spirit is still there, since this house of worship has loopholes in its walls for rifles and sharpshooters are sitting in its tower.

On a hillock about 500 yards southeast of town rests a stone fort called El Viso, now surrounded by trenches protected with rolls of barbed wire and a series of blockhouses. This stronghold is being defended by only 520 men, while nearly half of the American force, 6,653 men, is deployed to assault it. Shafter still thinks the place can be reduced in short order, after which the troops will be ready for the main attack on Santiago. The mistake is that he has thought of El Caney as merely an outpost. Instead, it's much the strongest point on the San Juan Hills, and as everyone has known from the start, it's essential to capture it before any attack can be made on the capital.

In command of all these defenses is General Joaquin Vara del Rey, an imposing man with a full beard, intersected by a broad, drooping mustache. The Spanish general may understand more than his opponents do, that the battle he's about to fight is crucial. If the Americans win it, the way is open to Santiago, more or less. If he wins, the whole American effort is going to be stalled, and if the Spaniards don't defeat them, fever will do the job.

As usual, the artillerymen begin the battle, although in this case it's a limited barrage because of Shafter's parsimony with his guns. About six-thirty in the morning, after the barrage begins,

John Fox, Jr., who in a few years will find himself a bestselling author with his romantic *Trail of the Lonesome Pine*, approaches the battery and finds it commanded by Allyn Capron, father of the gallant captain who was killed at Las Guásimas with Hamilton Fish. Fox learns that the first shells have been wide of the mark and the answering fire light. However, since the Spaniards have the advantage of smokeless powder, all the gunners can see of their work is the straw hats of the Spaniards bobbing about. But the artillerymen press on, and before they stop about ten o'clock, they've put a hole through the wall of the fort, followed it with another, while a third shatters the flagstaff and brings down its emblem. Wilder shots blow furrows in the earth all around the fort. Satisfied by this damage, the gunners lob a few shells toward the town and quit.

Meanwhile, as the Americans, led by General Chaffee's men, begin to inch up the slope, they're in a skirmish line, taking advantage of every tree, bush, or cover they can find. About fifty Cubans under General De Coro fight alongside them. Resistance is stubborn and it's clear that the Spaniards mean to fight it out to the grim end. Nevertheless, Chaffee and the Cubans push forward on the right at a slow but steady pace.

General Ludlow's brigade also moves ahead rapidly until it finds itself on a sunken trail, no more than fifty yards from the town, a depression too shallow to protect them from the fire of sharpshooters emanating from the village's shabby houses. The general's horse is shot out from under him. Nearby, troops of the 2nd Massachusetts are taking a beating since their old Springfield rifles use black powder and that makes it easy for the Spanish sharpshooters to pick them off.

By nine o'clock the crescendo of battle has swelled to a full-throated war as all three brigades move inexorably forward. Ludlow's men are only a hundred yards away from El Caney and they're coming within range of the sharpshooters in the houses. Fortunately for everyone, the Spaniards don't have any cannon in their fort.

At ten o'clock, Lawton orders a halt. Everyone's exhausted after the forced marches of the night before and nearly four hours of fighting. They need a rest. Shortly after one o'clock, however, Lawton calls for action again, this time aimed at the blockhouses, now wrecked shells as a result of Capron's gun, but their defenders fight on desperately. Chaffee's brigade has attacked the fort and suffered under a withering fire from both it and the blockhouses.

But the Americans' advance is inexorable. By two-thirty, the 12th Regiment is at the foot of the hill, just out of reach of the rifle pits, while General Miles's brigade is closing in on the town from the west and all these units are now ready for an assault on the fort. As far as he's concerned, the main action is at San Juan and he's afraid if these divisions outside El Caney linger there, they won't be able to join the main thrust at the San Juan entrenchments. He sends up a message to Lawton: "I wouldn't bother with the little blockhouses. They can't hurt us," and orders him to join the main assault. Fortunately, Lawton never sees this message, since it arrives too late and his men are already so deeply involved they can't be pulled out.

For the troops on the slope below El Caney, it's becoming a frightening and confusing day. A black regiment, the 25th Infantry, has been held back in reserve all morning, but now it's advanced to the firing line shortly after noon, about 800 yards from El Viso.

Lieutenant James A. Moss writes: "The dead, dying and wounded are being taken past to the rear; the wounded and their attendants are telling the Twenty-fifth: 'Give them hell, boys, they've been doing us dirty all morning.'...The process is indeed terrible. Men with arms in slings, men with bandaged legs and bloody faces; men stripped to the waist, with a crimson bandage around the chest or shoulder, men staggering along unaided; men in litters, some groaning, some silent, with hats or bloodstained handkerchiefs over their faces; some dead, some dying.

"Some of the soldiers are supplied with wire-cutters--the command at once cuts its way through, and crossing a lane, enters an open pineapple patch. Ye gods! It is raining lead! The line recoils like a mighty serpent, and then, in confusion, advances again! The Spaniards now see them and are pouring a most murderous fire into their ranks! Men are dropping everywhere!...The bullets are cutting the pineapples under our very feet---the slaughter is awful!...The bullets are coming into our very faces. A soldier comes running up, and cries out, 'Lieutenant, we're advancing into our own men!'...

"The officers in the pineapple patch hold a consultation, and decide there is only one thing for the United States

Regulars to do--advance. Advance until they find the enemy. The onward movement is just about to start. Lieutenant McCorkle is under a small cherry tree, kneeling on one knee; unbuttoning his shirt, he lowers his head and beholds in the pit of his right arm a ghastly wound, and then, poor fellow, he falls over, mortally wounded. Lieutenants Caldwell and Kinnison have been gradually working their way up another stream and are now about two hundred yards from the fort, and for the first time since the firing line was formed our men see the Spaniards.

"A general fusillading for a few minutes, and then orders are given for no one but marksmen and sharpshooters to fire. Thirty or forty of these dead shots are pouring lead into every rifle-pit, door, window, and porthole in sight. The Spaniards are shaken and demoralized; bareheaded and without rifles, they are frantically running from their rifle-pits to the fort, and from the fort to the rifle-pits! Our men are shooting them down like dogs!...'Remember the *Maine*!' shouts a sergeant. Four are shot down in the door of the fort.

"A Spaniard appears...and presents a white flag but is shot down before the firing line can be controlled. Another takes up the flag and he too falls. The fort has been silenced!...The line is now being formed for the final rush. One company of the Twelfth Infantry is also rushing up [it had led the charge at El Viso]. Men are still dropping by the wayside but on, on, up, up, they go, those dusky boys of blue!

"The line is now occupying its new position--some of the men are shooting into the town, and others are shooting down through the roof of the block-house. The Spaniards are falling over one another to get out! The heavy firing has ceased and after twenty-five or thirty minutes of desultory firing, El Caney itself surrenders!"

It's a glorious day for the black 25th. Not only have they spearheaded the advance to victory, but in another sense, they have also given the lie to at least some part of the American social order. These men, with their headquarters at Fort Missoula, were scattered all over western Montana at the time the *Maine* sank, doing garrison duty. The regiment had been born in Texas but was stationed in the West in 1880. Its job heretofore had been fighting Indians and building roads for Montana and New Mexico. Army people know about them, but the general public outside their immediate vicinity doesn't know they exist, since they've always been stationed in remote places.

These are tough soldiers, hardened by the rugged Montana winters, and suddenly, after the *Maine* goes down, they emerge into the American consciousness when they're ordered east at last, first to the Dry Tortugas, a place almost as remote as Montana, where rebel prisoners were turned loose to die or not in the Civil War, since there was no means of escape from the islands.

Gradually, however, the 25th has been drawn into the war with Spain. First they went to Key West, then to Chickamauga Park, in Georgia, before being sent to Cuba. They haven't forgotten their experiences at Chickamauga. When they left Missoula for the East, the whole town had turned out to give them a send-off, but when they arrived in Georgia, they were an unwelcome curiosity, almost a tourist attraction. People, both white and black, came from all over to see them, some from as far away as Chattanooga. Many of these whites had never seen a black soldier. The 25th had no trouble to speak of in town, but outside Chickamauga they were just "niggers," treated with the usual Southern contempt.

When they embarked for Cuba on June 7, they were on board the transport *Concho*, in company with the 14th United States Infantry, a battalion of the 2nd Massachusetts Volunteers, and the personnel of brigade headquarters. This ship, as the black historian Edward Johnson observes, was "not fit for man or beast," although it had once been a cattle ship. Officers naturally took the best quarters, and the enlisted men got what was left.

The *Concho* was scarcely out of sight of land before an order issued from the brigade commander forbidding intermingling. The white regiment was to stay on the port side, the black on starboard, and never the colors should meet. This came as a surprise to the regulars on both sides, since many of them had served together during the mining troubles in Montana and had no problem mixing. Another order followed, decreeing that the white regiment should make its coffee first, and although it was a smaller matter, this hurt. So they sailed on for fourteen long, miserable days, arriving in Cuba on June 22.

They showed what they were made of first at Las Guásimas, as we've seen, and when some of the white soldiers called them "smoked Yankees" afterward, it was said with admiration for their fighting qualities. Still, Ham Fish emerged as one of the heroes and no one seems to remember how much Corporal Brown contributed to the day with his Hotchkiss gun; he was found lying beside it, dead.

Now, at El Caney, the 25th has truly distinguished itself, fighting alone, so it's galling when the official reports say the 12th Infantry did the job, even though only one unit of it was present and not in the forefront at that. In fact, Private T. C. Butler, of the 25th's Company H, is first to enter the blockhouse by the fort and seize the Spanish flag for his regiment. However, an officer of the 12th orders him to give it up. Butler manages to take a piece of it to show his colonel. According to eyewitnesses, the 25th saved the day at El Caney, but they don't get official credit for it.

If one alien element in the day's work has more than justified its presence, another is still to be heard from--the fearless publisher of the *Journal*, W.R. himself. Hearst has come fully prepared to cover the war. The *Sylvia*, chartered from the Baltimore Fruit Company and refitted at considerable expense, has its own captain and crew, and besides a complement of reporters and photographers, it has typesetters who are prepared to operate in its hold a lightweight printing press, on which Hearst plans to publish the first American newspaper in Cuba, the *Journal-Examiner*. Ostensibly intended for a military audience, it's actually a Hearst promotional stunt and at the same time will provide a Cuban space for his coverage of the war, which he means to do himself. He also has an eye on the future. William Britz, a "biograph expert," is on board. He intends to put the action on motion picture film for the first time in history. Is Hearst already envisioning his own newsreel company?

Before he landed in Cuba, W.R. had typically combined pleasure with business, stopping off en route at Kingston, Jamaica, where everyone dined splendidly at the Crystal Springs Hotel. Later, Hearst went to the races and bought a few polo ponies he planned to use in Cuba; they had to share the *Sylvia*'s hold with his printing plant.

Arriving in the war zone, Hearst makes contact first at Admiral Sampson's flagship, the *New York*, and attempts an interview. The admiral says as little as possible, causing Hearst to characterize him as a "stiff, severe kind of man." His virtual rebuff of the publisher earns him mocking references in the *Journal* as a "tea-going admiral--a rear admiral, always in the rear."

Once on the scene in Cuba, Hearst as a correspondent is considerably overshadowed by his ace reporter, James Creelman, a short man with a black goatee, who presents a dapper appearance in khaki uniform with highly polished leather puttees. He's not much interested in interviewing the commanders, who are tame subjects for one who's talked with the Pope, Henry Stanley, Sitting Bull, Leo Tolstoy, and even "Butcher" Weyler, among many others. Beside him, Hearst looks almost nondescript in a white duck suit and a broad straw hat.

Creelman and the boss have already interviewed García, and this one goes well for a change, since García is well aware of all the *Journal* has done to promote the Cuban cause and, unlike Gómez, he's grateful. He greets his guests, flanked by a few aides, on the veranda of a tile-roofed house near Siboney. The general speaks excellent English, and there is no sign of the volcanic temper for which he is well known. It's a fault he sees in himself and has instructed an aide to watch for. If it appears he's ready to lose his cool, the aide is to whisper, "Ave Maria."

No need for that now. Everyone's in good humor, coffee is served, and Jack Hemment snaps pictures of the scene. Then a little ceremony occurs. A Cuban officer brings in a tattered battle flag, the lone star of Cuba shining on it, and García, handling it reverently, presents it to Hearst, saying: "I present to the New York Journal in commemoration of its services to liberty, the headquarters flag of the Second Department of the Republic. You see upon it the marks of Mauser bullets. This flag has been brought through many battles, and hundreds of brave men have died under it. Its colors are faded, but it is the best thing the Cuban Republic can offer its best friend." As the exchange is made, García shouts the battle cry Hearst has done so much to advertise: "Viva Cuba Libre!" The others present echo him.

After the interview, Hearst and his party climb a hill not far away, and Hearst takes copious notes with his pencil and notebook while he surveys the scene. Later, he writes his first story as a war correspondent, a 3,000-word description of the situation which, although Creelman isn't likely to admit it, is as good as that world traveler could have done.

After he files it, Hearst lands a cargo of ice from the *Sylvia* and gives it to the surgeons at the field hospital in Siboney, where it's badly needed, along with a large quantity of the ship's food. Then the *Sylvia* sails for Port Antonio, Jamaica, while Hemment, down in her hold, works frantically in his darkroom to develop the pictures that will go with Hearst's moment of glory at El Caney.

On the morning of July 1, the publisher, along with Follansbee, Hemment, and Honoré Laine, a Cuban army colonel who's been doubling as a *Journal* correspondent for several months, ride off on their horses to see the war. Creelman isn't with them. Having been tipped off that El Caney was to be the main objective, he sneaked away from his fellow correspondents soon after midnight and climbed to the top of a hill, the stone fort of El Caney clearly visible to him. Crawling forward to another hill, he joined Chaffee, who finds him valuable because he's the only one who seems to know of the existence of a back road up the hill. While they talk, a stray bullet clips a button from the general's uniform.

As Hearst and his merry men catch up with the troops, who are already under fire, shots begin to whistle overhead and they ride hastily into what they believe is the shelter of trees and sword grass.

"What the hell do you fellows think you're doing?" a passing officer addresses them. "Don't you see you're drawing the fire of those batteries? For God's sake, get off your horses."

"Well," Hearst replies mildly, "I guess possibly we *are* drawing fire." They dismount and take up a new position on a hill nearby, with a better view of the action. Hearst straps on his revolver, and they prepare to follow the troops.

Creelman, who is up ahead with the men heading for the top of the ridge at El Caney, has a different view of his trip to the front. "Presently we were trudging along in the mire," he writes, "tortured by the sour smells of the trampled vegetation, which yesterday's fierce sun had fermented, and the tropical fever, from which few escaped. Monstrous land crabs, green and scarlet, with leprous blotches of white, writhed across our path. Birds sang softly into the tangled chaparral and soft grass. Crimson and yellow blossoms glowed in the dense green growths. Troops of vultures wheeled lazily against the dawn-tinged clouds, or sat in the tall coconut palms. As the sun rose, it struck sparkles from the dripping foliage. Before us were thousands of men preparing to die; nine miles behind us were steam vessels ready to carry out dispatches."

Creelman is taking more than a journalistic interest in this battle. Two years earlier, he's seen what the Spaniards did to the *reconcentrados*, and since then he's been a determined partisan himself, dedicated to ending Spanish rule. Consequently he keeps begging Chaffee for permission to join in the charge on the stone fort. When the order for that assault is given, Chaffee nods consent and Creelman, revolver in hand, sweeps up the hill with the others as they take the fort.

Once inside, the Americans look upon a bloody scene. Dead and dying men are lying in their own gore. Some survivors are simply sitting on the floor, stunned. Creelman looks around for a Spanish flag and finds one in the grass behind the blockhouse. "I wanted it for the *Journal*," he writes later. "The *Journal* had provoked the war, and it was only fair that the *Journal* should have the first flag captured in the greatest land battle of the war." (Evidently he doesn't know about the flag the 25th recovered.)

Picking up the emblem, Creelman waves it derisively in the direction of the village, where a few of the Spanish are still holding out. He throws it to some soldiers, and they pass it along hand to hand, "cheering like madmen." That irritates the Spanish holdouts in the village and they open up. A bullet passes through Creelman's left arm and lodges in his back. They carry him down the hill and lay him among wounded soldiers. Someone throws the captured flag over him.

While he's lying there, in shock, something remarkable happens. As he reports later: "A strange yellow light on everything. Voices of thunder...blurred figures...a horse twenty feet high. Little fiery blobs kept dropping down from somewhere and the world was whirling upside down." Someone seems to be asking him about copy. A voice calls, "Copy! Copy! An hour to spare before the paper goes to press!"

Creelman opens his eyes and an apparition appears. He writes in his memoirs: "Someone knelt in the grass beside me and put his hand on my fevered head. Opening my eyes, I saw Mr. Hearst, the proprietor of the New York *Journal*, a straw hat with a bright ribbon on his head. The man who provoked the war had come to see the result with his own eyes and, finding one of his own correspondents prostrate, was doing the work himself. Slowly he took down my story of the fight. Again the tinging of Mauser bullets interrupted. But he seemed unmoved. That battle had to be reported somehow. 'I'm sorry you're hurt, but'--and his face was radiant with enthusiasm--'wasn't it a splendid fight? We must beat every paper in the world.'"

So Creelman gets the glory, and his boss gets the byline. Well, not quite. Hearst does his own story of the day's work, a more than competent job, but it's Creelman's vivid, dictated version of his own part in the assault that gives readers of the *Journal* the best sense of what it was like.

"To turn the left of the Spanish position," Creelman reports, "it was necessary to get a blockhouse, which held the right of our line. Chaffee detailed Capt. Clarke to approach and occupy this blockhouse as soon as the artillery had sufficiently harried the Spanish defenders.

"Clarke and Capt. Haskell started up the slope. I told them I had been on the ridge and knew the condition of affairs, so would show them the way. We pushed right up to the trench around the fort, and getting out our wire cutters severed the barbed wire in front of it. I jumped over the several strands and got into the trench. It was a horrible blood-splashed thing, an inferno of agony. Many men lay dead, with gleaming teeth, and hands clutching their throats. Others were crawling there alive. I shouted to the survivors to surrender, and they held up their hands. Then I ran into the fort, and found there a Spanish officer and four men alive, while seven lay dead in one room. The whole floor ran with blood. Blood splashed all the walls. It was a perfect hogpen of butchery.

"Three poor wretches put their hands together in supplication. One had a white handkerchief on a stick. This he lifted and moved it toward me. The officer held up his hands, while the others began to pray and plead. I took the guns from all and threw them outside the fort. Then I called some of our men and put them in charge of the prisoners. I then got out of the fort, ran around to the other side, and secured the Spanish flag."

As the battle of El Caney winds down, other Hearst minions are busy. Jack Follansbee, who speaks fluent Spanish, blithely places himself in command of a small detachment and leads them through the town, looking for surviving Spaniards. Hearst himself hurries off to Siboney to file his story, which the

Sylvia will take to Port Antonio. Next day, he encounters Honoré Laine, whom he hasn't seen since they set out the previous morning. Laine tells him his Cubans have been the happy recipients of forty Spanish prisoners taken by the Americans.

"And what did you do with them?" Hearst inquires.

"We cut their heads off, of course," Laine tells him matter-of-factly.

But the Spanish defenders die hard at El Caney. Out of ammunition, they keep on fighting as best they can even after the town itself surrenders. At the western edge of the village, on the road to Santiago, they make a last stand inside a small thatched fort, protected by trenches. For hours they block any further American progress and they die like heroes. General del Rey, who's presided over that day's disaster, rides up and down the lines, encouraging his men, until finally he's struck down with bullets in his legs. While they're helping him onto a stretcher, another shot strikes his head and kills him instantly. He adds to the day's dismal Spanish casualty statistics: 235 killed and wounded, 120 taken prisoners. The Americans have also suffered a severe toll at El Caney: 81 killed, 360 wounded.

During the battle, fought so fiercely, the two sides have arrived at a reluctant admiration for each other's valor. The Americans bury Del Rey with military honors, and one of his staff officers says later: "I have never seen anything to equal the courage and dash of those Americans. Their gallantry was heroic."

Surveying the scene, Charles M. Sheldon, British correspondent for *Leslie's Weekly*, assesses the outcome: "There is no doubt that if the Spaniards had held their stone fort at Caney with sharpshooters we would have been defeated with terrible loss, because our artillery was entirely inadequate for the work before us." A countryman, Captain Lee, the British military attaché, echoes him: "This was a heavy price to pay for possession of an outlying post, defended by an inferior force. That the attack succeeded was entirely due to the magnificent courage and endurance of the infantry officers and men."

As night falls, an uneasy quiet settles on the hills where American troops are now spread across the length of a ridge, sitting ducks for an attack from Santiago, especially if Governor Blanco can persuade Cervera to dismount his ships' guns and turn them on the heights. The men on the ridge are exhausted, and the officers are uneasy. When General Wheeler makes a tour of inspection just before dark, several of them urge him to persuade Shafter to order a pullback.

Now that we think of it, where *is* Shafter, anyway--this absentee architect of a close call for the entire V Corps? At least he's seen some of the battle from a vantage point on El Pozo. "I stood on the hill," he testifies later, "or sat on my horse on the hill, and about 2 o'clock I was fearful I had made a terrible mistake in engaging my whole army at 6 mile intervals."

Just how mistaken becomes apparent as reports from the front come in. At the end of the day, with the attack subsiding on the outer ridges, for all Shafter knows the Spaniards in Santiago may now have enough reinforcements to come out and sweep them away. If they have, he's ready to blame the Cubans who were supposed to block the reinforcements from getting there, and who have left the northern road open all day.

Instead of pulling back from a precarious position, Shafter is intent on holding the troops there, so he keeps the weary men up all night, making the rifle pits larger, digging new entrenchments. He doesn't even take pity on the men who have voluntarily fallen back to El Pozo, worn out and unfed. He orders them back at once to shore up the northern gap in the American lines. Nor does the general understand the extent of the day's damage when jolting wagons begin to bring in the wounded from El Caney and Bloody Bend. He isn't aware that ten percent of his effective forces have been lost, although he's shaken when someone gives him a lower estimate. "Sick in mind and body," as Leech tells us, "he shrank from exposing the army to further combat."

At least he doesn't conceal much of the truth from Washington. He reports the heavy losses of the day, and in a follow-up message, admits that he may have underestimated the casualties and asks for the immediate dispatch of a large hospital ship. The President and his men decide to give the press both these dispatches verbatim. Maybe full disclosure will stiffen the public's morale.

Those in the White House still don't have any details of the battle and have no idea of what the Army's true situation may be. They simply assume that Shafter is going to push on, and as the tension grows next day, the President and Alger virtually camp out beside the telegraph office into the evening, waiting for further word from their general. At one o'clock in the morning, they send a telegram to him, almost pleading for news. No reply. The President sits up for three more hours and then goes to bed.

While everyone's waiting, Davis decides it's time the world should know the reality. He writes a story for the *Herald*, date-lined "The Trenches of San Juan," describing the campaign as "prepared in ignorance and conducted in a series of blunders." Another such victory, he warns, and the troops will be compelled to retreat. "This may sound hysterical," he admits, "but it is written with the most serious and earnest intentions. This is written with the sole purpose that the entire press of the country will force instant action at Washington to relieve the strained situation." But when the *Herald* gets this story, the editors withhold it. Too inflammatory, they say.

No wonder. In his article, Davis charges, among other things, that Shafter used his artillery suicidally, even leaving some of it behind, and he follows this up, urged on by both Wood and T.R., by asserting that the situation is alarming and disaster is just around the corner. The commanding general, he says, has never been closer than two miles from the scene of action, and "the presence of some man with absolute authority is necessary at the front."

When the war is over, Shafter will write that, if he had known what was in those dispatches, he would have arrested Davis and deported him. He accuses the reporter-- "descriptive writer" or not--of giving military information to the enemy, and for years he will conduct a private campaign to restrain and censor all correspondents.

Davis's effort doesn't do much for the troops occupying the ridge on the day after the battle, but Crane files a story that brings the war home with stunning reality. "Pushing through the throng on the plaza [in El Caney]," he writes, "we came in sight of the door of the church, and there was a strange scene. The church had been turned into a hospital for Spanish wounded who had fallen into American hands. The interior of the church was too cave-like in its gloom for the eyes of the operating surgeons, so they had the altar-table carried to the doorway where there was a bright light.

"Framed in the black archway was the altar-table with the figure of a man upon it. He was naked save for a breech-clout, and so close, so clear was the ecclesiastic suggestion that one's mind leaped to a fantasy that this thin, plain figure had just been torn down from a cross. The flash of the impression was like light, and for this instant it illumined all the dark recesses of sacrilege, ghastly and wanton.

"An American surgeon and his assistants were intent upon the prone figure. They wore white aprons. Something small and silvery flashed in the surgeon's hand. An assistant held the merciful sponge close to the man's nostrils, but he was writhing and moaning in some horrible dream of his artificial sleep. As the surgeon's instrument played...'Good morning,' said the surgeon. He changed his knife to his left hand and gave me a wet palm. The tips of his fingers were wrinkled, shrunken, like those of a boy who has been in swimming too long."

The man with the scalpel is a veteran Army surgeon, Dr. Bangs, who has been operating all day on wounded Spanish prisoners of war, waiting patiently in the chancel, under a statue of Our Lady of Sorrows, for their turn. One by one they come in and lie down on the altar, and Dr. Bangs, wearing an oversize white apron, as do his assistants, moves his scalpel with astonishing speed over the shattered bodies. He's so busy at the moment he doesn't even have time to indulge his habit, as Milton tells us, "of popping his glass eye out of its socket and cleaning it on his pants leg."

Among the American survivors, worry and tension are increasing. T.R. declares: "We are within measurable distance of a terrible military disaster." The fighting has resumed, and it's clear the Americans don't have much more than a toehold on their ridge.

Some of the officers want to retreat to a stronger position, but Shafter is adamant. Doesn't he understand that the Spaniards are only 300 yards away? The troops, having fought for twelve hours and dug entrenchments half the night, are so exhausted some of them even forget to eat. The water supply is inadequate, and the wounded are still being picked up by ambulances and wagons. There isn't even time or strength enough to bury all the dead. No one has yet totaled the human cost to the V Corps in this war, but when it's added up, the total is going to come to 216 killed and 1,318 wounded, a 6:1 ratio of wounded to dead. At this point, however, Shafter isn't admitting any more than a possible ten percent loss in one day.

On the morning of July 2, at dawn, the Spaniards open up with fire from both artillery and rifles. Grimes has managed to get one of the two American artillery pieces only 500 yards from the Spanish infantry trenches during the night, and *he* opens with a barrage in the general direction of Santiago. The white smoke from his gun betrays the position, and the Spaniards concentrate fire on it. Smoke is so thick the Americans can't even see their own plight.

The worst fears are being realized. Men are in the open and under merciless fire. They take refuge in the trenches they captured the day before, as the artillery retreats to El Pozo. All day long heavy firing goes on, although neither side launches an attack. It would have been suicidal for the Americans to try it. These Spanish positions are stronger and more heavily defended than those they occupied on San Juan. So the miserable day drags on, with the casualties mounting again and General Hawkins listed with the wounded.

Frank Knox writes home: "I spent most of the night digging trenches. After the last relief I lay down under a little tree and slept until early dawn, when I was awakened from a deep sleep by a volley from the enemy. To the tune of wheeling bullets we danced for the trenches. If any one has discovered a more uncomfortable place to spend a hot day than a four-foot trench, I have yet to hear of it. About one o'clock our relief came up from behind the brow of the hill. They had to rush across an open space exposed to the fire of the enemy and then lay down beside the trenches. Then we crawled out and they crawled in. And then we made our run. When I reached the other side of the hill I was so weak I could hardly stand."

For the wounded, it's an interminable day and this situation seems to be going from bad to worse. The luckiest are those who can get as far as the base hospital at Siboney. George Kennan, now operating for the Red Cross, writes later: "As fast as the wounded arrived, they walked, or were carried on stretchers, to two or three large tents, pitched end to end and opening into one another, where hospital stewards and nurses placed them on tables, and the surgeons, some of them stripped naked to the waist, examined their injuries by candle light, and performed such operations as were necessary to give them relief. They were then taken or led away, and as far as possible, furnished with blankets and shelter. The wounded who came in after midnight were laid in a row on the ground and covered with a long strip of canvas."

Away from Siboney, however, it's a different story. Kennan inspects the 1st Division Field Hospital, in a clearing near the Aguadores River, where the lack of supplies is appalling. Only two ambulances are available (there are others back in Tampa), and one tent is shelter for about 100 wounded men. A few surgeons are working heroically under impossible conditions, overwhelmed, as Kennan puts it, by a "great bloody wave of human agony."

The surgeons stand at the operating tables, sleepless and hungry, because they have no time to eat, sometimes for as long as twenty-four hours at a time. They simply can't keep up with the bloody wave. Hundreds of men, seriously or even dangerously wounded, most of them half naked, lie on the ground for hours, unprotected from the tropical sun or the chilly dew at night, waiting to be attended to. There seems to be no organized plan to feed these men or give them the water they call for, so they get neither for as long as twelve hours.

Even after a man has been operated on, the orderlies who lift him from the table can do no more than lay him on the ground again outside the packed tents. Kennan writes, with hardly concealed horror: "Weak and shaken from agony under the surgeon's knife and probe, there he had to lie in the high, wet grass, with no one to look after him. Many brought in from the extreme right flank at El Caney had nothing to eat or drink in more than 24 hours. At midnight, the number brought into the hospital was about 800. All who could walk after their wounds were dressed, or could bear transport, were taken to Siboney and put on board hospital steamers and transports. Several hundred were too seriously hurt to be moved."

It's too much for Kennan. On Saturday afternoon, the day after El Caney, he calls Clara Barton, seventy-six-year-old founder of the Red Cross, from Shafter's headquarters, urging her to send supplies, and on Sunday afternoon Clara herself appears in camp at the head of a line of wagons filled with enough equipment to put up a small Red Cross emergency station. Two hours later, she's directing the feeding of all men in camp with cornmeal gruel, hot malted milk, beef extract, coffee, and what the men call "Red Cross cider." The worst of the food and drink crisis is over in at least one place.

But why are there so few skilled and caring hands to take care of these wounded men, when surely they're available? More mismanagement, this time liberally mixed with nineteenth-century male chauvinism. On June 26, Clara Barton had landed at Siboney with a contingent of trained nurses, ready for duty. The Army's head surgeon, a Dr. Winter (aptly named), greeted them coldly. He told them their help was "not desired." It seems the Army had a policy forbidding female nurses in camp.

If the Americans won't have her, Clara says, maybe the Cubans will, and she offers the entire Red Cross contingent she's brought with her to General Castillo. He accepts and they go to work in the Cuban field hospital, segregated but just as busy. It isn't until later in July, when hostilities are over and a fever epidemic is overwhelming the Army's hospitals, that Clara and her nurses are called in at this last desperate moment.

In spite of appalling conditions, the rate of recovery in this field hospital is remarkably good, Kennan notes. In fact, it's higher than in any previous American war. Kennan decides it's because the Mauser bullets leave small, clean wounds and antiseptic methods of treatment are available now that were absent in the Civil War. But there are exceptions. The recovery rate among those who have to endure abdominal operations in the field is zero, and in fact the surgeons stop performing them after the first day because it's so hot and damp. The surgeons also know that, if they do operate, the patients aren't going to get proper nursing and care.

In spite of their travails, the survivors can't help feeling sorry for the plight of the Spanish prisoners. Captain John Bigelow, of the 10th Cavalry, arrives at the Siboney hospital after a painful, jolting ride in a wagon, and observes some of these prisoners being marched in. "Like Cubans," he writes, "they were small, lightly built men. They marched at a good gait, keeping up with the long-legged horses of their escort. They bore themselves, I thought, with true Spanish dignity, holding their heads high even when glancing to right or left at the staring crowd. Cuban women hung over the railings of the porches, pointing and jeering at them. The Cuban men watched them with comparative gravity."

Back on the ridge, meanwhile, the troops are busy strengthening their lines when they aren't firing. Reinforcements arrive for Lawton's right wing, which is now extended.

Fresh troops come in, the 9th Massachusetts and the 34th Michigan, hurried off the transports that brought them and rushed to the front.

Nevertheless, T.R. is still sending urgent messages to Lodge, telling him disaster is impending and the President must be told to send every regiment and battery he can lay hands on. There's so much pressure from the officers to withdraw that Shafter grudgingly consents to consider the matter at a conference that evening. As dusk falls, the commanders gather on the grass outside his headquarters, with sentinels posted to keep out everyone, friend or foe. The general is still so weak they have to take down a door from one of the buildings and lay it on the grass for him to lie on.

Shafter begins by saying that he's aware some of his officers think he's pushed the Army too far. If they can prove it, he says, he'll agree to withdraw until he thinks the force is strong enough to take Santiago. He asks for opinions, and it's soon clear that not everyone agrees, one way or the other. "Well, gentlemen," Shafter says at last, "it's possible I've gotten you too far to the front, but I've always thought I had the courage to admit an error if I made one, and if we fall back I will take all the blame. Unless, however, you get orders to the contrary, you will hold your position." The officers leave silently. Any who thought the general might listen to the voice of reason are disillusioned. Obviously, the old man is going to do whatever he likes, and the hell with the rest.

Officers and men on the ridge have slipped off into a restless sleep when, a little later, the very air suddenly seems to explode in firing. Confusion is once more the order of the night. Some think the Spaniards are trying to blast their way into the American lines. It turns out afterward that the Spaniards thought the same thing. When the air clears, and it's over, officers decide the sudden outbreak on both sides must have been caused by nervous, tired men who startled each other somehow and began firing. Once again T.R. emerges as a hero. A lieutenant of the Rough Riders tells Ray Stannard Baker, who will be celebrated as a muckraker in a few years, that at the peak of the firing he thought he saw Spaniards "in a dense dark line at the top of the hill." He goes on: "For a moment the men in the trenches stirred restlessly, and then they saw Colonel Roosevelt walking calmly along the top of the entrenchment with a faded

The **World**

" Circulation Books Open to All." | " Circulation Books Open to All.

NEW YORK, SATURDAY, JULY 2, 1898   PRICE

SHAFTER ROUTS SPANISH AT SANTIAGO W
OF 400 BRAVE AMERICANS KILLED AN

Those Killed Are Comparatively Few in Number--The Engage
ment Lasted All Day and the Enemy's Outposts Were
Carried, and Reinforcements Brought Up for
Another Attack This Morning.

LAWTON AT
CANEY NOW.

Less than a Mile
Between the
Forces.

WASHINGTON,
July 1.—The War De-
partment has received the
following from Gen.
Shafter, dated at Siboney,
July 1:

"Had a very heavy en-
gagement to-day which
lasted from 8 A. M. un-
til sundown.

"We have carried their
out-works and are now
in possession of them.

There is now about
three-quarters of a mile
of open between my lines
and the city.

"By morning troops
will be intrenched and
considerable augmenta
tion of forces will be
there.

"Gen. Lawton's divi-
sion and Gen. Bates's
brigade, which have been
engaged all day in carry-
ing El Caney, which was
accomplished at 4 P. M.,
will be in line and in
front of Santiago during
the night.

"I regret to say that
our casualties will be
above four hundred.

"Of these not many
were killed.

"SHAFTER."

A second despatch from

BEGINNING OF BATTLE AT CANEY.

COMPARISON OF OPPOSING
FORCES AT SANTIAGO

20,000 SPANIARDS MARCHING
TO THE RELIEF OF SANTIAGO.

DETAILS OF GEN. SHAFTER'S GEORIOE

At 9.45 A. M. yesterday Major-Gen. Shafter, com
cabled to the War Department: "Action now going on, fl
that Gen. Lawton's division began the fight by attacking
and closed his brief despatch by saying: "Will keep you co

New York World, July 2, 1898

blue handkerchief flapping from the back of his hat, wholly unmindful of the bullets which hummed about him like a hiss of bees. A cheer went up, and calls for the Colonel to come down, and that was the end of the restlessness."

Roosevelt has his own theory about what precipitated the incident. He says one of his pickets was attacked and wounded, and this burst of firing touched off the fusillade on both sides.

Next morning, July 3, the firing begins again but it's much more desultory and it looks as though everyone's settling down to a state of siege. In Santiago, the defenders are greatly cheered by the arrival of reinforcements--Colonel Federico Escario, leading 3,600 Spanish troops. García's men were supposed to block them, but they got around him somehow. Even so, there aren't enough men in Santiago to risk trying to break the siege lines, and a crisis is quickly approaching because the Americans are cutting off the city's water and food supplies.

While the reinforcements are arriving, Alger is cabling to Shafter: "I waited with the President until 4 o'clock this morning for news from you relative to Saturday's battle." Alger wants him to report at the end of each day. Shafter replies that he has Santiago under siege, but with a thin line, and there is no possibility that he can storm into the city with the forces he has at present. He tells Alger that he's considering pulling back five miles to a safer position, where getting supplies will be much easier. For good measure, he complains about the heavy losses, the illness of two good generals, Wheeler and Young, besides his own incapacity. Just to be sure no one gets the wrong idea, he adds that he intends to retain command.

This communication hits Washington with the force of a Spanish barrage. No one has even considered the situation Shafter has laid out for them. From so far away, it seemed to the President and his Cabinet that it would be no problem at all to reduce this provincial capital, which has been tightly blockaded for some time and is desperately in need of food.

As for the Navy, the news is a major--and highly irritating--disappointment. They thought the land war would be over in a hurry and Sampson's ships could then finish off Cervera's fleet and if necessary blockade the whole southern coast of Cuba, as well as the port of San Juan in Puerto Rico. There is also the presumably urgent need to free as many ships as possible to reinforce Dewey in Manila. Now, if

Shafter withdraws, all the plans to end the war quickly will have to be put on hold. Besides, it's humiliating to think that a country just now aspiring to be a world power is tied down and made helpless by a few stubborn Spaniards and an indecisive general.

Poor old Alger tries to salvage something from the mess. He virtually pleads with Shafter. If the general will only hold his present positions, especially those on the San Juan Heights, "the effect upon the country would be much better than falling back." Incontrovertibly true. In fact, during the night of July 2, Shafter has decided to demand Santiago's surrender, and McClernand writes out the ultimatum at eight-thirty the next morning. The demand is a masterpiece of diplomatic courtesy with intent to kill: "I shall be obliged, unless you surrender, to shell Santiago de Cuba. Please inform the citizens of foreign countries, and all women and children, that they should leave the city before ten o'clock tomorrow morning." As Friedel observes, he's done everything but sign it, "Very respectfully, your obedient servant."

But even as the messages fly back and forth between Washington and headquarters, and while Shafter makes his polite demand for capitulation, Cervera and the United States Navy take the problem out of everybody's hands and virtually end the war in less than two hours on the high seas off Cuba.

7

A SUNDAY ON THE SEA

WHILE THE ARMY IS VALIANTLY CLOSING IN ON SANTIAGO, another kind of drama has been taking place in the city itself. Instead of persuading (he could even try ordering) Cervera to remove his ships' guns and turn them on the San Juan Heights, which would have completely shattered the American positions, Captain General Blanco is planning ways to save face, convinced that defeat is at hand.

What worries Blanco most is that the fleet will be scuttled in the harbor, an unimaginable humiliation. He tells Cervera and General Linares that they have to avoid this outcome at all costs. "If we must lose the squadron without fighting," he says, "the moral effect would be terrible, both in Spain and abroad." The alternative is to sail out of the harbor and escape if possible.

Cervera doesn't think it's possible. At first he says he will never consent to such a move, "for I should consider myself responsible to God and history for lives sacrificed on the altar of vanity, and not in the true defense of country." Blanco isn't going to take no for an answer, however. This time it's an order, and Cervera is forced to give in against his best judgment. But he insists on trying to make his escape in broad daylight, certainly the worst possible time. It's a maneuver that has the sound of heroic sacrifice.

On Saturday afternoon, July 2, watchers on the blockade ships see plumes of smoke drifting up from inside the harbor. What's going on? If Cervera's getting up steam, he must be coming out, since there's nowhere else to go. But the day ends with no further indication of activity. The Americans know that Hobson's sunken *Merrimac* hasn't blocked the harbor, but they can't believe Cervera would emerge to challenge a force so far superior in numbers to his own.

Sunday morning, July 3, dawns quiet and sunny, the blockade ships rolling, gently rolling, on a placid surface. Captain

Robley "Fightin' Bob" Evans is sitting in his cabin on the *Iowa*, enjoying an after-breakfast cigar and talking to his son Frank, a naval cadet on the *Massachusetts*. On Schley's flagship, the *Brooklyn*, Captain Francis Cook gets out his last laundered white coat and lays it on his bunk. Admiral Sampson, on the *New York*, is putting on leggings and spurs, a most un-Navy-like action. He's taking his flagship to Daiquiri, from where he plans on riding to Shafter's headquarters, hoping to get his agreement on some kind of plan for joint operations. He isn't looking forward to it. Early in the morning he's sent the *Massachusetts* and the *Suwanee* to Guantánamo for refueling.

A little before nine o'clock, the *New York* pulls out of the battle line, flying a signal, "Disregard movements of commander-in-chief," and heads for Daiquiri. Five ships remain: the *Iowa*, at the center and just opposite the harbor's mouth; the *Oregon* and the *Indiana*, flanking on the east; and the *Texas* and *Brooklyn* at the west flank. Supporting them, the gunboats *Gloucester* and *Vixen* are lying close to shore. All of them are a little out of position because of the tide, and some, trying to cut down coal consumption, have unhooked several of their engines, reducing their speed, and it will take awhile to start them again. However, the *Oregon* has steam up in her eleven boilers. On all the ships, battle hatches have been taken off temporarily so the sweating crews below can get a little air. All is serene; morning prayer services have just ended.

"At thirty-one minutes after nine," Bob Evans recalls later, "the general alarm for action rang all over the ship. My son jumped to his feet, exclaiming, 'Papa, the enemy's ships are coming out' and we both started as fast as we could go for the bridge."

The Spaniards are, indeed, coming out, beginning the day that Lieutenant José Muller y Tejeiro, of the Spanish Navy, will always remember. "If I were to live a thousand years and a thousand centuries," he writes, "never should I forget that third day of July, nor do I believe that Spain will ever forget it."

Led by his flagship, the *Infanta María Teresa*, the doomed Spanish vessels follow in a line: the *Vizcaya*, so recently seen as a courtesy exchange ship in New York Harbor; the *Cristóbal Colón*, and the *Almirante Oquendo*, golden figureheads reflecting the morning sun, scarlet and yellow battle flags stirring in the breeze of their passage.

As the *Teresa* steams out into plain view, moving around Smith Cay in front of the Punta Gorda battery, Captain Victor M. Concas y Palau, her captain, asks Cervera for permission to open fire. "It was a signal," Concas laments later, "that the history of four centuries of grandeur was at an end and that Spain was becoming a nation of the fourth class. 'Poor Spain!' I said to my noble and beloved admiral, and he answered by an expressive motion, as though to say that he had done everything possible to avoid it, and that his conscience was clear, and this was true."

Cervera is saying his own farewell as he drops the pilot, Miguel López, when his ship emerges from the harbor's mouth. "Goodbye, pilot, for now," he says, "and be sure you let them pay you, because you have earned it well." He knows he's taking the fleet to almost certain destruction. With the bottoms of his vessels fouled, there's no possibility of making enough speed to escape. Worse, about eighty-five percent of his ammunition is defective and of no use. The *Colón* is his fastest ship, but she has no heavy armament. All the ships are decked and ornamented with wood, invitations to devastating fires; it should have been ripped out before the fleet left but no one bothered.

In retrospect, Cervera may be thinking Blanco might have been right and he could have had at least some chance of escaping if he had slipped out at night. But he had been afraid that searchlights from the American ships, sweeping the harbor entrance from time to time, would have made it impossible for López, or any other pilot, to guide the fleet past the wreck of the *Merrimac* and through the treacherous channel.

Even now, as some American naval officers will speculate later, he might still escape if he steers for the open sea, but he's a cautious man. He orders the entire squadron to swing toward the east, where only one ship, the *Brooklyn*, stands in his way. Cervera believes that by sailing together the ships are certain to attract heavy fire, but there is a forlorn hope that maybe one may escape and reach Cienfuegos or Havana. If not, he plans to beach the vessels rather than let them sink in deep water with all hands. As Freidel remarks, "Cervera's strategy was more humane than daring."

There they go, then, sailing to certain defeat and some of the Americans, at least, can't help admiring them. Captain

John W. Philip, of the *Texas*, recalls: "The Spanish ships came out as gaily as brides to the altar. Handsome vessels they certainly were, and with flags enough flying for a celebration parade. Just as I reached the bridge the foremost of the advancing Spanish ships poked her nose around Puntilla. As she swung around, she fired, and almost immediately afterward our forward six-inch guns spoke. The first shell fired by Cervera threw up a column of water short of us and between the *Texas* and the *Iowa*. On each side of the *Texas*, the *Brooklyn* and the *Iowa* were coming up with a tremendous rush. The dash of these two ships, as soon as the alarm was given, straight for the enemy, with cascades of water pouring away from their bows...was one of the most beautiful sights of the battle. Farther east, the *Oregon* and the *Indiana* were also headed in, ready for business."

A young lieutenant sees something missing. By comparison, the gaily bedecked Spanish ships make the nearly flagless American vessels look shabby; only the *Texas* has a battle flag at her stern.

"What's a battle without battle flags?" the lieutenant yells. Even as the roaring volleys begin, he smashes in a locker and hauls out a few flags to dress up the rusty old *Texas* as much as possible.

Everyone else is too busy. Schley has hurried to a small platform he had built around the *Brooklyn*'s conning tower, where he's joined by Captain Cook and the navigator, Lieutenant Albon C. Hodgson.

"Commodore, they're coming right at us," Hodgson sings out.

"Well, go right for them," Schley answers.

The commodore sees a moment of overdue recognition approaching. By this time the *New York* is out of sight, and although Sampson never officially notified Schley that he was leaving that morning, Schley is aware of it, and even more aware that he is now the senior officer in command. What a marvelous opportunity!

In the next few minutes, he almost blows it. To him, it looks as though Cervera is trying to avoid the battleships by running between the *Brooklyn* and the shore, so Schley orders his ship turned away from the battle line, putting the vessel in a wide loop that carries her across the bows of the *Texas*. A narrow escape. To avoid a collision, the *Texas* has to back water, and for a few minutes comes to a dead stop. At the same time,

Captain Clark is bringing up the *Oregon* at full speed, with the *Iowa* close behind, and with the support of their powerful guns, Schley can now forge ahead.

Nevertheless, the Spaniards have succeeded in passing the battleship line while they were sailing in opposite directions and are now in a position to begin firing on the Americans. Aboard the *Teresa*, Captain Concas recalls later: "The second gun of the deck battery was the first to open fire and brought us back to this reality, too dreadful to allow us to think of other things. Giving the cruiser all her speed, we poured out a frantic fire with our whole battery, except the forward gun, which we reserved to fire at close quarters. In compliance with the orders received, I put our bow toward the armored cruiser *Brooklyn*, which, putting to starboard, her stern to us and fired her two after turret guns, moving to southward."

Prospects of complete disaster open up immediately. The *Texas* and the *Iowa* are coming between the *Teresa* and the *Brooklyn*, raising the possibility that the Spanish ship could be rammed by both of them. Concas hurriedly consults Cervera, who orders the *Teresa*'s prow pointed coastward, since it's suicidal to continue her present course. Just in time, too. The *Brooklyn* is now about 5,000 yards away, and the *Texas* and the *Iowa* only a little more than 3,000.

But the *Teresa* is in peril for another reason. She came out of the harbor ahead of the others, and for nearly ten minutes she's alone, exposed to the fire of all the American ships, with only two guns for defense, and knowing she's going to be a prime target. Miraculously, she escapes from this desperate situation without serious damage and breaks past the converging lines of American ships.

It was this moment Schley chose to make his controversial loop, nearly resulting in collision. Oddly enough, he thought the danger came from the Spaniards. At the time the turn was made, he testifies later, the nearest Spanish ship was only 1,100 yards away--so near, as he says, "that I could see, with the naked eye, men running from her turret to her superstructure deck; and I observed daylight between their legs, as they ran. I never saw the starboard side of the *Texas* at all. I only saw her port side, and she never approached any position that was within six hundred yards of the *Brooklyn*. She was so distant that she never entered my head as a menace or danger."

Maybe so, but on the *Texas*, Captain Philip gets a different impression, as he relates: "The smoke from our guns began to hang so heavily and densely over the ship that for a few minutes we could see nothing. We might as well have had a blanket tied over our heads. Suddenly a whiff of breeze and a lull in the firing lifted the pall and there, bearing toward us and across our bows and great clouds of black smoke pouring from her funnels, was the *Brooklyn*. She looked as big as half a dozen *Great Easterns*, and seemed so near that it took our breath away.

"Back both engines hard!' went down the tube to the astonished engineers, and in a twinkling the old ship was racing against herself. The collision which seemed imminent, even if it was not, was averted, and as the big cruiser glided past, all of us on the bridge gave a sigh of relief. Had the *Brooklyn* struck us then, it would probably have been the end of the *Texas* and her half-thousand men."

While the *Brooklyn* is coming about in a circle, all four of the Spanish ships, and guns at the harbor's fort, are laying down simultaneous barrages, and for the next ten or fifteen minutes the most furious exchanges of the day occur. Jets of water from falling shells spurt up, the air is filled with the noise of the guns and the dense smoke from them. Momentarily, it looks as though Cervera might actually pull it off and get away.

Watching them, Bob Evans thinks the Spanish ships, headed westward in a column, "presented the finest spectacle that has probably ever been seen on the water. Their broadsides came with mechanical rapidity, and in striking contrast to the deliberate fire of the American ships. A torrent of projectiles was sailing over us, harmlessly exploding in the water beyond...It was soon evident to me that I could not ram either the first or the second ship, which, up to this time, it had been my intention to do."

Instead, he gives the *Teresa* a broadside at 2,500 yards, then heads in again, opening up the port guns at Cervera's flagship, while the starboard battery fires at the *Vizcaya* and the *Oquendo*. The *Indiana* and the *Oregon* join in this assault.

The *Teresa*, under the heaviest fire, gives up first. A shell from the *Indiana* strikes her early on, causing great destruction, and soon after she's in flames, headed toward the beach. The *Vizcaya* is hit by a shell near the funnels and her ammunition explodes. The *Oquendo* is staggering under blows from the *Indiana* and the *Iowa*. Spanish gunners keep up a brisk fire through it all, but they're highly inaccurate. The Americans, on the other hand, have for weeks been measuring distances from Morro Castle to the blockade line with sextants and stadiometers, so they have a fairly good idea of ranges and do better.

The problem now is that there's so much smoke no one can be sure how accurate the fleet's guns are, and exactly how much damage they're doing. Captain Philip writes: "It got in our ears, noses, and mouths, blackened our faces and blinded our eyes. Often for minutes at a time, for all we could see, we might as well have been down in the double bottoms as on the bridge. One had the sensation of standing up against an unseen foe, the most disagreeable sensation in warfare."

Besides the smoke, Philip soon has other problems. A Spanish shell hits the door of the pilot house and bursts inside. Then another shell explodes over the forward superstructure. Philip recalls: "The concussion lifted the bridge contingent off their feet. I remember pitching up in the air, with my coat-tails flying out behind me, as if I had been thrown by one of Roosevelt's broncos. No one was hurt except Cadet Reynolds, one of whose ear-drums was split." And the ordeal isn't over. Still another shell strikes a few minutes later, harming no one but doing considerable damage.

The armed yacht *Gloucester* (in its earlier life J. P. Morgan's yacht, the *Corsair*) has been building up steam in its boilers as its captain, Commander Richard P. Wainwright, carries out a mission against two torpedo-carrying destroyers, streaking from the harbor with intent to launch their missiles at the battleships. The *Gloucester* has no armor to protect her, but Wainwright boldly attacks the destroyers, under fire from both of them, and shore batteries as well, and sinks the two small ships, which gives him particular satisfaction since he had been executive officer of the *Maine*.

He can't take all the credit, though. The destroyers are also under fire from the guns of the *Iowa* and the *Indiana*. A shell from the *Iowa* cuts one of the destroyers in two, and another hits its boilers. Not, however, before this doomed ship has fired a shell that sails by within six feet of Wainwright's head. But the *Gloucester* turns on this destroyer, the *Pluton*, and sends her crashing on the rocks, where she blows up.

The other destroyer, the *Furor*, is disabled so badly she can't escape up the harbor, and at this point, the *New York* appears on the scene to finish her off. Sampson had heard the sound of the big guns on his way to Daiquiri, quickly turned around, and by this time has reached the fringes of the battle. Although he's under fire from the shore batteries, Sampson sinks the *Furor* with just two shots and hurries to catch up.

Recounting the circumstances of his late arrival, Sampson testifies later that he was standing on the quarterdeck when he saw a puff of white smoke that morning, drifting up over Morro Castle, and even before he heard the guns, surmised that some kind of action was going on. "I at once sent to the bridge the order: 'Put the helm aport and turn back immediately.'" By ten-fifteen, he's at the harbor entrance, about forty-five minutes after the start of the battle.

Unfortunately for him, he's too late to take much of a part in the biggest naval engagement he'll ever see. As the fight goes on, the *New York* is always within sight of it, but also always out of range. It's galling to think that, while he's trailing after the action, Schley and the *Brooklyn* are in the thick of things.

At the start of the chase, Schley can't believe his ship will be able to keep up with the Spanish vessels; he doesn't know about the poor conditions that are reducing their speed. "We must stay with that crowd," he urges Captain Cook. They do, and it isn't long before all the American ships are firing at the Spaniards, with devastating effect. "The *Brooklyn* and the *Oregon* were a sheet of flame," Schley recalls. "I never saw such a fire and never realized what rapid gun firing meant before."

By this time the *Teresa* is so badly damaged that the other Spanish ships pass by her as she limps along. The *Oregon* pours a murderous fire into her at 2,000 yards. Smoke and flame burst from her, and she's obviously on fire. As she turns toward shore, the other battleships deliver more broadsides at her; soon she's drifting slowly toward the beach at Juan Gonzáles, only six miles from Santiago. It has taken her forty minutes to get that far. But Cervera takes care that she goes to her death gallantly, flags still flying, guns still blazing.

The *Oquendo* is the next victim. Closing rapidly, the *Oregon* pours in the shells from only 900 yards away, the day's most destructive fire, and within twelve minutes after the *Teresa* is totally out of commission, the *Oquendo*, ablaze from end to end, also heads for the beach. She's done for, but not without distinction. Of them all, she has suffered the most and fought back more fiercely. But at last her hull, torn and battered, comes to rest on the beach, a mile from the *Teresa*.

Now the *Oregon* hunts down the *Vizcaya*, two miles away, and the *Brooklyn* joins in. There's a furious exchange of fire from all three ships, and while they're at it, the only other surviving ship, the *Colón*, takes advantage of the fact that she's the fastest of the Spanish cruisers and increases her lead toward a hopeful escape.

Schley thinks the *Vizcaya* might be within range and sends Yeoman George Ellis to confirm it, but as he trots off, he's decapitated by a shell--the only American killed that day. Two officers want to throw his body overboard, but Schley stops them.

Except for the *Vizcaya* and the *Colón*, the Spanish jig is up. The *Brooklyn*, *Oregon*, and *Texas* are closing in on the former, and a shell has already exploded on her port bow. A few minutes later, a 12-inch shell hits her squarely amidships. Steam and smoke rise from this gaping wound. Blazing and crippled beyond recall, she too swings toward the shore.

By an odd chance, it's the *Oregon* that deals the final blow. Her turret officer is complaining to Captain Clark that he can't get his guns to bear on any of the fleeing Spanish ships when suddenly the *Vizcaya* appears off the starboard bow, burning and headed for the beach. "There's your chance," Clark tells him, pointing. With that, the full force of the turret guns is thrown at the *Vizcaya*, and by eleven o'clock, she's hauled down her flag and run aground at Aserradores, about eighteen miles from Morro.

So far, the score is Americans 5, Spaniards 0. It's taken just ninety minutes for the Navy to send three burning ships onto the beach. Two destroyers have been sunk as well. The only quarry left is the *Colón*, taking advantage of her superior speed and also protected by the heavy pall of smoke. She's pressing westward as fast as her boilers can take her, westward and close to shore.

Now begins what Freidel calls "the grandest chase in naval history." The *Colón* has a six-mile start, but the *Brooklyn* is belching black smoke as she hurries to overtake and cut her off, while the *Oregon* moves to block her flight to open water. On the

Oregon, Lieutenant Eberle remembers: "We sent our men to dinner by watches, but after getting a bite, they returned to the deck to follow the exciting chase and take a puff at their pipes." Since the American ships are so lightly damaged, the fight, as Freidel observes, "seemed to officers and men alike more a magnificent sporting spectacle than a grim and bloody battle."

A freshly minted cadet from Annapolis even stands on the forward turret of the *Iowa* with his camera and tries to get a snapshot of the *Oquendo* while its machine guns are still filling the air with lead. Captain Evans chews him out for this piece of unnecessary bravado, but on the *Oregon* another cadet, C. E. Miller, also has his camera out and is walking about the deck taking pictures as though the whole thing is some kind of holiday celebration. One of his snapshots will have a certain historical value. It shows Captain Clark standing beside William D. Leahy, the future fleet admiral.

Still a considerable distance away, Sampson can only watch the grand chase although his deck is trembling with vibrations from the screw as the *New York* struggles to stay within sight and, because of its superior power, begins to overtake the *Colón*. Everyone on board is speculating—can the flagship actually get into this thing? She's gaining on all the others, and shortly after noon, it's possible for her officers to see the *Colón*, moving as close to shore as the *New York* itself is.

But Sampson can't get there in time for the kill. The *Oregon* has kept pace with the fleeing Spanish ship, exciting the wonderment of the other crews because her maximum speed is sixteen knots and the *Colón* is estimated to be doing twenty. Even so, the *Brooklyn* is also gaining on her, and signals a somewhat mysterious message, "She seems built in Italy," to which Clark replies, "She may have been built in Italy, but she will end on the coast of Cuba."

That seems imminent as the fleeing vessel briefly turns toward the shore several times, as though looking for a place to beach. But the American ships are now within range. At twelve-forty, the *Oregon* strikes her with an 1,100-pound missile as the American crew crowds the forward turrets and some climb aloft to watch the climax of this chase. The *Brooklyn* is 9,500 yards away, nearly five miles, but she too fires a shot at the *Colón*, which drops just ahead of the ship. That seems to convince her commander. He heads for the beach.

Too late. At one-twelve her stern is struck by a 13-inch shell, severing the cords that hold up her colors. They drop in a heap. A bugle sounds the "cease fire" on the *Oregon*, repeated on the *Brooklyn* and other ships as the *Colón* surrenders. A band, hastily assembled, fills the air with the "Star-Spangled Banner," and the remaining ships gather around. Men swarm out on the decks, grimy, half naked, blackened by powder and coal dust, cheering lustily. The *Iowa*'s crew even cheers the *New York* as she comes up to the others at last and they see Sampson standing on the bridge. But again he's too late. Schley has already received the *Colón*'s surrender.

Given his chance, Schley is emerging as a heroic figure. Hundreds have seen him standing on the conning tower of the *Brooklyn* with the Spanish shells screaming by him, yelling to the gunners, "Give 'em hell, bullies!" His ship has been struck many times because, being faster than the others, it's been in the thick of conflict from the start. Miraculously, she isn't seriously damaged.

But the smoke has hardly cleared before the recriminations begin and Sampson takes his revenge on this hated subordinate who has managed to upstage him completely, through no fault of his own. The *New York* moves in between the *Brooklyn* and the *Colón*, and Cook is ordered to report on board the flagship. He goes over with a boatload of Spanish officers taken prisoner but comes back without them. There will be no prizes for the *Brooklyn*. Meanwhile, the *Colón* has opened her valves and is sinking.

Schley has already anticipated this rebuff, and knows who's going to get the credit, however undeserved. George Graham, a *Brooklyn* correspondent, describes the battle's aftermath: "Commodore Schley ordered the signal raised: 'A glorious victory has been achieved. Details later.' Vainly the signal officers on the bridge watched the *New York* for even the courtesy of an answering pennant showing that she understood the signal. Nevertheless, as the *New York* approached rapidly, Commodore Schley ordered another signal set, 'This is a great day for our country.' Instead of an answering pennant to this signal, there went up on the halyards of the *New York* a set of flags, which at first officers and men alike on the *Brooklyn* hoped to be a message of congratulations, but which proved to be a terse command, 'Report your casualties.' 'Report your casualties,' repeated

Schley, turning on his heel and walking over to the other side of the bridge, a pained expression on his face; and up to our signal masts went the flags, 'One dead, and two wounded.'"

It's after four o'clock when Sampson orders the *Oregon* to take command of the *Colón* as a prize ship, pointedly ignoring the *Brooklyn*'s (and Schley's) legitimate claim. She isn't much of a prize when the prize crew gets to her. The engine room is drowned in fifteen feet of water, and all the valves are open. Prisoners are transferred to one of the smaller American ships, the *Resolute*.

This particular crew is in sorry condition. Before Sunday, the firemen and coal-passers had been doing double duty ashore in the trenches defending Santiago. Hurried aboard, they'd been without food for thirty-six hours because, through some kind of foul-up, nothing had been prepared for them when they arrived. The Americans revive them with liberal doses of brandy, a remedy that backfires in the usual way, so that the prize crew has to spend some time sweeping up half-emptied brandy bottles and other residue lying on the deck, to be thrown overboard, and sweeping up the crew as well. Every effort is made to keep the *Colón* afloat, but she begins to list to starboard, and just as the prize crew gets clear of her, she turns over on her side, dead.

As they inspect the carnage they've created, neither officers nor men can help feeling sorry for the survivors. When his crew members cheer as the *Colón* steams to her death, Captain Philip reproves them with words that will travel from one end of America to the other and become part of the language. "Don't cheer, men," he admonishes, "those poor devils are dying." (The ship's chaplain tries to clean this up later; the captain said "fellows," not "devils," he insists.)

As long as there's light on that Sunday evening, the crews of all the American ships work tirelessly to salvage as much as they can of the human life they've shattered. Spanish soldiers are hoisted up from the water, taken off the beaches, rescued from still burning ships. When rescuers reach the *Oquendo*, they hear cries for help from men clustered on her bows. Burst plates from her guns and boilers are lying about, and it's clear she hasn't long to live.

The *Iowa* takes on the task of rescuing the officers and crew of the *Vizcaya*, who had to jump overboard when she went aground, still 400 yards from the beach. Many have taken refuge on a sandspit, standing in water up to their armpits. When Cuban rebels come down to the shore and see them, they start shooting as though the Spaniards were ducks in a barrel. Meanwhile, sharks, attracted by the blood flowing into the water from the wounded, are attacking savagely. It's almost better to be one of the wounded still on deck. They're clinging to the fore and aft ends of the sinking ship, where they're in danger of being burned to death. Up comes the torpedo boat *Ericsson*, with its auxiliary, the *Hist*, and they manage to rescue everyone.

The *Iowa* has arrived to help with this rescue effort, and its crewmen bring on board the *Vizcaya*'s commander, Captain Don Antonio Eulate. Evans greets him with all the respect due a fellow officer and gentleman, and the ship's other officers follow suit. This is quite natural, because many of these men on both sides know each other, having met when they happened to be in foreign ports at the same time, as well as occasionally at naval reviews.

Eulate is suffering from minor wounds, so a chair has to be lowered to bring him aboard. The boat that brought him, one of the *Vizcaya*'s life rafts, has a foot of water in it, and two dead men torn apart by shell fragments are rolling around in the bloody liquid. Supported by a cadet, Eulate is carried in his chair to the quarterdeck, where the ship's guard presents arms, the officer of the deck salutes, and Spanish prisoners come to attention.

Protocol is being strictly observed. Hoisting himself up with an effort, Eulate unbuckles his sword belt, kisses this ceremonial weapon on its hilt, and presents it to Evans. As he's expected to do, Evans declines to accept it, and instead takes the injured captain by the arm and helps him to a room where doctors are waiting to dress his wounds. The ceremony had to come first, however.

Before he ascends the ladder to go below, Eulate makes a grand gesture right out of the Spanish theater. He turns toward the wreck of his ship, extends his right arm toward it, and says, "*Adiós, Vizcaya.*" At that moment, as though the gesture had been a signal, the broken ship's forward magazine explodes, sending up a column of smoke visible fifteen miles away.

Cervera's rescue is not as dramatic but just as impressive in its own way. He's had a hard time reaching the shore after the

Teresa was beached on a sand bar. He had to swim, and finally was pulled to safety from the surf by means of a lifeline cast out by one of the *Gloucester*'s boats. Supervising the rescue, Lieutenant Wainwright remarks later: "When I saw that gallant gentleman in his wringing wet underclothes, I felt as if I were a culprit."

Bedraggled he may be, but Cervera is happier than he's been since his decrepit fleet left the Cape Verde Islands last April. He has done what was expected of him, carried out official orders as best he could, and finds himself alive and well, relieved of any other responsibilities in this war which he never wanted to fight. Sitting down to lunch with his fellow officers and Lieutenant Harry P. Huse, the gloomy, foreboding Cervera of the past few months is replaced by the genial Cervera his friends knew back home. Besides, he's glad to be eating again, having had only a cup of chocolate that morning before he left the harbor. While he's dining, he remarks about his long fast, and a sudden silence falls. Everyone's thinking of the mighty events that have taken place in just a few hours that day.

When the pluses and minuses are added up, Cervera really has nothing to be ashamed of. His guns and ammunition had been both defective and scanty. The gunners had not had any target practice for some time, but that's not his fault. His four heavy ships were outnumbered by the Americans' six, with their fourteen 12- and 13-inch guns opposed to his six 11-inch and thirty American 8-inch guns against none. From there on down, through every category of armament, the Spanish fleet has been outgunned and outmanned.

The worst figure he's going to have to explain when he gets home is 323 men killed, besides the 152 wounded, out of a complement of 2,227 men. Furthermore, 1,813 have been taken prisoner. Only a few managed to swim ashore and reach the Spanish lines at Santiago.

For the Americans, it's an overwhelming victory, but in the aftermath, when the cheering stops, there's a little less to gloat over. Besides the glaring disparity in armaments, there's the undeniable fact that the Navy's ships overhauled the Spanish fleet only because its bottoms were foul, reducing their speed to six knots. Everyone can cheer the fact that only one American was killed, but that can be attributed to the dismal marksmanship of the Spanish gunners, otherwise the toll would have been much higher on these badly armored vessels. Good luck had a lot to do with it too.

As for the American gunners, they were more often on the mark but the worst damage they did resulted from fires in the flooring and all that woodwork which should have been removed. When a Navy board examines what's left of the Spanish fleet, it can find only 122 certified hits, although 9,433 shots had been fired--hardly an impressive ratio. But then, the end results are happier. When the Navy finishes its assessment after the war, the result will pave the way for a badly needed modernization of the entire fleet.

More complicated, and much more brutal, is the assessment of credit after the battle. When Schley comes over the side of the *New York* to report, there's no question that he's the commander who won the battle, but Sampson is determined that as few people as possible beyond the eyewitnesses are going to know about it, particularly the authorities in Washington. There's nothing he can do to stop the press reports, but he can take immediate control and he does.

First he orders Schley to send the *Brooklyn* at once on a chase after an entirely mythical vessel reported up the coast. The idea is to give Sampson time to file a report before Schley does. The commodore, however, is not to be trapped so easily. He has already written his report and given it to a flag lieutenant for cabling ashore. Sampson writes his version too and gives it to *his* flag lieutenant, with instructions that it be sent first. The two lieutenants meet in the Siboney telegraph office, where Sampson's man, following instructions, pulls rank on the other and sends his first, meanwhile turning away Schley's emissary.

Sampson's message reads: "The fleet under my command offers the nation as a Fourth of July present the whole of Cervera's fleet." Schley's message is never sent.

Meanwhile, the *New York* steams back to Santiago Bay, and in the brilliance of a full moon, observes the wreckage of the Spanish fleet as it passes by. Charred timber and woodwork float on the water, along with boxes, trunks, and the uniforms that were in them. The red glow from still burning ships illuminates the beach. Having achieved a great victory through no effort of his own, and managed to take exclusive credit for it, Sampson should be a happy man this night. Officers observing him, however, note that his face is even bleaker than usual. He has the look not of a victor but of a man stunned by what's happened. As Leech notes, he "looked worse than Cervera."

In Washington, the official dispatch is received with much less enthusiasm than one might expect at first. Everyone with a knowledge of history knows that Sampson, or more likely his flag lieutenant, has phrased the report to recall General Sherman's famous telegram, offering Savannah's conquest to Lincoln as a Christmas present. But isn't this comparison more than a little far-fetched? people are asking. And what about "the fleet under my command" and no mention of the part played by Schley or anyone else? Isn't that a monument to self-conceit? All this seems more blatant when the correspondents' stories catch up with the official dispatch and it's disclosed that Sampson's part in the battle was minimal. The reporters' stories are loud in praise of Schley. They call his conduct heroic and make it clear that he was in command. In the end, for all his conniving about the transmission, the most Sampson gets is ridicule in many quarters.

Not surprisingly, the tension between the two commanders festers and grows in the time (more than a month) they're still together in Havana. To Schley's credit, he makes an attempt at magnanimity. Speaking to reporters, he declares that the victory was big enough for everyone, and he lets the Navy Department know that he's embarrassed over his sudden celebrity, adding that the honor of victory must naturally go to the commander-in-chief. But Schley makes a mistake. He thinks the celebrity he's acquired is going to be lasting. When it wears off, his magnanimity disappears with it.

Before long, the acrimonious dispute spills over into official Washington and filters down to the public consciousness. It refuses to die. Sampson finds support among his fellow officers and the Navy Department, while Schley has a smaller but more devoted following in Washington. What he lacks officially is more than made up for by the continuing acclaim of the press and public it reaches, not to mention a few influential politicians.

Senators show their support of Schley by opposing Sampson's list of promotions, while the admiral's supporters demonstrate *their* loyalty by starting a whispering campaign against Schley, charging him with incompetence and disobedience when he was trying to find Cervera's fleet and bottle it up.

They also revive the nearly fatal accident he so narrowly avoided when he pulled the *Brooklyn* out of the battle line and sent it on a collision course with the *Texas*. Sampson's partisans even question Schley's personal courage, which no one has thought to do before.

Suffering under this assault, Schley will ask for a Naval Board of Inquiry in 1903, where at last he'll be able to prove that Sampson's flag lieutenant, under orders, played a dirty and no doubt illegal trick on him. However, the board will fail to clear him, and only the loyalty of his followers will make Schley, in effect, the ultimate winner. He will rest on his honors and savor their support while Sampson will slip away into obscurity, steadily failing in both mind and body until his death.

So the victory of Santiago Bay, greatly hastening the end of the war in Cuba, disintegrates into a messy clash of personalities and partisan bitterness. As far as the commanders are concerned, the actual event ended on July 3, but next day there's a seriocomic postscript, courtesy of W. R. Hearst.

Lying off Siboney, Hearst hears the sound of the naval battle and, after carefully staying out of harm's way, spends the Fourth of July helping the Navy to mop up while he's compiling grist for the *Journal*'s mill. Nattily dressed in blue flannels and a yachting cap, he sails aboard the *Sylvia* to the theater of yesterday's battle.

He comes first upon the *Vizcaya*, the ship he had warned his readers was prepared to shell New York when it lay in the harbor last spring. Followed by Hemment, Follansbee, and his close friend, George Pancoast, Hearst goes on board the half-sunken hulk. Even now the decks are so hot you can burn your fingers by touching them. Hemment reports: "The girders which supported the main deck were twisted into every conceivable grotesque shape. The charred remains of many of the sailors were strewn around."

In the story he writes about has salvage operation, Hearst mentions a lump of Spanish coins melted together by the heat and, carried away, he exclaims: "Great heavens! Is this rent and twisted hulk, black and battered, blistered and burned, with the gaping chasm in its bow...is this the noble boat we all admired so much and dreaded not a little as she lay in New York Harbor, just before the war? Is this the deck from which Captain Eulate trained his guns on the tall buildings of New York?"

No one can say Hearst isn't consistent, regardless of what the facts may be.

Sailing on, the *Sylvia* comes upon the wreck of the *Oquendo*. Fires still burn on her and they occasionally touch off a surviving shell. In spite of this serious danger, the Hearstian crew go aboard for a brief inspection. Retreating again to a safe distance, they're hailed by an officer on the Marine cutter *Dixie*, which comes up alongside the *Sylvia*.

"What were you doing aboard that ship?" the officer demands.

"Just looking around, sir, at the results of the battle," Hearst tells him, judiciously meek.

When the officer finds out they're a passel of reporters, he gives them a short lecture on the dangers damn fools like them are likely to encounter if they continue messing around, and the *Dixie* buzzes off.

As Hearst leaves this scene, someone on the *Sylvia* spots twenty Spanish seamen from the *Oquendo* who are sitting on the beach, waiting to be rescued. Taking the *Sylvia*'s gig, Hearst and a few of his men head toward them. In his report of the event, Hearst writes: "We shouted at them and made a demonstration with out firearms, and the poor, cowed fellows, with great alacrity, waved a white handkerchief or shirt as a token of surrender. I jumped overboard, swam ashore, and told them we were going to take them aboard our boat to see the Admiral. They appeared rather gratified than otherwise, and seemed to dread the Cubans far more than Americans."

Hearst makes his twenty-nine prisoners bury some corpses that have washed up on shore, then takes them to the *Sylvia*. He informs them that it's the Fourth of July, which they're willing to admit, and orders them to give three cheers for George Washington and President McKinley, while Hemment takes pictures of them for the *Journal*. They respond with something less than enthusiasm.

But Hearst shows the genuinely compassionate side of his nature as well by filling his prisoners with food and drink, after which he takes them to an American warship, the *St. Louis*, where he asks for a receipt and gets it. If Sampson can give the President a Fourth of July present of the entire Spanish fleet, he's prepared to offer some of its refugees as a token of his support. This task accomplished, he takes the *Sylvia* back to

Siboney, where Hearst wants to check on Creelman's condition. Taking his wounded correspondent aboard, he heads his ship toward Baltimore. For seventeen days, he's covered the war he did so much to launch, and he returns well satisfied with himself and the result.

The *Journal*'s faithful tug, the *Three Friends*, which has been pottering about in Hearst's wake, has made a brief survey of the battle scene, then heads for Siboney. Frances Scovel is on board. She knows Harry is there somewhere but, beyond that, has no further knowledge and needs to find out what's happened to him.

As the tug approaches the dock in Siboney, it's hailed by a courier rowing out in a dinghy. He's carrying a two-word message from Scovel: "Don't land." The messenger explains. Three soldiers from the Michigan National Guard are down with yellow fever, and if the crew of the *Three Friends* comes ashore, there's a good chance the authorities in Jamaica won't let them land there.

Having been warned, the tug prepares to return to Port Antonio, but Frances has been expecting to take Harry with her and he hasn't appeared. Something must be very wrong, she decides, and persuades one of the tug's firemen to row her close enough to the shore so she can struggle through the surf. She's not going without Harry, but the *Three Friends* steams off without her.

It's easy enough to find Scovel, as it turns out. He's lying on a hammock in a hut on the outskirts of the camp, too weak to leave it. The doctors say he's suffering from a virulent form of malaria, but he's a lucky man. He doesn't have yellow fever.

The shortage of nursing care is so acute by this time that no official objections are raised when Frances announces she's going to stay and nurse him. As the days go by and Harry begins to improve, she extends her nursing duties to other ailing members of the press corps, performing a notable humanitarian service for which no official, or the *World* for that matter, even so much as thanks her. Harry recovers, of course. He's going to end the war in a much more spectacular fashion.

At home, after the battle, there is universal acclaim, in spite of the ugly controversies. People feel that the worst is over, even if Shafter is still at the edge of, but not in, Santiago. If there's a truly sour note, it comes from--who else?--Ambrose

Bierce. Readers of the Hearst papers, full of enthusiasm from news accounts of the Battle of Santiago Bay, are astonished by what they read in Bierce's curmudgeonly column. On July 10, he writes:

"Captain Philip, of the battleship 'Texas,' appears to be something of a naval freak. He runs to religion. After he had assisted in sinking Cervera's fugitive fleet he summoned the entire ship's company to the quarter-deck and said: 'I want to make public acknowledgment here that I believe in God, the Father Almighty, and I want all you officers and men to lift your hats and from your hearts offer silent thanks to the Almighty.' The wholesale slaughter of our fellow men in this or any war should, I think, be regarded rather as a political rather than a religious day. Captain Philip is reported to have said: 'As far back as history goes, in the days of Joshua, at Manila, here, everywhere, the man who fires the first shot of a battle on the Sabbath is sure of defeat. These Spaniards are a godless race and their cause is unrighteous; that accounts for our easy victories.'"

Outrageous!

Also surprising news for the "godless race," which is composed mostly of devout Catholics. At least Bierce demonstrates that for now diversity of opinion is not threatened in America.

Back in Cuba, however, there's still a good deal of work to do, and some of it is going to be even more controversial in this war of nearly total confusion.

8

NOT WITH A BANG, BUT A WHISPER

As the guns of Santiago Bay shatter the peaceful Sunday quiet, they're heard by the men in the trenches, who listen uneasily, having no idea what may be happening. Shafter hears them, too, but unaccountably attaches no importance to this sound of battle. Nor is he concerned when Sampson fails to keep his appointment for a conference that morning. In the afternoon, for reasons never explained satisfactorily, he convinces himself that indeed there's been a battle and the Spanish fleet has escaped, an erroneous idea he at once passes on to Washington where it arrives in the early evening.

To the President and his anxious men, this is the most depressing news so far. Sampson's report hasn't yet been received, so when the Army chief signal officer cables from Guantánamo that Cervera's fleet has been destroyed, they hesitate to believe it until he sends a second, confirming message, followed by Sampson's.

As for Shafter, he feels only relief in believing the opposite outcome. Now the Navy can really finish the job and he won't have to risk any more casualties, which is his primary concern. When he learns the true situation next day, he quickly reports that he has demanded Santiago's surrender. The double dose of good news creates a mood of euphoria in Washington and the nation. When Secretary Alger walks home from the White House in the early morning hours of July 4, the opening words of Shafter's cable are still sounding happily in his mind: "I shall hold my present position." While he's savoring them, he's hearing the cries of newsboys proclaiming the Spanish fleet's destruction.

But what, in fact, is Shafter's actual "present position"? As Freidel points out, it's "the height of irony in an ironic war" that in spite of the Navy's victory the land forces are facing imminent defeat. Having lost more than 1,600 men killed so far, no one is anxious to storm the barbed wire and strong fortifications protecting Santiago. Rain has begun to fall heavily and more or less constantly on the men in their steamy, muddy trenches. Worst of all, they have a deadly enemy within their own ranks: fever is quickly going to become an epidemic.

Shafter is in a dilemma. He has some face-saving to do, of the same kind that undid the Spaniards. How is he going to justify all the lives and money spent in this campaign, not to mention national honor, if he can't take Santiago? Assault seems to him far too risky, even though reinforcements are being rushed to him from home–2,000 are on the way from Tampa, 3,000 coming from Newport News, and 4,000 more sailing from Charleston.

With Cervera's fleet gone, he hopes that Santiago will surrender, but General José Toral, who has succeeded the wounded Linares, has already refused the ultimatum of July 3. Toral thinks Shafter's bluffing. The most he'll agree to is a temporary truce, much welcomed by both sides. Apart from Shafter, however, most of the Americans believe they'll have to destroy Santiago and they expect to do so. After climbing to a place where he can see people moving around the city, and the cooking fires of the defenders, Frank Knox writes home: "Santiago is a pretty place. It seems a shame to lay it in ruins."

The soldiers have spent a nervous Sunday. At first they heard a rumor that Cervera had sunk the blockading fleet and was now heading back toward Santiago, intent on finishing off the American invaders. Late in the afternoon, the good news filters in and there's general rejoicing. The men have already had a Fourth of July celebration--of sorts. Under Shafter's orders, the regimental bands played, the regiments formed in line at a safe distance, except for those who couldn't leave the trenches, Lieutenant Pershing read a telegram from the President, meant to be inspirational, as his regiment listened. Over in the Rough Riders' camp, a few homesick alumni boosted their spirits by singing "Fair Harvard."

Meanwhile, on both sides, matters are moving toward crisis proportions. The truce continues after Toral sends the British and other foreign consuls to ask Shafter for an extension.

Fearing a bombardment, 20,000 women and children are preparing to flee the city into the countryside, where there's neither food nor shelter. Already the *Massachusetts*, returning from being refueled at Guantánamo (thus missing the battle) has encountered the *Reina Mercedes*, a rusting old hulk of a cruiser whose guns had been used to defend the city, making a belated escape. Toral hopes she'll be sunk in the channel, thus blocking the American fleet from entering the harbor, but the *Massachusetts* sinks her in the wrong place. The belated thunder of this event, coming after a day of nerve-wrenching gunfire they had hoped was ended, is enough to start a premature evacuation from Santiago.

As these refugees trail past the American lines, Pershing observes them and writes: "All day along the hot dusty trail, hungry women carried a bundle of clothing, a parcel of food or an infant, while weak and helpless children trailed wearily at the skirts of their wretched mothers. An old man tottered along on his cane and behind him a pony had helped an aged woman; old and young, women, children and decrepit men of every class–those refined and used to luxury, together with the ragged beggar–crowded with each other in this narrow column...the suffering of the innocent is not the least of the horrors of war."

Another observer of these pitiful refugees, the victims of all wars, is Stephen Crane, who writes of them: "The vivid thing was the fact that these people did not visibly suffer. Somehow they were numb. There was not a tear. But the town [El Caney] was now a vast parrot-cage of chattering refugees."

Difficult as it is to take care of their own countrymen, the medical and supply forces of both the Army and the Red Cross somehow manage to keep many of the refugees alive--no small task, since they number 15,000 in these early days of July, and the number will grow. Help is coming from America, though. As fast as lighters can be unloaded through the surf at Siboney, tons of food and medical materials are sent by wagon to the front. Even the Spanish prisoners help out. Shafter asks Toral if he'll take some dangerously wounded soldiers back into Santiago, and the general agrees. Twenty-seven of them go at once, under military escort, jubilant to be rejoining friends and comrades. An unplanned fallout results. As they tell their stories to those in the city, the Spanish Army's commanders get an idea, for the first time, of what's occurring beyond their lines and it provides a new push toward eventual peace.

Shafter follows up this unprecedented return of prisoners

with a proposal to Toral that he return Hobson and the crew of the sunken *Merrimac* in exchange for captured Army officers and soldiers. The general agrees.

Crane witnesses the exchange: "Some of our staff officers rode out with those Spanish officers--prisoners--these latter being blindfolded before they were taken through the American position. The army was majestically minding its own business in the long line of trenches when its eye caught sight of this little procession. 'What's that? What they goin' to do?' 'They're goin' to exchange Hobson.' Whereupon every man who was foot-free staked out a claim where he could get a good view of the liberated heroes, and two bands prepared to collaborate on 'The Star-Spangled Banner.' There was a very long wait through the sunshiny afternoon.

"But suddenly the moment came. Along the cut roadway toward the crowded soldiers, rode three men, and it could be seen that the central one wore the undress uniform of an officer of the United States Navy. Most of the soldiers were sprawled out on the grass, bored and wearied in the sunshine. However, they aroused at the old circus-parade, torchlight-procession cry, 'Here they come!'

"Then the men of the regular army did a thing. They arose en masse and came to 'Attention.' Then the men of the regular army did another thing. They slowly lifted every weather-beaten hat and drooped it until it touched the knee. Then there was a magnificent silence, broken only by the measured hoof-beats of the little company's horses as they rode through the gap. It was solemn, funereal, this splendid silent welcome of a brave man by men who stood on a hill which they had earned out of blood and death.

"Then suddenly the whole scene went to rubbish. Before he reached the bottom of the hill, Hobson was bowing to right and left like another Boulanger. However, one could thrill again when the tail of the procession appeared--an army waggon [sic] containing the blue-jackets of the Merrimac adventure. I remember grinning heads stuck out from under the canvas cover of the waggon. And the army spoke to the navy. 'Well, Jackie, how does it feel?' And the navy up and answered, 'Great! Much obliged to you fellers for comin' here.' 'Say, Jackie, what did they arrest ye for anyhow? Stealin' a dawg?' The navy still grinned. Here was no rubbish."

Another observer of Hobson's return is Davis, who's been living in the rifle pits with the men for sixteen days. In his memoirs, he recalls: "The trail on which they came was a broad one between high banks, with great trees meeting in an arch overhead. Hobson's coming was one of the most dramatic pictures of the war. The sun was setting behind the trail, and he came up over the crest, he was outlined against it under this triumphal arch of palms. The soldiers saw a young man in the uniform of the navy, his face white with prison pallor, and strangely in contrast with the fierce tan of their own, and with serious eyes, who looked down at them steadily.

"For a moment he sat motionless, and then the waiting band struck up 'The Star-Spangled Banner.' No one cheered or shouted or gave an order, but every one rose to his feet slowly, took off his hat slowly, and stood so, looking up at Hobson in absolute silence.

"It was one of the most impressive things one could imagine. No noise, no blare, nor shouted tribute could have touched the meaning or the depths of feeling there was in that silence.

"And then a red-headed, red-faced trooper leaped down into the trail and shouted, 'Three cheers for Hobson,' and the mob rushed at him with a roar of ecstasy, with a wild welcome of friendly cheers. Few men, certainly very few young men, have ever tasted such a triumph. As brave men they honored a brave man; and this sun-tanned, dirty, half-starved, fever-racked mob of regulars danced about the educated, clever engineer as though the moment was his, and forgot that at the risk of their lives they had set him free, that the ground he rode over had been splashed with their blood.

"It was the same story all the way to Siboney. Every group of soldiers we came across stood at attention at the unusual sight of a navy uniform. When they recognized the man they waved their hats and cheered. It was the most wonderful ride a young man of twenty-eight had ever undertaken. Best of all, perhaps, was when he rode through the twilight and reached the coast and saw again...the lights of the flag-ship, his floating home, and heard from across the water the jubilant cheers of the blue-jackets, who could not even see him, who did not know he had already arrived, but who cheered because they had heard he was coming, because he was free."

Hobson's arrival is an unexpected and welcome interlude

in the lives of those men clinging to the forward positions out-side Santiago. They can't retreat, but neither can they advance. As Davis remembers: "Their own point of view and sense of relief and surprise were thus best expressed in the words of Stephen Crane's trooper, who sank upon the crest of the hill, panting, bleeding, and sweating, and cried: 'Well, hell, here we are!'"

Not much more than that, it seems at first. Casualties are still being taken out to the hospitals below, where their chances of surviving are precarious. Francis Nichols, the only member of the *World* staff on the scene, with Scovel still recovering back in Siboney, files a scathing report about conditions, noting that seventeen wounded men had died the night before, and every-thing needed to care for the living is in extremely short supply. Quinine tablets, he says, are so rare that they bring several dol-lars each in the black market. Dozens of wounded men are still lying on the ridge, waiting for transportation to Siboney.

Nichols writes indignantly: "Why ambulances that should have been at the front are now in the holds of transports, why there is no field hospital within two miles of the front, are ques-tions that men have asked as they died out in the cactus under the burning sun--died because there was no one to care for their wounds. Someone has blundered and blundered badly." The name of the chief blunderer is hardly a secret.

Conditions could scarcely be worse, but they soon are. The rainy season sets in and the soldiers in the rifle pits are periodi-cally deluged by tropical torrents of rain. Staying dry isn't mere-ly a matter of comfort. The men believe (erroneously, of course) that their other enemies, malaria and yellow fever, are caused by "vapors" rising from the soaked pits, so they spend most of the time trying to keep dry. It isn't easy. Davis writes: "It was not at all an unusual experience to sleep through the greater part of the night with the head lifted just clear of the water and the shoulders and one-half of the body down in it."

When the sun comes out two days after the naval victory, everyone greets it as a savior of lives, and it illuminates the exchange of Hobson and the other captives while General Shafter--his first appearance at the front--presides.

Crane, as we've seen, has been momentarily disgusted by what he thought was Hobson's playing the role of hero. As he and Davis ride back to Siboney in Hobson's wake, they argue about it. Davis says the country needs heroes and let's not write anything to disillusion them. Crane doesn't have much energy to argue. He's suffering from dizziness and backache again, as he did earlier in the war, and keeps himself going with the aid of a brandy bottle. When the brandy runs out, he falls from the saddle.

George Rea and Harry Scovel, just out of his sickbed hammock, are also in this little party of correspondents, and they help carry Crane to a grassy spot along the trail where he can rest for a while, then they go on to Shafter's headquarters in Sevilla, where they spend the night. By the time they all get to Siboney early the next evening, they find the cable office closed for the night and their patient delirious. Against Crane's protests, they haul him off to the base hospital, where the doctors give them the bad news. He has yellow fever.

Feeling a little better the next day, he gets to thinking about the adulation given Hobson, and earlier to Hamilton Fish, Jr., while the sacrifices of "the unknowns," as he calls them, aren't properly recognized. Asking for pencil and paper, he pens his last dispatch from Cuba, titled "Regulars Get No Glory," before Rea succeeds in getting him on a transport, the *City of Washington*, that will take him to a military hospital in Old Point Comfort, Virginia.

As he leaves the scene, Crane doesn't know he will be fired before the month is over. Don Carlos Seitz, business manager of the *World*, is the hatchet man. In his 1924 biography of Pulitzer, he'll assert that Crane filed only one dispatch of any merit (in reality, he'd sent more than twenty) and that one was the controversial account of the New York 71st's conduct at San Juan Hill.

Appearing in the *World* on July 18, filed from Jamaica the previous day, this story cast a more unfavorable light on the paper than it did on the 71st in the public's view--and the *Journal*'s. For years, the belief that Crane was the author appeared repeatedly in reputable accounts of these events, but in fact Crane never wrote it. When the dispatch was filed, Crane was lying ill in the Virginia hospital. The real culprit was his friend Scovel, who had strong opinions on the subject. There had been no by-line on the story; Crane had signed all his other war dispatches.

The firing was unique. Crane's bosses simply refused to

reimburse him for expenses; he got the point and quit. Joining the *Journal*, he was back in time to cover the Puerto Rico campaign. As it turned out, he had been misdiagnosed and didn't have yellow fever after all.

Meanwhile, back at the gates of Santiago, there's fever enough to spare. It's reached epidemic proportions in the V Corps. Only a week after the seizure of San Juan Heights, one regiment has lost 400 out of 900 men fit for duty. Buglers can't be found to blow their calls. By July 14, Captain Brown's command has only forty out of sixty-six fit and ready; two weeks later, only seventeen are able to answer roll call. When the black 24th Infantry is marched to Siboney, where many are to serve as hospital volunteers, only twenty-four are left standing. By this time, the surrender is under way, but some estimate only ten percent of the Army is fit to enforce it.

Official Washington tries to minimize this disaster at first, but when the boys return later on, Secretary Alger will reluctantly admit that ninety percent of the V Corps is either sick or convalescent. What a shock to those back home when they get their first look at the returning troops! One officer who weighed 170 is down to 80 pounds, and when he holds his hands to the light, they're transparent. Men no more than twenty-five years old look fifty. While the Army suffers only 345 deaths from battle, 5,462 are victims of fever, a 1:15 ratio.

Could this appalling toll have been avoided, or at least mitigated? As Linderman points out, the Marines prove it could have been. Isolated at Guantánamo, under the command of Lieutenant Colonel Robert W. Huntington, these men have survived ten weeks in a climate and on a terrain not much different than Santiago's, but they have only a two and one-half percent sick rate and no deaths.

That's because Huntington has insisted on following and enforcing the surgeon-general's orders about sanitation. Elsewhere, commanders have simply reflected the general attitude of Americans toward war: combat is the killer, and disease isn't even considered as the enemy it can be. Too late, people realize that proper supply and medical care would have greatly reduced these casualty figures.

In early July, Santiago is still standing in the way of relieving the V Corps's situation. Toral is defiant and rejects all demands for surrender. He has the same problem the higher authorities have been wrestling with--how to get out of this mess with a minimum loss of face. For his part, Shafter is aware of the mounting peril generated by delay, but malaria has left him weak and depressed. His recurring gout has so crippled him that he can scarcely get on his horse, even by means of the specially built platform constructed for him earlier. He has to wrap his foot in a gunnysack. He's obsessed with worry about the size of the Spanish garrison; he's been informed that García's negligent army has failed to prevent large reinforcements from reaching Santiago. He tells Washington that he can't consider attacking unless he has double the number of troops. In short, he's suffering from a failure of will as well as from gout.

In Washington they're already talking about replacing him. On July 4, McKinley begins discussions with his advisers about what to do with a command whose two ranking generals are disabled. The answer is to send General Nelson Miles, the Army's top commander, to take over. No one could be happier about this decision than Miles. He's been fiddling around in Washington, trying to organize an expedition to take Puerto Rico but not making much progress. He's been able to assemble an advance force of only 3,500 militia, who will follow him to Santiago. He's promised regulars, when Santiago falls.

Shafter is not getting much sympathy outside Washington either. Newspapers are full of stories about his physical problems, and the editorials are beginning to talk about "blunders." Consequently, everyone feels relieved at the news Miles will replace him. But when the general talks to reporters before he leaves, he disclaims any idea of replacement. Miles says he has genuine sympathy for Shafter's condition and has nothing but praise for his campaign. Could it be that the old Army boys are hanging together? On the day Miles arrives in Siboney, Shafter sends a terse message to Washington: "I am quite well." Translation: "I am not about to be replaced."

A more immediate problem is the inter-service rivalry and bad feeling between Shafter and Sampson, just when cooperation is needed. The day before the big battle, Shafter had sent Sampson a somewhat petulant demand for help, but the admiral still thought it too risky to try to force an entrance into the harbor, as Shafter wanted him to do. He made one concession. If Shafter was going to be insistent, he'd bring up some experts from Guantánamo and see if the channel could be cleared of mines, an offer the general simply ignored.

Next day the great naval battle interrupted this frustrating dialogue between the commanders, but on the following day, even before the smoke cleared, Shafter was on the cable to Washington, asserting that Sampson must use his entire fleet and force an entrance to the harbor, whatever the cost. Alger agreed, confidentially, but then he disclosed the addled condition of his mind by seriously suggesting to Shafter that he could shame the Navy by sending into the harbor a chartered steamer manned by Army officers, showing the way to Sampson. Talking to the President, Alger also charged that the Navy was dragging its feet. McKinley's answer was unhelpful; the two commanders should confer.

Of course they should, but Sampson is not about to put on his leggings and spurs again to make the trip to Sevilla. Instead, he directs his aide, Captain Chadwick, to act for him. So now it's Chadwick who puts on the spurs and makes the pilgrimage. Shafter greets him lying on a cot in a grove of trees near his tent. Chadwick offers a naval bombardment of Santiago, and Shafter agrees, without enthusiasm. He's never believed in bombardments, as we know. But Chadwick gets something from Shafter the Navy's never had before--a map of the city, showing the American positions outside it. When Shafter mentions his desire to have the Navy blast its way into the harbor, Chadwick points out that, since the waters of the channel are mined, Marines should be sent to capture the defenses at the harbor's mouth on the west side of the city, while Shafter's forces attack from the east.

Through the entire conversation, Shafter doesn't argue with Chadwick, doesn't appear to have much interest in what the Navy is doing, and sometimes seems not to be listening. To end the agony, Chadwick makes a half-hearted concession. Maybe he'll get some smaller ships to bring up the mines, he says, and takes his leave. The Army-Navy conference is, as usual, a failure.

Obviously, Washington is the only engine able to move these rivals off center, and a few days after the conference, McKinley orders the resumption of hostilities. The men in the rifle pits are delighted. They know nothing of diplomacy, but they've been profoundly irritated and affronted by the constant exchange of white truce flags. They hang out their own flags,

American ones, along the trenches, regardless of the fact that this move marks their positions clearly, and thus lays them open to enemy fire.

They're quite happy with their flags, fluttering along a five-mile front. When they see the white truce banners moving along the valley below them, they take them as a mockery of their vigilance, and scoff at them as another enemy. Some are reminded-so frequently are these truce flags exchanged-of the numerous editions of newspapers in large cities back home. "Is this the baseball edition coming out now, or is it an entry?" They yell in disdain.

The troops are ready to fight, not negotiate, so a cheer goes up on July 10 when the armistice expires and the latest Spanish truce flag starts to come down. Before it hits the ground, they open fire. The response is half-hearted and by dusk the exchange has stopped, but two more Americans are dead.

Meanwhile, the Navy begins bombarding late that afternoon, on into the early morning of July 11--not to accommodate Shafter, but because Washington has ordered it. A barrage of 8-inch shells from the *Brooklyn* and *Indiana* pour into the city, and then the *New York* joins in. A devastating fire descends on the helpless city from nine thirty-five until twelve forty-five, when the gunners knock off to get some sleep before resuming next morning. Santiago suffers severe property damage, and some inhabitants join the pathetic parade of refugees.

Shafter isn't willing to risk any more casualties, so the men in the rifle pits get no order to advance under cover of the bombardment. In fact, Shafter even has the gall to complain to Washington that Sampson didn't do what he asked, and even though another truce has been called, he insists that the Navy enter the harbor immediately.

Sampson isn't about to do anything of the kind, and he has the Navy Department's support. Don't risk any fighting ships, Long says. The Department isn't much interested in doing anything more for Shafter; its mind is on the Philippines now. The *Oregon* and the *Massachusetts* have already been detached and sent to Guantánamo, where Commodore Watson is organizing an expedition to the Pacific front. Long is also urging Sampson to relieve Dewey, keeping his priorities straight. Two days after the bombardment of Santiago, consequently, Sampson issues secret orders to get the squadron ready for a voyage to Manila.

When he hears about this move, Alger is upset. The Army in Cuba is being ignored, he declares, and the Navy and Sampson are defrauding the public. Many editorial writers share his opinion. They don't like Sampson either. But in the White House, tempers are flaring between Alger and Captain Mahan. They have a knock-down argument one day when Alger begins to denounce Sampson and Mahan "sailed into him," according to later reports, warning Alger that he isn't going to permit the Navy to be attacked in his presence. Secretary Long observes later: "It was a very pretty scrimmage. It rather pleased the President, who, I think, was glad of the rebuke." Alger later apologizes, but tensions aren't reduced. On the battlefield in Cuba, Shafter pointedly excludes Sampson from the negotiations with General Toral that are now resuming.

Shafter has been conducting these parleys pretty much on his own. Before the bombardment, he had warned Toral that his situation was hopeless, and if he didn't give in, the bombardment would begin. He gave the general time to cable Madrid, and Toral came back with a counteroffer. If the Americans let him and his troops go without an attack, he proposed, he was willing to give up Santiago and half the province as well.

Shafter and all his generals are willing to settle for that, but McKinley cables Shafter: "What you were sent to Santiago for was the Spanish Army. If you allow it to evacuate with its arms you must meet it somewhere else. This is not war." The only concession he'll make is to send the Spanish prisoners of war home at American expense. That leaves Shafter no alternative but to renew negotiations, which he feels better about because he's now dealing from strength, or so he believes. Heavy reinforcements have begun landing at Siboney. Miles's arrival is imminent, but Shafter isn't worried about that. He's also aware that influential officers like T.R. are accusing him of "incompetence and timidity," but he says it doesn't bother him. And if they're worried about his health, he insists, he never felt better except for his gout, as he informs General Adelbert Ames, who writes to his wife: "I found General Shafter sitting on a camp stool dressed in hickory shirt and a pair of blue trousers with a pair of dirty suspenders. One foot was swathed in a dirty white cloth. His immense abdomen hung down, yes, actually hung down between his legs. He was not a pleasing object in either figure or face."

Miles arrives and agrees with Ames about Shafter's condition, but he's far more concerned about the health of the troops. Three cases of yellow fever at the Siboney hospital have been diagnosed just before his arrival. Thinking the building must be infected, Miles orders it burned, but that only creates a new problem--what to do with the displaced patients.

George Kennan says that the Army has neglected to apply chloride of lime to the privies overflowing behind Siboney's houses. The village, in fact, is redolent and no one seems inclined to clean it up, much less disinfect it. Whatever health regulations exist aren't being enforced. On the beach, homeless Cuban refugees are living on the sand, going into the bushes to relieve themselves and throwing on the ground what food they don't eat. In a pond behind the village, the decaying remains of a mule pollutes the stagnant water. No wonder there are more than thirty cases of fever already in Siboney.

Sanitation is even worse in the rifle pits, where it's impossible to carry out such measures in any case. Flies and mosquitoes feast on more dead mules lying on the slopes, and the stench is nearly intolerable. It's easy to see why the troops would rather go into battle than rot in this place. Even the simplest actions are perilous. When soldiers are thirsty they can't wait to boil their water, which comes from streams still stinking with human and animal bodies.

To add to everyone's discomfort, the summer rains begin again on July 11, and tropical storms sweep the trenches day after day, creating more misery there and new problems at Siboney, where it's much more dangerous to unload transports, and getting their cargoes inland is nearly impossible because what pass for roads are small muddy rivers. Even when supplies get through, there's no shelter for them on the firing line.

It may be some consolation to know that the Spaniards are feeling just as desperate at this point. General Linares is ill in bed himself, but he manages to cable Madrid: "Our troops are exhausted and sickly in an alarming proportion. Cannot be brought to the hospital--needing them in trenches. Cattle without fodder or hay. Soldiers without permanent shelter. The only food rice, and not much of that. Our losses were very heavy. Unfortunately, the situation is desperate. The surrender is imminent, otherwise we will only gain time to prolong our agony. The honor of arms has its limits."

The problem for the Spaniards is still how to get out of Cuba with honor, so the negotiations continue. Shafter is willing to help, but he's getting no support from Washington. On July 12, he urges the President to accept Toral's earlier offer to withdraw, but in the early hours of July 13, a reply comes back from McKinley: emphatically no. Later that day, however, Miles makes the same plea and that's a different matter. McKinley calls a Cabinet meeting to discuss the problem. There was something in Miles's message that he hadn't known before. Shafter had hinted at serious illness in the Army, but Miles urgently confirms it. If negotiations aren't concluded very soon, it's clear, the victory of those brave men (and future voters) will be lost. On the other hand, only total surrender is going to justify the lives already lost in this war, to say nothing of the expense.

McKinley and his men are also well aware of a rising tide of public anxiety. Details of the battles on San Juan Heights, delayed by military censorship and heavy cable traffic, are coming in to be splashed over front pages. Some correspondents are returning on hospital ships, and for the first time, people are beginning to understand what their sons and husbands have been enduring, and what dangers they're still in. The reporters haven't spared Shafter, since he's never spared *them*, and it's becoming clearer every day what an incredibly botched war this has been from the start, and continues to be. Some uncensored telegrams are also coming through, disclosing the ravages fever is inflicting on the V Corps.

Supporters of the Administration may call the correspondents bringing back these dismal reports "natural allies of the war party in Madrid," but the truth is coming out in a flood. Miles himself has informed the President that there are already 100 cases of yellow fever, and the surgeons tell him it will reach epidemic proportions unless the Army is removed quickly.

But Washington isn't talking yet about removing the Army, although plans have been approved for its disposal after the surrender. The President and his men know how the public reacts when it's even rumored that troops might be recalled--without a victory. Further delay seems intolerable, but both the President and the Cabinet are determined not to let the Spaniards get away on easy terms. Miles is told once more to demand total surrender, and if he's refused, to order an assault--that is, if he thinks the Army is in any condition to bring it off successfully.

Miles asks Toral to meet him between the lines, and at noon at July 13, he and Shafter talk with the Spanish general. At first it looks as though they're going to get nowhere. Miles tells the general he's prepared to bring in 50,000 more men, and insists that the American terms for surrender are liberal, except that it must be unconditional. Toral says he *can't* surrender. Spanish law forbids it as long as he has ammunition and food, however scanty. Otherwise, he's required to maintain Spanish honor.

At this point, Miles gets a little testy about it. He assures Toral that the United States has done everything it can to preserve Spanish honor, and if he doesn't surrender now, he will have to face the consequences, which are going to be dreadful. He can have until daylight the next morning to make up his mind. He can't do that, Toral protests desperately. He has to talk it over with Madrid before he can give an answer. All right, Miles says, make it tomorrow noon then.

The deadline arrives and Toral says, very well, he's prepared to surrender but he hasn't been able to get Madrid's approval yet. Fair enough, Miles says, but he's going to insist on the terms already laid down. He renews the promise that Spanish troops will be repatriated by the United States. Does that include the entire command? Toral inquires.

This brings up a question the Americans have wanted to resolve for some time--just how big *is* his command? Toral provides the surprising answer readily: 11,500 men in Santiago, 2,000 more at Guantánamo, 3,500 in San Luis, and maybe 1,500 others in the interior within a twenty-five- or thirty-mile radius. This is considerably more than the Americans thought, and Shafter is happy to see that they're all going to be included. "I was absolutely thunderstruck," he says later, "that of their own free will, they should give me 12,000 men that were beyond my reach."

It takes two more days of negotiations, full of misunderstandings and exasperating delays, before the deal is made. At one point, discouraged, Shafter cables Washington: "We may have to fight them yet." But at last the documents are duly signed and the ceremony of surrender is set for Sunday,

July 17.

Toral gets more out of it than he may have expected. He's pleaded with passion for a token surrender and the honors of war, and the peace negotiators at last agree to let the Spaniards return home with their arms. That makes it a "capitulation," not a "surrender," and Spanish honor is saved. The agreement also has some other articles reflecting what Leech calls "verbal concessions to the chivalry of Spain." On the other hand, the Americans now have all of Toral's troops and all of the eastern half of Oriente Province immediately, with the remainder of Cuba to follow.

So we're ready for the grand spectacle of Santiago's fall, whether capitulation or surrender doesn't matter to the Americans. Something else matters to Shafter. He wants this ceremony to be a tribute to him and the troops, especially to himself, and he isn't going to invite all those people who have opposed him or given him trouble. That includes, first of all, the Cuban Army of Liberation, which has considered itself an ally of the United States until this moment. Shafter won't permit them to enter the city for the ceremonies, nor, as it turns out, any other time.

The press--particularly the press--isn't invited either. Shafter makes it clear that not only are they unwelcome, but he tells one of them that they will "goddamned never" be allowed inside the city if he can prevent it. Beyond them, the uninvited also include Sampson. Shafter has already snubbed him. The admiral had to make an official request before he could get a copy of the articles of capitulation, and when they came, Shafter had written on them, "for your information."

At the last minute, on Sunday morning, after he's insulted everyone, Shafter changes his mind and issues invitations, although he's careful to see that by the time Sampson and Chadwick get theirs it will be too late for them to arrive on time. As for the correspondents, they don't take Shafter seriously. More than a hundred of them are getting ready to follow the troops into the city that Sunday morning, like it or not. Shafter had issued a handful of passes to reporters he thought were relatively guiltless, notably George Clarke Musgrave, a British reporter who has spent the past year in Cuba. But Musgrave says this kind of discrimination is unfair and refuses to join the party.

Among the others who are coming, invited or not, is Harry

Scovel, still weak but in motion again. After the ceremony is over, he's planning to follow Miles on the Puerto Rico expedition. George Rea is with him, and he's preparing to sail for the Philippines. Some of the correspondents are in poor physical shape, and all of them are exhausted. During the past four months, Scovel has lost fifty pounds. He's bothered by intermittent attacks of nausea, and in the two days before the entry, he gets only four hours of sleep.

Capitulation Sunday begins as a beautiful morning, with religious services held on San Juan Hill, after which General Wheeler, recovering from his fever, makes the formal announcement of surrender. Shafter gets his gouty foot in the stirrup and is hoisted onto his large horse for the ride to the ceremony. His mount creaks along between lines of jubilant troops, and behind ride the divisional commanders and their staffs, plus a troop of mounted cavalry--the only one Shafter possesses at this point.

The American officers ride to a large field just outside Santiago and there they meet General Toral and an honor guard of a hundred men. Shafter rides up to him and presents him with the sword and spurs retrieved from the body of General Del Rey, the Spanish hero of El Caney, and Toral's guard presents arms. In the city, the Spanish flag is lowered--after three hundred and eighty-three years of colonial rule. At the meeting field, the Americans present arms as the Spaniards file away to the left and return to the city, where all the troops lay down their arms temporarily at the arsenal.

Now we're ready for the triumphal entry. The Americans ride in columns of twos, Shafter and Wheeler in the lead, followed by all the others in order of rank. It's quite an educational trip, this entry. Wheeler describes it later: "As we rode for the first time into Santiago, we were struck by the excellent manner in which the Spanish lines were entrenched, and more especially by the formidable defenses with which they had barricaded roads."

Barbed-wire entanglements on the road, he recalls, look like "nothing so much as a huge thick spider's web with an enormous mass in the center. Behind this some ten or fifteen feet were barrels of an extraordinarily large size, filled with sand, stones and concrete. It would indeed have been a hard task for American troops, were they ever so brave and courageous, to have taken a city by storm which was protected by defences such as these." Noting them as he rides, Shafter considers himself an extremely lucky man. And there's an extra bonus. If he'd tried to storm the city on July 2 and succeeded, the prisoner bag would have been only 8,000. Now nearly 25,000 are going to fall into his enormous lap.

The actual entry turns out to be just as sloppy as the war itself. These conquerors have to break ranks to get around the barbed wire and sandbags so the line of march becomes disorganized and never gets itself together again.

One element is missing from the parade. It's García and his men, who feel they have every right to be there. Shafter disinvited the rebel general at first, but when he reversed himself at the last minute, García swallowed his pride and, with an honor guard, rides toward the city. Before he can get there, he encounters a road block. A private dressed in the uniform of the 1st Volunteer Cavalry--that is, the Rough Riders--stops him, pulls a pistol from his belt and aims it at García's head. This young man is one of T.R.'s protégés, Edwin Emerson, Jr., who had been sworn in by Roosevelt just a few days before. His first assignment is this road block and he intends to carry out orders.

"You'll have to turn back," he tells the general. "I have orders not to permit any Cuban soldiers to enter the city."

Emerson will say later that it was only coincidence that he happened to be there, it wasn't some dark plot by T.R., Shafter, or anyone else, and he will also claim that he didn't recognize García, but it doesn't help. The final insult has been given. Deeply humiliated, García rides back to headquarters, and some time later, sends off a letter to Gómez, resigning his command. He's had enough of the Americans. Then he tells his officers that the war isn't over. They should keep on fighting against this "army of the intervention."

In Santiago, the troops amble rather than march to the governor's palace, where Shafter has organized what he believes is going to be a rather fancy occasion. All the city officials turn out to meet the conquerors, including the foreign consuls. Thousands of inhabitants have gathered in the plaza to watch the surrender--pardon, the capitulation--ceremonies. As the clock in the cathedral tower strikes noon, the American flag is about to be raised. But not without a final, bizarre incident.

Captain McKittrick, Shafter's son-in-law, has been given

the honor of hoisting the flag, with the help of General Wheeler's son and Shafter's ever present loyal aide, Lieutenant Miley. An interested spectator is Harry Scovel, who, in the spirit of the occasion, even gives Miley, who doesn't recognize him, a boost onto a projection where he'll be in a better position to see the actual flag raising.

Scovel himself, notebook in hand, is determined to get the best possible view of the ceremony, so he slips around the side of the palace, where he's only thirty feet from the flagstaff, and climbs a tree. Those in the front of the building can't see him, but his head and shoulders are above the roofline. General Wheeler notices him, though, bows in his direction and smiles. McKittrick, standing near Wheeler, follows the direction of the general's salute and observes Scovel.

"Who is that man?" he demands.

Scovel answers for himself, calling down his name. Hearing it, recognition dawns on Lieutenant Miley and he glowers. "Get down from there," he orders.

Scovel, who has hoisted himself onto the roof for a better view, climbs back into the tree, but that's not good enough for Miley, who apparently wanted him to flutter down on wings.

"There's a man up here on the roof and he won't get down," Miley yells, inaccurately.

Shafter hears him. "Then throw him down," he orders.

Scovel is already down and stands there while the flag goes up, a 21-gun salute resounds, and the 6th Cavalry's band plays "Hail Columbia," followed by the inevitable "Star-Spangled Banner," as the 9th Infantry presents arms to the colors. The troops still in the rifle pits, now lined up by regiments, can see the flag ascend, and they begin cheering.

Shafter's officers line up to give him formal congratulations, while Scovel, only a few feet away, joins George Rea and some other correspondents. With the flag up, the celebration seems to be falling apart, since nothing else has been planned, so a reporter from the New York *Sun* suggests that Shafter permit the troops to cheer the flag, an odd request in itself. A few reporters think so too, and they mutter a few sarcastic "good ideas" while Shafter tells McKittrick to give the order, but he hesitates. He seems to think his father-in-law isn't being given sufficient recognition.

"Three cheers for General Shafter," he calls out. A dutiful

but weak response comes from the men, and some are even seen to smirk and nudge one another. Shafter can't help noticing and he looks grim.

This is the moment Scovel chooses to make one of the biggest mistakes in his life. Carried away by the spirit of the occasion, and believing that bygones are bygones, he approaches Shafter, meaning to apologize. He starts to explain that he was the man on the roof but had meant no harm. Shafter wheels on him and interrupts.

"You son-of-a-bitch," he says, "you and all your tribe are goddamned nuisances."

Scovel, shocked, says the first thing that comes to mind. "You shouldn't use such language to me, sir."

With that, Shafter takes a swing at him, a move he will later refer to as "a flamboyant gesture of dismissal." Some gesture. The blow strikes Scovel in the face, knocks off his hat, and he staggers a bit before he does what comes naturally and swings back.

"You!" he shouts. "A Major General of the United States Army! You ought to be ashamed of yourself."

Shafter explodes. His voice is ordinarily high-pitched but now it's a hysterical scream: "Let no one see that man. Let no one speak to him."

Scovel describes later what followed: "Next thing I knew, about 281 Marines were all over me. For the first time since I came to Cuba, I was really scared."

In the idiom of a later day, it's déjà vu all over again for Scovel that night. He's sitting in a Cuban jail. He hears first that Shafter wants him shot, but next morning he learns that wiser heads have prevailed and the general is going to drop the charges. He's released and an Army tug takes him to Siboney, where he's put on a transport bound for New York.

The extraordinary thing about this incident is that more than a hundred correspondents are witnesses and not one writes a word about it. What kind of professional loyalty is this--not to mention that it's a news story of some consequence? Well, they tell themselves, it's true Shafter has come off very badly in this affair, but to write about it seems unpatriotic in the hour of triumph.

There's one exception. Thomas F. Millard, a *Herald* reporter, wasn't there but he hears about it next day from Shafter and McKittrick, and files a story that is most uncomplimentary to Scovel. Consequently, when Harry reaches New York, he's fired; like Crane, he's another victim of internal politics. But Millard's story is picked up joyfully by the anti-interventionist press as an example of the evils of yellow journalism.

Scovel's chief defender is Davis, who is so outraged by Shafter's conduct that he spends his time while he's traveling to Puerto Rico writing a dispatch characterizing Shafter as a "self-promoting incompetent," and goes so far as to call him a coward and a bully. For the first time in his life, Davis is censored by his own paper. The *Herald* refuses to print his story. Nothing is going to save Shafter, however, nor his conduct of the war. Only two months after the ceremony at Santiago, the papers are full of exposés.

Scovel also acquires an unlikely supporter in the aftermath. Pulitzer, who's become a full-fledged anti-imperialist, assembles the facts on the Scovel incident and invites him to write a letter to the editor, relating how it really happened, an account syndicated across the country, swinging public opinion back to Scovel, as editorials testify.

In the wake of Santiago, the rejection of García is also bearing bitter fruit. Shafter has forbidden all armed insurgents to enter the city, and he rubs it in by telling García the Spanish authorities in Santiago are going to remain in charge until the Americans can replace them. Shafter doesn't see why García can't understand and accept this move (the general hasn't yet resigned). "I explained this to him fully," he complains, "that we were at war with Spain, and that the question of Cuban independence could not be considered by me." The embittered García takes his troops, leads them back into the interior, and refuses to have anything to do with Shafter.

Ironically, in the days after the surrender, it's the Cubans who seem to be replacing the Spaniards as the enemy. Shafter and Lawton are convinced they're a threat to American control. On August 6, Lawton warns the War Department: "Definite instructions as to policy to be observed toward the Cuban Army should be given. These people will maintain their organization, are scattered through the country in the vicinity of the city, are threatening in their attitude, and keep the inhabitants stirred up and panicky by threats and acts of violence." Shafter's opinion of Cubans is lower than ever. These people won't disband and they won't go to work, he says, and so they'll have to live by robbery. "A dual government can't exist here," he concludes. "We have got to have full sway of the Cubans."

McKinley doesn't give the generals much sympathy. He reminds them that the United States is responsible for peace and quiet in conquered Cuba, and the insurgents must be treated fairly. But they must recognize that the war is over, McKinley continues in his high-level, unrealistic way, and they must recognize American military authority. He instructs Lawton to acquaint the rebel leaders with these decrees, and then, in one sentence, gets to the heart of the matter: "Interference from any quarter will not be permitted."

Soon after, Wood appoints Lawton commander of Santiago Province, with his headquarters in the city. García comes to him there, demanding work and rations for his men. Lawton reports: "I told him they could have neither, while they remained under arms." In that case, García replies, it's war. When Wood hears this, he says, "The sooner the better," and adds, "because, as we had taken a mean job on our hands, that might be the best way out of it." These sentiments are conveyed to García and he backs away from any talk of war, more deeply angry than ever.

Before the troops can be moved out, they develop an intense hatred of Cubans, which is not simple bias but pure racism. Crane puts it simply after San Juan: "Both officers and men have the most lively contempt for the Cubans. They despise them." Crane himself isn't free of this hostility. One of his stories has charged that García's men stayed in the rear and wouldn't fight, instead stealing from the soldiers and eating up supplies. By the time Santiago falls, there's general agreement that Cubans won't fight and they won't work, they're no damn good and to hell with them.

All this is grossly unfair, as historian David Healey points out. In reality, they had been more than useful on several occasions. They had covered the American landings, and acted as scouts and guides, a service acknowledged by grateful letters from both Lawton and General Ludlow. Humiliating to them as it must have been, they did a great deal of carrying and digging when it was most needed. They had bottled up 8,000 Spanish regulars in Holguín, seventy miles northwest of Santiago, and prevented them from entering the city, in spite of Shafter's belief to the contrary. A thousand of them helped Marines hold

6,000 Spanish troops on Guantánamo.

So why is everyone ready to ignore these substantial contributions? It's easy enough to see why the troops feel the way they do. With them, it's not simple racism entirely, although that's a large part of it. But they also believe that, for them, the war consisted chiefly of the battles on San Juan Heights, where the Cuban contribution was minimal. Then, too, there's the fear and loathing of people who are not like us. Our men see dirty, ragged soldiers who are always begging, always hungry. When García, who knows more about American history than the average American soldier, points out that much of George Washington's army was in the same condition, and was despised by the British, they just shrug. They know more mythology than reality about the American past. Racism raises its ugly head when Southerners and Westerners see that there's a large representation of black soldiers in the Cuban army.

A correspondent from the *Manchester Guardian* sums it all up neatly: "The fact is that the United States Army made the very old mistake of judging the allies by its own standards." They don't understand guerrilla warfare any more than the Spanish regulars did. And most of all, from many generals and high officials on down to the men in the rifle pits, the Cubans are held to be inferior people. Six months after the war is over, here's Shafter, talking to reporters in Savannah, and saying in answer to a question: "Self-government? Why, these people are no more fit for self-government than gun-powder is for hell."

Meanwhile, as the war ebbs away after surrender, the War Department faces a monumental job. It has to evacuate two armies. Spanish prisoners have to be sent home, while the American troops must not only be taken out but occupation forces must be sent in to replace them, a double load to contend with when shipping is severely short and the large problems of sanitary conditions and sickness are yet to be faced. Shafter is particularly devoted to helping the Spanish prisoners. As Leech tells us, he "took an instant liking to these tractable men." His chief task is to protect them from García's troops, who would like to kill them all before they can get away. When Washington inquires how Shafter is doing with the problems of his own men, he's evasive. He says he'll move those in the rifle pits three miles back from Santiago, but he can't move any more until the Spanish prisoners leave.

By this time, the only word for Shafter's behavior is insubordination. The surgeon general's office is much concerned about preventing a serious yellow fever epidemic and urges the War Department to move all the troops it can up into the mountains, away from the truly desperate conditions below. But when this order is conveyed to Shafter, he flatly refuses to follow it. Without saying as much, in so many words, he makes it clear he's not moving *anyone* to higher altitudes. Meanwhile, the lists of men stricken with fever get longer every day. When the War Department presses him, Shafter says these are mild cases, not to worry.

In Santiago, now an American-ruled city, everything is lovely, if you can believe the upbeat stories being filed by the correspondents. Unbelievably, these reporters who were so hostile to Shafter just the other day now seem to back him in the controversy about what to do with the troops. Is this spurious patriotism once more? Their stories speak of troops moved to the mountains (although none are), Siboney's dirty huts burned, clean white tents around the hospitals, fever patients isolated. Like Shafter, they belittle the severity of the burgeoning fever epidemic. Look at the Marines on Guantánamo, they say, see how healthy these men are--for reasons we've already discovered. So the folks back home are lulled into believing conditions are normal. Only Shafter's officers refuse to endorse what he's doing and saying.

As always, someone leaks the truth--not a reporter, but Charles Dick, the President's old friend and political aide, a lieutenant colonel in the 8th Ohio. On July 25, he writes a personal letter to McKinley, speaking for himself and his fellow officers. He says there's an "appalling situation" in Cuba. If Shafter doesn't get these troops out right away, he declares, no one knows what may happen when the yellow fever season really develops in late summer. Don't delay a moment, he pleads. Dick tells the President he's been unable to contain himself because his heart bleeds for these troops. The true story of the Santiago campaign, he concludes, will constitute one of the most shameful pages in our history.

Dick and the other officers are reaching a point of desperation because of Shafter's stonewalling. Every day they see the awful and dangerous conditions of the camps and hospitals, watch those still alive and well trying to subsist on short rations of fat bacon or hardtack, or canned beef which is often wormy. There's a rising tide of resentment among these men about how they're being treated. They want to go home, not to Siboney, an assignment they look upon as a death sentence. Those who survive tell their comrades about life and death in the hospitals--men tossing about helplessly on the ground, those lucky enough to recover too weak to pitch a tent. Yet it's these same troops that the War Department wants to march off to the mountains.

They just don't get it back in Washington. McKinley doesn't have Dick's letter until August 12, eight days after he sent it. For public consumption, he declares: "Our occupation should be as free from severity as possible," and the editorial writers praise him. Public opinion shares the contempt for Cubans evident everywhere in the American establishment. Nothing is said about their terrible poverty, which isn't going to end when the Americans leave, nor of the many years they've endured foreign rule, nor their simple devotion to the cause of freedom, to which they believed their American allies were equally devoted. Nor, for that matter, is anything being said about the fact that the Spanish prisoners are getting much more supplies from the commissary than American soldiers. That only adds to the general hatred, but Shafter insists his men are so friendly with the prisoners he can scarcely keep them apart.

But the truth continues to seep out, accelerated when the transports begin to bring men home. The trip itself is an ordeal not much water and sometimes it's undrinkable. Food is so bad sick men can't digest it, and sometimes can't even swallow it. Two returning ships, the *Seneca* and the *Concho*, themselves rotten with the complaints of old age, carry such pitiful cargoes they get the public's attention at last. The *Seneca* has more than a hundred badly wounded men, most of whom were in the charge at San Juan Hill. They tell of being packed into a hole almost without air, and left there with no one to care for them. When the *Concho* arrives, it disgorges another lot of half-starved and neglected men stricken with malaria.

The pressure is too much. The War Department begins at once to make plans for evacuating the V Corps, except for a cavalry division Shafter claims is healthy enough to stay. He's beginning to wake up. On August 2, he tells Washington that a yellow fever epidemic is imminent--it's already happening, in fact--and advises that all the troops be moved as soon as possible.

What about those Spanish prisoners he's so fond of? the War Department wants to know. Their transports haven't even arrived, and only one American replacement regiment has disembarked. Alger thinks Shafter is being unreasonable to demand immediate action now, when there are simply not enough ships available for such a large operation. In any case, the rest camp at Montauk Point isn't ready to take even a cavalry regiment, much less the entire army. All right, says Alger, the surgeon general has assured him you can't get yellow fever at high altitudes, so he renews his offer to move the men to the mountains.

What Shafter hasn't told him about his sudden change of mind is that he's just found out that, even if he moves the men, it won't save them. No matter what the surgeon general may believe, the mountains are no refuge from fever and camps there can't be made suitable anyway. Shafter hasn't been paying much attention to his army, preoccupied with the prisoners as he has been, and when he takes a good look, he realizes that he's seeing a shadow of what was once a spirited and eager collection of men. He hastens to root out and disperse bits of good food, camp equipment and medicine which surprisingly turn up, but it's the old story-too late. These soldiers can't go anywhere but home.

What to do? Shafter does what he should have done before. He calls a meeting of his commanding and medical officers in the governor's palace, which is now his headquarters. The officers are ready for him. At T.R.'s instigation, they've prepared the famous round-robin letter to Shafter, really intended for the eyes of the War Department. It virtually demands the withdrawal of the entire army, asserts that a mountain camp is impossible, reports the prevalence of malaria, and warns that a severe yellow fever epidemic can be expected any time. The tone of the letter is threatening, even dictatorial, but it's signed by all the divisional and brigade commanders, nine generals, and a colonel. General Lawton is the only holdout. He doesn't like the "mandatory language," and thinks the illnesses are mostly caused by "homesickness and other depressing influences."

Under such pressure, Shafter has no alternative but to present the War Department with the facts he's been withholding, and Washington learns for the first time that he is presiding over "an army of convalescents" who can only be saved if they're transported home at once. Any delay will mean that very few can be moved. Alger and the other officials are horrified. Evacuation of all but the yellow fever cases is ordered immediately. A small force will be left to maintain authority until replacements arrive.

Washington has something else to worry about. Negotiations for a peace treaty are about to get under way, and if the Spaniards find out they're dealing with a crippled enemy, the negotiating won't be easy.

That means rigid censorship, but Alger hasn't reckoned with the enterprise of the correspondents still in Santiago. One of them, an Associated Press reporter, somehow obtains a copy of the round-robin letter, and on August 4, it's published in full. He also gets T.R.'s letter, and those at home learn from Roosevelt's own pen that the Rough Riders are "so weakened and shattered as to be ripe for dying like rotten sheep." T.R. wants to save these men from "a doom as fearful as it is unnecessary and undeserved."

When he reads these revelations in the evening papers, McKinley becomes "very much excited and indignant," as Leech says, because this is the war's worst indiscretion. Since the peace discussions are in full swing, it also couldn't have come at a worse time. What a revelation it's going to be for the losers! Plainly the Americans aren't capable of holding what they've won if the Spaniards want to dispute it, and in the bargain their Army's officers are openly insubordinate. From the Administration's viewpoint, the whole thing has become a political nightmare. So the negotiations plod on in the midst of an uproar never seen before in such parleys when the victors are presumably in a position to dictate the terms.

Informed readers of Ambrose Bierce's column are inclined to agree with him when he writes on August 2, under the heading "A Freak War": "Of all wars concerning which we have knowledge--and history is mainly a narrative of wars--none has been distinguished by so many odd features as this one of ours. If in the opera bouffe the sovereign of Novagonia, whom their wicked rulers were starving, were to undertake their deliverance by a strict blockade of the country, we should call it great fun. The notion of 'starving out' the oppressors, with all the resources of the country at their command, in order to succor their landless and penniless victims, would nimbly and sweetly recommend itself unto our gentle sense of humor. Yet that is what we (without a smile) have done to our Cuban reconcentrados.

"In both Cuba and the Philippines--we are confronted with a possibility that is as droll as anything known on the stage. At Manila, indeed, it is more than a possibility; it has the imminence of a reasonable expectation. All signs foreshadow the necessity of an alliance with those whom we want to conquer against those whom we want to aid."

Ah, yes--Manila and the Philippines. Those in Cuba have been too busy to think about these islands, but the planners in Washington are already preparing to write another ugly chapter in the story of America's imperialism. First, however, there's Puerto Rico to take care of--and the problem of how to get the troops home from Cuba Libre, American-style. One thing at a time.

9

PUERTO RICO: A POSTSCRIPT

WHEN THE EXPEDITIONARY FORCE SAILS FROM
Guantánamo Bay on July 21, with intent to subdue Puerto Rico,
the happiest man aboard is Nelson Miles, its commander. A few
more days in Cuba and the general might have exploded from
sheer frustration.

Some of it, of course, can be attributed to his obsession
with yellow fever. An arbitrary man to begin with, Miles has
exceeded mere caution in preparing for this invasion. When he
learned the number of cases already existing in Siboney, he
refused to permit any of the regulars in Cuba to sail with him.
He'll go with a few thousand volunteers, he declares. Fresh
troops are arriving from Tampa and Charleston, but he won't let
them disembark to breathe the infectious Cuban air; the ships
will have to stay well out to sea.

Miles is almost paralyzed by his fear of the fever. He won't
use any of the transports that have carried back home soldiers
infected with malaria or dysentery, nor will he have objects of
any kind on his ship that might have been exposed to Cuban air.
His obsession will later make him highly unpopular with his
men when paymasters from Santiago arrive in Puerto Rico after
the landing, and Miles won't permit this possibly infected
money to be distributed because he's heard that two men on the
ship fell ill on the way. He demands and gets new paymasters
and new bills sent from clean old New York. To cap it all, Miles
orders malarial and feverish Siboney burned to the ground, creating new problems for Shafter.

Aside from his obsession, however, Miles has behaved
well during his brief stay in Cuba, doing his best to save
Shafter's face. To help him in this endeavor, Shafter has treated him like a visitor, one who is there "more in an advisory
character," as he puts it. Miles goes along with it, sending
back complimentary reports, not intruding in the surrender

discussions with Toral, even leaving the parleys before they're concluded.

Virtue is not rewarded. Back in Siboney, he gets a message from Shafter purporting to explain his instructions from Alger, but the message implies that he and Alger are working together and Miles, commander-in-chief of the Army, is not much more than a bystander. That convinces Miles he's the victim of a conspiracy between Shafter and the War Department, and he pulls rank on everybody. No one's going to subordinate *him*. He prepares to leave for Puerto Rico at once, with or without orders from Washington, sending terse messages to both Sampson and the War Department that he's leaving as soon as possible.

When Alger gets this cable, he and McKinley are aghast at what they believe is sheer folly. They haven't even assembled a proper army and the ships to carry them. Alger cables Miles to come back to Washington, or else establish a base in eastern Cuba and await reinforcements. Miles simply ignores the order, which seems to be a not uncommon course to take in the upper echelons of the armed services these days. He's determined to assemble the few thousand volunteers he already possesses, plus whatever artillery hasn't been unloaded from the ships in Santiago Bay, and set off for Puerto Rico. He'll organize after he gets there.

To carry out this plan, however, he's going to need help from the Navy and so he goes off to Guantánamo Bay for a consultation with Sampson. The admiral is busy. He's preparing to transport his squadrons from Cuba to the Philippines and he already has orders to take all the armor-clads with him. Two of them--armed auxiliary cruisers--are in the general's hands and Miles is not prepared to unload the troops waiting on them.

Sampson is confused by the onslaught of this sudden summer storm and doesn't understand that Miles wants support on a far more substantial scale than the admiral is prepared to provide. The cables are flying back and forth between Guantánamo Bay and Washington, where Alger feels that he has to defend Miles and succeeds in convincing McKinley that he has to put some pressure on Sampson to cooperate. The President agrees. He orders the Philippine expedition put on hold temporarily and tells Sampson he must support the Puerto Rico invasion.

So at last the expedition gets under way: 3,415 men, with artillery, two companies of engineers and one from the Signal Corps. They are carried by nine transports, convoyed by the *Massachusetts* and two Ivy League small vessels, the *Yale* and *Columbia*. This force is going to face 8,223 Spanish regulars and 9,107 volunteers, who haven't heard any news about surrender. Miles intends to land at Fajardo, on the northeast end of Puerto Rico, forty miles from the capital city, San Juan, where the island's only fortress is still in Spanish hands.

Getting there isn't even half the fun. In spite of all Miles's precautions, there is typhoid aboard the ships. The decks are filthy, and there's too little fresh water. Ignoring these uncomfortable facts, a correspondent from the Chicago *Record* reports: "It was like being set free from prison to leave the harbor of Guantánamo. We passed slowly along the northern coast of Haiti, running at night without lights so as to make our coming entirely unexpected, and on the early morning of July 25, a serene, beautiful day, we made directly for the port of Guánica."

Why not Fajardo, as planned? Miles had hoped to deceive the Spaniards by landing there, but when he neared this port, he learned that the launches and lighters he needs to land haven't caught up with him yet, so he shifts to the safer harbor of Guánica, where he believes landing craft will be available. Guánica is near Ponce, at the opposite end of the island from San Juan, but that fits the general's plan. He's convinced himself that it will be good for the troops to march cross-country to San Juan because it will have a pacifying effect on the inhabitants. It doesn't occur to him that the mountainous terrain might produce another San Juan Heights on a different island.

There's just one more little problem. Miles is landing at a point exactly opposite from the place where his reinforcements are headed, and they're unaware of it. Correspondents, learning of the change, disembark from their press tug following the expedition fleet and use the cable station at St. Thomas, then a part of the Danish West Indies, to report the change of course.

More consternation in Washington. When Alger hears of this alteration, he uses the same station to ask frantically: "Why did you change?" Miles gives him a curt reply: "I deemed it advisable," and he adds, "Spaniards surprised." Not any more than Alger, who gives up. Later, Miles finds out that his switch was a lucky one. The Spaniards had intercepted cable messages and knew he was planning to land at Fajardo, where they had prepared a nasty surprise for him.

As far as that goes, no one is sure about Guánica just yet. The *Record*'s man reports: "Not knowing just what might be ahead, we went in fighting shape, the crews standing at their stations by their guns, which were trained, loaded and ready to fire. The saucy *Gloucester* ran ahead of us into the little harbor, flying an enormous American flag at her topmast, without stopping to inquire about batteries or torpedoes."

In fact, there's no opposition. The *Gloucester* sends twenty-eight men ashore in a cutter, and they deploy to cover the beach. Since no one appears, they haul down the Spanish flag and send up the American emblem instead. That brings the first fire, a desultory volley from the underbrush, which injures no one. Quickly, the men build a wall across the only highway leading out of the village and station one of the new Colt guns there as an outpost. Fortunately, there's a large lighter in the harbor and Miles uses it to begin landing his troops from the transports. When the enemy fire is resumed, the *Gloucester* opens up with her guns and the enemy vanishes.

The engineers land first and move inland, leaving a few men behind to construct a pier. Miles himself circles around in his launch, offering help by picking up pontoons for the task. Ten more lighters have been discovered by this time, and so the troops are able to disembark quickly. Davis, who's already on the scene, reports that in only a few hours 2,000 men of the Illinois Volunteer Infantry and the 6th Massachusetts are encamped along the village street. Guánica's residents have already emerged from the bush to which they had fled and are busy selling horses to the American invaders.

Davis reports: "The volunteers made themselves at home on the doorsteps of the village, and dandled the naked yellow [!] babies on their knees." There's a skirmish at the outpost next morning, but the boys from Massachusetts make quick work of it. Another alarm sounds in the evening, but it proves to be false.

"To those of us who had just come from Santiago," Davis writes, "the sight of the women sitting on porches and rocking in bent-wood chairs, the lighted swinging lamps with cut-glass pendants, and the pictures and mirrors on the walls which we saw that night through the open doors as we rode out to the pickets, seemed a part of some long forgotten existence."

The present existence is lively enough for everyone. That night some stray mules wandering the hills look like Spaniards to the sentries at the farthest outposts and they fire on them. There are no casualties among the mules but some stray bullets fall on the transport where General Miles is sleeping, and on another ship sheltering some Red Cross nurses. Whether this is "friendly fire" or not depends on who's under it. The nurses, as Davis reports, are "delighted at being under fire, even though the fire came from the 6th Illinois." Not so the commander. "From remarks made the next morning by General Miles," says Davis, "he did not seem to share in their delight."

There's some more skirmishing the next day, in which the Massachusetts and Illinois men take a hill and send some Spanish cavalry galloping away, with no casualties, while the Spaniards lose eight killed and several more wounded. Although they don't realize it at once, this proves to be a decisive battle because it opens up both railway and highway to Ponce.

Two days after the landing, the *Dixie*, one of Sampson's escort vessels, steams into the harbor of Ponce, finding it free of mines and without any fortifications. On the following morning, the remainder of the convoy ships and transports enter the harbor and Ponce is occupied, while the Spaniards who had held the town retreat toward San Juan.

Henry Barrett Chamberlin, of the Chicago *Record*, describes the unexpectedly warm reception Ponce gives the Americans: "As the transports steamed into the harbor hundreds of small boats filled with Puerto Ricans came out to extend a welcome. When the cutter in which the general rowed ashore started, the Puerto Ricans followed in seemingly endless procession, shouting, '*Viva los Americanos*,' while one hoarse-voiced individual...roared in broken English, 'Long live Washington.' The entire population participated in the rejoicing. There was music in the streets and plazas; the houses were decorated with brilliant colors; the flags of a dozen nations flying over the consulates along the water front gave the place the appearance of a most energetic midway, while anything that bore the least likeness to the colors in the American flag was profusely used for decorative purposes. Streamers of red, white and blue flew from every balcony and every roof. The wharf, the stores, the roofs, the balconies were crowded with men, women and children in holiday attire.

"The firemen and the volunteers of the Puerto Rican army paraded in uniform and petitioned General Miles to be permitted to enlist in our army. Hardly had the landing commenced than the commanding general and staff received invitations to dine with public officials, and the outlook for a social campaign of a month was more promising than the chances of bloodletting."

It's the kind of welcome the Americans had expected from the Cubans. Never was a conquering army received with so much joy. This is not news to Davis and Crane when they sit drinking in a Ponce bar on the first night of the American occupation. Crane is an alarming sight physically but his spirit is restored. As Milton tells us, he "shocked" the others "by his concave chest, wasted muscles, and legs like pipestems." One of his fellow correspondents, Charlie Michelson, describes him as "one of the most unprepossessing figures that ever served as a nucleus for apocryphal romances...the very antithesis of the conquering male."

But he's full of life. As he sits drinking with Davis, he remarks that it's so easy to capture a Puerto Rican town that even a correspondent could do it. Davis picks up the challenge quickly. Drawing out a map, he chooses at random a town called Juana Díaz, halfway between Ponce and Coamo, as a candidate for surrender, and says they should start early the next morning before the troops get there. But Davis oversleeps and Michelson persuades Crane to leave without him.

Eluding the early morning pickets, Crane easily finds the town and enters it, looking military in a khaki suit with leggings. The mayor receives this conquering hero cordially and gives him the keys to the city jail. (If it had been Scovel, he might have considered this a hint.) Crane immediately takes command. Milton describes how he lines up all the town's men and divides them at random into "good fellows and suspects." He orders the suspects confined to their homes, which no one takes very seriously. The others are invited to help celebrate Crane's great American victory, which they do all night.

Davis reports the episode later, but some of Crane's friends, who weren't there, say it doesn't fit his character. What does fit it beyond doubt is his subsequent exploit. Leaving Puerto Rico, he makes his way back to Havana where he finds that the American authorities have interned a dozen or so reporters on a ship in the harbor and won't let them into the city, since they might possibly report something truthful, or at least embarrassing. Resourcefully, Crane re-enters from the Bahamas, posing as a British tobacco merchant.

He finds the city in an uproarious controversy over an announcement by the departing Spanish officials that, when they leave, they're going to take the bones of Columbus from the Havana cathedral where they've been reposing and repatriate them in Madrid. Of course Columbus never moved about on these bones; his real skeleton is in Santo Domingo, but no one in Havana believes such a fable.

Otherwise, Crane reports, the city is in a postwar boom. One of its newspapers is busy printing copies of the United States Constitution and sending out newsboys to sell them in the streets. A popular saying runs, "Better a lion's tail than a rat's head."

Back in Puerto Rico, Davis was sorry to see Crane leave, but he's still determined to see for himself whether a Puerto Rican village will surrender to a reporter, and since the 16th Pennsylvania Volunteers and the Wisconsin Volunteers are headed toward Coamo, he tags along.

Arriving at the outskirts, General James H. Wilson employs his artillery to demolish a blockhouse that looks threatening. While the main body rests, about two minutes away from the village, the Pennsylvanians advance and find themselves in a hot skirmish. Through his glasses, Davis watches the 2nd Wisconsin, under General Oswald J. Ernst, come up to help. Observing them, it appears to Davis that Ernst is going to be the first general to enter Coamo, and thus take the surrender.

"I had never seen five thousand people surrender to one man," Davis writes later, "and it seemed that, if I were to witness that ceremony, my best plan was to pursue the 2nd Wisconsin. I did not want to share in the spectacle of surrender with my brother correspondents, so I tried to steal away from the three who were present. By dodging through a coffee *central* I came out a half mile from them and in advance of the Third [sic] Wisconsin. There I encountered two 'boy officers,' Captain John C. Breckinridge and Lieutenant Frederic S. Titus, who had temporarily abandoned their thankless duties in the Commissariat Department in order to seek death or glory in the skirmish-line."

Davis can't shake his fellow correspondents, however. They observe his maneuver and, with British naval attaché Captain Alfred Paget, they catch up. The party now consists of eight men, counting "Jimmy," a young boy who would ordinarily be selling papers in Herald Square but now is on duty carrying Thomas Millard's copy to the nearest press post. They are riding Puerto Rican ponies which, possibly scenting fodder in the town, suddenly break into a charge of their own, while their riders pull on the Mexican bits in a futile effort to slow them down.

Looking back, Davis can see that the Volunteers, who had intended to cross on a bridge into town, have found it destroyed and are now headed for a ford the correspondents had crossed a half hour earlier, so, as Davis writes: "Instead of a town which had surrendered to a thousand American soldiers, we seven unarmed men and Jimmy were being swept into a hostile city as fast as the enemy's ponies could take us there."

No time to debate protocol--is it correct, or even wise, to beat the general into town?--or to deal with the embarrassing fact that Jimmy's faster pony is well ahead of the others. "We all raced forward," Davis relates, "bunched together, and swept into the main street of Coama [sic]. The place is empty. No soldiers on either side in sight."

Is it an ambush? The intrepid reporters wonder if they've been *too* intrepid. Then, Davis writes, "a lonely man dashed into the middle of the street, hurled a white flag in front of us, and then dived headlong under the porch of a house. The next instant, as though at a signal, a hundred citizens, each with a white flag in both hands, ran from cover, waving their banners, and gasping in weak and terror-stricken tones, '*Viva los Americanos.*'" Embraces all around, accompanied by presents of wine, cigars, and rum.

In his brave Spanish, Davis speaks to a man who says he's the mayor and begs to surrender the town of Coamo into American hands. Davis takes him aside, fearing that, if he hesitates, the mayor might surrender to someone else, possibly even Jimmy. The mayor escorts Davis to his official residence and gives him the key to the *cartel*, which is the staff of office, made of gold and ebony, as well as the town's flag, prudently hidden behind a writing desk.

"It was a fine Spanish flag," Davis writes, "with the coat of arms embroidered in gold. I decided that, with whatever else I might part, that flag would always be mine, that the chance of my again receiving the surrender of a town of five thousand people was slender, and that this token would be wrapped around me in my coffin. I accordingly hid it in my poncho and strapped it to my saddle. Then I appointed a hotel-keeper, who spoke a little English, as my official interpreter, and told the *alcalde* that I was Military Governor, Mayor, and Chief of Police, and that I wanted the seals of the town.

"He gave me a rubber stamp with a coat of arms cut in it, and I wrote myself three letters, which, to insure their safe arrival, I addressed to three different places, and stamped them with the rubber seals. In time all three reached me, and I now have them as documentary proof of the fact that for twenty minutes I was Military Governor and Mayor of Coama [sic]."

In a few minutes, General Wilson arrives with three thousand men and Davis's brief moment of glory is over.

But it isn't such a big deal after all, this one-man conquest of Coamo. Puerto Ricans are surrendering all over the place, with wild enthusiasm. There had been virtually no revolutionary sentiment on the island, and in fact the Spanish had permitted the citizens to have an autonomous government. However, the Puerto Ricans understand which side their political future is buttered on, and they much prefer a country like America, a symbol of self-government, than Spanish colonialism. Making a speech of welcome, one prominent merchant declares: "We are glad that the United States is to be our country."

When the troops land at Ponce, they make themselves right at home, sleeping that first night on the piazzas of houses, or sharing a bedroom with a citizen. Next day they explore the town and find such wonders as cheap cigars, cheap meals of rice and beans, and--a miracle--an occasional egg. Trooper Irving Ruhland, of the New York Volunteer Cavalry, can scarcely believe what he's seeing. He writes home: "Milkmen appeared at dawn. The milkmen milked the cows at the doorsteps directly into small-necked bottles. Ox carts loaded with commissary stores soon filled the street. Our horses began to come ashore as the day dragged along, and were picketed to the fence where the native washerwomen had been hanging their clothes."

Shelter tents are pitched outside of town, artillery is brought ashore and drawn through the streets past awed citizens, and regiment after regiment marches behind them. The total effect is of an invincible America, and no one is inclined to argue the point.

Miles takes charge of the town. A rate of exchange is established, and a system for collecting taxes and customs duties is set up. Local laws are reconciled with martial law as much as possible. Captured Spanish volunteers swear allegiance to the United States, while Puerto Ricans take their oaths as judges and registrars. An American post office is opened up, and the damaged telephone system is repaired by the Signal Corps. Trains begin to run on the railroad. Nearly every shop hangs out a sign, "English spoken here," with qualifications.

In the plaza, where Ponce's residents are accustomed to hearing the Spanish band playing such alien tunes as "The March of Isabella," the bandstand now shelters a regimental ensemble playing equally alien but more colorful ditties, such as "Sweet Rosie O'Grady" and "The Banks of the Wabash." The opera house is reopened and an American company offers the dazzled citizens a variety performance. Within twenty-four hours of the landing, a new newspaper, *La Nueva Era*, appears on the street, half in Spanish, half in English.

Near Coamo, where two roads meet, an enterprising Wisconsin volunteer hangs up a sign on a tree, with a hand pointing north and the legend below it reading, "Go to James Getts for Clothing, Warrington, Wis." The market economy may die, but it never surrenders.

Davis writes: "The people of Ponce were certainly the most friendly souls in the world. Nothing could surpass their enthusiasm or shake their loyalty. If a drunken soldier, of whom there were surprisingly few, entered the shop or home of a Porto Rican [sic], the owner could not be persuaded to make a charge against him. The natives gave our men freely of everything; and the richer and better class of Porto Ricans opened a Red Cross hospital at their own expense and contributed money, medicines, cots, and doctors for our sick soldiers. They also placed two American Red Cross nurses in charge, and allowed them absolute authority."

Only the early advent of peace prevents Miles and his staff from completely Americanizing the island. After the bungling and scandal of Santiago, the treatment of the sick on the transports and in camps, the occupation of Puerto Rico is a triumph.

From the military standpoint, Miles's slow but steady conquest of the island is equally successful. He has devised a plan, which Davis somewhat obscurely terms "*a fête des fleurs*" in comparison with the "Santiago nightmare." Essentially, it was a plan to outflank the enemy at every point and gradually herd the Spanish defenders into San Juan, then capture that city.

Some enemy generals, like Juan Díaz, surrender without fighting. Others put up what seem like desperation defenses. In the terrain outside Coamo, after its one-man surrender, the only real skirmish of the expedition takes place. Witnessing it, the town's former mayor, Davis, writes: "The Spanish commander seemed to wish to die. He galloped out on the road and into the meadow, where he was conspicuous from the top of his head to the hoofs of his horse. At one time he stood motionless, holding his reins easily and looking up at the firing line above. After he was killed the men in the trench along the road raised a white handkerchief on a stock and ceased firing." In this, the only encounter of the campaign that could be called a battle, six Americans are wounded and a half dozen Spaniards are killed.

That is the only serious resistance to Miles's advance. Guamá, defended by only 400 Spaniards, surrenders after a short skirmish in which one officer and four men, all from the 4th Ohio, are wounded.

The enemy is entrenched in force at Las Marías, but the American regulars drive them back and on to Mayagüez, a city with a population of 30,000, which they aren't strong enough to hold. At Adjuntas, it's the same story. A night skirmish is enough. The Navy captures Fajardo, and the end of the Spanish occupation is very near when news of the armistice arrives on August 11, much to the relief of the Spaniards, whose defense of the island has been less than enthusiastic. Most of the American troops are ready to go home only a month after they landed.

For some of them, it's been a kind of potentially deadly outdoor jaunt in the countryside, and the ease of the American victory has caused popular humorists back home, like Finley Peter Dunne, to call it a "moonlight picnic." It takes Davis to reply to Dunne's jibe and set things straight: "The reason the Spanish bull gored our men in Cuba and failed to touch them in Porto Rico [sic] was entirely due to the fact that Miles was an expert matador, so it was hardly fair to the commanding General and the gentlemen under him to send the Porto Rican campaign down into history as a picnic." So much for Shafter.

Most informed people back home, as Leech points out, are happy about Miles's success without really understanding how skillfully he did the job. Other citizens are more interested in the fact that the armistice has been declared and the war in Cuba is over, and they're pleased that the War Department isn't going to be wasting any more public funds there. They don't know yet how much occupation is going to cost them.

If there's any disappointment, it comes from the nearly 140,000 militia who feel cheated because they didn't get to go into combat and be shot and starved and laid low by fever for the greater glory of the nation. State governors and politically influential officers are still bombarding the War Department with appeals on behalf of men who want to serve. Many of them had hoped to be sent to Puerto Rico, and Alger had dispatched as many as he could, taking full credit for this semi-spectacular movement of volunteers.

Only McKinley has had serious doubts. He says: "What do you think people will say if they believe we unnecessarily and at great expense sent these boys out of the country? Is it either necessary or expedient?" Neither, as it turns out, and when McKinley asks the same question at a Cabinet meeting, Cortelyou reports that "the discussion of the subject ended abruptly."

Both sides are pleased that the armistice has been fairly speedy. Washington is thinking now about Manila, and so is Madrid. More American troops are being sent there, because so far the conquest, after Dewey, has extended no father than from Cavite to, as Leech puts it, "a peanut field outside Manila." No one's even thinking about that other part of Spain's Pacific empire, Guam. Spain doesn't care much about Guam but it does care about Manila, and under the circumstances, Madrid is prepared to let Cuba go if it can save Manila and the rest of the archipelago.

In Washington, there's much confusion about the Philippines, and some angry divisions in the Cabinet. Up to now, McKinley has been willing enough to let the Philippines go, except for Manila, but now he's having second thoughts. The rebel forces under Emilio Aguinaldo--the Philippine equivalent of Gómez--have been having some notable successes against the Spaniards, and have in fact surrounded Manila. But now comes the doubt. It's that old Cuban problem all over again. Is a dedicated revolutionary like Aguinaldo, who also wants independence for *his* country, likely to submit to American authority? Not if he's like Gómez and García. The Cabinet shudders. He might take over Manila and go on to establish a Philippine republic. Unthinkable!

The trouble is they don't yet know enough about this man. Dewey is his champion for the moment, but what does that mean? The Navy isn't going to be fighting on land. Aguinaldo himself, in an interview, has been saying some alarming things about independence. Washington has been encouraging him to join in with America against the Spaniards, but independence is another matter.

Hoping to get a clearer idea of the situation, Long has asked Dewey for a full report on the situation, and the admiral's reply arrived on June 27, just as things were heating up in Cuba. Relations with Aguinaldo are cordial and correct, Dewey says; no commitments have been made on either side. He thinks the rebels can't take Manila without help, but Aguinaldo is going to try and just might do it.

Dewey sounds relaxed about it all. He says Aguinaldo is going to form a civil government, and he believes the Filipinos, unlike the Cubans, are intelligent and capable enough to do it. Four days after Santiago Bay, Aguinaldo indeed proclaims himself president of a republic not yet in existence. *Déjà vu*, Cuba.

The Americans already have a considerable force in the islands--nearly 17,000 men, which the Cabinet thinks is quite enough to dispose of Aguinaldo if he proves to be difficult. But if Dewey is to be believed--and Long, for one, believes him--we're not going to have any trouble with this native upstart.

Reporters on the scene already know more than Washington does about what's going on. When they read their morning papers, Cabinet members learn that the busy German fleet is disregarding the American blockade of Manila, and is suspected of being in cahoots with Aguinaldo. There's been an incident at Subic Bay, when a German cruiser prevented rebel troops from seizing an island there (which knocks a temporary hole in the conspiracy theory). Dewey acts quickly, sending two cruisers to the island, which is seized, discouraging the German vessels from further activity.

Things are moving rapidly now. After Aguinaldo declares independence, he decrees martial law in all the islands. General Merritt lands with more troops, and expects the Spaniards will soon surrender. Dewey tells Washington the situation is critical and now believes Aguinaldo is more enemy than friend. It seems clear in Washington that its occupation forces are going to clash with the rebels.

For four days, the Cabinet debates what its peace policy is going to be. Draft after draft of a treaty with Spain is submitted, altered, and redrawn. Summing up the State Department's position, McKinley says: "Judge Day only wants a hitching post." Seeking to lighten things, the President engages in a little friendly banter with old James Wilson.

"Yes," he says, "you Scotch favor keeping everything-- including the Sabbath."

Wilson doesn't smile. "You didn't put my motion for a naval base," he answers.

"No, Judge, I was afraid it would be carried," the President admits with a chuckle.

The French ambassador, Jules Cambon, acting for Spain, is summoned to the White House to hear proposed terms for a treaty, and gets a severe shock when he hears them. His instructions from Madrid are that an armistice is highly desirable, but nothing should be given away except Cuba. He asks for easier terms. If granted, he adds, it could mean American acquisition of all the islands. Indeed.

Well, McKinley counters, that all depends on the terms of the treaty. He's willing to change one word--"possession" to "disposition." Cambon asks that Puerto Rico be omitted on the matter of indemnification, but McKinley will not even discuss it. Then Cambon asks for a clarification of the Philippines clause. McKinley tells him he hasn't made up his mind about it. Could he be a little clearer, at least? Cambon wants to know. Unfortunately, he can't, the President replies. Only one agreement emerges from this session: the final conference will be held in Paris.

Plainly, the Spanish government is gagging on these terms, scarcely believing it may lose its Pacific empire. Madrid tries various ploys. Maybe the Americans will agree to limit further negotiations to administrative reform. They won't. McKinley and Day are beginning to be annoyed by this diplomatic dance, and once they threaten to break off the talks. But at last a protocol, the prelude to a formal armistice, is signed. (The armistice has already been in effect for some time.)

The signing takes place on a sultry August afternoon, the twelfth, while a thunderstorm booms and flashes outside. Reporters and photographers have been banished, but news about the document spreads rapidly, as might be expected. Its immediate effect has been to end the Puerto Rican campaign, as we've seen, but the news doesn't reach Manila until the morning of August 13, too late to stop American troops from closing in on the city.

In the Cabinet Room, Secretary Day spins a globe and muses, "Let's see what we get by this." But all over the country, as Leech tells us, "Americans were wondering what they had got in their rash and sentimental adventure on behalf of Cuba Libre," after four months of war. It hasn't cost much in human lives, to be sure (if you don't count the fever victims), and business hasn't been greatly disturbed by it. Maybe it's been too easily won. But already the lines are being drawn.

There are those who see a grand new destiny for America, the acquisition of a modest empire, like those the big boys in Europe have been running for centuries. A country that was united only thirty-three years ago, at a cost of more than 600,000 lives of its own citizens, is surely not going to back away from the conquest of small foreign countries at so little cost. And we have such a noble motive: to free the native populations from the oppression of a colonial power. If these people really want to be independent, however, they'll have to wait until American politicians are convinced such backward people are capable of governing themselves.

Strong feelings of national pride are involved in the emergence of the United States on the world scene, abandoning its previous isolation. Patriotism has propelled this war, and it's going to determine the conditions of peace, although not everyone is convinced of that scenario by any means. In New England, the Anti-Imperialist League is forming to impede, or stop if possible, the creation of an American empire. But these are mostly the voices of intellectuals, perennial enemies of honest patriots.

Meanwhile, before we plunge into the Philippines, there's one problem remaining--getting the boys home from Cuba, or as many, at least, as can still be saved from malaria and yellow fever. Like the rest of the war, it's going to be one more lesson in bungling.

10

COMING HOME

No one in America, apparently, knows how to take care of an army, whether in sickness or in health. From the beginning, this has been the domestic scandal of the war with Spain, and so it will continue to the unhappy end.

Sometimes it seems as though the trouble is simply the result of bureaucracy, the perennial enemy of efficient government, and this is easy to believe when we hear the conversation quoted by Leech between the French attaché and Commissary General Charles F. Eagan. The attaché wants to know how the Americans provision their army, and the dialogue, according to Leech, runs as follows:

"You buy the stores in Chicago and you turn them over to the quartermaster and take them to Tampa?"

"Yes, sir."

"And they arrive in Tampa and are turned over to the commissary?"

"Yes, sir."

"And then they are turned over to the quartermaster to take them to Siboney?"

"Yes, sir."

"They arrive at Daiquiri and you turn them back to the commissary again?"

"Yes, sir."

"And you want to get them to the troops, and you give them to the quartermaster again?"

"Yes, sir."

What the attaché reports back to his superiors is no doubt unlikely to improve Franco-American understanding.

If there's anyone worse off than the commissary officers when it comes to getting anything accomplished, it's the surgeons. Some medical supplies and stores were left behind in Tampa after the expeditionary force sailed, and some of what managed to be loaded on the transports was ruined by careless handling and inadequate packing. There wasn't much remaining to be taken ashore. When medicines and hospital supplies, badly needed in Cuba, finally got there in July, a large part went right on to Puerto Rico with Miles. Other shipments were still sitting in transports off Siboney in early August.

In Washington, the Medical Bureau has its own problems, most of them self-imposed. Surgeon General George W. Sternberg is a distinguished scientist but he resists any kind of innovation or reform, particularly if it seems to limit his prerogatives. Otherwise, he is hampered by the great difficulty of getting enough surgeons and attendants into the field. But it's nursing that resistance to change and simple short-sightedness can hurt most.

In April, before the war was under way, the Daughters of the American Revolution volunteered to help process the piles of applications for nursing duty piling up at the Bureau. In spite of Ambrose Bierce's cynicism, American women *do* want to help, and many want to use their nursing skills. But when the D.A.R. finished its processing and gave the Bureau a list of qualified nurses, nothing whatever happened for week after week.

Why? Because conservative medical officers just don't want female nurses if they can avoid it, in spite of the notable track record of such women in the Civil War. Sternberg sides with these medical dinosaurs. Even though the need becomes more acute every day, he won't assign female nurses to hospitals unless the surgeon in charge asks for them, which in most cases is never. By the time the need was so desperate that a few nurses succeeded in getting to the overcrowded and ruinous hospitals in Cuba, the war was nearly over.

Overcrowding is a disgrace in itself, because Sternberg won't do anything about it even though everyone knows relieving it is one way to prevent epidemics. It isn't as though Sternberg doesn't know all about these elementary facts; he's known them since his service in the Civil War, but here he is, a generation later, repeating the same mistakes. He closes his ears when he's told that sick soldiers are avoiding going into the hospitals if they can. Conditions there and in the camps are often indescribable, as we've seen.

All this makes it a little more understandable, though not excusable, when the business of bringing the boys home gets underway. Even so, it's hard to believe that it's the end of July before a lease is signed to construct a receiving hospital and base on the sands of Montauk, at the tip of Long Island. The obstacles have been formidable, to be sure--and familiar in our own time. Hotel owners argue that their business is going to be ruined by bringing all these infectious soldiers into their resort territory. Some residents protest, too, although they're assured that the risk is minimal.

The Bureau is congratulating itself that at least the transports are not going to be compelled to land in New York, which would surely touch off a public uproar, but on the other hand, where can they land at the sandy tip of Long Island? Not at Montauk, certainly, where the water isn't deep enough. The nearest reasonable point for disembarkation is Fresh Pond Bay, which is several miles away, and where the only facilities available are sand dunes. There is a shortage of fresh water at both sites.

To build the kind of huge facility needed, materials in great quantities have to be brought in, and the only link to supply depots in New York is the Long Island Railroad, even at that stage in its history a subject of controversy. Whatever its failings may be, it simply wasn't built to undertake such an enormous mission. Nevertheless, we're going right ahead. The War Department calls in the president of the line, W. H. Baldwin, and instructs him to add on substantial quantities of rolling stock and personnel in a hurry, while he's building miles of new sidings to accommodate freight cars and constructing a metropolitan railroad station out of the Montauk depot. Baldwin will make transportation history if he can do it, especially since the entire effort is a race against time. The soldiers have to be brought home, and they're already on the way.

The new installation, when it's brought into existence, will be called Camp Wikoff, in memory of a gallant colonel of the regulars who fell at San Juan Hill. By mid-August, scores of workmen swarm onto the site, laying pipelines for wells that haven't yet been drilled, stretching telephone and telegraph lines across the dunes, bringing in lumber and tents. All the familiar near disasters occur. There aren't nearly enough wagons to transport everything. Brooklyn carpenters go on strike. Supplies begin to trickle in, but no warehouses have

General Joseph "Fightin' Joe" Wheeler

reproduced from the collections of the Library of Congress

been constructed to receive them, so they remain unloaded. Hastily built sidings are so inadequate that freight cars are stacked up as far to the west as Amagansett.

And then the first troops begin arriving, more than 4,000 of them, and there isn't a single tent ready. These are cavalrymen brought up from Florida, some of them already showing the first symptoms of typhoid and malaria, all of them hungry because the travel rations were inadequate. Along with them come boxcars filled with more than 5,000 horses and mules, all of whom need to be fed and stabled as soon as possible. The men are still in their tropical uniforms, at least those who finally got them, and they're shivering in the cool offshore winds from the ocean. This is the stuff of nightmares.

But we shouldn't underestimate the American can-do spirit. A week later, the pier has been lengthened and strengthened to make unloading easier, a quarantine station has been established, and men and their equipment are made clean again on a disinfecting barge anchored offshore. Baldwin has outdone himself, too. Not only has he erected a large new station at Montauk, but it boasts a restaurant and has a more than adequate platform. Sheds are rising like mushrooms. Electric light, telephone, and telegraph services are in and working. Fresh water from new wells flows through new pipes--or will as soon as the pumps arrive.

Still unfinished are the hospital and detention camp, but the remainder of the establishment is impressive. At some point the officials have grasped the fact that they're going to need three times what they'd planned originally, so now 10,000 tents in neat rows are spread across the sandy plain. Floors and cots haven't arrived, but everything's going to be in place by the end of the month.

Unfortunately, it isn't a full-blown miracle. What this camp is ready to receive, as Leech points out, are "able-bodied, resourceful soldiers," but what it gets are "convalescents unable to help themselves, nearly all requiring special attendance and special diets."

So the first week is Nightmare Alley: men lying on blanketed stretchers, others half carried into ambulances, some passed through quarantine as sound when they can scarcely walk. It's a village of ghosts, blank eyes looking out of skeleton faces. There are those who don't make it into camp and fall beside the road, because they've been forced to walk miles to reach this safe haven, and there aren't enough ambulances to pick them up and carry them the rest of the way. Carpenters are frantically putting up new hospitals before the first one is completed, and meanwhile, men are lying helpless on the ground, as though they were still in Cuba.

There's only one immediate solution, and that's to delay disembarking the transports when they arrive, more of them every day. This creates new suffering on the ships, where it's already unbearable.

Everything is in short supply, not just lumber and tents but doctors and nurses. When the chief surgeon appeals to Sternberg for help, he's told to find what he needs locally. Obviously, more women are needed and some determined Sisters of Mercy show up to offer their services, as do professional nurses from everywhere, but nothing has been built to accommodate women. The pressure on Sternberg is now so great, however, that he has to send in more women and provide for them, as well as recruit male attendants. Doctors are being contracted for as rapidly as possible.

General Wheeler has arrived from Cuba to run Camp Wikoff, and he begins by knocking a few heads together. Even in these circumstances, it seems, men will be boys. The hospital and regimental surgeons are quarreling over the disposition of medical supplies and preventing efficient use of these badly needed materials until Wheeler straightens them out. He sees to it that the commissary department issues something besides red tape.

But as Wheeler discovers, it's almost impossible to eliminate, or even alleviate, well-established inefficiency, or overcome the usual shortage of everything. He's done his best, though, seeing to it that plenty of light, nourishing food is requisitioned, along with ice to keep it fresh, and enough beef and bread for everyone. Yet these provisions can't be evenly distributed because there are only two wagons available. The quartermaster hasn't provided any more.

When men well enough to take care of themselves arrive, they raid these commissary wagons, and troops have to be sent to guard the storehouses because the carpenters haven't put doors on them. The guards steal quantities of the provisions they've been assigned to guard. This situation becomes so serious that there's a question of whether Camp Wikoff isn't going to record some cases of starvation.

This camp has been built in great haste and with little provision for anything but essentials, so the men are nearly overcome with joy when charitable donations begin to provide some of the comforts they haven't enjoyed since they left home. Convalescents line up for these delicacies.

For some lucky men, especially for the Rough Riders and two militia regiments, the home front comes through with packages. Others are also beginning to come to the aid of the beleaguered soldiers. Red Cross workers are busily setting up kitchens, and women from Ladies' Aid societies turn out to help them. New York socialite Helen Gould makes an inspection tour of the hospitals and afterward this Lady Bountiful raids the kitchens of her rich friends, including William K. Vanderbilt, and sends out a corps of chefs to set up kitchens. This is a real novelty for men serving in an army which has never made any attempt to provide or train cooks, and pleads it has no money to hire any. In that department, nothing has changed since the Civil War.

When the tide of help really starts to roll in from the public, it becomes a flood. So much squab and pheasant, whiskey and brandy, champagne, and hundreds of other delicacies arrive that these survivors of the war are delirious with happiness instead of fever. For most, it's the best they've ever eaten in their lives. The commissaries look like the storerooms at the Ritz. So much butter and cream is available that former scarecrows are likely to become round balls. The sudden change in diet and the excesses of good will from people who can afford it creates some new illnesses, the result of overindulgence.

Yet *everyone* isn't being overfed, as the newspapers remind their readers, and as the visitors to Camp Wikoff report. There are still emaciated men there, not yet ready for a solid diet, and others--especially the recovering typhoid patients--who have to live on a liquid diet, according to the erroneous medical beliefs of the time. Not understanding why some feast and some don't, there are visitors who complain of the War Department's "inhumanity," which T.R. calls "hysteric nonsense."

When Shafter arrives at the end of August, he calls Montauk "the best camp I ever saw," and he's not as far wrong as he usually is. An authentic miracle has been accomplished in less than a month. On these windswept dunes, after an initial period of total confusion and bungling, a small city has been created. True, it looks like "a Western boom town," as Leech describes it, but that's because it was put up in haste with sometimes crude materials. The Western touch can be seen in the hitching rails outside the railroad station, and the rough plank sheds.

Somehow the epidemic everyone feared when all those malaria and typhoid cases were brought in never develops, nor does the yellow fever scare turn into reality. With good care available for the first time, the death rate is only two percent.

But Camp Wikoff is condemned by many of the public in spite of the facts. Visitors have never seen so many still wretched men in one place before, and the impression is overwhelming. When the War Department tries to relieve the congestion by a liberal policy of granting sick leaves, people complain because they say the soldiers are sent home before they're able to travel. The Department pays no attention to these complaints. Sternberg and the others know that autumn is about to come on; the nights are already chilly in September. Camp Wikoff wasn't constructed to last through a winter, and its life must necessarily be a short one. Those too sick to leave on their own feet are taken by ambulance to city and suburban hospitals. The volunteers are discharged as soon as they're able, and the regulars are transferred to Army posts.

After the middle of September, a dwindling number of visitors can see the Montauk boom ending before their eyes. Tents are being struck, freight cars roll off empty, the station has fewer and fewer travelers and its restaurant closes. By the time bleak November arrives, only empty storehouses remain. Another narrow escape, in retrospect.

Now it's finger-pointing time. A grumbling press and public want to know just who fouled things up in this war. The politicians promise to investigate themselves. Much of the criticism is directed against poor old Alger, but he'll have to share the blame because the President, recognizing a political crisis when he sees one, orders a complete investigation of the conduct of the war. He hopes this will sidetrack any effort by Congress to do the same.

There's a new player on the field by this time. Miles has returned from Puerto Rico, still smoldering from his presumed humiliations, and he's ready to declare war on the War Department, a move which he hopes will also advance his political ambitions. He's already laid the groundwork by telling his troubles to the Kansas City *Star*'s Puerto Rican correspondent. Consequently, when he arrives in New York on September 7, a herd of reporters crowds onto the pier to ask him some pointed questions. Miles is ready for them. He's prepared a handout, a long statement constituting his brief against the War Department. The subsequent stories in the papers give him a public relations edge because he's widely praised for compelling McKinley to act. As for Alger, he's doing his own smoldering. He's angry and scornful, hinting broadly that the attacks on him are coming from people who kick dogs.

"What do you want me to do?" Alger cries after a reporter asks him a particularly embarrassing question. "To get down into the sewer with these people?" This attitude only produces more questions. Even papers friendly to him deplore editorially his unwillingness to discuss the subject frankly. A Detroit paper, once a supporter, accuses him of "concentrated self-righteousness."

McKinley is discovering that finding investigators willing to investigate is no easy matter. Where are you going to find jurors who aren't already convinced the defendants are guilty? Many of those asked to serve flatly refuse to get involved in a mess that may have unforeseen political consequences. But at last a panel is sworn in to investigate the military aspects of the case--nine men, all veterans of the Civil War, but only one from the Confederacy.

The panel goes to work during the last week in September, with the President promising to make available any papers or people it may want to examine. Just tell the truth, he instructs the members, that's all he wants. That's all everyone wants, of course. The chairman is a man not entirely above suspicion--General Granville M. Dodge, a promoter who is best known for building railroads, and less known for his White House and congressional connections. There are at least two men known to be friends of Miles.

At first, as the commission pursues its labors, public opinion verges on hysteria but then it subsides as the weeks drag on, and by December, the inquiry has vanished from the front pages. That is, until Miles is called, shortly before Christmas.

Those who know him expect the general to use his appearance as a public rehearsal of his grievances, but instead he takes a much more popular course, attacking the commissariat. He brings up the emotion-charged subject of the tainted beef sold to the Army (or so he alleges), both the refrigerated and canned varieties, and points out that even when this particular supposed scandal was uncovered, no one in Washington did anything about it. This is an adroit maneuver. By seeming to be devoted to improving food for the troops, which everyone supports, he's pointing an accusing finger at those in the Administration who allowed this disgraceful thing to happen, and he emerges for the moment as the whistle-blower, a selfless servant of the public.

Miles's testimony makes him so popular with Democrats that he begins to believe in his own self-image and falls victim to White House fever, an ailment that has humbled better men. As a witness he makes a carefully staged impression, refusing to be either sworn in or affirmed, taking full responsibility for his testimony. When he gives it, the chief villain appears to be the Subsistence Bureau, as it's euphemistically named, which supplied the beef and other tainted food, causing serious illness among the troops, as charged. He says the canned beef was not part of the legal ration, although in fact it was, and he drops a chilling hint of what he thinks was the reason for its distribution. "The pretense is that it was sent as an experiment," he tells the commission.

As the testimony about tainted meat continues, one horror story after another edifies newspaper readers and dismays the Administration. Miles has collected statements from regimental commanders who swear to the bad appearance and flavor of the meat. It is said to have been compounded from "scraps and tailings," even "refuse" from soups found in the stores. One volunteer surgeon expresses his belief that someone had injected the meat with secret chemicals, turning the committee's collective stomach by saying it smelled like a dead body.

On the stand, Miles repeatedly calls the meat "embalmed beef," enhancing the surgeon's image of it, and he repeats the phrase again and again when he talks to reporters. Apparently he believes it is literally true. Hearst and Pulitzer are so delighted with his testimony and his out-of-the-committee-room views that he achieves more publicity than any general was able to acquire during the war. He's given credit for moral courage, at least, from other papers because it becomes clear that the President is probably going to relieve him of his command and order a military court of inquiry, if not a full-fledged court-martial.

Some of those attacked by Miles fight back. General Eagan is horrified when he reads in the *Journal* that he stands accused of experimenting on troops by giving them refuse and meat injected with undertakers' chemicals. "General Miles has crucified me on a cross of falsehood and misrepresentation," he cries in the papers. He can't sue for slander because Miles is protected by the immunity McKinley granted to witnesses. In a letter to him, Eagan demands that he verify these accusations but Miles gives him no satisfaction. Then they must let him testify on his own behalf, he tells the commission, and he is granted a January hearing, about three weeks after Miles leaves the stand.

Eagan is rapidly becoming Miles's chief victim. He's getting much abuse from the editorial writers, and there are demands that he be fired from the Army. No wonder he can't sleep and that his health is rapidly declining. He finds it intolerable that Miles has raised the suspicion, convincing to many, that he made money from the beef contracts he negotiated, or at least approved.

Pushed to the limit, Eagan self-destructs when he finally gets to testify. He spends days before his appearance drawing up a long statement to be distributed to the press, a summary of what he's going to say on the stand. It's an emotional denunciation of Miles, not a measured defense. Holding the complete document in his shaking hands as he testifies, Eagan makes an almost hysterical attack on his accuser, calling Miles a liar who ought to be dismissed from the Army, if not imprisoned. His indictment of a fellow general is comprehensive: "Miles lies in his heart, he lies in every hair of his head and every part of his body. I wish to force the lie back into his throat, covered with the contents of a camp latrine."

The commissioners hear this in disbelieving silence. They rule that Eagan's statement won't be accepted unless he revises it. These veterans of another war are appalled by what they've heard--not because of the accusations, but because Eagan has done the unthinkable and the impermissible. He has struck at Army morale and brought into public view the bitter divisions in the War Department which both the Army and the Administration have been trying to sweep under the rug.

So now there's hell to pay. The press wants Eagan court-martialed, and so does the Army officer corps and much of Congress. Alger is not eager to initiate any such proceeding. After all, Eagan has only said publicly what he himself has suspected. But there's no way out of this pressure cooker. The court-martial is duly ordered; Eagan is to be tried on charges of conduct unbecoming an officer, not to mention "conduct prejudicial to good order and military discipline."

When the military court finally meets in the red plush precincts of the Ebbitt House, it finds a much different Eagan confronting it--a man who knows his career is over. He sits there, his face gray with fatigue and despair, saying little. On the stand, he rehearses his military life: volunteer in the Union Army, a second lieutenant of regulars in the Indian wars on the Western plains, wounded in the Modoc War, the recipient of a brevet promotion. Eagan is in tears as he sees it all slipping away. His sole defense is that he was provoked by Miles's charges. After all, he asks his fellow officers, isn't a soldier's honor as sacred as a woman's? His most dramatic display of emotion comes when his lawyer asks him directly if he ever profited from any contracts he negotiated. "Before God, not one cent!" he bursts out.

It's no good. The court finds him guilty, and it isn't much consolation that clemency is recommended. This is bad enough, but perhaps the worst Eagan endures is the knowledge that no one is giving him any sympathy because no one believes him. When McKinley commutes his sentence to suspension from duty for six years, there's a fresh wave of hostility toward him. The public wants to hang him, and they think McKinley himself sympathizes with the meat packers, if not something more sinister. Eagan fades away into disgrace for the six years of suspension that will bring him to his date of retirement.

But Miles has gone too far. On a broader scale, he's guiltier than Eagan, in the eyes of many, because he has attacked a major American industry, the meat packers, and the government itself while still the ranking general in an Army presumably demanding unquestionable loyalty. He's acquired powerful enemies among the packers because the inquiry has hurt their markets both at home and abroad. They've brought pressure to bear on their political friends, with the result that the investigation has also become an inquiry directed toward exonerating the industry from any wrongdoing.

For nearly five months the Dodge Commission, as it's called, examines and deliberates, finally producing a report in February. This report has in it something for nearly everybody. The military system is faulty, it says, and needs to be fixed; several suggestions are made about fixing it. The monumental bungling in preparing for war is deplored; no disagreement there. Alger is condemned in a quaint phrase for "want of grasp." But the Commission fails to find any evidence of corruption by Alger or anyone else, and on the evidence, there does seem to be far more simple incompetence on the part of government officials than intent to defraud.

Naturally, the Commission's report convinces nobody. "Whitewash" is the word generally applied to it. People do have some reason to doubt. Dodge, it appears, had already been defending the War Department before he was named as chairman. Moreover, McKinley either neglected or purposely omitted giving the Commission power to call witnesses or have them be sworn. That gave any Army officers who might testify, a number near zero, an opportunity to evade responsibility. Later, McKinley will say that he promised potential witnesses that they would be protected from the consequences of their testimony, but it all adds up to the public's derisive name for this body, "The Alger Relief Commission."

In the end, Miles fares no better than Eagan, and in some ways he's worse off. The charges he has made are dismissed, and he himself is censured. He can see now that he's made a great mistake. His vision of the White House is fading away. Obscurity, the last thing he wanted, awaits him. Meanwhile, he's regarded by the public as just another part of the "whitewash." The editorial writers are calling for that last resort, the special prosecutor (they call it a special tribunal), to investigate, find the smoking guns, and get on with a few convictions. They want to know what is the "overwhelming evidence" Miles told the commissioners he possessed that chemical preservatives had been used in Army meat.

McKinley isn't prepared to satisfy them. If he orders a military court of inquiry, it will give Miles reason to proclaim that he's being persecuted for telling the truth. Insiders think they know why Miles has launched this attack on the War Department; the scent of political ambition is too strong to be ignored. As Henry Adams writes, in his sardonic way, the general's brother-in-law, Colgate Hoyt, had "actually threatened the members of the Administration in Washington with electing Miles President, to their face." That prospect didn't frighten McKinley, but the Administration is beginning to get into increasingly hot water over its expansionist policy toward the Philippines, and the President wants no showdown with Miles, a situation that would certainly be counterproductive.

That's why McKinley steers further inquiry toward Miles's allegations, not the general himself, who isn't even temporarily suspended. The President creates what is immediately christened a "Beef Court," and gives it ample power. That earns him numerous Brownie points in the press, where he's praised for his determination to have a thorough and impartial investigation of the charges.

While the public at large is convinced Miles has been telling the truth, some of his friends aren't so sure. They've never thought he could prove his charges about the beef. For one thing, he's certain to bog down in confusing definitions of what is "pulp" and what is "refuse" in canned meat, and whether it's the same thing as "embalmed" refrigerated beef. Miles's evidence is mostly directed at the canned product, not the refrigerated kind. It's no secret that chemical preservatives are used in meat packing, but Miles can't prove that fresh beef is inedible because there's overwhelming evidence that it isn't in most cases. If any of it has been bad, it's the result of careless handling and bungling delays in transportation.

Miles won't listen to any of these qualifications. Instead, he draws up a list of witnesses for the inquiry that McKinley's ordered, and works with the lawyers on their plans for examination. Friends keep urging him to retract his charges and resign from the service to save what's left of his career, but he can't hear them. As Henry Adams writes, he's "dead-bent on breaking his head."

That occurs when the "Beef Court" brings in its verdict three months later. For Miles, it's devastating. No evidence to justify a charge that the fresh beef was "embalmed," or was otherwise unfit. There was nothing wrong with the canned beef, the court rules, except that the commissary bought far too much of it. Eagan made a "colossal error," the court finds, but his only motive was "the earnest desire to procure the best possible food for the troops," a verdict that comes too late to help Eagan. Worse than all this, Miles is censured for being so late in reporting what he thought was contamination of the beef supply. The court recommends, however, that no further action be taken against him.

McKinley approves the verdict, but the whole proceeding has not been enough to silence critics in and out of the general public. Some newspapers charge that Alger packed the court, although few of the papers had been willing to give the War Department a fair hearing. If McKinley had chosen, he could have silenced the criticism, at least in loyal Republican papers, by a discreet word to the publishers, but he chose, as usual, to be silent.

The press isn't willing to let the matter end there. A renewed campaign against the meat packers begins, prompted by the revelation during the hearing that they did indeed use chemical preservatives in meat, and that canned meat of any kind is likely to be processed by dubious means and end up as an equally doubtful product, as far as quality is concerned. People across the country react with turning stomachs and renewed suspicions. These facts lay the groundwork for the muckrakers a few years later, and the passage of the Meat Inspection Act.

McKinley takes a Republican position in the controversy. Let's not do anything to hurt a great American industry, he seems to be saying. This isn't a consideration, however, with the packers' foreign customers, who are greatly disturbed by the scandal, particularly the Germans. But nothing more is done for the moment. The War Department continues to treat the packers respectfully and to buy meat from them. Eagan praises the work of the Department's contractors and what they buy. Alger has nothing at all to say. Some even belatedly hail Miles for "the highest kind of courage," a phrase coined by Harvard President Charles W. Eliot But nothing, by this time, can make Miles the national hero he expected to be. For a while during the controversy, crowds cheer him when he appears, but in a surprisingly short time it's "Nelson who?"

On this ironic note, the Cuban phase of the Spanish-American War ends. "Cuba Libre" would be *libre* if the American occupiers weren't there, and the country's future under dictators of both left and right lies ahead of it.

Something of the terrible irony implicit in what Cuba has just gone through is the fate of García, who dies suddenly on December 11. This authentic freedom fighter, held back from Santiago's surrender at gunpoint and scorned by the Americans, gets a first-class military funeral in Washington, complete with a large bodyguard from the Army, plus a covey of high-ranking generals and Administration officials who reverently (no cynicism visible) escort his body to a temporary grave in Arlington.

Americans who fought in the war forget the combat and medical horrors almost before they're over, at least those who escaped with whole bodies. They can't abandon the dreams of glory they carried into the struggle, and revive them at veterans' encampments for decades afterward.

A case in point is Colonel Theodore Roosevelt. When the Rough Riders are mustered out on September 15, he writes, "Oh, well! So all things pass away. But those were beautiful days." As President, shortly before he dies, he's still remembering the glory: "San Juan was the great day of my life," says this man who has known more great days than most will ever see.

Now we're off to the Philippines. There it won't be so easy to forget.

Part Three

LIBERATING THE PHILIPPINES

1

LOOKING WESTWARD

"IF OLD DEWEY HAD JUST SAILED AWAY WHEN HE SMASHED THAT Spanish fleet," McKinley remarks to Herman Kohlsaat, "what a lot of trouble he would have saved us." How true! No doubt a great deal of inconvenience *would* have been avoided, particularly to the Filipinos, if old Dewey had picked up his battleships and come home.

Why didn't he do it then, and why is he still there, three months after Manila Bay, with the fighting in Cuba over and Spain beginning to negotiate a peace treaty? The answer is simple. No one has any intention of recalling him because, whether they're acknowledging it or not, the American government means to have the Philippines, first by treaty if that's possible, and if not, by force.

But why would any sensible nation, even a budding world power, want this immensely complicated piece of Pacific real estate? In that far-flung archipelago there are 7,100 islands and islets. Asia is only 500 miles southeast. The islands cover 115,800 square miles, surrounded on the east by the Philippine Sea, on the south by the Celebes Sea, and on the west and north by the much larger South China Sea.

Since the sixteenth century, when King Philip II of Spain conquered the islands and gave them his name, the inhabitants have been living under harsh colonial rule, three hundred thirty-three years of it. They have been ruled with little mercy by the Spanish civil authorities, and with even less from the friars, who have brought not only their religion but a talent for exploiting the natives to their own ends. Both kinds of occupiers are cordially hated, the friars more than the civilians.

Things were not much better before the Spanish arrived. The islands were settled by Malaysians and Indonesians, providing a mixed Filipino-Chinese heritage before the Spaniards came and complicated matters.

In the end, after further mixing, the Philippines have wound up as a country speaking at least seventy languages and dialects. Although the friars succeeded in imposing the Catholic faith on most of these people, Muslims, Buddhists, and others crept in, and eventually with the Americans will come the Protestants. This, then, is the polyglot puzzle toward which America is casting acquisitive eyes.

There are any number of mixed motives for wanting these islands, but three stand out. Some of those already fighting American expansion think the politicians in Washington want them simply because, like Everest, they're there. Businessmen have a more definite motive. Acquiring the Philippines, they know, will be a major step toward opening up vast new markets in what they like to call the Orient. The churches constitute a third group. They want what religions in American have wanted since the Catholic French and the Protestant British fought each other for control of the continent--an opportunity to harvest untold quantities of unsaved souls.

It hardly matters to them that most of the souls in the Philippines have already been saved, at least as far as the Catholics are concerned. If Spain has done nothing else there, it has created the largest number of Catholics anywhere in the Far East. If we omit the so-called "wild tribes," who are always being omitted by someone, most of the islands' 6.5 million inhabitants are members of the Church.

Protestant Americans don't quite grasp this fact. Somehow they've gotten the idea that the revolt of the natives against Spain, which has been going on for some time, is a revolt against the Church. "Cuba Libre" they could understand, but since the Filipinos have their own language, it doesn't translate. Consequently, much of the religious push toward annexing the Philippines comes from the Protestant missionary societies, infused wtih large doses of bigotry and self-interest. Catholics want annexation too, but they're quiet about it. The score is already heavily in their favor.

People in these three groups aren't unanimous, of course. There are Protestant divines who attack what they call "gunpowder gospel," meaning forced conversions. There are also big businessmen like Andrew Carnegie who oppose invading the Philippines and annexing them. Former President Grover Cleveland calls such moves "dangerous perversions" of conquest.

Republicans who fought in the Civil War thinking they were abolishing slavery don't like the idea of possibly enslaving, so to speak, another nation; it isn't Republican, they say. All these opponents are united against one word, "imperialism," the word that's dividing America.

Yet there are also many who can't forget that Spain recognized the Confederacy and has never been suitably punished for it. They want blood--in Cuba, the Philippines, or elsewhere, just as long as it's Spanish blood. These people are the hard core of unabashed imperialism, which has been flourishing in America for years. Citizens in 1891, for example, paid respectful attention to Rear Admiral S. B. Luce when he wrote: "War is one of the great agencies by which human progress is effected. [War] stimulates natural growth, solves otherwise insoluble problems of domestic and political economy, and purges a nation of its humors. War arouses all the latent energies of a people, stimulates them to the highest exertion, and develops their mental and material resources.

"So in the economy of nature, or the providence of God, war is sent...for the forming of national character, the shaping of a people's destiny, and the spreading of civilization. With the United States as the dominant power of the western world lies the obligation of contributing her share to the further extension of civilization, to the spreading of the gospel, and conveying to less favored nations the most enlightened views of civil government. The time will come...when the nation in its manhood will 'put away childish things,' assume its own high responsibilities, and organize its forces for practical use."

Who's going to argue with a man like the admiral, the architect of the modern American Navy, first president of the Naval War College, the man who launched Alfred Mahan on his career? Luce and Mahan have both influenced T.R. and, like ripples from a stone thrown into a pond, these views spread in influential circles and raise the blood pressure and anxieties of those who oppose war, foreign entanglements, and especially imperialism.

The strident voices of Hearst and Pulitzer are strangely silent in this controversy, for the most part. On the face of it, the basic situation in the Philippines would appear to be much the same as it was in Cuba--that is, a native people exploited by the same ruthless European colonizer that brought Cubans to revolt. But having invented one war, the "yellow kids" of the New York press appear to be indifferent about inventing another.

There was something amateurish, in a way, about the war in Cuba. It was a badly managed, slap-happy war, full of volunteer enthusiasm and covered by superstars of the press. The war in the Philippines, on the other hand, is going to be serious business, as it turns out--a war fought mostly by American professionals who get whatever they need without foul-ups, and it's reported not by journalists of the Davis-Crane stripe but by hardworking correspondents whose names are hardly household words.

What is about to happen in the Philippines was foreshadowed, at least in one respect, two years after Admiral Luce's xenophobic pronouncement, when the nation found itself in a splendid illustration of what he was saying, a sort of warmup for the Philippines. In January 1893 occurs what the historian E. Berkeley Tompkins calls the "comic opera coup d'état," that is, the annexation of Hawaii, in which Queen Liliuokalani is dethroned and the islands are made available to the United States for annexation.

Is this an indigenous struggle for freedom from a ruler notorious for her imperial intransigence? Not at all. It's a revolt by a small number of property holders, nearly all of them Americans, who are determined to protect their economic, social, and political interests, none of which have much to do with the people of Hawaii. They are rich, powerful, and influential, these men, controllers of the sugar interests and all the smaller industries that have sprung from it.

They have it made. Their great plantations, worked by cheap Oriental labor, produced vast quantities of sugar as a highly profitable crop until the Tariff of 1890 put it on the free list, causing a heavy loss of market. A year later, Queen Liliuokalani ascended the throne and there was trouble in River City.

The Queen has a simple philosophy. She doesn't like foreigners and thinks Hawaii should be for the Hawaiians, hardly a novelty in human history, but she's just tough enough to try to make it work. She means to rule by fiat, but there's a viper in her political bosom. It's the American Minister to Hawaii, John L. Stevens, a friend of former Secretary of State

James G. Blaine, and a man who intends that Hawaii will be annexed if possible. It's Stevens who's really behind the revolution of the property owners on January 16, 1893, in which a white elite calmly overthrows the Hawaiians. The excuse is that, two days earlier, the Queen had tried to set aside the Constitution of 1889, which was largely the product of this same white elite.

Stevens and his friends carry out the revolution with the greatest of ease, employing 160 Marines from the cruiser *Boston*, whose captain is also pro-annexation. There has to be some alibi for this precipitous takeover, and Stevens has enough chutzpa to declare solemnly that American lives and property are in danger and must be protected. The idea is to show the Queen that, tough as she is, she isn't tough enough to defy the United States Government when it wants something. Raging will do her no good.

After the coup, Stevens moves swiftly. A provisional government is organized and a commission appointed to arrange a treaty of annexation in Washington. If this body is supposed to be a committee of Hawaiians supplicating to be annexed, it has an odd composition--three Americans and a British citizen. When it arrives and its mission becomes known, there's an explosion in the American newspapers that the annexers hadn't quite counted on. Anti-imperialists are on the barricades everywhere, and they find plenty of support from people who just don't like the idea of annexing another country, obviously against its wishes.

Secretary of State John Foster has to move fast, and he does. The commissioners arrive in San Francisco on January 29, and by February 14, they and Foster have prepared a loving valentine for the Hawaiians, duly signed. The deal is a bargain. We get the island by assuming its debt of only $3.24 million and paying the Queen $20,000 a month for life, while her daughter, Princess Kaiulani, gets a lump sum of $150,000 for agreeing not to bring up any nonsense about succession. Two days later, the House Committee on Foreign Relations speeds it through, but then it runs into a roadblock in the Senate.

The brutal tactics leading to this point are deplored in passionate speeches, and the Senate tacticians manage to stall the treaty until newly elected Grover Cleveland, a known anti-imperialist, takes office. Once in the White House, he does what the anti-interventionists have been demanding: he appoints a special investigator with full powers to look into the whole affair. James B. Blount, former chairman of the Senate Foreign Affairs Committee, is named to do the job.

First Blount sees to it that the treaty is withdrawn from the Senate, then he ends the Stevens protectorate, has the Marines ordered back to their ship, and succeeds in getting the United States flag lowered from the Hawaiian Government Building. This last act is too much for the imperialists, who burst out in righteous anger over the insult to "Old Glory." Once the flag has been raised somewhere, they say, it amounts to treason if it's voluntarily lowered, a notion providing fuel for a debate that goes on for decades.

Suddenly, however, the triumphal march of the anti-imperialists is halted when Mahan steams to the rescue with an article called "Hawaii and Our Future Sea Power," which later appears as a chapter in his equally influential 1889 book, *The Interest of America in Sea Power, Present and Future*. Everyone's talking about Mahan's Navy-inspired views, with scarcely any middle ground to be seen.

Cleveland takes matters into his own hands. He says he believes American representatives (read "Stevens") acted improperly in dethroning the Queen, and if American ethics mean anything she will have to be restored. The new American Minister, Albert Willis, gets instructions on October 18 to convey to the Queen the President's regrets for what happened, particularly the use of American troops, and after implying that she will be reinstated, suggests that royal tolerance should dictate complete amnesty for the revolutionaries, who are, after all, Americans.

Amnesty! Cleveland can almost hear an outraged shriek from the truculent Queen across thousands of miles of land and water. As far as amnesty is concerned, she lets the President know, it is her considered opinion that "such persons should be beheaded and their property confiscated by the government." So much for amnesty. So much, too, for any easy transition back to monarchy, obviously of the absolute kind. With the best political intentions, Cleveland has painted himself into a corner. He's made a high-minded case for restoring the monarchy, but if he does, it's quite possible the Marines will have to be called in again to prevent the Queen and the American community from doing something rash.

The matter reverts back to Congress, where it's debated endlessly for two months until, on May 31, 1894, the Senate passes a resolution, like one passed earlier by the House, which states: "Resolved, that of right it [Hawaii] belongs wholly to the people of the Hawaiian Islands to establish and maintain their own form of government and domestic policy; that the United States ought in no way to interfere therewith, and that any intervention in the political affairs of these islands by any other government [especially Spain] will be regarded as an act unfriendly to the United States."

While the anti-imperialists are congratulating themselves on a victory, the consensus otherwise seems to be that what Congress has done is to devise a stalemate. So matters rest for the time being, just as the rumblings of war in Cuba are beginning to be heard. But the national argument has stirred up emotions which are still propelling actions and ideas today. The word "jingo" is beginning to be heard, although few people know that its origins are British, dating to a popular music-hall ballad of 1877, when war between Great Britain and Russia seemed a grim possibility. The refrain ran:

We don't want to fight
By by Jingo if we do,
We've got the ships, we've got the men,
We've got the money too!

In America, the conflict shaping up appears to be what politicians are always calling "traditional American values" as against those who think these values are code words for something else. On the editorial page of the New York *Post*, E. L. Godkin, nearing the end of his career as the country's most influential voice with the smallest circulation, contrasts "true Patriotism" with "sham patriotism." Using the newly popular word, he rails against the "fury of our political Jingoes," who have created, he says, a "most tiresome and meaningless jargon about 'the flag' and 'a vigorous foreign policy,' and making ourselves 'respected in the eyes of the world.' Hence have proceeded the efforts to work up the American people into a towering rage over some far-off island, which nine-tenths of them know nothing and care less about, or to get up a foreign war with some weak power which it would be a disgrace to fight."

Then Godkin works *himself* into full cry: "The medium through which the newspaper acts most effectively on the enthusiastic temperament is what is known as 'true Americanism,' or 'intense Americanism.' An 'intense American' is constantly on the lookout for somebody who expresses or implies doubts about the ability of the United States to thrash all other nations, or one who fails to acknowledge the right of the United States to occupy such territories, canals, isthmuses, or peninsulas, as they may think desirable."

All this is against the predominant national grain, however. In the United States, as the war with Spain approached, more and more people, many of them influential, appeared to be actually longing for imperial conquest. Mahan is one of their chief spokesmen. "The best hopes of the world," he tells readers of the *North American Review* in November 1894, don't rest "in fond dreams of unbroken peace." He exults in the idea that men are welcoming the "jarring sounds which betoken that there is no immediate danger of the leading peoples turning their swords into plowshares." In the same magazine two years later, Captain H. C. Taylor, who succeeded Mahan as president of the Naval War College, tells the country why war is good for you. "Not only," says the captain, "do nations that practice too long the arts of peace in forgetfulness of war become enfeebled and the natural prey of neighbors grown strong through combat, but they grow corrupt internally as well and race decadence hastens its steps. The corrupt ease, the luxurious immorality of life, towards which a total absence of war always leads nations, has in it something more degrading for the human race than simple savagery."

Such sentiments help explain why Hearst and Pulitzer found it so easy to push Americans into the war with Spain, with all its unforeseen consequences, and why the prospect of annexing the Hawaiian Islands, and later the Philippines, appalls only a vociferous minority of Americans. One move leads to the other. Three days after Santiago Bay, the Senate passes a joint resolution to annex the Hawaiian Islands by a vote of 42 to 21, with 26 abstentions. The division in the House is just about the same. As one Representative puts it, members have changed their minds and voted "yes" because "the war fever has gotten into their blood." McKinley signs the resolution the day after it's passed.

A day later, former President Cleveland writes to Richard Olney: "Hawaii is ours. As I look back upon the first steps in this miserable business and as I contemplate the means used to complete the outrage, I am ashamed of the whole affair."

Hawaii is one thing, the Philippines are another. Only one irate old lady stood in the way on the nearer islands, but the other territory is Asian, and Spain still has to be euchred out of it, not to mention the presumptuous idea that the Filipinos, like the Cubans, seem to want their independence. No wonder that McKinley, sensing the issue is strewn with land mines, can't make up his mind what to do.

While the War Department and General Miles are trying to destroy each other, the President pleads for people, in and out of government, to give him their thoughts on the Philippines. For his part, he says, he's studying the question constantly, and praying in-between studies. Now and then he talks to editors and other prominent citizens, who aren't much help in arriving at a consensus. By doing nothing, he's opened the door to a national debate.

Those who don't want annexation propose calling it a protectorate instead, but with Dewey and his fleet there, with more American troops arriving, the Administration can't very well withdraw on the basis of this fuzzy definition. So there it is again: Dewey hasn't sailed away, and America, shrouded in folds of the flag, can't back off now.

There are practical reasons for staying in the Philippines, especially if you're a Republican. The European nations are threatening to partition China, and rosy visions of huge trade opportunities in Asia are illuminating the horizon. Manila would at least give us a foothold, the President believes. He doesn't want a lot of territory, though, and certainly this deeply conservative man is not anxious to take any kind of radical step. Forcible annexation would be "criminal aggression," he declares.

For McKinley, it's one of the hardest decisions he's ever had to make. Leech describes how he paces the White House floor night after night and, before he sleeps, kneels by his bedside in the hope of getting some help from a Higher Authority. Conscience tells him he ought to renounce any claim to the Philippines, but he simply can't bring himself to do it. If he decides for annexation, it will mean peace in the Pacific and Manila needn't be given up, because that would be another blow to conscience if he simply abandoned the islands to the

Spaniards. Well, suppose we kept Manila and let Spain have the rest, could the country manage without the revenue coming from its only large port and big city? Wouldn't Spain be forced to sell to the Americans?

That's about as near as McKinley gets to arriving at a conclusion before he begins to draw up instructions for the commissioners he's sending to the peace conference in Paris, headed by a man in whom he doesn't have a great deal of confidence, Secretary of State William Day.

A major problem for McKinley is that he doesn't really know what's happening in Manila, and before making a decision, he decides to send an emissary, General Francis V. Greene, a New York militia officer, to survey the scene for him. Greene has impressive qualifications. A former officer in the Regular Army, he taught engineering at West Point and has had a notable career in business. He's literate, observant, and articulate.

Greene makes his report to the President on September 27, 1898, after six weeks in the Philippines. The Spanish governmental machinery is in a state of disorganization, he reports, and the officers of the American occupying forces are the only central authority. The Spaniards are in deadly fear of the insurgents, whose hatred for them is virulent. Catholicism may have been planted firmly, but for many of the people, it's bloomed into hate for the friars who planted it. Greene believes the Filipinos will fight hard if there's any attempt to restore Spanish rule, and that would surely lead to war and anarchy.

On the other hand, Greene doesn't think much of Aguinaldo's ideas about self-government. He calls them despotic and asserts, incorrectly as it turns out, that the insurgents can't count on the native population of the other islands to back them. But then he notes--and now he's on the right track--that well-educated Filipinos with property are not supporting the rebels and don't particularly want to be independent.

Greene concludes that the protection of a strong nation will be necessary for years and comes out foursquare for annexation. In that spirit, he makes an enthusiastic inventory of the potential wealth of the islands, only waiting to be exploited. If the natives offer any serious resistance, he adds, the military won't have much trouble overcoming it, and so the insurgency isn't really important.

McKinley disagrees. As a politician, he sees what Greene doesn't: that these matters are fraught with political dangers, already evident in the national debate. Nor does he believe the insurgency is as ineffective as Greene thinks it is. After all, they've overrun Luzon, captured its Spanish garrison, and set up a revolutionary capital at Malolos, the biggest town north of Manila. Moreover, Aguinaldo has also organized and set in motion the first Congress of the Philippine Republic. This is going to be "Cuba Libre" all over again, with a different cast of characters.

Who is this man, Emilio Aguinaldo, who's created such a serious problem for the American government, and whom Mark Twain will compare with George Washington and Joan of Arc? Born about 1869 in Cavite Viejo, his father was a farmer who sold vegetables impartially to the Spaniards and the natives, meanwhile dabbling in politics and rising to be mayor of Cavite. Emilio's mother was a *mestiza*, whose father was Chinese.

Growing up, Aguinaldo never learned enough Spanish to speak with the conquerors and had to be content with the minimal education provided by the Tagalog school. An ambitious young man, he went to Manila and got a better education at the Jesuit school, where he was quick to learn. Returning home, he took the oath of office from the Spanish government to become Captain Municipal of Cavite, giving him his first opportunity to show his strength as a leader. But his father died, and in order to take care of his mother, he had to go back to peddling vegetables for a time. The insurgency he began to lead has increased in strength until it's overrun Luzon and established the revolutionary government Greene reports is nothing to worry about.

McKinley and his fellow Republicans have a dilemma on their hands. To establish American rule in Luzon is going to be taken as American colonialism, replacing the Spanish variety. To the troops on the ground, this idea is already a betrayal. They thought all they had to do was throw the Spaniards out and go home.

Their unhappiness flows back to America in letters, until William Jennings Bryan protests in the Cabinet Room one day: "Many of the Nebraska volunteers feel that they have a right to be mustered out, on the ground that the issues of the war have changed. They volunteered to break the yoke of Spain in

Cuba, and for nothing else. They did not volunteer to attempt the subjugation of other peoples, or establish United States sovereignty elsewhere."

There's still time for equivocation. The peace commissioners begin their talks in Paris on October 1, with divided opinions and with the impetus toward annexation. It's going to be a long battle there, but events won't wait in the Philippines. They've been building toward a climax for a long time.

2

TAKING MANILA

As far as the armed forces are concerned, the war in the Philippines is older than the one in Cuba. In fact, forty-nine days before the United States declared war on Spain, the American consul in Manila told the State Department in a dispatch on February 22, 1898: "Conditions here and in Cuba are practically alike. War exists, and battles are of almost daily occurrence. Prisoners are brought here and shot without trial, and Manila is under martial law."

It's Spain's war with the rebels he's talking about; we're still on the sidelines. "The Crown forces," the consul goes on, "have been unable to dislodge a rebel army within ten miles of Manila, and last Saturday, February 19, a battle was fought there. A republic is organized here as in Cuba. Insurgents are being armed and drilled, are rapidly increasing in number and efficiency, and all agree that a general uprising will come as soon as the Governor-General embarks for Spain, which is fixed for March 8."

America has its own plans for Manila. Long before the *Maine* blew up, the city's capture was being planned. As early as the fall of 1897, while Dewey was sitting in the Gulf of California commanding the *Narragansett*, he was planning what he'd do if war was declared. He'd sail over with his ship and take the city. To do that he needed help, so that's why he asked for command of the Asiatic Squadron and got it. Two months before the *Maine* disaster, on December 7, 1898, he sailed for Hong Kong. On the following February 25, Roosevelt cabled him: "In the event of declaration of war with Spain, your duty will be to see that the Spanish squadron does not leave the Asiatic coast, and start offensive operations in Philippine Islands." He's certainly prevented the Spanish squadron from doing anything but sink. "Offensive operations" come next.

What they're thinking about in Washington, except for the waffling McKinley, is expressed early in 1898 by Frank A. Vanderlip, Secretary of the Treasury: "The possession of the Philippines by a progressive commercial power, if the Nicaragua Canal project should be completed, would change the course of ocean navigation as it concerns a large percentage of the water-borne traffic of the world.

"The project is alluring. In the undeveloped resources of the Philippines the sanguine radicals see a great opportunity for our genius. They recognize that in a decade we might make a change greater than has been wrought since Magellan's discovery until the present time. They see great development companies formed to test the richness of the unknown mineral deposits, and still others to develop transportation or to reap the treasures of the forests. We thus see with sudden clearness that some of the most revered of our political maxims have outlived their force." Then he adds: "A new mainspring...has become the directing force...the mainspring of commercialism."

This contribution to the department of utter frankness is the kind of thing upstanding businessmen can understand. A glorious vision rises before them: the United States (and of course themselves) in command of a great distributing center in the Philippines, dispensing the fruits of unobstructed capitalism to that half of the world's entire population living within a radius of 3,500 miles from Manila.

With such visions, the Administration begins its movement westward. Fresh from his triumph at Manila Bay, Dewey informs the government on May 13 that he's going to need 5,000 men to subdue the islands, surely one of the worst wrong guesses in history. The government is quick to supply what he wants. On May 25, the first ships of a very large expeditionary force, three transports, carrying 117 officers and 2,382 men under command of Brigadier General Thomas M. Anderson, sail from San Francisco. About the same time, the Navy confirms a rumor that on June 13 a Spanish fleet of six armored cruisers, six converted cruisers, and four destroyers had been reported off Ceuta, sailing east. Since this force is larger than the entire Asiatic Squadron, the Navy worries that it might reach Manila Bay and destroy Dewey, then wait for the pitifully vulnerable American transports to arrive. Dewey is warned and says he's ready. As for the commanders of the transports, who are out of touch with everyone for thirty days, they have no idea what may be waiting for them on the other side of the Pacific.

But this mighty Spanish fleet proves to be as ghostly as the unfortunate Cervera's moth-eaten armada was reputed to be while the Americans were still trying to find it. The transports proceed peacefully on their way, stopping at Honolulu to pick up a convoy ship, the cruiser *Charleston*. Its commander, Captain Henry Glass, has instructions to stop along the way and pluck Guam off the Spanish Empire's colonial tree.

Thinking the place must be heavily fortified, Glass approaches cautiously, sending several shots across the bow, figuratively speaking, of Fort Santa Cruz. No reply. When he lands, Glass discovers that the Spanish authorities don't even know war has broken out, and the fort's guns have long since been taken elsewhere. Its commander tells Glass: "Why, Captain, we are without defenses at this port, as all of our forts have been dismantled. If it were that you were entitled to a salute from us, we would not have fired it...as we have not even a field-piece on this bay." Guam gives in without a murmur.

Next day Glass and the transports arrive at Manila and begin disembarking at Cavite. The captain talks to Aguinaldo and reports later, "He did not seem pleased at the incoming of our land forces," although this force isn't large enough to do more than hold the base.

But the Yanks are coming. On June 15, Brigadier General Francis V. Greene, who will soon be on a more diplomatic mission for the President, sails with 3,000 men, and on June 27 and 28, the largest force yet, nearly 5,000 officers and men, slip out of San Francisco under the command of Brigadier General Arthur MacArthur, the forerunner of that other commander, his son Douglas. Hot on their heels is the final group of the expedition, its commanding general, Major General Wesley Merritt, and his staff.

What a contrast to the incredible bungling at Tampa. This expeditionary force is launched with the kind of fanfare reserved for conquering heroes. Writing home, a Signal Corps sergeant reports: "What a magnificent send-off San Francisco gave us as we sailed out of the harbor. The numberless steam whistles, the guns, flags flying everywhere, handkerchiefs waving. Then the boys of the Indiana realized what the parting really meant, but we did not dwell long upon that, for as we passed [through the Golden Gate] a strong wind was blowing which steadily increased. After crossing the bar the sea was very rough, and I think nine hundred and ninety of the one thousand men on board were sea-sick. It was an exceedingly rough night--one might say a night of horror--you must know how crowded we were. It was simply suffocating. A porthole leaked somewhere, and the water washed back and forth over our deck, carrying with it various articles which had been broken loose. I saw a large roast of beef, two boxes of hard-tack, two large coffee-pots, and some pans float past our room several times, making a most unearthly racket."

For the sergeant, things aren't much better the next day. Lashed to a stanchion, he has to perform his task of waving signals to the other ships. "It was the wildest work I ever did," he writes. "The seas were tremendous. Half a gale was blowing. We were in the trough of the sea, rolling so heavily it seemed as if every roll would be our last." After such a voyage, the stopover in Hawaii is a short visit to heaven.

On the way again, the commanders have some apprehension about Admiral Cámara's phantom fleet, not knowing yet that after Santiago Bay the Navy dispatched a flying squadron to harass the Spanish on their own coast. Cámara had got as far as Suez, but when he learned of this move, he retraced his steps. He's lucky. If he had gone on, it's virtually certain he would have arrived in the Philippines with his ships in worse shape than Cervera's, sitting ducks for Dewey.

The War Department has turned itself inside out to ensure the success of Merritt's expedition, even requisitioning men and material the struggling troops in Cuba are going to need. There's something almost indecent in this rush toward the Philippines, and it isn't entirely on the American side by any means. At this point, Spain and the United States are in agreement on only one thing: both of them want to keep the rebels out of Manila, and they're quite frankly racist about it. Dewey customarily refers to the Filipinos as "the Indians," and promises he will "enter the city and keep the Indians out."

When he arrives on July 25, General Merritt says he has been given orders not to deal with "the Indians." He is instructed to treat them as non-people. He won't recognize them, won't promise them anything, and as far as he's concerned, "Aguinaldo is just the same to me as a boy in the street." As for the Spanish commander in Manila, General Fermín Jáudenes, he's vehement about it. His interpreter tells Merritt: "For himself, he was willing to surrender to white people, but never to niggers."

Greene's troops land on a peanut field a little south of Manila, well within range of the Spaniards' field guns, but the gunners aren't anxious to do more than make a few perfunctory gestures, knowing that anything else would unleash a barrage from Dewey's fleet. Greene and MacArthur land next, using native lighters that resemble sail-less Chinese junks.

All the invading forces are now joined in what they're calling Camp Dewey. Days go by while entrenchments are dug, interrupted only by a few wild and unenthusiastic volleys from the Spaniards. The Americans don't answer until the night of July 31, when a heavier outburst from the Spanish guns provokes them into a reply.

The Cuban mistake is repeated. Now the enemy knows exactly where the Americans are and they pour in a much more accurate fire, leaving ten men killed and forty-three wounded. Thinking they've got onto a good thing, the Spaniards keep up their fire for the next few nights, but Dewey won't let the troops fire back. He's philosophical about it. "Better to have small losses, night after night, in the trenches, than to run the risk of greater losses by premature attack." However, he's not dogmatic. If Greene wants to return fire, he'll order a bombardment from the fleet.

Bombarding always seems like a good idea anyway to the Navy, as Shafter knows, and so, on August 7, Dewey sends a message to General Jáudenes that unless he stops firing on the American positions he will get a heavy load of shells in forty-eight hours' time. That's enough not only to end the firing but to start negotiations. Jáudenes has no wish to commit suicide.

The problem with surrendering is much the same as it was in Santiago. Jáudenes wants to do it, but there's the troublesome matter of Spanish honor, not to mention preserving his image in Madrid. The negotiations open with both sides agreeing that the city will be surrendered in return for Dewey's promise to keep Aguinaldo and his army out, something both sides want. Then, on August 13, they will fight what Freidel calls "one of the most unusual battles in military and naval history," with the outcome prearranged. Jáudenes will make a show of resistance, weakening his troops facing the Americans so they can be used to bolster defenses against the insurgents. At the same time, Dewey and Merritt tell Aguinaldo that their troops will fire on the rebels if they try to enter the city. Nevertheless, since the commanders don't know about the armistice just signed, because of Dewey's by now notorious cut cable, it's going to be virtually impossible to pull off a bloodless battle.

The scenario starts unfolding at 9 A.M. on the thirteenth when Dewey's ships open fire on Fort San Augustín at Malate, without damaging anyone since it had already been evacuated. As the American troops wade in the water along the beach, they signal their position to Dewey's ships. Then the Colorado volunteers cross an inlet and storm the empty fort.

That should have been the end of the battle, but the rebels aren't cooperating. They're firing on the Spaniards, who are firing back. And something else seems to have gone wrong with the scenario. When MacArthur's men encounter a Spanish blockhouse near the beach, they're greeted with heavy fire. For hours the two sides exchange volleys as the Americans push their way forward, tramping through gardens, edging around houses and the huts of the poor until a civilian appears and tells them a white flag has been raised over the blockhouse.

That opens the door to Manila. Greene has a half-dozen others jump on their horses and gallop up the street beyond the blockhouse into the Luneta, as the city's public promenade is called. Spanish infantry, who also aren't following the script, fire on them from the city walls, but Greene and his men ride on until they encounter a heavy barricade of railway iron thrown across the sea-front promenade.

Pulling up, Greene sees a Spanish officer and a private standing at an embrasure and inquires if the town is surrendering. The officer says he doesn't know. All he's been told is to put up a white flag, which he immediately produces. While this conversation is going on, American troops are moving up behind Greene, exchanging occasional shots with unseen Spanish not-very-sharpshooters.

A medieval-looking bridge crosses over a grassy moat at the entrance to this walled city (as it was then), but it isn't Horatio who's at this bridge, just B company of the 23rd Regulars. Beyond the wall they can see a long street along which Spanish troops are trying to retreat. Captain O'Connor, of the 23rd, halts them until he gets further orders.

Everything seems to have gone wrong with the bloodless surrender. Brown-uniformed American troops are confronting white-uniformed Spaniards in several places, while the sound of firing is nearly continuous. Momentarily, the whole plan stands in terrible danger of disintegrating if some careless soldier on either side fires in the wrong place and sets off a massacre.

Greene demonstrates that he's equal to the occasion. Looking back, he sees the main body of troops advancing and orders them to hold the gates. Then he tells the Spanish officers to march their troops into the city. At this point, a carriage rolls up, bearing two men in livery, who give Greene a note from Dewey. It says that Army and Navy officers are even now negotiating the actual surrender.

Greene returns with the messengers, but he comes back later and orders the 3rd Artillery into a position where they can stop the rebels from entering the city. Other regiments are sent to push back over the bridges those who have already entered. This comes as a considerable shock to the rebels, who haven't been told they aren't going to share the victory. They had expected to plant their flag on the walls. Greene completes the initial conquest. "I marched down the river to the captain of the port's office," he writes, "where I ordered the Spanish flag hauled down and the American flag raised in its place."

Not quite bloodless--six Americans and forty-nine Spaniards are killed--but a reasonable facsimile of a battle for Manila. Jáudenes can report to Madrid that he did his best in the face of superior numbers. The Americans are in and the Spaniards are literally out, their troops milling around outside the walls until they can be concentrated in prisoner-of-war camps. Aguinaldo's men are also outside the walls and they're bitter about it.

Spanish authorities still inside Manila are terrified the rebels will get in and take a terrible vengeance for decades of brutal misrule, but they needn't worry, even though the furious insurgents have broken through and taken a small part of the city near its outer limits. Dewey asks Washington for instructions on how to deal with Aguinaldo, who is demanding a joint occupation. McKinley's answer is unequivocal: "The President directs that there must be no joint occupation with

MANILA HAS FALLEN, HONG KONG REPORTS.

Capital of the Philippines, Long Menaced, Said to Be Occupied by the American Troops.

New York Journal, August 15, 1898

the insurgents. The insurgents and all others must recognize the military occupation and authority of the United States. Use whatever means in your judgment are necessary to this end. All law-abiding people must be treated alike."

Madrid is nearly as angry as the rebels. They protest vociferously that Manila was captured after they had signed an armistice, but Dewey's cut cable prevented the news from reaching the city in time, so the Americans win on a technicality. If Spain wants to get Manila back, it will have to re-fight the entire war. Not a chance. The United States is in sole possession of Cavite and about three quarters of Manila, the stubborn rebels holding on to the other quarter. But we want it all--not just Manila but the entire Philippine Islands. At that moment, however, we're under siege from several thousand insurgents, who are entrenching themselves in the old Spanish earthworks, some of them within a revolver shot of barracks being occupied by Americans.

A few days later, these presumptuous Filipinos are demanding joint occupation of the city once more. Again, Dewey asks the White House for advice about "forcing obedience of the insurgents in this matter and others that may arise." McKinley's answer is loud and clear: "Use any means in your judgment to that end."

With the lessons of Cuba barely behind them, the American commanders still don't understand these people who want their own country. General Anderson, who has been conducting the negotiations, finds an "astonishing" change in them from "reasonable" to "aggressive." Anderson thinks this is because Aguinaldo has decided that the Americans mean to hold the Philippines under military rule, which is not far from the truth. And if that's true, there's not much to talk about.

In Paris, however, there is still plenty to negotiate, and the commissioners from both countries have been doing it since the first of October. By December 10, the wrangling is over and both parties sign the Treaty of Paris. The United States gets Guam, Puerto Rico, and the Philippines. The latter acquisition will cost us $20 million, a bargain. In the *Harvard Law Review*, Carmen F. Randolph writes: "Assuming that the annexation of the Philippines is embodied in the treaty, it is the most questionable project of domestic concern that a President has ever submitted to the Senate."

No one doubts a battle will take place there, reflecting the heated debate sweeping the country. Mr. Dooley, Finley Peter Dunne's creation, conveys at least part of the national conflict when he asks his friend Hennessey for *his* opinion. "I know what I'd do if I was Mac," Hennessey responds forthrightly. "I'd hist a flag over th' Philipeens, an' I'd take in th' whole lot iv thim. an' yet," said Mr. Dooley, "'tis not more than two months since we learned whether they were islands or canned goods." Mr. Dooley also has some thoughts on future trade: "We import jute, hemp, cigar wrappers, sugar an' fairy tales fr'm th' Ph'lippes, an' export six-inch wheels an' the like."

The President has a different vision, and expounds it in a burst of historic honesty that leaves a permanent blot on his image. After meeting with the Methodist Episcopal Church's General Missionary Committee, an extremely active expansionist pressure group, he raises a hand as they're leaving and says: "Not quite yet, gentlemen! Before you go I would like to say just a word about the Philippines business." He rehearses his dilemma once again for them and concludes: "I walked the floor of the White House night after night until midnight, and I am not ashamed to tell you, gentlemen, that I went down on my knees and prayed to Almighty God for light and guidance more than one night. And one night late it came to me this way--I don't know how it was, but it came...that there was nothing left for me to do but take them all, and to educate the Filipinos, and uplift them and civilize them and Christianize them, and by God's grace do the very best we could by them, as our fellow-men for whom Christ also died. And then I went to bed, and went to sleep, and slept soundly, and the next morning I sent for the Chief Engineer of the War Department (our map-maker) and I told him to put the Philippines on the map of the United States, and there they are, and there they will stay while I am President."

Plainly, the President is a long way from reality. He thinks the Filipinos are impoverished, which most of them are by American standards, and mostly illiterate, which is not the case. He means to impose a just and merciful American government on them. As for Aguinaldo's insurgents, he regards them as a lawless lot only interested in loot, alienated from the gentle masses who just want peace. He believes they have been stirred to commit foul deeds by unscrupulous native politicians like Aguinaldo. As soon as they and all the others understand what a blessing Big Papa is giving them by annexation, they will happily submit.

Neither the President nor his Cabinet members have any realistic conception of what's going on in the Philippines, in spite of all the official papers. Dewey warned them in October that Luzon was in a state of anarchy, which could be expected to spread to the other islands. But no one in the White House pays much attention because they keep getting cheery reports from General Elwell S. Otis, whom General Merritt has placed in command of the troops so that he can devote all his time to administration.

This isn't entirely Otis's fault--in a way. He often finds himself without accurate information, since most of what he knows comes from the people he associates with--upper-class men of property in Manila. These people supported the government Aguinaldo set up in Malolos at the beginning simply because they hated Spain so much, but when it comes down to cases, they really don't want independence. They prefer to be protected by their American friends, who will make them even richer.

These friends, however, don't seem overly anxious to win hearts and minds. Supporters of the Americans in Manila may have money and property, but they're the wrong color. Even American officers are sometimes tactless and discourteous, and the troops are frankly racist in their dealings with the natives. More than the regulars, the volunteers are angry at finding themselves hated and it's Cuba all over again. They loathe the "niggers."

Everything now depends on whether the peace treaty is ratified by the Senate, where a furious debate is under way. If it's confirmed and the Philippines are ceded to the United States, according to its terms, Aguinaldo's government in Malolos is ready to declare a revolution, and they advertise it by posting manifestos in places where they will do the most good. It's becoming brown against white, whether Spanish or American, and revolutionary fervor spreads rapidly from island to island. Most Filipinos don't have any clear conception of broad ideas like nationalism and unity, but they have no trouble understanding what freedom means, and the word is sweet.

Aguinaldo's name is synonymous with it, and even in the remote interior, tribesmen are rallying to him.

Now that it seems imminent, annexation isn't making McKinley any more popular at home. He's abused by press and pulpit. To many people, it looks like a clear case of military takeover for the sake of those who have always been considered McKinley's close allies--the business community and especially Wall Street. His opponents in Congress warn him angrily about abusing executive power and deplore the President's seeming indifference to public opinion.

Meanwhile, Manila under siege is a tinderbox waiting to explode. Otis has instructions to "preserve the peace," and he takes every precaution to avoid open hostilities while the debate over the treaty is going on. He publishes a proclamation from the President to the Philippines, which has already been denounced at home as "contemptuous" and "insulting," but takes the liberty of deleting from it any reference to American sovereignty. The general in command of the American post at Iloilo, not knowing of this judicious censorship, publishes the document in its original form, and predictably it enrages the insurgents anew.

Aguinaldo gives up hope at this point and begins preparing for war. While Congress is debating the treaty, he's getting his artillery into position on the siege line and strengthening his defense. He decides, however, to make one more move toward peace and asks Otis for a meeting to see if the tensions can't be reduced. Otis sends a commission of officers, who hear their Filipino counterparts present a compromise proposal. The Americans can have a protectorate, they say, if independence is also granted. But at the same time, they register strong protests against being excluded from Manila and against American encroachments on their territory outside the city limits. Otis pays no attention to their grievances, but he does forward the compromise proposal to Washington. No reply. In his usual manner, Otis then issues soothing statements to the press and to Washington.

This is part of a deliberate campaign to assure that Americans at home will be kept in as much ignorance as possible about what's going on in the Philippines. As early as July, the correspondents were protesting the establishment of censorship, and American reporters in Manila more or less smuggled out a statement telling people at home what was being done to them. Sent on the mail boat to Hong Kong and then by cable to America, their statement says: "We believe that owing to official dispatches from Manila made public in Washington the people of the United States have not received a correct impression of the situation in the Philippines. The censorship has compelled us to participate in these misrepresentations by excising or altering uncontroversial statements of fact, on the plea as General Otis stated, that 'they would alarm the people at home, or have the people of the United States by the ears.'"

Robert M. Collins, the Associated Press's man in Manila, writes to his boss, Melville Stone: "Recently I filed what I thought was the most inoffensive statement that the business men who had appeared before the commission had advocated a retention of the existing system of currency. The censor said, 'I ought not to let that go. That would be a lift for William Jennings Bryan. My instructions are to shut off everything that would hurt McKinley's administration.'"

Why is the Administration so intent on keeping as much news as possible from the public? The answer is embodied in the message Alger sends to Otis on January 21: "Give copy to Dewey of all official documents to you relating to joint operations." This means that the treaty is signed and all but approved, and McKinley is determined to go ahead with a military takeover. To prepare the public, the War Department issues a statement quoting Otis that the insurgents are about "to force an issue. If this occurs, the results cannot be foreseen." Otis has permission to do battle, the Department says candidly, and "it must be understood that there is nothing in General Otis's instructions to prevent him [from] most vigorously defending himself and the interests confided to him."

Otis, meanwhile, is laying down his own cheerful propaganda line. Americans are completely in control of Manila, he reports, and the insurgent leaders have instructed their troops to take defensive action only. He calls the notion that they might attack the city both "ridiculous and suicidal." But on January 24, the War Department asserts that Otis holds just the opposite opinion.

In fact, Otis is following specific orders. On January 21, he asked Dewey to get the fleet's guns in position to support his troops, and at the same time, ordered the men stationed at Iloilo to return to Manila. He also instructed General MacArthur to get his artillery in place to support the troops at Pandacan.

Aguinaldo isn't unaware of what the Americans are up to. On the same day Otis issued his orders, he learned that the joint negotiating commission had decided not to hold any more sessions and was ready to "complete the execution of its plans." A few days later, he's told that Dewey has fired all the Filipinos who have been doing dogsbody work for the American ships. No reason given.

We're at a point of crisis as the Senate prepares to vote on ratification of the treaty. Henry Adams writes from Washington on January 29: "Old Hoar is quite frantic. [He means Senator George F. Hoar, of Massachusetts.] In executive session the other day he declared to the Senate that if he could only prevent ratification of the Treaty, he would willingly lay his head upon the block before the Vice-President's chair. So Cabot told me with a gasp. I would gladly see the execution on the same condition, if I could see how under the scaffold of this sainted man, I could find an escape from the Philippines. *Nous y sommes*, and as far as I can see, Treaty or no Treaty, we must stay and fight the Philippines [sic]. No one wants it. Poor [Senator Eugene] Hale is at last whipped till he cowers. There is no fight left in him. Our army is in as bad a condition as the French. It needs complete reconstruction. In case of serious operations in the Philippines, I really do not see a hope of escaping awful disaster. Of course we can thrash the Philippines and kill them by the hundred thousand, but it will cost in one season at least fifty thousand men, fifty million of money, and indefinite loss of reputation."

Charles Francis Adams, Jr. makes a rather far-fetched historical comparison. It's as though the French, after Yorktown, had taken the colonies as a transfer from England, he says, then put down the rebels because they thought we couldn't govern ourselves. Only the French conscience would have stood in the way, he goes on, and "neither would there have been anything in the record of the next years under the old federation to have shown that they were not right in such a conclusion. On the contrary, Shays' rebellion in Massachusetts would have quite justified them in such a course of reasoning and line of procedure." His Anti-Imperialist League audience in Boston's Tremont Temple gives him a round of applause.

Now, in Manila, things are moving rapidly toward a climax. On February 2, Lieutenant F. Hall, of the 20th Kansas Volunteer Infantry, gets some secret orders from Colonel Frederick Funston. He's told to start a shooting war with the insurgents if it's possible. Other regiments get similar orders.

About the same time, an unplanned tinderbox explosion almost occurs in another area when Colonel John M. Stotsenberg, of the 54th Nebraska, finds himself in a shouting match with a Filipino officer commanding troops in Santol, a small town near the colonel's outpost, in the Pandacan area. Violence is averted because at the moment the Americans have orders not to fire, and negotiations take place instead. The Americans demand that the rebels withdraw from the town. Under protest, the Filipinos do so, and the Nebraska troops move in.

Next day, February 3, Senator Hoar gets a cable from Howard Bray, an Englishman working with the rebel junta in Hong Kong (the equivalent of the Cuban Peanut Club in New York). Bray wants Hoar to view news of hostilities with caution, adding that the Stotsenberg incident was only "a political move to influence votes in the Senate. In any case an insignificant skirmish due to intentional provocation." For some reason, Hoar makes no mention of this in the closing hours of the treaty debate, and Otis proceeds to carry out his plan of provocation without further interference from home.

On February 4 comes the flash point we've been waiting for. Otis orders the Nebraskans to feel free to fire if they spot any more rebel "intruders," and Colonel Stotsenberg carries out the plan's final details. During the afternoon, rumors circulate through Manila that American troops have been placed under arms.

In the end, the start of the entire war to put down Aguinaldo and secure the Philippines comes down to two men, Private Willie Grayson and a friend named Miller. They're on sentry duty outside Santol, ordered to patrol a hundred yards into an unoccupied area the insurgents claim as belonging to them. As Grayson tells us later, they carried out their orders, then "waited to see if there were any insurgents in the vicinity."

There were. Grayson reports: "About eight o'clock...something rose slowly up not twenty feet in front of us. It was a Filipino. I yelled 'Halt!'...He immediately shouted 'Halto!' at me. Well, I thought the best thing to do was to shoot him. He dropped. Then two Filipinos sprang out of a gateway about fifteen feet from us. I called, 'Halt!' and Miller fired and dropped one. I saw that another was left. Well, I think I got my second Filipino that time. We retreated to where our six other fellows were, and I said, 'Line up, fellows, the niggers are in here all through these yards.'" Shots blaze out on both sides.

General MacArthur confirms that the start of the war is no accident. "We had a pre-arranged plan," he writes. "Our tactical arrangements there were very perfect, indeed. Everything was connected by wire...and within an instant after the firing at the outpost I received a message from Stotsenberg. 'The pipe line outpost has been fired on; I am moving out with my entire regiment.' ...When I got Colonel Stotsenberg's report I simply wired all commanders to carry out pre-arranged plans, and the whole division was placed on the firing line."

On the lowest military echelons, conscience still lives. Private Grayson had been ordered to shoot if he had to, but when he sees the result, it dawns on him that he may have been designated as the cheese that tripped the mousetrap. On his way home when the war is over for his outfit, he talks about "the damn bull-headedness" of the officers who ordered the advance of his outfit into territory that didn't belong to the Americans, a move that led to his firing of the fatal shot. What Grayson doesn't know is that on the day of the precipitating incident Otis had countermanded long-standing orders to guards at the outposts to avoid any such incitement, and that behind the decoy sentries was a large part of the American army.

Dewey's ships have joined in as the Americans advance and firing breaks out along the entire siege line. The rebels begin to fall back under the weight of the Americans' onrush. Casualties are so great among them that the next day Aguinaldo does what must have been humiliating. He sends a conciliatory message to Otis. The fighting last night was an accident, he says, and not the result of any orders he gave. He asks for a cease-fire and establishment of a neutral area between the two sides. Otis gives him a discouraging answer. The fighting has begun, he says sententiously, and it must go on until it stops--when, he doesn't say.

There's a good reason why Otis refuses a cease-fire. By this time he's heard from Washington. When McKinley got the news just before midnight the day before, he told the press Manila had been attacked by insurgents. After meeting with the Cabinet next morning, he instructs Otis "to follow up his victory over the insurgents and crush the power of Aguinaldo in the Philippines." Nothing could be clearer.

A White House reporter for the San Francisco *Call* supplies some interesting details. After McKinley got the midnight call, the paper says, he told an intimate friend that "the Manila engagement would, in his opinion, insure the ratification of the treaty tomorrow." The *Call* reporter talks to Senator Lodge next day and he has the same opinion.

One last bolt from the anti-treaty side is cast next day in the Senate when Benjamin "Pitchfork Ben" Tillman, of South Carolina, an unabashed white supremacist, takes the Senate floor and thunders: "Time alone will tell whether this battle was provoked by the Filipinos for purposes of their own, or by the Americans...to sway men in this Senate to ratify the treaty and change the status."

The tumult ends on February 6, when the treaty passes-- by one vote. What Tillman implied is fairly clear to a good many people and they're outraged by it, but the Administration blandly insists that the rebels "fired on the flag" and it's all their fault. It will be a little while before the inevitable truth gets through to the public, and meanwhile there's one brutal fact everyone has to face: the war for the Philippines has begun.

3

INTO THE QUAGMIRE

A SHOCK WAVE SPREADS ACROSS AMERICA WHEN THE NEWS Otis can't completely suppress informs the people back home that our boys aren't simply occupying Manila but fighting an all-out war with the insurgents. Obviously, men are going to be killed, and this isn't what we bargained for. Cuba should have been the end of it.

Republicans are in disarray because they see themselves as instruments of an increasingly unpopular public policy with an election year nearly at hand. Immediate damage control is called for, and McKinley does his best to provide it by braving the New England winter to make a speech in Boston at the Home Market Club on February 16.

The President isn't devious. He explains once more, sincerely and forthrightly, how he got from there to here, and concludes: "I do not prophesy. The present is all- absorbing to me. But I cannot bound my vision by the blood-stained trenches around Manila--where every red drop, whether from the veins of an American soldier or a misguided Filipino, is anguish to my heart--but by the broad range of future years...[that people's] children shall for ages hence bless the American republic because it emancipated and redeemed their fatherland, and set them in the pathway of the world's best civilization."

His audience isn't listening to these pious promises of redemption for the Filipinos. What it feels and hears is that phrase, "the blood-stained trenches around Manila." The red drops he's talking about could be falling from the veins of someone they love. The applause is perfunctory. Not even the President can make this war truly popular. Nevertheless, it's the imperialists who are in power, and for a few months, the anti-imperialists are reduced to defensive gestures.

Then, in the spring, comes a dramatic change in public sentiment. Letters from the troops have been coming in, and it's the ones from the volunteers that are causing a sea change, creating a rising popular opposition to the war. There are 12,000 of these volunteers out of about 30,000 troops now in the Philippines--men who had volunteered to fight Spain, not the Filipinos. The regulars go where they're told, but these men believe they should have been sent home when Spain capitulated, unless they wanted to re-enlist. Their families agree with them.

Most of these volunteers come from the South and West, and the tide of discontent is rising rapidly there, shocking the Administration when its intensity begins to be felt. Hostilities have barely got under way in February when the California Senate asks McKinley to order the 1st California Regiment home as soon as they can be spared.

As the deaths and casualties among the volunteers mount, the clamor for recall increases, especially when it becomes clear that Otis is suppressing the bad news, which leaks out anyway in letters home that have escaped sloppy censorship, and in smuggled dispatches from the correspondents. In March, influential politicians in Pennsylvania start trying to get the state's militiamen recalled, and by April, the movement is mushrooming. Crowds at a public meeting in Nashville call for a return of the Tennessee troops. Newspapers in Oregon lead a drive to return that state's men, "who never enlisted for such a war."

In Minnesota, the governor sends a special message to the legislature, urging that it order a mustering out of the troops from that state immediately. South Dakota follows suit when Governor Lee joins the parade and writes McKinley that the war is "repugnant to the fundamental principles of government." He thinks the men from his state are being held against their will, a common belief. Parents of volunteers in the 1st Nebraska send the President a joint letter demanding that "the government send back home those who have not contributed their precious fever-stricken or bullet-torn bodies to enrich the soil of Luzon."

If the people at home are unhappy, the soldiers themselves are even more so, as a flood of letters from them testifies. On March 30, the Boston *Transcript*, which has become virtually the organ of the Anti-Imperialist League, carries a smuggled dispatch from its man in Manila declaring that "a majority of the

United States volunteers are eager to return home. 'We did not enlist to fight niggers,' is a remark that is constantly heard."

The reporter quotes an anonymous general's belief that it will take 100,000 men to control the islands. The Philadelphia *Times* prints a letter from a volunteer reporting that the 10th Pennsylvania has voted unanimously against serving when their original enlistments expire, recalling the reluctant militia of the American Revolution. The 13th Minnesota sends a public telegram demanding that "the regiment be ordered home and mustered out of the service at once." The Republicans in Washington find all this most embarrassing. They've been passing on Otis's rosy reports, including his most recent observation that the war is nearly over, and predicting that the volunteers would re-enlist so no more troops need be sent. But the volunteers want to come home and they don't re-enlist in any large numbers, the Army is plainly going to need more troops, and the war goes on. The last thing in the world McKinley wants to do in the present domestic climate is to call up more troops, but it's unavoidable. What he realizes he must do is bring at least some of the militia home, and on April 16, he announces who the lucky fellows are going to be. Minnesota, South Dakota, and Pennsylvania will get their boys back; it would be most unwise to lose these Republican states. But let's not kid ourselves, they'll have to be replaced, and on the nineteenth, it's announced that 14,000 regulars will soon be on their way to the Philippines.

Not a moment too soon. A correspondent in Manila writes to a London friend: "The volunteers, or at least a portion of them, were at one point on the verge of mutiny, and unless General Otis had begun sending them homeward there would have been sensational developments."

These moves take some of the pressure off the Republicans, but it's necessary, even in these earliest days of public relations, to put the blame on someone else, and in the traditional way, a leak is arranged from the White House to a few newspapers known to be pro-war. It appears that at a Cabinet meeting there was revealed a sinister plot, discovering that "anti-expansionists in this country, believed to be connected with the Anti-Imperialist League, or influenced by it, have been sending letters or telegrams to the volunteers in the Philippines and stirred them up to discontent, and that this is at the bottom of the pessimistic reports from Manila by way of Hong Kong, and the appeal for the recall of the volunteer regiments." Otis himself, it's said, has reported "seditious" telegrams sent to volunteer regiments and has decided to "expose the men who have been hampering the government."

In the midst of our winter of discontent in America, Rudyard Kipling drops a small poetic bomb, a poem entitled "The White Man's Burden," intended not only to inspire Americans in their new role but to stir up more British support for subduing the pesky Boers in South Africa, who are also having outrageous ideas about freedom. Published in February 1899, the Kiplingesque message is concentrated in one much-quoted exhortatory stanza:

Take up the White Man's burden,
Send forth the best ye breed
To wait in heavy harness
On fluttering folk and wild---
Your new-caught sullen peoples,
Half devil and half child.

Just what McKinley's been telling us all along--"Christianize" and "civilize" these "sullen peoples." Perhaps no poem has ever, before or since, caught such universal public attention in so short a time. As one observer writes: "In winged words it circled the earth in a day, and by repetition became hackneyed in a week." As summarized by a sympathizer, its message "revealed a necessary but thankless task to be performed by the white race under the restraints of conscience."

Kipling's poem is the kind that invites parody, and the parodists oblige. In the New York *Times*, one of them writes:

Take up the White Main's Burden,
Send forth your sturdy sons
And load them down with whiskey
And Testaments and guns,
Throw in a few diseases
To spread in tropic climes,
For there the healthy niggers
Are quite behind the times.
And don't forget the factories!
On these benighted shores
They never work for twelve hours a day,
And live in strange content.

The "twelve hours a day" line is especially popular. Labor discontent is rising again, and it will be only a little more than two decades before the president of Republic Steel is denouncing the eight-hour day as a communist plot.

Suddenly anti-imperialism is more popular. As the campaign of 1900 begins to warm up, Richard Croker, the eminent if dishonest Democratic boss of New York City, is asked to give his definition of anti-imperialism, and delivers some one-liner ammunition: "My idea of anti-imperialism is opposition to the fashion of shooting everyone who doesn't speak English."

The parodies go on, and in some of them any kind of civility is being dropped. "Marse Henry" Watterson, the Voice of the Old South, who is publisher and editor of the Louisville *Courier-Journal*, contributes his own editorial-page parody, in which he accepts the white man's burden, yet complains:

But the riff-raff; Lord, the riff-raff; injun,
nigger, beggar man, thief---
Both mongrel, puppy, whelp, and hound
And cur of low degree.

William Howard Taft, the portly future President who will soon be High Commissioner in charge of the American occupation, launches a memorable phrase, "little brown brother," in an otherwise forgettable interventionist speech, and it quickly becomes a part of the popular vocabulary, also an object of ridicule. A much-quoted two-liner written by an American soldier complains:

He may be a brother of Big Bill Taft
But he ain't no brother of mine.

This is part of a longer effort which Mark Sullivan tracks down in later years as appearing first in the Manila *Sunday Sun*, beginning:

I'm only a common soldier-man, in the blasted Philippines.
They say I've got Brown Brothers here, but I
dunno what it means.
I like the word Fraternity, but still I draw the line;
He may be a brother of William H. Taft, but he ain't no
friend of mine.
I never had a brother who begged to get a drink to keep
himself from dying when he hovered on the brink;
And when my Pal had give it him, and emptied out his sack
Would take the opportunity to stick him in the back.

Echoes of Cuba. Another soldier is even more emphatic in a poem he begins: "Damn, damn, damn the Filipino," and advises, "Underneath the starry flag/Civilize him with a Krag," meaning the Krag-Jorgenson rifle.

Paradoxically, a public unable to put two and two together is expressing sympathy for the Boers who, at the moment, are coming out from under the British guns. On November 15, 1899, *Life* magazine (whose name Henry Luce will one day appropriate) remarks: "A small boy with diamonds is no match for a large burglar with experience." Why this sympathy? No doubt traditional dislike of the British by those who can't forget the Revolution, but as John Hay, speaking of the war with Spain, writes to Henry Cabot Lodge, "Great Britain is the only European country whose sympathies are not openly against us."

Judge magazine, *Life*'s rival on the newsstands, comes to McKinley's aid with an issue featuring a lurid cover on which Aguinaldo is depicted standing with one foot on a dead American soldier. Superimposed is an equally lurid title: "What is Behind Aguinaldo, That Fiend Who Has Slain Many American Soldiers?" Anticipating future gimmicky magazine design, *Judge* prints a flag ingeniously cut so it can be lifted, revealing the benign features of William Jennings Bryan.

On the anti-imperialist side, the tone is becoming vitriolic. That renegade former Republican leader, Carl Schurz, describes McKinley's actions as those of a "contemptible rascal." When the President casts another memorable phrase on the troubled waters, "benevolent assimilation," he sets off another flood of abuse. The New York *World* inquires caustically: "Of course Aguinaldo's punishment should fit his crime, but what is his crime?"

Another Republican leader, one of the ablest, former Speaker Thomas Reed, retires from Congress out of disgust with the President's expansionist policies and privately unleashes a torrent of sardonic irony on the President and all his works. One morning, after reading in the paper that Aguinaldo's son has been killed, Reed goes to his law office and, seeing his partner at work, exclaims: "What, are you working today? I should think you would be celebrating. I see by the papers that the American army has captured the infant son of Aguinaldo and at last accounts was in hot pursuit of his mother."

Even Andrew Carnegie joins the chorus. Writing to a former friend in the Administration, he says, "You seem to have about finished your work of civilizing the Filipinos; it is thought that about 8,000 of them have been completely civilized and sent to Heaven; I hope you like it."

While the storm rages at home in the spring and summer of 1899, the killing fields in the Philippines are enriching themselves with that blood McKinley was talking about in Boston, and most of it is coming from Filipino veins. However, the American commanders in the field are beginning to realize just what kind of war they've gotten into. Six days after the fighting began at Manila, General Lawton, last seen assaulting El Caney, drove out 4,000 Filipinos from Caloocan, on the city's outskirts, and MacArthur, moving ahead on another part of the front, writes later: "When I first started in against these rebels, I believed that Aguinaldo's troops represented only a fraction. I did not like to believe that the whole population of Luzon... was opposed to us, but having come thus far, and having been brought much in contact with both insurgents and amigos, I have been reluctantly compelled to believe that the Filipino masses are loyal to Aguinaldo and the government which he leads."

It wasn't all hammer and tongs at the war's beginning, though. When General Miller, early in December 1898, led an expedition of troops fresh off the boat from San Francisco against Iloilo, the largest city on the Visayan Islands, about 400 miles south of Manila, he asked the Filipinos commanding this outpost, in courteous words, if he might land there. They said no. He tried again on January 1, 1899, this time handing out McKinley's "Benevolent Proclamation," claiming sovereignty. The Filipinos inquired if he had any instructions from Aguinaldo, since they were not empowered to act on anything affecting the federal government without orders. In a letter, they laid down a direct challenge: "The supposed authority of the United States began with the Treaty of Paris. The authority of the Central Government of Malolos [then the seat of the insurgents' government] is founded in the sacred and natural bonds of blood, language, uses, customs, ideas [and] sacrifices."

In the face of this moving declaration, Miller decided not to attempt a landing and sailed back to Manila. But when the war actually begins in February, he returns with two armed vessels, the *Baltimore* and the *Petrel*, along with more troops, and takes Iloilo with no trouble. Cebu, the island's third largest city, is soon taken too, and on March 31, MacArthur captures the rebel capital, Malolos, driving out the insurgent army during the next few weeks, after which a northward push is resumed.

On a parallel line with MacArthur, Lawton is sweeping through the countryside with little resistance, eventually establishing a base in San Fernando, forty miles north of Manila. Vera Cruz is captured and Calumpit falls by the end of April. The Americans are pushing the insurgents before them, and the rebel army is breaking up. During April and May, Aguinaldo tries desperately to reach some kind of peace, sending emissaries with white flags behind the American lines. He wants to stop the fighting and negotiate a peaceful settlement, but Otis pays no attention.

These victories are not without cost to the Americans, but the folks back home aren't getting the casualty figures, or much else of substance. On July 9, all the American correspondents in Manila, representing everything from the most radical expansionist journals to the neutral news associations, submit a round robin letter to Otis, protesting censorship of their dispatches, and eight days later, the letter appears in the papers at home. The reporters renew their previous charge that Otis is preventing them from writing the whole truth, arguing that the official dispatches present "an optimistic view...not shared by the general officers in the field."

When he reads this, McKinley calls a Cabinet meeting where it is decided to do nothing. The President, in fact, is much in favor of censorship and has no intention of restricting it. Still, there's widespread public agitation about this letter, and a scapegoat has to be found. It turns out to be Alger, who is asked to step down and take the blame.

Aguinaldo may have lost the organized war by this time, but he tells his followers in November 1899 to disperse and spread out, conducting a guerrilla warfare which he would direct from new headquarters in the mountains. He hopes that, after the election of 1900, McKinley will be overthrown by Bryan and maybe then Otis will be compelled to listen to reason. By his action, Aguinaldo has drawn a line that marks a turning point in the war for the Philippines. From now on, these American

generals, who are old Indian fighters, are going to be conducting the same kind of search-and-destroy missions that beat the
native people of the Plains, the Southwest, and the Northwest
into submission. The terrain may be different, but the purpose
is the same. We're launched now on a guerrilla war that won't
end until July 1902.

Before the close of 1899, the Anti-Imperialist League, now
becoming a national organization, is publishing scores of letters
from soldiers to their families, filtering through the leak in censorship. Typically, an artilleryman writes home about the village
of Titatia:

"The town...surrendered to us a few days ago, and two
companies occupy the same. Last night one of our boys was
found shot and his stomach cut open. Immediately orders were
received from [the] General...to burn the town and kill every
native in sight, which was done to a finish. About one thousand
men, women, and children were reported killed. I am probably
growing hard-hearted, for I am in my glory when I can sight my
gun on some dark-skin and pull the trigger."

There are so many of these letters, assiduously circulated
by the League, that the Army hurries around getting the enlisted men, at least, to recant, which takes no extraordinary pressure in the circumstances. Stories of atrocities by American
troops are indignantly denied, but the evidence piles up.

Racism by the soldiers in the conduct of this war is the
same brand they exhibited in Cuba, and if anything it's more
virulent. These inferior Filipinos fighting for their freedom are
"monkey men," "niggers," and the more popular "goo-goos."
They are believed to be dirty people. A widely circulated piece
of doggerel runs:

O, Aguinaldo leads a sloppy life,
He eats potatoes with his knife,
And once a year he takes a scrub,
And leaves the water in the tub.

On more exalted levels, the vocabulary is different but the
feelings are the same. Senator Albert J. Beveridge, for instance,
after he's elected to the Senate by the Indiana State Legislature
in 1899, visits the Philippines, the very model of a modern
young imperialist, and is given a VIP tour of the killing fields--
"into the field," as he puts it. Returning home, he writes a
report of his visit for his friend, George Horace Lorimer, who

two years ago became editor of the *Saturday Evening Post*. With Beveridge, as with Otis, everything is coming up roses. Morale is high, all the men are brave, and in addition Beveridge has discovered "a remarkable and striking ethnological fact."

Our active fighting force, this freshly minted senator writes, is dominated by "the Saxon type. Everywhere the blue or gray eyes, everywhere the fair skin, everywhere the tawny hair and beard. Those thoroughbred soldiers from the plantations of the South, from the plains and valleys and farms of the west, look the thoroughbred, physically considered. The fine line is everywhere. The nose is straight, the mouth is sensitive and delicate. There are very few bulldog jaws. There is, instead, the steel-trap jaw of the lion. The whole face and figure is the face and figure of the thoroughbred fighter, who has always been the fine-featured, delicate nostriled, thin-eared and generally clean-cut featured man."

This is the great mind who will soon become an ornament of the United States Senate.

He is far from being alone. In a more restrained way, others join the chorus. An editorial written in the New York *Times* condemns Aguinaldo's "insane attack" and his "stupendous folly," which only goes to show that the Filipinos are undisciplined children. To give such people the power to govern themselves, says the *Times*, is like giving "a dynamite cartridge to a baby for a plaything." The historian Richard E. Welch, Jr., summarizes the *Times* viewpoint: "If the American-born black man was judged incapable and so inferior, how much more 'the Filipino nigger,' for he was stunted, foreign, and rebellious."

The obsession with the Filipinos' alleged uncleanliness is turned to profit by a soap company in an advertisement on the inside cover of *McClure's* magazine for October 1899. "The first step toward lightening The White Man's Burden is through teaching the virtues of cleanliness. Pears' Soap is a potent factor in brightening the dark corners of the earth, as civilization advances, while amongst the cultured of all nations it holds the highest place."

As the campaign of 1900 warms up, the Republican promise to "civilize and Christianize" the benighted (and of course dirty) people of the Philippines is sounded in his usual ringing terms by T.R., the former Rough Rider, soon to enter the White House himself. The Filipinos, he tells his audiences, are just as savage and irrational as the Apaches, those other unfortunate freedom fighters we recently subdued. Aguinaldo, he says, mixing his tribes and metaphors freely, is the "Osceola of the Philippines" (referring to the Seminole chief in Florida) and "a renegade Pawnee," no easy simultaneous feat.

T.R. finds himself in agreement with the editor of the New York *Tribune*, Whitelaw Reid, that "if men will not govern themselves with respect for civilization and its agencies, then, when they get in the way, they must be governed." It has to be understood that progress can't be achieved "without some blood having been shed," preferably not ours.

In Emporia, Kansas, another friend of George Lorimer's, William Allen White, assures the readers of the Emporia *Gazette* that as good Christians they must deplore those dreadful lynchings in the South, but at the same time they must not forget that "only the Anglo-Saxons can govern themselves," and we have a Manifest Destiny to press on "as a world conqueror." The Negro at home, says this ultimate small-town editor, must be regarded as American society's backward child, deserving of our benevolence since he is otherwise incapable. Obviously, Social Darwinism lives and thrives in post-Civil War America.

Not surprisingly, the struggling black press disagrees. Its readers have no voice whatever in domestic policy, much less foreign, but clearly they have an identity with "the colored peoples of the Philippines." This is not, however, a unanimous opinion. Some journals (a minority) regard the Filipinos simply as foreigners with no particular claim to the sympathy of American blacks. But the majority of the papers are bitterly anti-imperialist, and the *Broad Ax*, published in both Salt Lake City and Chicago, sees the conflict as just another war "to satisfy the robbers, murderers, and unscrupulous monopolists, who are ever crying for more blood."

In Philadelphia, R. C. Atwood, editor of the influential *Defender*, condemns the bloodletting going on in the Philippines as "one of the most unrighteous acts ever perpetrated by any government." But other papers are reluctant to criticize the troops in the islands because some of them are black regulars, and there's still a high sense of pride in what these regiments contributed to the conquest of Cuba.

Such divisions of opinion are reflected in the black community generally. Journalists see the war as pure racism, for the most part, but church leaders are divided, although there are more for than against. In academia, the anti-imperialists find a strong minority voice in Kelly Miller, professor of mathematics at Howard University, who writes burning prose against the war for black journals like the Washington *Bee*, joining forces with Frederick Douglass's son, Lewis, who contributes to the New York *Age*.

The anti-war writers, however, can't ignore the fact that, besides the black regiments in the Philippines, there are also two such regiments recruited especially for service there, the 48th and 49th Volunteers. All told, there are six black regiments and they seem to have no morale problems except a slightly high desertion rate. As Welch points out, these troops may be unhappy to find themselves aiding white colonialism, and they're angry about the "nigger" and "goo-goo" epithets, but for many of these soldiers, mostly from the South, the horrors of war represent an escape from the horrors of civilian life in racist America. The Army has had no trouble filling up its black regiments.

Sergeant M. W. Sadler, of Company K, 25th Infantry, sums up the feelings of most of these recruits when he writes in the Indianapolis *Freeman*: "Whether it is right to reduce these people to submission is not a question for the soldier to decide. Our oath of allegiance knows neither race, [nor] color." A comrade in Company K, however, after suffering an ambush by the guerrillas, has no doubt that the Filipinos are his enemies when he sees three of his comrades the victims of "butchery." When black soldiers desert, it isn't because they have any trouble fighting people of a different shade but because they can't stand their white officers.

Of the deserters from the six regiments, only nine join the insurgents, most notably Corporal David Fagan, of the 24th, who attaches himself to Lacuna's guerrillas and becomes a commissioned captain. Acquiring a Filipino girl as his common-law wife, he takes up the rebel cause as his own. This change of climate earns him two distinctions: he becomes the most despised insurgent in the Philippines (next to Aguinaldo) in the eyes of American officers, and a large sum of money is offered for his capture, dead or alive, but preferably dead.

It's this same "Captain" Fagan who's involved in one of the war's most dramatic episodes when he leads an ambushing party and traps a detachment of the 24th Regiment doing garrison duty in Magalang, a town in central Luzon. These men of the 24th are escorting a line of mule wagons when Fagan's guerrillas surprise and kill them, after which the ambushers wait for the rescue party they're sure will soon arrive. The rescuers prove to be scouts and would have been cut down too if reinforcements hadn't suddenly arrived on both sides. In the subsequent battle, the black soldiers of the 24th can hear above the gunfire taunting shouts from Fagan, and it drives them to fight with such ferocity that their white officers are in awe. One of the battlers is a Sergeant Washington, whom a scout remembers as "a white-haired Negro grown old in his Uncle Sam's army," who is injured but refuses to leave the field, and according to the scout, "stood there flat-footed, cursing and...fighting like a madman."

But the heroics of the black soldiers are lost on men like William Howard Taft, who will shortly bring the blessings of civil administration to the islands. Taft deplores what he calls the affinity black soldiers have for Filipino women. Not only do they have native mistresses, he complains, but they're creating "a good deal of demoralization in the towns where they are stationed." It's no surprise, when the war eventually winds down, that the black regiments are brought home first.

But in 1899 their relief is more than two years away as a divided country begins to understand what the President and his party have committed themselves to do. The people's resentments and anxieties are many but racism is not among them, except for the intellectuals who constitute the Anti-Imperialist League, and its followers among the general public. The trouble with the League is not only that it's a minority movement, but it has no political clout. The imperialists are solidly in power, even though they're uneasy about the label. They prefer to call themselves expansionists, believers in "territorial growth," not to mention Manifest Destiny. They like to talk about the great colossus of America as driven by "destiny," or "duty," or, in the pulpit, by "Providence," meaning the Higher Authority McKinley believes is on his and America's side.

Kipling's exhortation to assume "the white man's burden" is taken literally in the imperialist camp, and they're only bewildered when the intellectuals of the League question whether they understand the poem or have even read it. Couldn't they see the irony in it? these gadflies want to know. And haven't they grasped the fact that Kipling is pessimistic the burden will ever be taken up? Senator Tillman tells the Senate, in one of his still impassioned speeches, that the imperialists ought to ignore Kipling's exhortation and pay more attention to the poem's admonition.

Small needles are constantly stuck in the imperialists' hide, as in the New York *World's* parody, whose closing stanza reads:

We've taken up the white man's burden
of ebony and brown.
Now will you kindly tell us, Rudyard,
How we may put it down?

In the uneasy America of 1899, with the election of 1900 looming and the Philippines showing every sign of becoming the quagmire no one thought it would be, it's a tremendous relief to find something to cheer about in September when Dewey leaves Manila for home, after seventeen months. An outburst of sheer exultation occurs in America. At last, an authentic hero returns to show us we were right all along.

We simply can't do enough for this man. All the newspaper clippings about him since Manila Bay are brought together in a 150-pound album, bound in solid silver, for a formal presenta-tion. *Life* magazine publishes a special "Admiral's Number." At Madison Square in New York, a jerry-built but impressive arch is erected for his triumphal procession.

Dewey loves it all. Humility has never been one of his virtues. Later, in his autobiography, he gives such an unabashed description of his homecoming:

"From all parts of the United Sates had come requests for a journey across the country by rail. Our inland cities seemed to be vieing [sic] with one another in plans for magnificent recep-tions. Towns, children, and articles of commerce were named after me. I was assured that nothing like the enthusiasm for a man and a deed had ever been known. I knew what to do in command of the American squadron, but being of flesh and blood and not a superman, it seemed impossible to live up to all that was expected of me as a returning hero...Dewey arches, Dewey flags, and 'Welcome, Dewey!' in electric lights on the span of the Brooklyn Bridge!

"The great city of New York made holiday. Its crowds banked the piers, the roofs, and Riverside Drive, when the

Olympia, leading the North Atlantic squadron, which won Santiago, proceeded up the North River; and they packed the streets for the land parade in token of public emotion, while the gold loving-cup which came to me with the freedom of the city expressed the municipality's official tribute. I was no less deeply affected when I stood on the steps of the State House at Montpelier, with the grounds filled with 'home folks,' and when on the steps of the east front of the Capitol I received from the hands of the President the sword of honor which Congress had voted me."

A few days after he gets the sword, Dewey is given something much more valuable. A committee has been formed to collect money for the purchase of a house as a further mark of honor. (General Grant got two of them.) Dewey not only accepts this substantial gift, but he tells the committee what part of town he wants to live in, and asks for a "modest" house with a small dining room suitable for entertaining eighteen guests at dinner.

When this story leaks out, public and press are already beginning to have second thoughts. Whatever happened to the simple sailor who now wants eighteen chairs around his dining table? In any case, should he have looked a gift horse in the mouth?

But Dewey has other matters on his mind. Less than two months after his arrival, he's married at a fashionable wedding in St. Paul's Catholic Church in Washington. And all this time, the American people thought he was married to *them*. They react like rejected suitors. What is he doing, anyway, marrying again at his age? The bride is thoroughly dissected in the newspapers and they can't find much to say about her that's favorable. It's all wrong. She's been widowed herself, she's much younger, and worst of all, she's a Catholic, stirring up still further the anti-Church prejudices generated by the so-called American Protective Association. The best they can find to say of her is that her first husband, W. B. Hazen, while not a hero, was distinguished and a general himself. Her brother is the equally distinguished John R. McLean, owner of the Washington *Post* and the Cincinnati *Enquirer*.

The real shocker comes only a few days after the wedding, however. Dewey deeds to his bride the house given him by a grateful public. Besides the dubious ethics of this transaction, the anti-Catholic propagandists spread the word that the house will become the seat of the papacy when the Pope takes over Washington.

There's no end to the scandal. It's said that Mrs. McKinley doesn't approve of the new Mrs. Dewey's Paris gowns and expensive jewelry, but that's nothing new in the bride's life. She was also criticized on the same grounds when her husband was the military attaché at the American embassy in Vienna. But the final nail in her marital coffin is driven when it's disclosed that this Catholic was brought up a Presbyterian, then became an Episcopalian, and didn't find Catholicism until she lived in Vienna. Can't this woman make up her ecclesiastical mind? The country disapproves.

Unperturbed, Dewey waits it out, and for a time he's still popular, with a lecture and social schedule of staggering proportions all over the country. Inevitably, a less-than-grass-roots movement develops to propose him for the White House in 1900. Anti-Bryan Democrats see an opportunity to unhorse the Great Commoner and run an authentic, still popular hero--or so they think. When they ask Dewey privately how he feels about it, Dewey all but accepts before the prize is even offered, in a way that suggests it's no more than he deserves.

When he announces his candidacy, on April 3, 1900, he gives an exclusive to a New York *World* reporter, and this sensational development rates a three-column headline in that paper and most of the others. Then comes a swift, astonishing reaction. Do we *really* want Dewey to be President? On the day after the announcement, the Atlanta *Constitution* has a headline that cuts the hero of Manila Bay a little beyond the quick: "Leaders Laugh at Poor Dewey. The Entire Capital Is Laughing at the Former Hero." It's the "former hero" that hurts most.

Ridicule, mingled with some regret, is prevalent in the country. Many blame the new Mrs. Dewey, who indeed is enchanted by the idea and says so freely to reporters. But *Life* writes sardonically: "The report that George Dewey, formerly known as a hero of Manila Bay, will stump the country for Bryan and Stevenson is said to be a canard. Mrs. Dewey has denied that the report is not true."

Summing it up, when the reaction dies down, Senator Augustus O. Bacon, of Georgia, remarks that while "Admiral Dewey was a hero, he was a dangerous presidential possibility, but since he became a human being and indulged his fancies as others have done, he has lost his hold upon the hero-worshipers."

Dewey's humiliation is complete. Even the controversy about him has to give way in the papers to the Boer War and the mess in the Philippines, as well as the coming presidential campaign. So Dewey sinks into oblivion, and as a final irony, when he dies on January 16, 1917, the volley fired over his grave at Arlington by Annapolis midshipmen can scarcely be heard in the public consciousness above the roar of the guns on the Hindenburg Line, as Mark Sullivan notes later.

All that's left for some time after his departure from public life into the slow fade-out of obscurity is the Dewey Arch at Fifth Avenue and Twenty-third Street. It was a splendid thing, this arch, conceived by some of the period's best sculptors, modeled after the Arch of Titus in Rome. True, it was put together out of laths, wood, and plaster on rather short notice, so that Dewey could ride under it followed by a parade of soldiers, sailors, and assorted politicians, but the intention at the time was to make a permanent marble and granite structure out of it later. In the disillusionment following Dewey's announcement, however, it's too difficult to raise the necessary contributions, and soon the weather begins to disintegrate it in a shower of peeling paint and falling plaster. In the end, dirty and bedraggled, it's carried off by the Sanitation Department.

Mr. Dooley has the next to last word on Dewey's arch: "When a grateful republic, Mr. Hinnessy, builds an ar'rch to its conquering hero, it should be made of brick, so that we can have something convenient to hurl after him when he has passed by."

The New York *Times* takes a moral tone: "For our own sake and for Dewey's sake, it is too bad, not merely because it makes us appear ridiculous in the eyes of foreigners, but because these alternating currents of emotion, this most abrupt substitution of the cold shoulder for the warm heart, argues a want of steadiness in our make-up." Amen.

Dewey will never hear or even know about the final stab to his heart. When his picture flashes on the screen at a Biograph entertainment in Washington, a hissing as of a thousand serpents rises from the audience.

As the new century begins, Dewey is the last distraction from the reality of the Philippines, where the killing has begun in earnest.

4

CIVILIZING THEM

THEY'RE ON THE MARCH IN THE PHILIPPINES AS 1900 BEGINS. Troops move aggressively into the province of Cavite. In February, General James F. Bell takes an expedition by water to the southern islands, capturing the provinces of North and South Camarines, as well as West Albay. Other troops occupy the Viscayan Islands, setting up garrisons wherever they can. Spreading out, the Army manages to establish 400 different posts.

It hasn't been all that easy. General Lawton comes to have a grudging admiration for the little brown brothers: "Taking into account the disadvantages they have to fight against in arms, equipment, and military discipline--without artillery, short of ammunition, powder inferior, shells reloaded until they are defective, inferior in every particular of equipment and supplies--they are the bravest men I have ever seen. What we want is to stop this accursed war. These men are indomitable. At Bacoor Bridge, they waited until the Americans had brought their cannon to within thirty-five yards of their trenches. Such men have the right to be heard. All they want is a little justice."

That's a scarce commodity in American foreign policy. What McKinley wants is to subdue the population as quickly as possible, establish some kind of government we can control, probably our own military at the beginning, and get the boys home. That's why he's more than willing to listen to the lullabies Otis keeps singing to him. When Aguinaldo asks for an armistice, the War Department proclaims that the end is near and there's a sigh of relief in America. Then Otis denies there will be any armistice, and the fighting goes on. After Aguinaldo once more sends a flag of truce from his mountain headquarters, the Administration proclaims total submission, and announces that the President is sending commissioners to establish a civil government. The commissioners depart, but the war goes on.

Everyone involved would like to end it before the rainy season begins in the summer, and when that doesn't happen, a cry goes up from Bryan in this election year, while the Democratic papers and the Anti-Imperialist League charge that the Administration's policy of subjugation is a failure. They want to declare victory and get out at once. Republican papers say nonsense, all we need is to send an army large enough to crush the rebellion.

Disturbing items trickle in from Hong Kong and in soldiers' letters to increase public anxiety. We don't have enough men to hold the positions we've won, it's said. The troops are suffering greatly from the heat, and might not survive the rains either. Barbarism on both sides appears to be emerging. Although it's denied, reports persist that no prisoners are taken by either side.

Why are we in this stalemate, anyway? The answer seems to be that the President has total confidence in Otis. McKinley can't understand what his favorite commander is doing, but seems determined to let him keep doing it--even when he disobeys orders. They tell him to load up the transports that bring him regulars with volunteers going home, but these ships keep coming back with only a handful of men. It's June before McKinley can get him to return the state volunteer regiments he needs for political safety.

Otis is beginning to move away from his earlier estimate that 30,000 men could do the job. Slowly he's escalating that figure, and he stops promising the whole affair will be over soon-- that is, until he gets fresh troops. Then his optimism quickly returns. He seems to believe the rebels are only holding on until after the American election, when a more sympathetic Administration might give them the justice they keep jabbering about. Besides, the new Secretary of War, Elihu Root, who succeeded Alger, is keeping a steady flow of men coming over from San Francisco.

But Root is having his doubts about Otis. He believes what the correspondents are saying about him, when they can get past the censor, and he's impatient with the general's constant ambiguity. Root can't get a straight answer from him about how many men he's likely to need. He suggests that Otis have a meeting with his general officers, who will give him some kind of consensus figure. Otis replies that everyone agrees more men are going to be needed, but in his maddening way, he omits fixing a firm figure, except to say that few think more than 50,000 effectives will be needed.

Otis admits that rebel strength has been underestimated, but if Root could let him have, say, fifteen more volunteer regiments, it would probably be enough. Root has no power to produce such a volunteer army, which the President would like to avoid. But McKinley can't say no to Otis, and he orders up ten more volunteer units while he's doubling the enlistments already approved. Soon Otis has more than 65,000 men to command, and before it's all over, there will be more than 100,000 American soldiers in the Philippines.

None of this is calculated to reassure the public. Otis does his best to suppress anything unfavorable about either him or the war, but disturbing stories continue to seep out of Manila from the ingenious correspondents, depicting Otis as a deeply flawed general whom no one particularly likes. The Democrats dislike him so much they're keeping up a public clamor to have him recalled, as well as demanding the establishment of a new policy of peace and conciliation toward the Filipinos. Much of the public agrees with them.

Who *is* Otis, the man everyone but McKinley seems to want removed? Behind his back, they call him "Nervous Nellie" Otis, but that hardly does justice to his complicated personality. This sixty-one-year old Civil War veteran still has a hole in his head made by a Confederate bullet, which sometimes troubles him and which some of his critics unkindly believe is the source of what they consider his lunacy. But again, that isn't the answer. The truth is that Otis is a workaholic, a man who has few interests in life except to work at what he's assigned to do, in this case to subdue the Filipinos and bring them to heel.

In pursuit of that mission, he doesn't trust anyone else to do anything he can possibly do himself. Consequently, he's preoccupied with political problems in Manila and at home, reforming the judicial system of the Philippines, acting as the senior diplomat on duty, dealing with matters of commerce and business, public health, education, even religion. There is also, of course, the war. This incredible collection of self-assigned problems keeps Otis at his desk sixteen hours a day.

Such devotion ought to merit admiration, but the best Otis can hope for is respect for his all-around competence, and wonder at how he stands it physically.

Fair-minded critics have to give him his due. After all, he *has* sent a well-equipped, well-trained army into the field, placed the Manila judicial system under the control of native lawyers, set up municipal governments in towns the Americans have seized, and demands a strict honesty in every aspect of his work.

But people just don't like him. He fusses endlessly over trifles in a way that drives others up the wall. He stubbornly refuses to accept anyone's opinions but his own. Further, Otis is just plain surly by nature. When he has to confer with others, his attitude ranges from total indifference to short-tempered snapping, rising to a crescendo when anyone opposes him. He was never able to get along with Dewey, and he can't get along with anyone else either, especially the correspondents, as we might expect. Like the other commanders in the Army and Navy, with a few exceptions, he hates the press because he can't totally control the correspondents, and there's always the danger they'll disclose an embarrassing truth. At various times, he threatens to court-martial or expel offending correspondents.

One of the many things Otis can't understand is why his rigid system of censorship doesn't work. It enrages him to find some piece of information he thought he had successfully suppressed appearing in one of the Manila papers. When his enemies charge him with trying to mislead American public opinion, they're right. That's exactly what he's doing.

But it's the refusal of the rebels to give up in the face of far superior force that maddens him most. As an old Indian fighter, he should know better, but the reason he keeps thinking the war must end quickly is that a large, well-equipped army like his must soon overcome any enemy whose only commission is a bag of rice, and who fights with primitive arms and strategy.

Commanders in the field understand it. They see their troops winning the battles but losing them immediately afterward as the rebels simply regroup in the jungle to try again, and reclaim villages as soon as the Americans leave them. Advance and withdraw. That seems to be the order of the day for Otis's army.

Disquiet among the field commanders finds a focus in the figure of General Lawton, who wants more men, as Otis does, but believes the American strategy is all wrong. Lawton likes the correspondents and they like him, so his views are getting through to the American public while Otis's often do not. The result is that a growing number of people think if Otis were thrown out and replaced by Lawton the war would be over.

In some way, these two men are alike. They're both Regular Army, veterans of the Civil War and the Indian wars, devoted to the service, with strict conceptions of duty and a strong belief that they are incontestably right. Lawton, however, is five years younger, and where Otis is content to spend sixteen hours a day at his desk, his rival is never happier than when he's on the front lines, indulging himself in what he likes to call "beautiful battle." Pursuing those earlier freedom fighters, the Indians of the Plains, he was considered the most daring of the young cavalry officers carrying out that other civilizing mission. Tall, erect, with iron-gray hair, he's the very model of a modern major general. You can't miss him. He rides his big black horse up and down the lines, where that's possible, or just strides along on foot. In both cases, he's a conspicuous figure, especially wearing the white sun helmet he acquired for the Luzon campaign. His fearless exposure to enemy fire wins him the admiration of soldiers and correspondents alike, until eventually a stray rebel bullet kills him.

But for now, as Leech reminds us, there's "some hidden instability, some painful tension that found release in danger, or in drink." Alcohol almost undid him after the conquest of Santiago. Appointed military governor of that district, he drank so heavily that an alarmed War Department hurriedly appointed Leonard Wood to replace him and spirited Lawton back home on the pretext of ill health. In Washington, he began to deal with his alcoholism, and it wasn't long before McKinley, coming to know and admire him, was ready to send him to the Philippines, first taking him aside and giving him a stern temperance lecture, ending with a promise extracted from Lawton to stop drinking. Until now, he's kept his promise.

Not that he's a happy camper, by any means. He'd come expecting to be the field commander, but Otis isn't about to give up any of his perquisites. No one tells Lawton that this is the situation. It isn't long, however, before he realizes he's not there to become a man of distinction on the battlefield. Apparently the best he can hope for is command of a division, and just to rub it in, Otis gives command of the next big campaign to MacArthur, leaving Lawton with what he considers nothing more thrilling than a reconnaissance in force.

But you can't keep a man like Lawton down for long. It quickly becomes obvious that by temperament and training he's ideally equipped for the kind of guerrilla warfare Aguinaldo is conducting. Unlike Otis, he remembers what he learned on the Plains. He molds his small force into a unit of daring scouts, a flexible body able to adapt instantly to changing conditions. He keeps on talking to correspondents, and he's careful to have them within earshot when he observes that 100,000 men are going to be needed--thus becoming the anonymous general of the dispatches.

Inevitably, a gulf widens between Otis and his talented rival. Lawton doesn't seem to understand that everything he tells the reporters, or even hints at, is going to find its way to America and advertise the rivalry springing up. When he learns that his remarks have stirred a stormy controversy at home, he denies everything. As a dedicated Army man, he knows he's on dangerous ground here. Just the same, he's bitter about his situation. He firmly believes that if they let him loose on the field of battle he could turn the war around.

Everything comes to a head when the spring offensive peters out, the rains begin, and hope of peace seems distant. Lawton has been sent north on a diversionary operation in support of MacArthur's communications, but he's changed this maneuver brilliantly into a major action. Before he can claim a real victory, however, a series of detailed and confusing orders flows in from Otis, just as Lawton is convinced he can capture the fleeing Aguinaldo and end the war. He wants to keep going, but Otis orders him to come back. So his entire campaign is wasted.

Returning to Manila, Lawton decides things can't go on like this and he means to confront Otis and settle matters. Knowing that he's in perilous territory, he takes along a witness, Professor Dean C. Worcester, a member of the commission McKinley has sent over to survey the scene in preparation for a new government. Lawton certainly has his nerve, but after all, he's the man who accepted Geronimo's surrender, and he has no hesitation in confronting Otis with a plan to capture Aguinaldo and achieve peace.

While Otis gives him scowling attention, Lawton outlines his plan. Give him two regiments to command, he says, with permission to arm and equip them as he sees fit, and he'll guarantee results. Then he holds out a carrot. If Otis agrees to this, he will bet his reputation and his rank that he'll deliver Aguinaldo, dead or alive, in two months.

The effect on Otis is extraordinary. No one has ever seen him laugh out loud, and General Funston has been heard to say that he would no more think of telling a joke in the general's presence than to pluck his beard. But now Otis opens his mouth and emits a loud guffaw. That's his way of telling Lawton he thinks this is the most preposterous request he's ever heard. He regards Aguinaldo as no more than a figurehead, a man who "never amounted to anything." Hell, no, Lawton can't go.

So the war rumbles on, and these rebels who want freedom so much simply refuse to give up, even though their army is broken and several of Aguinaldo's cabinet are prisoners. All organized opposition is ended, but the fighting continues as fiercely as ever. Otis doggedly pursues the enemy, but plainly he's not winning the war, and in May of 1900, he abruptly asks to be relieved of his command and goes home, the Army's first top-level casualty. It's hard to believe, but he goes declaring that the insurrection is a "thing of the past," and that the Filipinos are "thoroughly content to submit." Maybe there *is* something to that canard about the effect of the Confederate bullet in his head.

In a way, though, he's no crazier than a good many other Americans, some of them in high places. Washington policy-makers never get it through their heads that all the Filipinos really want is their freedom, first from Spain, then from America. Not every Filipino supports Aguinaldo, to be sure, and, as Otis claims, they are afraid to say so out of fear of reprisals, but these people are in the minority. The whole situation apparently is too complicated for Americans to understand. Even when the anti-imperialist press manages to get a good deal of the unpleasant truth out in the open, McKinley keeps on insisting that nearly all the Filipinos want American sovereignty.

MacArthur, succeeding Otis in command, knows better. He understands that the Filipinos are mostly united, and as the occupation spreads, he tries a different approach in June by offering amnesty, and a promise of civil rights when hostilities cease. They don't buy it. MacArthur has to abandon the carrot and go back to the stick, issuing a proclamation declaring that the "laws of war" will be enforced, referring particularly to those Filipinos, safe in American-occupied towns, who are sending aid to the enemy.

At least the Republicans and Democrats are finding something to agree on. Both are beginning to hate the war, and both are disgusted by the way it's being conducted. And they still don't like Otis, even in retrospect. Anti-expansionists don't like him because they think the Filipinos are patriots. Republicans don't like him because he didn't win quickly.

On the question of the militia and their services, however, the parties are far apart. In August, those men who think they shouldn't have been sent "to fight niggers" in the first place begin to come home, now that Otis isn't around to keep them there, and they're still angry, believing they've been victimized by Republican policy in what they regard as a war that's more political than military. There's talk about how Otis isolated these men mentally by forbidding League pamphlets to be sent through Army mails.

McKinley feels it's essential to put on his damage control clothes and see what can be done to restore some confidence in the party, with the election almost at hand. The occasion is chosen carefully--the homecoming celebration for the 10th Pennsylvania Volunteers, who spent the past year in the Philippines. Pittsburgh is going all out to welcome these men home. As the sun-browned veterans tumble from the train, they're formed into parade formation, led by the President in his carriage. Cheering crowds jam the sidewalk on the line of march, and thousands more await the ceremony in Schenley Park, where McKinley is to review the troops before he speaks.

One thing can be said for this President, he backs down only under the most severe pressure, and he has no intention of doing so now. He makes a call-to-the-colors speech, laying out the Administration line as patriotic gospel. Conciliation in the islands isn't going to bring peace; force of arms is the only way to do it. Otis is defended fervently. McKinley takes personal responsibility for any mistakes made. The war will go on without pause until American authority is firmly established. Those poor benighted Filipinos who follow Aguinaldo, he says, are simply misguided and deserving of our pity.

McKinley reserves his best oratorical flourishes for the volunteers, some of whom may be surprised to learn that they're the saviors of humanity and Western civilization as we know it. McKinley turns and addresses the soldiers directly while he eulogizes them, promising at the end to give every man a special medal of honor. Cheers from the soldiers, uproarious applause from the crowd. Without the volunteers, he concludes, "our flag would have had its first stain and the American name its first ignominy." America's obligation to civilization has been redeemed.

Not one to let a political opportunity slip by, McKinley excoriates the anti-imperialists (he calls them "anti-expansionists") as "the unpatriotic" and asserts they are "few in number." He reads a roll call of those states, nineteen of them, which resisted the suggestion of these unpatriots that the boys should come home. The Pennsylvania troops cheer the mention of every name. Since they're at home now and certified heroes, they can afford to be generous.

The unpatriotic are ready to fight back, and at the end of 1900, with McKinley safely re-elected, casting doubt on how much influence they really have, they acquire a spokesman--Mark Twain, the most popular author in America. As one of Twain's biographers, Justin Kaplan, points out, he's thought the war in Cuba was a noble cause, but now the idea of men willing to fight for other men's freedom is being subverted in the Philippines, just as it was in the Boer War and the Boxer Rebellion in China.

In December, as the year draws to a stormy close, Twain is called upon to introduce young Winston Churchill to his first American lecture audience, at the Waldorf Hotel in New York. Churchill's mother isn't the only tie that binds England and America, Mark declares: "I think that England sinned when she got herself into a war in South Africa, just as we have sinned in getting into a similar war in the Philippines. And now that we are also akin in sin, there is nothing more to be desired."

By this time, Twain is convinced that the war, as Kaplan puts it, is "an unholy alliance of Christianity, cash, and colonialism going under the collective name of civilization," and on

December 30 in the New York *Herald*, he fires a historic salvo: "A Greeting From the Nineteenth to the Twentieth Century." He's burning over the suppression of the Boxers in China by the Great Powers, including 2,000 American troops, as well as events in South Africa and the Philippines.

"I bring you the stately matron named Christendom," Twain writes, in his best polemical style, "returning bedraggled, besmirched, and dishonored from irate raids in Kiao-Chou, Manchuria, South Africa, and the Philippines, with her soul full of meanness, her pocket full of bodies and her mouth full of pious hypocrisy. Give her soap and a towel, but hide the looking-glass."

A month later, in the February 1901 issue of *North American Review*, Twain lays down a formidable barrage, one of his best, "To the Person Sitting in Darkness." This is a vitriolic masterpiece, a stinging indictment of what he calls the "Blessings-of-Civilization Trust," with an international cast including McKinley, Joseph Chamberlain, the Kaiser, and the Tsar of Russia, not to forget the Christian missionaries. Reprinted in pamphlet form by the League, this fiery denunciation becomes the cutting edge of opposition to the war.

Twain covers the world in it, and by the time he gets to the Philippines in his indictment, he's in full cry. He quotes an American soldier, "We never left one alive. If one was wounded, we would run our bayonets through him." Such facts, Twain says, along with all the others, must be laid before the "person sitting in darkness" and then explained to him, saying:

"There have been lies, yes, but they were told in a good cause. We have been treacherous, but that was only in order that real good might come out of apparent evil. True, we have crushed a deceived and confiding people, we have turned against the weak and friendless who trusted us; we have stamped out a just and intelligent and well-ordered republic; we have stabbed an ally in the back and slapped the face of a guest; we have bought a shadow from an enemy that hadn't it to sell; we have robbed a trusting friend of his lands and his liberty; we have invited our clean young men to shoulder a discredited musket and do bandits' work under a flag which bandits have been accustomed to fear, not to follow; we have debauched America's honor and blackened her face before the world; but each detail was for the best.

"We know this. The head of every state and sovereignty in Christendom and 90 percent of every legislative body in Christendom, including our Congress and our fifty [sic] state legislatures, are members not only of the church but also of the blessings-of-civilization trust. This world-girdling accumulation of trained morals, high principles, and justice cannot do an upright thing, an unfair thing, an ungenerous thing, an unclean thing. It knows what it is about. Give yourself no uneasiness; it is alright."

We need a new American flag, Mark says, one with white stripes painted black, with the skull-and-crossbones replacing the stars. Every line of Twain's indictment expresses his hatred of colonialism, racism, slavery in whatever form, cruelty, exploitation, suffering, and misery, as Maxwell Geismar sums it up.

Twain expects the worst from this outburst. He writes to his old close friend of Hartford days, the Reverend Joseph Twitchell: "I am not expecting anything but kicks for scoffing, and am expecting a diminution of my bread and butter by it, but if Livy [Twain's wife] will let me, I will have my way." Livy proves sympathetic, but Twitchell is not, and Mark rages at him: "I can't understand it! You are a public guide and teacher, Joe, and are under a heavy responsibility to men, young and old; if you teach your people--as you teach me--to hide their opinions when they believe the flag is being abused and dishonored, lest the utterance do them and a publisher a damage, how do you answer for it to your conscience?"

Twitchell's conscience is solidly Republican, which is the answer to Twain's question. He sticks by his opinion and predicts that Twain is going to find himself in a good deal of trouble. The predicted storm soon breaks. A Congregationalist minister in New York denounces Twain as "a man of low birth and poor breeding," a small sample of the abuse descending on him from other quarters. Far from backing down, he fires a second volley with an article titled, "To My Missionary Critics." Later in the year, when he and his friend, William Dean Howells, are getting honorary degrees at Yale, the students and others give him an ovation, but T.R., who is also present, says privately, "When I hear what Mark Twain and others have said in criticism of the missionaries, I feel like skinning them alive." After the ceremony, however, there's no doubt how Yale feels about

Twain. As he tours the campus, cheers follow him, and he responds by removing his hat and bowing.

The Anti-Imperialist League members and their followers greet Twain's attacks with elation. One of them exclaims: "Praise to the Eternal! A voice has been found." Indeed. Twain is cast as the Conscience of America.

While the controversy over Twain's onslaught is still raging, a startling new development occurs in the Philippines, and it marks the war's turning point. The episode begins when an officer in General Funston's district in central Luzon intercepts a messenger from Aguinaldo. He's carrying dispatches to General Lacuna, calling for reinforcements to be sent to the leader's headquarters camp. So now the Americans know definitely where the camp is, and that means it becomes possible to capture Aguinaldo. MacArthur develops a plan to do it. As a tool, he uses a company of Filipino scouts from the Macabebe tribe--fierce, pure-blooded natives of the islands who had been loyal to the Spaniards before the Americans arrived. There are only about 25,000 of these people all told, living in Pampanga Province.

Early in March, these scouts are loaded on the *Vicksburg*, which slips quietly out of Manila Bay. Only their American commanders know what's going to happen, but once everybody's aboard, the plot begins to unfold. The Macabebes are told to take off their American uniforms and dress as though they were ragged members of Aguinaldo's guerrillas. They're informed that they will be in charge of five American "prisoners" they have presumably captured, one of whom is the little redheaded general from Georgia, Frederick Funston, who is rapidly earning the kind of reputation for derring-do he was only beginning to establish in Cuba.

The *Vicksburg* sidles up near the shore to discharge the conspirators, a hundred miles up the coast from Aguinaldo's camp so the vessel's smoke won't be seen. In the dead of night, with its lights screened, the *Vicksburg* discharges its cargo and slides away again, with orders to pick up the party at a nearby point eleven days later.

Before Funston starts out, he drills the Macabebes carefully in the little drama they're going to play. When they pass through villages on the way to Aguinaldo's camp, they're to tell curious villagers that the Americans were captured in the very act of drawing maps of the countryside, and after a skirmish in which some were killed or wounded, these five were seized as prisoners of war, to be taken to Aguinaldo. It's the kind of story that will assure them of hearty welcomes from the villagers, and Funston observes later that these people, as well as rebels they encounter along the way, are also courteous and kind to the American prisoners.

Still, it's a long march and everyone is exhausted when the expedition finally stops about eight miles from Aguinaldo's camp so that the Macabebe leader, Hilario Tal Plácido, can send a note on ahead to Aguinaldo, saying that he's bringing in prisoners but they've had to stop and rest. Food is urgently needed, he says. The idea is that if Aguinaldo sends the food it means he doesn't suspect. He sends the food. So far, so good.

But as the march is about to be resumed, a message comes from Aguinaldo saying that the Americans ought to be left where they are, under guard, so that they won't know the location of the rebels' secret headquarters. Funston doesn't panic. He instructs the scouts to go ahead, but later he sends Plácido a forged note from Aguinaldo saying that the prisoners should be taken to the camp after all.

The result is that, when Plácido arrives with his men at the headquarters hut, the Americans are out of sight but quite near. There's a guard of about fifteen men around the leader's quarters, and while Plácido is talking to the rebel chief, his men are quietly and unobtrusively throwing a cordon around the place. Plácido tells his plausible story to Aguinaldo while watching this maneuver out of the corner of his eye, and when he thinks the moment has arrived, he walks to the window and gives a prearranged signal. The guards are quickly overpowered. Some are shot outright, others are beaten and tortured. At the same time, Plácido, who is a very large and well-built man, grabs the 115-pound unsuspecting Aguinaldo, throws him to the floor of the hut, and sits on him until Funston and the Americans hurry up.

Pausing just long enough to rest, the kidnaping party hurries its victim along the eight miles of trail to where the *Vicksburg* is already waiting for them. When they reach Manila, MacArthur receives Aguinaldo with the courtesy one military commander gives another. Nevertheless, he's kept under close guard for three weeks, while the American generals try to convince him his cause is hopeless and he'd do well to give it up.

To their surprise, he permits himself to be convinced, takes the oath of allegiance, and issues a proclamation in which he "recommends"--a key word--that hostilities be abandoned.

For successfully carrying out this caper, Funston is promoted but when the story of his adventure is told in the papers it only divides America further. To the Administration and its supporters, he's a hero; to the Anti-Imperialist League and its sympathizers, Funston has done a despicable thing. Twain leads the onslaught with "A Defense of General Funston," in which he attacks the capture with heavy sarcasm, at the same time proudly accepting Funston's characterization of all those who oppose the Administration's policy as "traitors." To Mark Twain, such "traitors" are several notches higher in the scheme of things than "patriots." Since he wrote the piece on Washington's Birthday, Twain compares the two generals (most unlikely, in any case) and finds Funston the exact opposite. As Geismar puts it, Twain is afraid that Funston, "with all his duplicity, cruelty, and sadism, will become the model of the new American military hero."

Twain can't stand the thought of it. He writes: "It was left to a Brigadier General of Volunteers in the American army to put shame upon a custom which even the degraded Spanish friars had respected. *We promoted him for it.*"

Much to the surprise of everyone, Aguinaldo's capitulation not only doesn't stop the war but seems to make it bloodier. The rebels apparently believe Aguinaldo was coerced into giving up, and they have no intention of doing so. As a result, the war grows more brutal every day. Shortly after the rebel leader's capture, General Bell returns to America, leaving his command in southern Luzon, and in Washington makes a statement in an interview that the New York *Times* calls "remarkable." No one could doubt it. Bell reports: "One sixth of the natives of Luzon have either been killed or have died of the dengue fever in the last few years. The loss of life by killing alone has been very great, but I think that not one has been slain except where his death has served the legitimate purposes of war. It has been necessary to adopt what in other countries would probably be thought harsh measures."

And just what have these "harsh measures" done? Well, according to War Department figures, the population of Luzon was 3,727,488 before the war, and because dengue fever is the result of famine caused by war, it follows that Bell's figures show about 616,000 people dying as a direct result of the conflict. Is this what McKinley means by "benevolent assimilation"? The League reprints Bell's interview statement and distributes it widely.

More disturbing information comes from George Kennan, who writes in an *Outlook* article that the so-called "water cure"--pouring water in a man's mouth until he confesses or dies--is being used by American forces. The officers he quotes as sources say it is being done only by the ferocious Macabebe scouts, but at the same time, they don't condemn it.

Newspapers pay little attention to such charges, mostly because correspondents are finding it difficult to get hard evidence, and what they do find doesn't survive military censorship. But Senator Hoar and a crusading editor named Herbert Walsh are determined to expose American military brutality. We'll hear more about this, but not until the war is over.

Before he leaves Luzon, General Bell himself provides enough evidence to convict him, although he clearly believes he's doing the right thing. In an order, he declares it's necessary to "make the state of war as insupportable as possible, and there is no more efficacious way of accomplishing this than by keeping the minds of the people in such a state of anxiety and apprehension that living under such conditions will soon become unbearable. Little should be said. The less said the better. Let acts, not words, convey the intention."

What acts does the general have in mind? He's specific about it. A force of 2,500 men is organized in columns of fifty each. Their orders are to search for rebels in every mountain or valley, and in every last ravine. Any food found outside the towns must be destroyed. Captured rebels must be killed. "These people need a threshing," Bell says, taking a high moral tone, "to teach them some good common sense; and they should have it for the good of all concerned." Other commanders follow his example. The result of teaching good common sense is that a sixth of the native population of Luzon is killed, as Bell later reports, and that includes men, women, and children. We're calling this "pacification," a word so useful as to be employed decades later in Vietnam.

No wonder that a Republican congressman, after visiting the islands, says in an interview when he returns: "You never hear of any disturbances in northern Luzon; and the secret of its pacification is, in my opinion, the secret of pacification of the archipelago. They never rebel in northern Luzon because there isn't anybody there to rebel. The country was marched over and cleaned in a most resolute manner. The good Lord in heaven only knows the number of Filipinos that were put under ground. Our soldiers took no prisoners, they kept no records, they simply swept the country, and wherever or whenever they could get hold of a Filipino they killed him. The women and children were spared, and may now be noticed in disproportionate numbers in that part of the island." These victims of the war--and they *do* include the women and children so tactfully overlooked by the senator--are the same people who Secretary of War Root asserts "received us with open arms."

Otis, before he leaves, holds a press conference to deal with these horrendous facts as they trickle out to the public, and two reporters tell him they've seen soldiers bayoneting wounded men. When Otis points out that the ears of two Americans were cut off, Collins, of the AP, says this was only retaliation for the mutilations of deceased Filipinos. Otis has to admit that he's heard stories of looting and blackmailing, but he blames it all on the volunteers.

Collins writes later: "There has been, according to Otis himself and the personal knowledge of everyone here, a perfect orgy of looting and wanton destruction of property and most outrageous blackmailing of the natives and Chinamen in Manila, and various incidents like the shooting down of several Filipinos for attempting to run from arrest at a cock fight."

Soldiers' letters home provide first-hand accounts of atrocities. Private Charles Brenner, of a Kansas regiment, writes to his mother of a battle at Caloocan: "Company I had taken a few prisoners and stopped. The colonel ordered them up into the line time after time, and finally sent Captain Bishop back to start them. Then occurred the hardest sight I ever saw. They had four prisoners and didn't know what to do with them. They asked Captain Bishop what to do, and he said, 'You know the orders,' and four natives fell dead."

How in the world can Secretary Root say, in an official statement: "The war in the Philippines has been conducted by the American army with scrupulous regard for the rules of civilized warfare, with careful and genuine consideration for the prisoner and the non-combatant, with self-restraint, and with humanity never surpassed"? But he does say it, and a good part of a gullible public that would like to forget the whole thing believes him.

In mid-1901, the war is moving toward its excruciating end. MacArthur is relieved of his command in July and returns home. He is replaced by General Adna Chaffee, who has been spending his time since Santiago leading United States forces, in palship with the imperial powers of Europe, in putting down the Boxer Rebellion, which the Anti-Imperialists have been denouncing for some time as a terrible act, "one of unexampled brutality and ferocity," in Schirmer's words. Naturally, they denounce Chaffee's appointment too.

So successful has been the search-and-destroy campaign that, by late summer and early fall of 1901, the only major area still in active revolt is the island of Samar, and it's there that the conflict stumbles to its bloody end, for all practical purposes. The story of Samar embodies everything that's wrong with this war, foreshadowing Vietnam, as so much of the action in the Philippines has done. It should be an object lesson everyone can learn from, but it's forgotten as soon as the investigations and court-martials are over with, and the dubious peace between 1902 and 1917 begins.

5

THE HORROR OF SAMAR

WILLIAM HOWARD TAFT IS "A LIKEABLE MAN OF FORTY-TWO, jolly but impressive, with a big body and a big smile and a big judicial brain," as Leech describes him. He's also a man whose greatest ambition is to be appointed to the Supreme Court, so when the President summons him to the White House he's puzzled because no vacancy is presently available. What could McKinley have in mind?

Surprise, surprise! Taft still can't get over it nearly a decade later when he describes their conversation:

"Judge," McKinley begins, "I'd like to have you go to the Philippines."

"Mr. President, what do you mean by going to the Philippines?" Taft inquires.

"We must establish a government there and I'd like you to help," McKinley says.

"But, Mr. President," Taft protests, "I am sorry we have got the Philippines. I don't want them and I think you ought to have a man who is more in sympathy with the situation."

"You don't want them any less than I do," McKinley replies fervently, "but we have got them and in dealing with them I think I can trust the man who didn't want them better than I can the man who did."

Incontrovertible, if peculiar, logic. And that's how Taft, the future President, becomes Taft the first civil governor of the Philippines. Having extracted a promise from McKinley not to forget about that Supreme Court appointment while he's far away in the jungle, Taft departs without particular enthusiasm and arrives at the scene of conflict in July 1901.

Another unpleasant surprise awaits him. He'll have to share power with General Chaffee, who as Army commander of the Division of the Philippines has placed more than fifty of the islands' seventy-odd provinces under military rule.

Taft believes all the provinces should be brought under civil government at once. Chaffee disagrees. He insists, and publicly, that the necessity is to place the Filipinos under what he calls "bayonet rule" for an unforeseeable time to come.

Taft is left with what amounts to establishing a shadow civil government while Chaffee goes about the task of putting the bayonet to those provinces not yet under his rule. That leads him to the largest and most recalcitrant of the remaining holdouts, the island of Samar--5,000 square miles of hilly, jungle wilderness, whose annual rainfall measures anywhere from 100 to 170 inches. Samar is the third largest in the archipelago, after Luzon and Mindanao. It's the most eastern part of the Viscayan group, on the Viscaya Sea. The island has no roads at all, and not many trails, a place largely unmapped and uninhabited even today. The rebels are said to be well back in the hills from the narrow plain on the coast.

When Major Littleton Tazewell Waller, the Marine commandant leading the invasion, first sees Samar, he calls it "an evil-looking, humpbacked island." But he means to conquer it at all costs, which in time will nearly include his life and does include his career.

On August 11, 1901, the Army transport *Liscum* brings a force of Army regulars and a few Marines into the harbor of Balangiga, at the southern end of the island. Joseph Schott, the foremost chronicler of these events, describes the solders: "Troops, Army and Marines, wore floppy felt campaign hats, heavy blue wool shirts, and carried long, cumbersome Krag-Jorgenson rifles." The enemy awaiting them is General Vincente Luchan's army, if we could call it that, made up of all ages from children of ten or so to old men. Their arms are muskets, bolo knives, and bamboo cannon.

Waller means to conquer this wilderness by sending an initial force of less than eighty men, members of Company C, 9th U. S. Infantry, now looking disconsolate in rain-soaked gray campaign hats and black slickers. They gaze from the *Liscum* without enthusiasm at Balangiga, which is a community of about two hundred huts on stilts surrounding a central plaza, where there are two masonry buildings--the city hall (called the "tribunal"), and a combined Catholic church and convent. Behind the church on its west side is a river running into the sea, and on the north and east sides dense jungle encroaches.

Hills rise up behind the town, some of them high enough to be shrouded most of the time by low-hanging clouds.

Not a tropical paradise, to be sure, but here come the natives in their outrigger canoes to welcome us. The troops examine them. Some look familiar, that is, they're wearing the typical native costume of white shirts that look like pajama tops, and cotton pants. All have broad-brimmed straw hats circled by wide red bands. But they don't look quite like the other Filipinos the men of Company C have seen. They're dark and stocky, and more powerfully built. They are also a silent and sullen lot.

As the native boats surround the ship, Captain Thomas W. Connell, a tall West Pointer in his late twenties, and his second in command, 1st Lieutenant Edward A. Bumpus, a few years younger, watch the Filipinos, and Bumpus, with a laugh, says, "Boys, we're in Googoo Land for sure now." "Goo-goo" has replaced "nigger" as the troops' favorite description of the natives.

It isn't the first time Samar has been invaded by Americans. A year earlier, General William Kobbe had led troops ashore, to be greeted by natives charging them along the beach with bolo knives and hemp beaters used as clubs. Some of the Americans were slashed by the bolos but no one was killed, while most of the attackers were shot. Afterward, in his report to headquarters, in Manila, Kobbe noted ruefully, "I begin to understand why the Spanish would never permit these people to even own a table knife."

But things have changed, apparently. About the time Taft arrived to bring peace, the *presidente* of Balangiga, Pedro Abayan, had written to Manila headquarters asking for American troops to protect his people from raids by Moro pirates. That's why Company C is there now, Chaffee having convinced himself that the natives are tired of violence.

Now here's Presidente Abayan coming out to greet Captain Connell and his men, trailed by other officials wearing, incongruously, white cotton suits and black top hats. To Connell's surprise, there's also a priest in his black cassock, a white-brimmed straw hat shading his Spanish countenance and carrying a cane with a shiny gold head which he swings like a scepter. Abayan and the chief of police, Pedro Sánchez, address Connell and he surprises them by answering in fluent Spanish. But the captain doesn't like the look of these short, muscular men with their surly faces, and he doesn't much like the look in the priest's jaundice-yellowed eyes. Already he's wondering what he'll be able to report to his superior, Brigadier General Robert Hughes, who is in command of the Department of the Viscayas, of which Samar is a part. Many of his men may be wondering, too, what lies ahead. These are relatively innocent farm boys for the most part, many of them runaways from home, seeking adventure in the Regular Army. Adventure seems to be looking right back at them now. Some of these troops are immigrants who don't speak good English, let alone Spanish. The noncoms are mostly rough-and-ready Irishmen, so poorly educated they can't read the Articles of War.

Connell stands out from all the others. Fair-haired, he looks more priestlike than the priest. He was a native of New York City, had graduated from West Point in 1894, and served in Cuba and North China before he came to the Philippines. Oddly enough, he doesn't agree with Chaffee about "bayonet rule." He's a "benevolent assimilation" man, and he really intends to civilize and Christianize these people if he can, even though the priest may have beaten him to it. He regards this place as a kind of laboratory for his ideas.

So begins the terrible saga of Samar, this rugged island swept much of the year by rain, strong winds, and occasional typhoons, its population of something like 222,000 (no one is sure) struggling to survive the elements and each other. They're a mix of the original black population with invading Moros, Chinese, and Spaniards, living under hereditary chiefs, raising rice, sweet potatoes, tobacco, and a kind of banana plant called abaca, using the most primitive agricultural methods.

Since the Spanish were thrown out, the people of Samar have been living under the overall rule of General Luchan, who took over the capital, Catbalogan, with the aid of a hundred riflemen, and proclaimed himself governor under Aguinaldo's Philippine Republic. As a general, he's also the military commander. Luchan has turned out to be popular in his self-anointed role. He's half Chinese and half Tagalog, short and heavy, in his late fifties, his face distinguished by a luxuriant black mustache. In his earlier life, he had grown up in a rich Luzon family, but became a revolutionary almost from the beginning of the revolt. In Samar, he's been a no-nonsense ruler, cruel and dictatorial.

Connell, who has come to dethrone him, is not popular in Company C or elsewhere in the Army. The men not only don't like his views about assimilating the goo-goos but they resent his attempts to protect them from the wiles of native women. He wants to do the impossible--keep them pure and uncontaminated. Connell also believes in that old-fashioned word "trust." Consequently he orders that, when the men are at church or at mass, they must not carry guns, although he's not so foolish as to disarm the twenty-four-hour guard he sets up around Balangiga.

In August, a month after his arrival, Connell is visited by an Army inspector, Lieutenant Colonel Roger Foote, from headquarters at Leyte. Foote seems to like what he sees--good discipline, excellent sanitary arrangements, and a policy of peaceful penetration that seems to be working although it hasn't really been tried yet. Foote warns Connell against over-confidence. Just fifty miles up the coast, he says, an American patrol squad has been ambushed, with three men killed.

There's something Connell doesn't know. American troops have recently raided General Luchan's headquarters, and found among other items a letter containing serious threats against Company C's occupation force. The raiders, under Captain H. L. Jackson, of the 1st Infantry, had stumbled into their headquarters so suddenly that the rebels scarcely had time to flee. In the subsequent confusion, a little boy pointed to a woman holding a baby and said, "That's Mrs. Luchan," and so it is. While the slightly wounded general escapes, his wife and his mother are taken prisoner, along with a pair of staff officers, three riflemen, twenty bolomen, and a big stack of correspondence from the office. All of this booty, human and material, Jackson sent back to headquarters while he pursued the fleeing general.

When they sort out the letters at American headquarters, they find one from Abayan to the general dated May 30, only a few weeks before the petition for American troops was sent to the American command. In the letter, Abayan laid out a "fictitious policy" covering how to treat the Americans when they came. As soon as the time was right, he concluded, "the people will strategically rise against them."

Typically, this letter, which should have given Connell ample warning, spends so much time being passed around and analyzed by various military minds at various headquarters that, when they conclude it represents a clear and present danger, it's too late for Connell. One interesting fact has emerged from the analysis. The letter was written in excellent Spanish, but Abayan is not educated enough to have written such a letter. Only one person in town is equipped to do it: the priest.

September comes in hot and rainy. Back home, on September 6, the young immigrant Leon Czolgosz, believing he's also striking a blow for the liberation of humanity, approaches the President at the great Exposition in Buffalo, and with a gun in his bandaged left hand, raises it and fires the shot that kills McKinley, who dies eight days later. The shocking news reaches Manila some time after that, and he's given a mock funeral. More than 2,000 men of the Army, Navy, and Marines are lined up, and while the melancholy death march sounds from a regimental band, an artillery salute is fired, and then the troops sing McKinley's favorite, "Lead, Kindly Light."

At Balangiga, meanwhile, things are moving toward a climax, although Connell doesn't know it. He takes a patrol up the river on September 25, looking for rebels, leaving 1st Sergeant Randles in charge, telling him to keep his eyes open. But Connell hasn't been gone more than two hours before Abayan and Police Chief Sánchez approach Randles as he's writing orders and tell him they want to bring in eighty laborers from the countryside to clean up the plaza. It will help these peasants work off their unpaid taxes, Abayan says. Since cleaning up the plaza is something Connell has wanted, the sergeant is only too happy to give permission and tells the *presidente*, "Bring in as many as you can."

In the morning, forty husky laborers march in from the jungle, and a day later, forty more arrive. They go right to work, and by the time Connell gets back the place is looking much better. The captain is so happy he wants to thank the priest for helping him in his humanitarian program, since it's the Church that handles taxes, but the priest is nowhere about. No one's seen him. Then the news of McKinley's assassination arrives, and momentarily everyone's distracted. Connell discusses the prospect ahead with his men and predicts gloomily that T.R., who now succeeds McKinley, will go back to the "bullets-and-bayonets" policy. A lieutenant ventures to say that maybe that's the only policy these goo-goos will understand. As historian Daniel Schirmer records, Connell flares back: "How in God's name can they ever have any self-respect if we continually refer to them as Googoos?"

Something is definitely going on in Balangiga. That night, the sentries notice an unusually large number of women hurrying into the church. They're all wearing unusually heavy clothes and some are carrying small coffins. Suspicious, a sergeant stops a woman, pries open the coffin lid with his bayonet, and sees a dead child staring up at him. "Cholera," the mother tells him. With so many coffins, an epidemic must be going on, the sergeant thinks, but he's heard nothing about it. If he had only lifted the body, he would have found beneath it a cargo of cane-cutting bolo knives. And if he had parted the folds of the garments these heavily swathed women are wearing, he would have seen that most of them were men. Why didn't the sergeant act on his suspicions? Because Connell has ordered that there be no physical familiarity with native women.

After a busy night of coming and going, Sunday dawns peacefully and the men of Company C are eating or still asleep or reading letters from home. Sánchez's tax-free laborers are busy cutting grass around the plaza. Surveying this bucolic scene watchfully, the police chief walks over to a hut where Sergeant Betron and eight other soldiers are eating breakfast, with only three armed sentries to protect them. Approaching one of them, Private Adolph Gamlin, Sánchez suddenly grabs his rifle, opens Gamlin's skull with it, and fires one shot, a signal. At that sound, the church bell begins to peal, conch-shell whistles are heard everywhere from the jungle's edge, and out of the church doors rushes a body of bolomen. At the same time, the laborers in the plaza begin using their bolos on any American in sight, or hitting them with picks and shovels. Most of the soldiers are unarmed, and they fight their attackers fiercely as they try to get to their rifles. In the confusion, Sánchez himself is shot.

Schott describes the crimson shambles in the hut where Sergeant Betron and his comrades were eating breakfast only moments before: "The scene in the blood soaked hut was frightful. One man was sitting bolt upright on the ladder in front of the shack, dying, face covered with blood from a gaping wound in his forehead. Private Litto Armani lay on the floor moaning in agony. He was slashed across the abdomen and suffering intense pain. Private Jerry J. Driscoll was crawling about blindly on his hands and knees, his brains falling out through a broad crack in his skull. Survivors...on the outside joined together, armed with clubs, pots, bolos, anything they could find."

The attack is well timed. Mess tents are filled with unarmed soldiers eating breakfast, and these are the prime targets. The soldiers defend themselves with chairs and kitchen utensils against screaming, bolo-wielding Filipinos, until the attackers cut the tent ropes. In the first few minutes, Company C is virtually wiped out. It's like a wild, gory hunt as bolomen pursue soldiers in every direction, slashing and killing.

Connell is one of the victims. Still in his pajamas, he lies face down on the ground, a multitude of stab wounds in his back. Unbelievably, however, enough of Company C remains to get to the rifles, take over the town, and drive their attackers into the jungle. Only thirty-six out of seventy-four men in camp that morning are left alive, and thirty of these are wounded, some severely. It's a precarious victory.

Miraculously, Sergeant Betron is one of the survivors and he takes command. He briefly considers trying to hold the town but he knows most of the wounded will die if he doesn't get medical help, so he decides to load the survivors into five boats and attempt to reach Waller's headquarters at Basey, about thirty-six nautical miles up the coast. These boats are primitive craft, double-riggers hollowed out of logs.

While the enemy keeps up a constant harassing fire, some of them with the soldiers' own rifles, Betron manages to disable what weapons are left behind and marshals his men on the beach, with those wounded worst on stretchers. Sometimes the bearers have to drop the stretchers and fight off renewed attacks. They can hear conch shells whistling in the hills, signaling new assaults.

Just before he shoves off, Betron sends riflemen back into the village to shoot any native still living, and to drive Filipinos who are already looting the bodies back into the jungle. These rear-guard riflemen also make sure no Americans are still alive before they pour five gallons of gasoline on the church and set it ablaze. As they leave, the men salvage a case of whiskey.

The five boats shove off, the badly wounded lying in the largest boat, and they see something they've overlooked--the flag still flying above their parade ground. They won't leave without it. Private Claude Wingo, wounded though he is, leads three men to go back and get it. They succeed in pulling it down, but two of them are killed by rifle fire from the jungle while they're doing it. The other two make it to the boats, carrying the flag. It's still only eight o'clock on this bloody Sunday morning.

The survivors are far from being out of danger. Only half a mile from shore, enemy fire can still reach them. Two of the wounded are dead by noontime. The wind comes up and a rough sea threatens to swamp the boats; one does slide down a foot in the water but it's saved by the outrigging. The wind and water drive them toward shore and the men have to wade through the surf to the beach, only ten miles from Balangiga. They're half dead with thirst but they find some coconuts to chop open and drink the milk.

When daylight comes, five of the men are staggering along the beach when twenty to thirty natives charge toward them. Two soldiers and a native boy who's refused to leave manage to escape, staying ahead of their pursuers until they find a rotting boat they're able to launch and push off far enough from shore to be temporarily safe. Meanwhile, the other four boats, which have been tied together with ropes, are close by, trying to get around Capines Point, but the wind and sea are against them. When the bow of Private Wingo's boat looks like it's being pulled underwater, he cuts loose. "I'll have a better chance of paddling my own canoe," he shouts to the sergeant, who watches him and a single companion paddle away in the general direction of Leyte. They're never seen again.

Somehow, three of the boats manage to crawl up the shoreline, under constant watch from natives on the beach, who sometimes try to intercept them with their own boats but fail. The Americans shoot three of these harassers. The best of the boats never gets to Basey but comes to rest on the neighboring island of Leyte where the men reach safety at last. In the other boats, the water rations give out, and these survivors are so crazed with thirst that they begin to drink the sea water. Betron, in one of the boats, tries to land on the coast early in the morning, hoping to find water or coconuts, but the natives appear and the men have to shove off hastily. Blood dripping from the wounded trails in the water, attracting sharks, which join the pursuit. Wind-blown seawater slashes into the boats, aggravating the pain of the wounded. Near sunset, a small steamer passes by, far out, but doesn't see the survivors. In the dark as they go along, they can make out the shoreline by the light of native fires along it.

At dawn, with the wounded men crying out in delirium, the boats ground on a sandbar at the entrance to Basey Harbor, and a sentry on shore sees four men, still able to walk, sloshing crazily about in low water, trying to pull the boats off the bar. Betron attempts to shout but thirst has dried up his throat. Nor can the other men help him. Their tongues are black and swollen too.

Soldiers on shore finally see them and come to the rescue, pulling the two remaining boats to shore. There are twenty-six half-conscious men in them and eight die once they're ashore. Two from the other boats make it to Leyte, and four others are found in the jungle by a search party from Basey. Two more make it on foot later. So, at the final count, of the seventy-one men and three officers of Company C, only twenty-six all told have survived their awful ordeal.

Now Captain Edwin V. Bookmiller, commander of Company G of the 9th Infantry at Basey, takes charge. He wants to lead a force back to Balangiga to identify the dead, and asks for volunteers from C Company. One of the survivors steps forward, but a comrade says, "This man is wounded, sir," and he's sent off to the hospital. But by the following morning, Bookmiller has fifty-three men assembled and, with some hospital corpsmen, ready to go back to Balangiga on the gunboat *Pittsburgh*, to see if there's anything there worth saving. The force is protected by a Gatling gun and a one-pounder cannon. On the way, they pick up the half-fainting trio of two privates and the native boy who had escaped by running up the beach.

When the *Pittsburgh* arrives at Balangiga, a reception party is waiting for them--half-drunken natives running to the beach, waving spears and bolos. Behind them the town is half covered by black smoke. Since the Americans left, the Filipinos have been improving their time by getting drunk and trying to burn down their town. But now the party's over. Bookmiller turns his Gatling gun and cannon on the crowded beach, and in a burst of flame and smoke, bodies fly into the air and several score of the former inhabitants are killed. Then the soldiers come charging through the surf, bayonets fixed, and in a few minutes they've secured the town.

Another gory sight awaits them. There's poor 1st Sergeant Randles, headfirst in a water barrel, his feet chopped off. They find Captain Connell's head being roasted over a fire, and the rest of his nude, mutilated body jammed into the latrine. Someone has smeared strawberry jam into the deep bolo slashes on Lieutenant Bumpus's face. Near him lies the body of a man never identified who has had his stomach cut open and a sack of flour poured into it. In the kitchen, side by side, is a sergeant's headless body, his dog lying next to him. Both are covered with flour, and the dog's eyes have been gouged out, to be replaced by stones.

The rescue party buries thirty-six Americans in a mass grave, after which the few Company C men left pour kerosene on the bodies of the dead natives and burn them. When some women come out of hiding and beg to have the bodies buried because they're all Catholics, a religion in which cremation is forbidden, Bookmiller gives them an ecclesiastical response: "Their black souls are all burning in hell now, so let us dispose of their bodies in the same manner."

A corporal asks him what to do with twenty natives who didn't get away in time, and the captain leaves it up to the survivors of Company C, who shoot them on the spot. Houses still standing are burned to the ground, and Balangiga is left a smoldering ruin. If this isn't the end of benevolent assimilation on Samar, it will do.

Corporal Arnold Irish, looking back at the remains as the *Pittsburgh* moves off, says with pure hatred, "Damn the infernal googoos," and Bookmiller, who seems to be handy with biblical answers, quotes from the Book of Hosea: "They have sown the wind and they shall reap the whirlwind."

When the report on Balangiga reaches Manila, Taft, the new civil governor, is completely taken aback. "It was like a clap of thunder out of a clear sky," he writes home to his wife. Taft is in a bad way himself. He's just getting over dengue fever, and now he's suffering from severe intestinal cramps. Still, nothing prevents this huge man from growing even larger. The Chinese chef he brought out with him produces lavish meals in his kitchen and Taft manages to put them away, stomach pains or not. Nor does the news from Samar shake his confidence that his civil government is going to succeed, a view shared by the New York *Times*, which refers to Balangiga as "this painful little episode." Taft echoes the paper in a report to Secretary Root, calling it "a painful, but unimportant little episode." Otherwise, he says, almost all the natives are friendly. Or dead.

When he writes to his brother Horace, however, it appears that Taft doesn't have much use for the Army people with whom he's compelled to share power. "You know we have the ragtag and bobtail of America," he confides, "who are not only vicious but stupid. The Samar incident has furnished them with material and I regret to say that they have found in Army circles a great deal of sympathy for their position. The Army has been completely stampeded by the Samar affair. Chaffee...has mounted patrols running through Manila at night and has repeated to General Wright a number of times that they are standing on a volcano. The Army and Navy Club is filled with rumors of insurrection."

It's true that there's a bit of ragtag and bobtail in Manila-- men who see the war as a way to make quick money on the sly. Life in the city is pleasant enough, too, no matter what horrors may be taking place elsewhere. Vintage wines and champagne go untaxed and are imbibed freely in expensive restaurants. The wives of officers and civilians are discovering what so many British memsahibs have already found in India--servants are dirt cheap. They have a lot of them, native women who go back to their dreadful slums at night.

Everyone who can get away from work (and some who can't) goes to the races, and the city's luxurious clubs are con-stantly giving teas and balls. The club men make a nice distinc-tion: military men belong to the Army and Navy Club, civilian officials (if their rank is high enough) join the University Club. Women, of course, are excluded from both except for social events. Wherever Americans gather, in fact, the caste lines are sharply drawn. Charles Ballantine, of the AP, reports: "In the American and European life in Manila, the Filipino is a small quantity, and there is scarcely any communication between the two races."

As in Cuba, the older Army officers are nearly all Union veterans, so that when they gather to pass the time of day or evening at the Army and Navy Club, it sounds like a meeting of the G.A.R. An outsider is General Luke E. Wright, a member of the Philippine Commission, who was a Confederate general. He listens sympathetically to the others, which somehow irritates Taft.

The commanding general is Adna Chaffee, and he's becoming obsessed with the perilous situation which he believes everyone is in. His orderly recalls later that Chaffee's customary greeting in the morning at breakfast is, "Well, has it blown up yet?" And when the orderly queries, "What, sir?" the general roars, "The volcano, damn it! The volcano we're standing on." In his old age, militarily speaking, Chaffee is becoming irritable and humorless, but he has reason to be worried. Reading reports from the field, he hears that waves of insurrection keep on sweeping over even the conquered islands.

Chaffee keeps boring the War Department with cables citing ominous incidents here and there. On October 16, for example, he reports that forty-six men from Company E, 9th Regiment, have been attacked by 400 bolomen, leaving two killed and six wounded. Eighty-one natives were killed, he adds. Next day he passes on a new report from Samar, where it appears that the garrison at Weyler was assaulted by more than a hundred bolomen, some of whom also had rifles. The War Department cables back promptly; "Take appropriate action immediately to quell new insurgent uprisings Samar."

Just what Chaffee's been waiting for. Maybe he can stuff enough native bodies down the volcano to plug it shut. Immediately he creates a separate command and gives it an odd name, the Sixth Separate Brigade. To command it, he assigns Brigadier General Jacob R. Smith, an old pal of Civil War days who had also fought Indians with him on the Plains. His orders are brief: Subdue Samar, once and for all.

Smith establishes his headquarters at Tacloban, on Leyte, where he can see across a narrow strait the garrison town of Basey, in which the Balangiga survivors have found refuge. Smith thinks he'll need a thousand men to subdue Samar, and if he can't get enough regulars, he's willing to take a temporary loan of Marines. He gets 300 of them. The order for them goes to Waller, as commander of the Marine First Brigade, and it's the wording of this order that will cause a great deal of trouble later on.

The message is straightforward enough. It calls for a battalion to be ready immediately--meaning ready to go in twenty-four hours. Waller is to take personal charge of this force, consisting of four companies, seventy-five men in each, with fourteen other officers under him. These are hardened veterans he'll be taking to Samar, men who have fought in Cuba, Puerto Rico, and the Boxer Rebellion, always with distinction.

Waller himself is a forty-five-year-old officer his friends call "Tony," described by Schott as "an aggressive bantam, a swaggerer." He's been in the Marines for twenty-two years and has no illusions about war after leading men at San Juan, Santiago, and Puerto Rico. They gave him a special medal for his heroism at Santiago. Smedley Butler, another Marine commander who will turn against war in later life, describes Waller as "a little fellow with a fiery mustache and a distinguished bearing. His size made no difference. He dominated the others. The picture of him that stays with me is the Waller of his dashing prime in the Philippines. His men adored him. He had a magnificent face and carriage. I can see him, straight as a ruler, his head thrown back, his enormous nose outlined against the sky, as he saluted the flag. Waller may have liked to talk about himself, but he had plenty to talk about."

He marches his men to a wharf at Cavite and boards them on the *New York* early in the morning of October 22. These troops are well equipped. They have full field packs and weapons, also 40,000 pounds of rifle ammunition and 10,000 food rations, packed in wooden boxes. They have eight Colt automatic guns and a trio of three-inch artillery pieces, plus five pack mules.

As they leave shore, Chaplain Chadwick, who survived the *Maine*, gives the men a short inspirational speech, closing with a prayer. Then it's a short trip to Catbalogan, a port town on the west coast of Samar, where they dock next morning, and for the first time, Waller meets his superior, General Smith, who arrives on board with Major Edward F. Glenn, judge advocate of the Department of the Visayas.

The two men survey each other. Waller sees another veteran, sixty-two years old, who has spent forty years in the Army. He has a sour reputation among the men because of his harsh, loud voice, too frequently employed to dress down subordinates. Behind his back, he's known as "Hell Roarin' Jake." He's as short and aggressive as Waller, and in Schott's words, "his ragged, rather mournful, gray mustache made him look a bit like the old comedian of vaudeville and silent movies, Andy Clyde." Smith's service record is much like the other veteran generals'--enlistment in the Union Army in 1861, a survivor of several battles, including Shiloh, and fighting Indians in the West afterward.

Smith has some specific orders from General Chaffee, who wants to get back the arms that were lost at Balangiga. "You must get them back," he tells Smith. "You can have $5,000 in gold. Capture the arms if you can, buy them if you must; whichever course you adopt, get them back." Since the arms are probably well distributed in the interior by this time, that is likely to be an impossible task.

In their conversations, Smith informs Waller that all the garrisons in Samar are being reinforced to end the insurrection on the island by whatever means may be necessary. With a nice touch of commemorative spirit, Smith has promised to do that by Christmas Day. Waller's part in the campaign will be to clean out the district on the southern end of the island, where the rebels have been making sorties with the rifles captured at Balangiga.

In painfully specific terms, Smith gives his oral instructions to Waller: "I want no prisoners. I wish you to kill and burn, the more you kill and burn the better you will please me. I want all persons killed who are capable of bearing arms in actual hostilities against the United States."

"I'd like to know the limit of age to respect, sir," Waller says.

"Ten years," the general replies.

Waller wants to pin it down: "Persons of ten years and older are those designated as being capable of bearing arms?" Smith assures him this is the case, reminding him that some of those who took part in the Balangiga massacre were about that age.

Since Admiral Rodgers, Navy commander in the Philippines, is on the gunboat *Vicksburg*, which will stay near Waller's base, the Marine commander finds himself in the somewhat uncomfortable position of reporting to both the Army's General Smith and the Navy's chief as well. Consequently, when he dictates the orders to his officers and men he sees to it that they contain only General Smith's commands, or so he maintains later. But there's one exception. The last paragraph in his general orders is his own and it reads:

"We have also to avenge our late comrades in North China, the murdered men of the Ninth U.S. Infantry."

Waller sets up his headquarter in Basey. Determined to avoid any repetition of what happened at Balangiga, he instructs the men of his command to be armed at all times, even at meals. And now he's ready for his first search-and-destroy mission. He's told that his initial goal should be the village of San Antonio, only a few miles away on the coast, where the inhabitants are busy supplying the rebels with rice. Taking a single company, Waller surrounds the village as twenty men, waving their bolos in defiance, vanish into the jungle. Two are captured later. After administering the oath of allegiance to forty-eight male inhabitants of San Antonio, he burns the place to the ground. In spite of Smith's orders, he takes his prisoners, along with their families, back to Basey.

The rebels exact revenge. On October 26, they cut the telephone lines connecting Basey with Tacloban, and get away with it. Learning that the *presidente* of Gibasy, one Serrafino Elano, has twice been seen in Basey without reporting his presence, Waller has him arrested and burns down the town.

This is the pattern Waller follows at first. Patrols go out to devastate anything they can find--burning houses, killing pigs and chickens, destroying boats, as well as piles of dried hemp. No mercy is shown. When one patrol enters a hut where two women and a man are sitting with such incriminating evidence as a blue Army shirt and trousers, Army shoes, and three blood-stained bolos, everyone in sight is killed. The patrol marches on into serious danger of losing its own collective life. Once they're ambushed but fight their way out of it. At night, as they move along the trail, they extend long poles in front of the column to expose four-foot-deep pits whose bottoms are lined with poisoned spearheads.

They survive all this, but not the chills and fever that are a constant danger, as well as swollen feet, and the ravages of leeches on their skins. Ants and leeches are their worst non-human enemies, but it's also necessary to worry about lizards, centipedes, spiders, tarantulas, rats, and huge mosquitoes. Fortunately, there are only a few snakes, most of them tree boas.

Such attacks by the wide-ranging patrols begin to have an effect. Fewer and fewer natives are to be seen. Captured prisoners say the rebels have fallen back to the Soboton Cliffs, where as many as 5,000 of them may have taken up a strongly defended position. Examining his maps, Waller decides to take some troops down the river in boats and attack this stronghold, using platforms made of bamboo to mount his heavy guns.

This mission gets under way at 5:15 A.M. on the gray morning of November 6, when the *Vicksburg* disgorges a steam launch which pulls a whaleboat and a cutter, loaded with men, ashore. The rebels seem to know they're coming, and they greet the expedition with bamboo guns, killing two men. Nevertheless, two cutters, more whaleboats, and a gun platform start going up the river until they run into such heavy fire they're forced to retreat until only snipers endanger them.

Waller meanwhile is carrying out his policy of total destruction in every direction. Seven men with their wives and children are found in one house and it takes awhile to kill them all. Adding it up at the end of November, Waller figures he's destroyed 255 houses, killed thirty-nine men, captured eighteen others, destroyed seventeen bolos, a ton of hemp and a half ton of rice, besides thirteen innocent carabaos. Not bad, but it hardly amounts to the suppression of all resistance. He's got to get up the Cadocan River and destroy the stronghold sixteen miles inland, perched on the Soboton Cliffs. He sends a fifty-man force which is to meet and join a similar company from reconstituted Balangiga, now a functioning outpost again.

On the evening of November 16, these forces find themselves at the foot of the cliffs, which rear up 200 feet above them, looking like a honeycomb with their innumerable caves. The rebels have cut ledges and shelves into the cliff side, connecting one level with another by ladders. The immediate defense consists of bamboo cages containing huge rocks and secured by ropes which can be cut to send them crashing down on invaders. There are also bamboo cannon, loaded with black powder and homemade shrapnel compounded of rocks, scrap iron, and broken glass.

The rebels sight the Americans and fierce fighting breaks out at once, one of the hottest engagements of the war. The Marines try to get up the ladders while the rebels fire at them from their caves. Ropes are cut but the falling bamboo cages do surprisingly little damage. The tough Marines reach the cliff top and spill over it into hand-to-hand combat, while others of their comrades follow them up the ladders.

These rebels fight frantically, but they're no match for the Marines and flee, after which the Americans blow up their powder bags and destroy their rice. If this is the main center of the resistance on Samar, it serves that purpose no more. Astonishingly, the Marines suffer no casualties while they kill thirty rebels. Forty cannons are captured, stores of powder and food are destroyed. Chief damage to the Marines appears to be their uniforms, which are badly torn, and their shoes, worn through by the rough terrain. They're barefoot and their skins bear huge leech welts, but they are victorious.

Waller takes another party up the river on November 27 and travels eight miles inland, where he sends out patrols from the supply camp he establishes. One of the patrols finds a just-emptied rebel camp where the footprints on the ground are made by American shoes; the huts are filled with American kerosene cans, lamps, spades, and used-up tins of rations. Another burning reminder of Balangiga.

New orders arrive from Smith during the first week in December. It's getting closer to the Christmas Day deadline. "The interior of Samar must be made a howling wilderness," Smith says dramatically, but he doesn't sign the order. Is it an oversight? Waller asks the man who brought it, Lieutenant J. H. A. Day, and Day says, "Smith. Those are his instructions." We'll see much more of Day later.

On the eighth, Waller moves out of Basey again with two columns, one headed for the interior, the other advancing along the beach. They're joined by one of the companies now at Balangiga and for the next six weeks these combat patrols push the rebels toward the east, killing and burning along the way. The job isn't finished by Christmas Day, so they stop long enough to roast a carabao on a spit, finishing the holiday meal with boiled potatoes, onions, and biscuits, followed by games and potato races in the spirit of the holy day. Sixteen prisoners share this meal, but not the races. At night, Waller reads *A Christmas Carol* to the troops by the light of a coal oil lantern, after which they sing and dance, play poker, and tell yarns. Then, next morning, it's on to the killing again, pushing toward the east coast and at last returning to Basey.

They may have missed Smith's deadline, but Waller and the other commanders are optimistic they can get the job done soon. In Manila, there's a new vice-governor general, General

Luke E. Wright, another former Confederate leader. Wright notes that fighting is still going on at various places in the southern islands, especially Cebu and Samar, but he thinks things are looking up everywhere, especially on Samar. Chaffee isn't talking so much now about standing on the brink of a volcano, according to his orderly.

Back in Washington, enough stories about the conduct of the war have been circulated by the Anti-Imperialist League to bring about a Senate hearing, where T.R.'s new administration is going to have a hard time. The Democrats announce that they favor "an immediate declaration of national purpose to give the Philippines first, a stable form of government; second, independence; third, protection from outside influence."

Not if T.R. can help it. He's reported to be edgy and irritable these days. He intends to bring Taft home to testify (much to Big Bill's intense relief) and he counts on Senators Lodge and Beveridge to help him at the hearings.

Back at the ranch, on Samar, Waller is doing his best to make a howling wilderness out of the island, as per instructions. He's found a Spanish map, which may or may not be reliable, showing a trail starting near the Soboton Cliffs westward for nearly forty miles, or so he estimates. American troops have never crossed the island, but Waller thinks now is the time to do it. It won't be easy. This terrain is cut up by rivers and deep gullies, and is entirely covered by thick forest. So far, an exploring party hasn't even been able to find the trail shown on the map.

Waller's officers shudder at the idea of making such a march, especially when they hear he means to string telephone wires along the way, and they try to talk him out of it. But he's adamant. He tells them he has no choice; he has to obey Smith's orders. So off he goes with fifty men and thirty or so native carriers, plus rations, diminished from the six days' supply he asked for because that much isn't available. Again, the other officers warn that this four days' supply won't be enough.

On the day after Christmas, the expedition moves out, one part of it headed into the interior, the other in the direction of Balangiga. The rain's stopped, the sun's out, and the men are singing as they travel. These are troops Waller has picked with care, the strongest and ablest he commands. Two native guides from Basey, whom the soldiers call Slim and Smoke, the former an officer in the Basey police, lead the way. Even as they march off singing, however, at least two officers are still trying vainly to talk Waller out of the expedition.

They follow the river as far as their boats will take them, then send the craft back and head up a steep mountain ridge toward another river, the Soribao. Torrential rain begins again and the initial happy mood vanishes as water sores and chafe marks begin to take a toll on the men trudging through gritty volcanic soil. They have to cut their way through heavy vegetation, and prickly thorns rip at their uniforms, making entrances for the ever present leeches.

Coming to the Soboton River, which they'd intended to follow to the mountains of the same name, they find it in flood stage, making it necessary to cross and recross. Officers try to hurry the men along (the oldest is only twenty-six) but Waller restrains them because he's afraid the baggage and rear guard won't catch up, and he now takes complete charge, giving all the commands. Still, their progress is too slow, and that concerns him.

By December 30, they're only halfway there. Waller writes in his notebook: "Banks of river, high and mountainous, covered with massive timbers and a network of vines and undergrowth. Not even birds to break the monotony. Camped on a wretched little sand and shingle bar in the river. Cut rations to two slices of raw bacon each. No fire. Hard bread has given out."

Then a dismaying surprise. As they follow the river, it makes a sudden sharp bend and begins flowing back the way they've come--eastward. That "knocked the heart out of the officers," Waller notes. A council of war is called. Waller gives in a little, saying he'll go on if possible but will do whatever they decide. They decide to build rafts and float back to the east coast, a journey which Waller estimates will bring them out, in two days' time, not far from Broongon, and near a garrison town that could provide them with supplies.

But when they start out, on the day after New Year's, the first raft they build sinks at once. Looking for logs to build another, they find that nothing's available--all the wood is either too green or too water-soaked. Waller tries to maintain a calm, confident manner but he's getting apprehensive as he sees his men in their ragged uniforms looking ill, trying to walk on bleeding, swollen feet, their spirits at a low point. Some can't even keep up.

Once more they sit down to talk it over. Waller tells them he'll take two lieutenants and thirteen men able to travel, and try to reach the supply base at Soboton Cliffs, where a relief party can be formed to return and get the others, who will follow slowly behind as well as they can along a trail Waller will mark so plainly they can follow it with no trouble.

It doesn't work. Progress is so slow on their eastward journey that Waller decides to give up and go back to Lanang. He sends a native carrier with a message to the others, telling them his decision and ordering them to go back where they started from. He promises to join them there as soon as possible, and they'll try again to get down to the east coast on the river. But this plan doesn't work either. Rafts are almost impossible to build, as they've already discovered, and meanwhile, the native carriers are restless, finally refusing to cut any more logs. Captain Bearse, now in charge of this main body, starts out with a corporal named Murphy to see if he can find Waller and tell him the situation.

At that moment, Waller and his party have stumbled into a bit of luck--a clearing planted in banana trees, coconut palms, and sweet potatoes. Using the lens from his field glasses, Waller starts a fire and at last the men eat good food again. In a native hut, they find five Filipinos and take them prisoner, two of whom, a man and his son, say they know how to get to Basey, and agree to act as guides. Before they can start, Bearse and Murphy find them and Waller sends back one of his recalcitrant natives to tell the main body that the plans are changed yet again. They should give up on the rafts, start west once more, make camp in a clearing, and wait until help comes. Or, as an alternative, follow as best they can along his marked trail. He plans to push on to Basey.

It isn't long before Waller's native messenger comes back and reports he can't find the others because there are too many rebels in the area. That makes the captain suspicious, so he's hardly surprised the next night when he catches this same native trying to steal the bolo Waller always carries. Snatching it back, he kicks the thief and swears at him. Next day the party presses on to Basey and reaches it on the afternoon of January 6.

In his notebook, Waller reports their joy: "The men, realizing that all was over and they were safe and once more near home, gave up. Some quietly wept; others laughed hysterically. Most of them had no shoes. Cut, torn, bruised and dilapidated, they had marched without a murmur for twenty-nine days. My shirt was in rags, my hat was a hat only by courtesy. Torn as we were, with eyes suffused with blood from leech bites, I felt that appearance made no difference, we had come through."

A relief party is sent back at once to find the others, the indomitable Waller again in charge. They march for eleven days without finding anyone, meanwhile getting into a sorry condition themselves with fever and leech bites. Once more, as before. But Waller manages to get his party back to Basey by January 15, and there he himself collapses with a high fever, a sprained ankle, and a body hideous with leech stings. His eyes are swollen nearly shut. As Schott points out, the endurance of this forty-five-year-old man is incredible. Since the twenty-eighth of December, he's walked more than two hundred miles across a murderous terrain and in an equally evil climate that might have killed someone half his age.

Fortunately, Waller doesn't know what's happening to the men he couldn't find. Captain Porter, in charge of them, has split them up, taking those most able to travel toward Lanang and making all possible speed to get rations before the others starve. Lieutenant Williams, in charge of those left behind, was to wait as long as he could for Waller to find them, then he was to follow after Porter on a marked trail.

On January 11, Porter and three of his men stagger into Lanang and collapse, and a relief party is sent south to get the others. For those others, the expedition has become the worst nightmare they could imagine. In the sodden rain they have to cross swollen rivers. The native porters are sullen. After a while, the men are so weak they can't carry their rifles and belts. Nine of them simply fall down beside the trail; they can't make it. Another goes mad, and although he's still struggling along with the others, he's barking like a dog or else whistling forgotten melodies. Two men drop out and no one ever sees them again. Two others follow. At that point, no one in the party is able to travel any farther. All of them appear to be dying, and one has gone blind, but in any case is unable to walk. When a sergeant finds three privates slumped on the ground, unable to go on, one tells him, "Leave us be, Sarge. We all came into the outfit together and we've decided to go out together."

At night, a lone native attacks the sergeant but with no harm done. In the morning, however, the survivors agree that they'll have to kill all the natives still with them or they'll be killed themselves. Not easily done. There are more of the natives, and the Americans are too weak to organize any action. Nevertheless, Sergeant Williams tells them, "At the first false move tomorrow, we must start shooting and try to kill them all."

Fortunately, it isn't necessary to carry out this suicidal idea. A relief party from Lanang finds them in the morning, including four left behind by the riverbank at the original camp. Just in time for everyone. The Army carries these surviving Marines who can't walk down the mountain on their backs. The natives, it turns out, had been hiding food from the men and so *they're* in good shape. Nothing is done for the moment, but when the porters arrive at Lanang, a little behind the others, Williams describes the night attack on him, and their general bad conduct. All are arrested and put under guard.

Next morning the Marine survivors are loaded on a gunboat that will take them to medical facilities at Tacloban, and the natives are shackled and brought down below decks.

Writing his final report on this abortive campaign, Waller blames at least part of his troubles on 1st Lieutenant John Horace Arthur Day, a handsome, slender young man who speaks fluent Spanish, and of whom people feel a vague mistrust. Waller also has time to read a five-page circular issued on Christmas Day by General Smith. It proves to be a remarkable document. In it, Smith asserts that the Samar insurrection has been made possible by upper-class Filipinos and he demands harsh action, measures that will "create in the minds of all the people a burning desire for the war to cease; a desire or longing so intense, so personal, especially to every individual of the class mentioned, and so real that it will impel them to devote themselves in earnest to be bringing about a state of real peace. Short, severe wars are the most humane in the end. No civilized war, however civilized, can be carried out on a human basis. In waging this war officers will be guided by the provisions of General Order Number One Hundred A.G.O., 1863, which order promulgates the instructions for the government of the armies of the United States in the field."

What is this somewhat ancient order Smith is reviving? It was the first code of its kind when Abraham Lincoln issued it and was picked up by the Germans to be used as military field law in the Franco-Prussian War. The code lays down 157 rules for armies in the field, one of which sets forth at length the powers military commanders have over people in a conquered territory during wartime. General Sherman had taken it as gospel and followed it precisely on his way to Atlanta. No doubt it inspired his "War is hell" observation, and that's what Smith means to do in the Philippines.

But General Order 100 is about to undergo a severe and dramatic test, especially the latitude it gives to field officers, and with unforeseen consequences. While Waller was struggling through the jungles of Samar, a conspiracy had been exposed at Basey. Three men had been executed, and a priest imprisoned. When Waller returns, he's so ill with fever that he can't look into these or any other matters, although he senses a mood of almost despairing defeat at the base.

Everything comes to a head on January 19, but what actually happens on that day is still the subject of argument by historians. What emerges are two different versions, one by Waller and one by Day. Waller's story is somewhat clouded by the fact that his temperature was 105 degrees at the time, he was half delirious and occasionally vomited.

Day's story is that he followed a native prisoner upstairs at headquarters sometime between 11 A.M. and noon and saw him pushed into Waller's office by the town *presidente*. This official called to Waller through the open door of the patient's room, which was adjacent, and said that the prisoner, a man named Apolinar, was a spy. Waller heard the accusations as he lay on a cot with his bandaged right leg on two pillows. Day pushed into the office in time to hear the prisoner say (in Spanish) that if he did anything wrong it was only because he was poor and needed food for his family.

Weak and feverish as he was, Waller was only irritated by the intrusion on his misery. But Day persisted. "Colonel," he said, "this man is lying. He is not telling the truth. Let me take him outside and I will get all the information from him."

"All right, go ahead," Waller agreed, too sick to argue.

Now the story becomes more obscure. Some say Day gave the prisoner the water cure, but he denies it later, although witnesses testify he admitted it several days afterward while he was drunk. Day's story is that he questioned the prisoner in Spanish,

asking him why he came to Basey. He had come to take the oath
of allegiance, the man says. In that case, Day wants to know,
why hasn't he come in before? He has, the man asserts, twice,
taking the oath once from an enlisted man acting as interpreter
and again from Day himself at a time when the lieutenant was
adjutant.

Day doesn't recall any such incident, and adds that all the
natives look alike to him. In any case, he says, this man is a
member of Aguinaldo's Revolutionary Society and had been in
touch with General Colinares, leader of the rebel forces near
Basey, supplying him with information as to whether it would
be a good time to attack the post, since, with thirty men in the
hospital, there are only forty-five others fit for duty. Day says
the rebel leader had sent his prisoner to spy on the garrison.
Now Day is insisting again to Waller, lying on his bed of pain,
that this man ought to be shot at once, although Waller is scarcely able to make this or any other decision since he's half conscious. But Day testifies later that the colonel did, indeed, tell
him to go ahead.

With two men, Day marches the prisoner down to the
waterfront, a few hundred yards away from the town's plaza, and
stands him about twenty feet from his captors, with his back to
them. Day testifies later: "I stood between the prisoner and the
firing party and said, 'I am ordered to shoot you. You are a spy
and although I regret having to do it'--I did not finish it but
jumped to one side and swung my hat suddenly so as not to let
him know when he was going to be shot. The men fired. I
turned my head away and then turned back to see him in the act
of falling. He fell backwards and I stepped up to him. I thought
I saw a convulsive shudder in his shoulders. In my horror at seeing the man not dead, I drew my revolver and put it at his head
and I killed the man." Then he calls the local chief of police and
instructs him to put the body on view in the plaza as an example to others. This victim isn't buried until ten o'clock the next
morning. Day swears he reported the execution not only to
Waller but to several other officers, all of whom deny it.

Next day, the last survivors of the death march arrive.
Waller tries to greet them but his speech is still fever-blurred.
Sergeant Quick, in charge, reports that he's brought along those
natives who proved to be treacherous and wants to know what
to do with them, giving his own opinion: "I would shoot them

all down like mad dogs." Waller doesn't reply except to excuse him, but asks two other officers what should be done, and they agree with Quick. So Waller instructs Day to assemble a firing squad and have them shot as soon as all arrive in camp (a few are still on the last stage of the trip back), and he also orders a native already arrived to be shot at once. Day--"upset and excited," as he's described--is in charge of the killings and he executes these prisoners in the middle of the street at the center of town.

If Day was excited, some will testify, it was because he'd been drinking heavily and not sleeping much. He's been talking to a private named Russell, not on the march, who tells him that the native carriers have killed ten men, ten others died of starvation after the carriers stole their food, and there's poor Sergeant Williams, lying in the hospital nearby, dead from wounds inflicted on him.

After hearing this story, Day is in a cold rage by the time he meets the ship bringing in the prisoners at Basey wharf. He doesn't waste any time with such foolishness as charging them, or even interrogating them; he says an "investigation" has already been made and he's ready to act. At his court-martial, Day will claim the charges were treason, but if so, they were never set down in writing.

The final act begins. Day marches his nine prisoners from the guardhouse to a point in the center of the main street. Watching the scene is Sergeant Henry Slater, a survivor of the march, tottering in front of the hospital on swollen feet, waiting to be treated. As the prisoners are marched by, he hears they're going to be executed, and even though he's in his bare feet, he hobbles after them to see the show.

It's a militarily precise job. The men are shot three at a time, their backs to the firing squad. One breaks away and tries to run off, but they chase him down, and another is pushed into his place. Someone gives Sergeant Slater a rifle and he joins the firing squad. By the time the last two are ready for execution, a crowd of Marines has gathered, begging to join Slater. Day chooses four of them to shoot the last pair.

Later, Day asks Waller if he won't let Slim, the former native cop, go free, but the colonel won't wait for even a day to kill him. The lieutenant asks to be excused from this particular duty, so Waller gets two orderlies to do the shooting. Later that afternoon, Day has a conversation with Sergeant Quick about the whole affair, and Quick tells him Private Russell was wrong, and that the men he said had been killed by the natives had actually dropped out and died by themselves. Williams, he adds, is going to live. By that time, of course, it's too late to reverse what's been done without the semblance of due process.

It doesn't end there, on the dusty streets of the little garrison town. When Waller reports these executions to headquarters on January 22, his account is passed on to General Chaffee, who immediately senses danger. Next day he hurries to Tacloban, where Smith meets him at the wharf, and they ride to headquarters in a mule-drawn ambulance. Chaffee comes right to the point. "Smith," he says, "have you been having any promiscuous killing in Samar for fun?" Smith says no, having no idea what he's getting at.

"Well," Chaffee goes on, "I understand that at Basey they have been killing some people over there." Later, Smith says that this was the first time he had heard about it, and he orders an investigation. But next day another Smith appears in the office, Major F. A. Smith, of the Inspector General's Department, who has been instructed by Chaffee to take over the investigation and file a secret report. By this time Smith senses that some kind of sensational scandal may be developing, and if that happens, he might well be the designated scapegoat. The general doesn't intend to be caught, if he can help it.

Waller, meanwhile, is still weak, recovering slowly from his ordeal, but he finds the strength to begin writing his report of the death march. He has come to a few conclusions as a result of this experience, he says. One is that a large rebel force doesn't exist on Samar. As for the failure of his march, he blames the sodden, dripping weather. If the sun had been out, he asserts, the whole thing would have taken no more than five days. He admits that casualties were heavy: ten men lost during the march and two more who died after they reached Basey. The total is twenty-four percent of his original command, he notes carefully.

But his ordeal, and that of the survivors, is over now, or so he believes. On February 10, his battalion is detached from the Sixth Separate Brigade and ordered to leave Samar, returning to Cavite. The men are loaded on the transport *Lawton* and General Smith sees them off with laudatory words: "You are as fine a group of soldiers as has ever served under my command

and I have been an officer for forty years." Does this include Waller? Apparently not. As he describes it:

"Leaving Samar without the faintest suspicion of anything wrong, we reached Cavite. We looked forward to meeting our old chums and friends--we expected a warm welcome home. This welcome we received from the flagship New York--the ship's sides were lined and cheer after cheer after cheer went up for us. Then with that, to us, sweetest of all, compassion for the memory of brave, true men, held in reverence and honor by brave men, the flag was placed at half-staff and the band played, 'Home, Sweet Home' for those of us slumbering the last sleep in Samar. I went to report to my Commander-in-Chief and was met with the charge of murder." Chaffee has ordered the indictment, accusing Waller of murdering eleven natives. He is to be court-martialed in Manila within three weeks.

In a way, this signals the end of the war in the Philippines. Three months later, in May, all those who have been in the islands for more than three years will be sent home, including 600 soldiers and 300 Marines. About the same time, provincial governors are elected in the first free election, and on July 6 comes T.R.'s proclamation ending the insurrection officially, with amnesty for all who take the oath of allegiance, and military governments are withdrawn everywhere except where the Moros live.

But Waller's indictment ushers in the post-war finger-pointing and assessment of blame. His court-martial stirs up a hornet's nest of protest in America, and we're also going to have a congressional hearing about the way this war was run, just as we did after the Cuban phase ended. It will make a bitter story.

6

THE SOUR FRUITS OF VICTORY

WHEN THE NEWS OF WHAT HAPPENED ON SAMAR BEGINS to trickle in, Americans divide according to party and their own interests. For most citizens, what's occurring in the Philippines is like an uneasy sideshow to the general prosperity at home. Their consciences may bother some of them, but most are simply annoyed by the bitter arguments still going on in the newspapers and among the politicians. They wish the whole thing would just go away.

It does, but it dies hard. Imperialism and anti-imperialism are still unresolved questions. Republicans insist that there isn't any argument: the Philippines are ours and we may as well accept it. They applaud an editorial in the Washington *Post* that insists the public must face facts: we deliberately acquired these islands, and we intend to use them for our own profit.

Voices of dissent still are heard, but they come mostly from furious intellectuals like Mark Twain, or disgusted academics like William James, who has opposed the war with Spain from the beginning. At the start of the conflict, in a letter to his friend François Pilloon, James called the "Cuban War" a "curious episode of history, showing how a nation's ideals can be changed in the twinkling of an eye, by a succession of outward events partly accidental." Later, when McKinley applied the soothing phrase "benevolent assimilation" to the military occupation of the Philippines, James saw it as "the cold pot-grease of McKinley's eloquence," and loathed it. He viewed the nomination of McKinley and Roosevelt in 1900 as "a combination of grime and grit, soap and sand, that ought to scour away even the moral sense of the country."

In the Senate, after the islands are finally cleansed, Albert Beveridge rises to reveal that God has been in charge of the takeover all along: "We will not renounce our part in the mission of our race, trustees under God, of the civilization of the world.

God has not been preparing the English-speaking and Teutonic peoples for a thousand years for nothing but vain and idle self-admiration. No! He has made us the master organizers of the world to establish a system where chaos reigns." In a few years, he will find it difficult to explain why God gave the Teutonic peoples a slightly different plan for organizing the world.

Senator Hoar can't let this kind of rhetoric go unchallenged, and delivers some of his own, in his usual biblical style. Borrowing from the Bible, he declaims: "The devil taketh him up into an exceeding high mountain and showeth him all the kingdoms of the world, and the glory of them, and saith unto him: 'All these things will I give thee, if thou wilt fall down and worship me.' Then said Jesus unto him: 'Get thee behind me, Satan.'" Beveridge doesn't seem to get the point.

Southern newspapers are not enthusiastic about acquisition of the islands on the grounds, as one of them says, that "we have enough niggers"; consequently many of them are numbered among those who want to get to the bottom of the whole affair and find out exactly what was going on in that distant place. Senator Hoar hears their voices and a chorus of others. On January 12, 1902, while the horror of Samar is still unfolding, he submits a Senate resolution calling for a special committee to "examine and report on the conduct of the war."

Just what a good many people have been waiting for, but the Republicans are determined to sidetrack this investigation and run it under the political carpet if possible. The fact that the committee will be headed by Senator Lodge is a guarantee that the Democrats won't get much help from the chairman. Between the end of January and June 28, the hearings sputter along, and in spite of all precautions, some of the truth emerges and it is ugly.

To a veteran politician like Hoar, it becomes obvious in the first few weeks that how these facts will be interpreted and what their impact may be will be determined by the committee's composition. Here, for example, is the powerful Beveridge assuming what amounts to the position of defense counsel for the Army. Republican members manage to confine examinations of military conduct to about a third of the sessions, and see to it that most of the witnesses are those who understand the difficulties of pacification and civilizing. However, an embarrassing document turns up, a report submitted to the War

Department by Major Cornelius Gardner, who has been the civil governor of Tayabas Province, in Luzon.

One of the committee's Democratic members manages to introduce a letter to the Secretary of War from Nelson Miles, who's still hanging on as Chief of Staff in spite of the Cuban scandal. In it, Miles mentions Major Gardner's report as evidence to support his own belief that the Army's policy has been one of "marked severity." The committee's Democratic minority then demands that Gardner's report be produced, and in spite of Republican efforts to prevent it, the major's document is leaked to the press.

In it, Gardner complains that the conciliatory efforts of the Taft Commission earlier on were sabotaged by the animosity shown toward Filipinos by a hard core of enlisted men and their junior officers, who were responsible for harsh reprisals and for concealing Army brutality.

More evidence turns up. It appears that General Franklin Bell had set up concentration centers in Batangas Province. The AP had already reported at the time the hearings began that Bell's plan to isolate the guerrillas was to drive all the civilians into concentration centers--the *reconcentrados* of Cuba reinvented. These centers would be guarded by troops, and civilians found outside the camps after curfew would be shot with no questions asked. Some papers make the obvious comparison: Bell is the new Butcher Weyler.

Democrats on the committee introduce letters from soldiers, some of them already printed and distributed by the League, as examples of Army severity. One of these reports (later authenticated) is that American soldiers were using dumdum bullets. Others describe various forms of torture used by Army men. The water cure stories are revived, including the revelation that sometimes soldiers jumped up and down on the victim's distended stomach. Then there is the equally infamous "rope cure," in which the victim's neck and torso are tied together, after which the rope is twisted with a stick.

Some of this is old stuff to newspaper readers, but earlier stories are reintroduced. One is the New York *Journal*'s account of how officers had beaten to death, using rattan rods, the presidents of both San Miguel and San Nicolas because they would not admit contacts with the rebels. Two months later, the rival *World* printed its own atrocity story from a correspondent who wrote: "Our soldiers here and there resort to horrible measures with the natives. Captains and lieutenants are sometimes judges, sheriffs, and executioners. It is now the custom to avenge an American soldier by burning to the ground all the houses, and killing right and left the natives who are only 'suspects.'"

Then there are letters, printed and reprinted by Democratic newspapers, such as the one from Sergeant Howard MacFarlane, of the 43rd infantry, whose letter home appeared in the Fairfield, Maine, *Journal*, describing how "eighteen of my company killed seventy-five nigger bolomen and ten of the nigger gunners. When we find one that is not dead, we have bayonets."

In another letter, Lieutenant John F. Hall, of the 20th Kansas, says that his commander, General Funston, gave orders to shoot all prisoners and even justified, by preventing him from being court-martialed, the action of Major Wilder S. Metcalf, who ordered shot a prisoner who was down on his knees, begging for his life. No one pays much attention to Funston's denial.

Then there's Private Andrew E. Weir, of the 4th Cavalry, who writes to his uncle about Lieutenant Frederick T. Arnold and a Sergeant Edwards, who stripped a prisoner, gave him the water cure, whipped him with the popular rattan rods, and strung him up by his thumbs. Lieutenant Arnold explained, Weir relates, that Filipinos "had no feelings other than physical, and should not be treated as human beings," and as though to prove it, this same officer cut a strip of skin from a prisoner's ankle and attached it to a piece of wood, as a kind of ornament. The busy lieutenant also held an old man's head under water until he lost consciousness, and tied another prisoner to a saddled horse on a short length of rope, then spurred the horse to a gallop.

Republicans cry foul. Not all these stories are true, they assert, and an investigation shows that some of them aren't. A few of these writers back home are stationed in Manila and have never been in combat. To cover up their real lifestyles, they invent fanciful tales of life in the field to make it appear they're out in the front lines with the others. When they're not writing, they enjoy their native mistresses and make a whole generation of saloon and brothel keepers rich for life.

The committee makes a serious effort to separate the true from the untrue, which is difficult. Taft is on the stand testifying for two hours a day for a week or more, asserting that such instances of cruelty are isolated, and of course he blames the press, already an old American custom, for spreading these tales. His claims bring the Democrats and the press down on him with equal fervor.

A former Army surgeon, Dr. Henry C. Howland, tells the committee that chronic homesickness is the motivation for these stories, repeating a theory we've already heard in Cuba. Senator Lodge doesn't buy this notion. He writes to George Lyman: "When a soldier in a disturbed district going along the road found the body of his comrade by the roadside stabbed to death from behind and his private parts cut off and stuffed in the mouth of the corpse, he was very apt to do something pretty nasty to the next armed Filipino he met." When the testimony about what happened at Balangiga is introduced, it confirms Lodge's idea of why there is so much inhumanity of men toward men.

When Charles S. Riley, of Northampton, Massachusetts, sits down to testify, he blasts a large hole in the defense of the Army that Secretary Root had been giving the members previously. Riley is a sergeant in the 26th Infantry, and what he has to relate concerns the conduct of Captain F. Glenn on Panay in 1900. Glenn has been considered something of a hero up to now. Promoted to major, he is presently a staff officer of the Sixth Separate Brigade at Tacloban, as judge advocate of the Department of the Viscayas. Glenn has been commended for his service on several occasions, and is noted for his success in getting information out of the natives. How he got it is now disclosed by Sergeant Riley to the fascinated committee members.

A letter to his parents from Riley, dated November 25, 1900, is introduced, in which he reports on what happened in his company, commanded by Glenn: "Arriving at Igbarras [sic] at daylight, we found everything peaceful; it shortly developed that we were really 'treading on a volcano.' The presidente, the priest, and other leading men were assembled, and put on the rack of inquiry. The presidente evaded some questions and was soon bound and given the 'water cure.' This was done by throwing him on his back beneath a tank of water and running a stream into his mouth, a man kneeling on his stomach meanwhile to prevent him from drowning. The ordeal proved a tongue-loosener, and the crafty old fellow soon begged for mercy and made full confession. The presidente was asked for more information and had to take a second dose of 'water cure' before he would divulge."

On the stand, Riley confirms these facts in his letter and testifies in greater detail about the incident, adding that Glenn ordered Igbaras burned to the ground. It was a town with 10,000 inhabitants.

Separating wheat from chaff, it's clear to the committee--at least to all the Democrats and even a few Republicans--that if only part of what's been testified is true, there are serious violations of Lincoln's Order 100, not to mention the Articles of War.

While testimony is still being heard, the Waller controversy reaches Root's office and he orders his own investigation, with the help of Senator Lodge. There's no way of avoiding this unpleasant and possibly highly embarrassing duty. It's a squabble among officers at the highest level, and since a court-martial has already been ordered, there is no possibility of sweeping this affair under the official rug.

There have been earlier premonitions. On the previous November 4, the Manila *Times*, an English-language paper dutifully supporting everything the United States does, had reported: "Brigadier General Smith had been in Samar about 10 days and his strong policy was already making itself felt. He had already ordered all natives to present themselves in certain of the coast towns, saying that those who were found outside would be shot and no questions asked. [When] the time limit had expired...General Smith was as good as his word. His policy of reconcentration is said to be the most effective thing of the kind ever seen in these islands under any flag. All suspects, including Spaniards and half-breeds, were rounded up in big stockades and kept under guard." This story appears later in American newspapers.

In that same November, the Philadelphia *Ledger* printed a review of current military policy by its Manila correspondent, and since the paper was an Administration sympathizer, the story had to be taken seriously in the circumstances. The correspondent wrote:

"The present war is no bloodless, fake, opera bouffe engagement; our men have been relentless, have killed to exterminate men, women, children, prisoners and captives, active insurgents and suspected people from lads of 10 up, an idea prevailing that the Filipino as such was little better than a dog. Our soldiers have pumped salt water into men to 'make them talk,' and have taken prisoners people who have held up their hands and peacefully surrendered, and an hour later, without an atom of evidence to show that they were even insurrective, stood them on a bridge and shot them down one by one, to drop into the water below and float down, an example to those who found their bullet-loaded corpses. The new military plan of settling the trouble by setting them at each other looks promising."

In the face of all the accumulating evidence, President Roosevelt understands that it would be politically unwise to keep on denying, as Root continues to do, that nothing much has happened in the Philippines besides isolated incidents for which Army officers cannot really be blamed. On April 16, he officially orders the court-martial of General Smith. His heart isn't in it, though. A short time later he writes a letter of congratulations to General Bell on his Batangas campaign, where 300,000 Filipinos are presently sitting in concentration camps, and whose methods even Lodge has characterized as "cruel."

At the center of the storm and trying to avoid any unhappy consequences to himself, General Chaffee has decreed that Waller has to be punished, whether he's physically up to being tried or not. "He must be punished," Chaffee reiterates when queried. He's determined to make Waller the scapegoat for what happened on Samar. Some newspapers are already calling him the "Butcher of Samar." Move over, Weyler.

At the court-martial, Smith's testimony is a masterpiece of perjury and betrayal. He denies that he ever gave orders to "kill and burn" or to "take no prisoners," although the evidence is clear that he did. He has no hesitation about betraying both Waller and the Marines who took part in the Samar campaign. After hearing eighteen days of testimony, the court takes only a half hour to acquit Waller by an 11 - 2 vote. Lieutenant Day is also acquitted. Later, in the Great War, he will turn up again as a colonel in the Belgian Army, and when the war is over, will be granted the same rank in the United States Army Reserve, finally appearing in the twenties as an officer in, of all places, the Honduras Constabulary.

When Smith is given his own court-martial in Manila, on charges of "conduct to the prejudice of good order and military discipline" by giving the disputed orders to Waller, he pleads not guilty, but he is convicted anyway because he is plainly guilty. But these old Army boys stick together. Smith's punishment is a mere "admonishment," with the lame explanation that "the accused did not mean everything that his unexplained language implied." If you can believe that, you can believe Spain won the war. He's permitted to retire a year and a half early.

Other survivors of Samar face a variety of fates. The Army waits until 1925 to court-martial Lieutenant A. S. Williams, who led the death march column, but not for what he did there. He's convicted of "drunkenness and conduct unbecoming to an officer in a public place." There does seem to be something rotten here because later Williams drowns when his car plunges into San Francisco Bay at 4 A.M. Bearse and Porter live out routine lives as Marines. Major Glenn is court-martialed and convicted of giving the water cure and burning down Igbaras, but the penalty exacted for these crimes is a flat $50 fine, which some consider a gross insult to justice. In the end, Glenn retires from the Army as a brigadier general.

But it's Waller whose fate is seen by later historians as the worst example of miscarried justice. His acquittal is appealed and reviewed by the Judge Advocate General of the War Department, who certifies the validity of his original plea and confirms that his court-martial board "acted without jurisdiction and...its proceedings are, for that reason, null and void." His eighteen-day ordeal in court is ruled unnecessary. But some newspapers can't forget him, guilty or not, and periodically they haunt him for the remainder of his life. Moreover, Americans who've been shocked by the testimony before the Senate Committee and the court-martial proceedings are inclined to blame everyone for Army policy, acquitted or not.

Wherever he goes, Waller's past dogs him, through service in Panama, Mexico, and Haiti. They can't forget. When he's considered a strong contender in 1910 to be Commandant of Marines it appears that his lifelong ambition will be fulfilled, but President Taft can't think beyond Samar and appoints William P. Biddle instead. When Biddle retires four years later, Taft passes over Waller again. Promoted to major general (small consolation), he dies on July 13, 1926, and his old friend Smedley Butler says of him: "The doctor reported he had a stroke. What he really died of was a broken heart."

The Senate Committee breaks off the investigation in June 1902, inconclusively, and no one wants to resume it except the anti-imperialists, who sum up matters in a report of their own investigation:

"We have in fact destroyed the public buildings of the country, inflicted continuous crop losses during a period of six years, ravaged and burned large sections of the country, produced conditions leading to the death of most farm animals and to serious human and animal epidemics, brought foreign trade to an unprofitable condition by our tariff legislation, inaugurated tremendously expensive government for the benefit of foreign office-holders, established a partisan judiciary, crowded the prisons and deported or sent to the gallows the best and most patriotic leaders."

A damning indictment, but that's not all of it. More than 4,200 Americans have been killed in action, far exceeding the loss in Cuba. About 2,800 have been wounded. These figures don't include, as Geoffrey Perrett tells us, those who fell in "ones and twos, murdered in back alleys, in flyblown village bars, and in the arms of smiling girls." There are more of these, he believes, than those who fell in combat. As for the other side, we killed about 16,000 guerrillas, and more than 100,000 (who will ever know the exact figure?) of noncombatants, including those murdered outright and all those others who died from hunger and disease.

Summing it up, Perrett notes that the war in the Philippines "divided America more than any other between Appomattox and Vietnam, but it was quickly forgotten, except in the army," for whom it was a learning experience. Before the conflict with Spain and the Philippine insurrection, the Army had been out of practice since the Civil War, with only the Indians providing rehearsal time for learning destruction. "From this one small war," Perrett concludes, "would flow a century of consequences."

Yet no American war has been so quickly forgotten. It was a time when national honor and patriotic pride were elevated to the stature of a religion. People were optimistic because times were good, and they wallowed in romantic nationalism. The Flag was nearly always capitalized when it appeared in print. Editorials and public oratory were filled with such phrases as "the highest duty," "the supreme sacrifice," and "martial glory." Such phrases required neither quotation marks nor apology. Edward Everett Hale's "The Man Without a Country" appeared in 1902 and for a while was outsold only by the Bible. It was a cautionary tale about a young lieutenant named Philip Nolan who damned the United States and for his pains had his passport removed and his citizenship revoked, was denied residence in his native country, and spent the rest of his life on ships carrying him from country to country, all of which refused to take him in, thus upholding the patriotic ideals of a country founded on dissent.

As Welch puts it aptly, "This was our most quickly forgotten war, the war least celebrated in legend and song, least marked by cenotaph and monuments." Americans closed their eyes to any claim of other people's humanity, and whatever moral outrage there might be was confined to the intellectuals of the Anti-Imperialist League and Democratic newspapers. The war years, as Welch concludes, were "years of prosperity and expansion of the home market." Nothing else seemed to matter.

But once the idea of freedom has been entertained, it isn't easily given up. The Americans may forget, but some Filipinos don't. Fighting dies out slowly, and on Mindanao, largest of the islands, it doesn't stop entirely until 1916. In April and May of 1903, Captain John J. Pershing, working his way toward the Great War, finds himself attacked several times on Mindanao by the fierce Moros.

Who are these people who don't know when to quit? They are Muslim warriors with their own traditions, not all of them admirable by any means. They practice both polygamy and slavery, and for many Americans that's reason enough to kill them. But the carrot is offered first. Army and Navy officers attempt to seduce the Moro chiefs into peaceful pursuits by giving them elementary lessons in science and naval gunnery, and some are impressed enough to give up further resistance. This effort ends when Americans back home find out that these slave-owning polygamists are being wooed to become our allies.

So the bush war against them goes on fiercely, and when they show a remarkable resistance to being annihilated by what weapons the Army possesses, field commanders plead with the Ordnance Department to give them something more substantial than the .38-caliber semiautomatic pistol the Colt factory in Hartford has been producing since 1902. Ordnance turns the job over to John M. Browning, the country's chief designer of guns, asking him to produce a weapon capable of stopping a Moro warrior cold. These tough fighters have shown an annoying disposition to use their bolos even when they have absorbed one or two .38-caliber bullets. This challenge to Browning's genius produces first a .45-caliber bullet, around which he designs a gun, and shortly Hartford is turning out the Colt .45 automatic pistol, which not only destroys Moros but becomes standard military issue in 1911.

Those Moros who escape pacification retreat to the hills and mountains where they keep their culture alive and fight the continued Army presence in the Philippines whenever and wherever it's possible. Little about this bush warfare reaches the United States until 1906, when an event so terrible occurs that the American conscience is roused from its customary sleep.

This is an event that reawakens Mark Twain's anger and he writes a scathing account of it, titled "Comments on the Killing of 600 Moros." These "dark-skinned savages," as Twain calls them sarcastically, have been pursued by American troops until they take refuge in the bowl of an extinct volcano crater, near Jolo. As Twain puts it, "Since they were 'hostiles' and bitter at us because we have been trying for eight years to take their liberties away from them, their presence in that position was a menace."

General Wood, in charge of a search-and-destroy force, learns that the Moros, whose number he estimates (incorrectly) at 600, including women and children, are tucked away in the crater at an altitude of 2,200 feet--"very difficult of access for Christian troops and artillery," Twain notes. Wood gets his men to the top, however, without much difficulty and they look down into the bowl. There, at a distance of about fifty feet, are the Moros. The general mounts his artillery as near the rim as possible and prepares to attack, with about the same number of troops as the men, women, and children below him.

Twain describes what followed: "The battle began--it is officially called by that name--our forces firing down into the crater with their artillery and their deadly small arms of precision; the savages furiously returning the fire, probably with brickbats--though this is merely a surmise of mine. Heretofore the Moros have used knives and clubs mainly; also ineffectual trade-muskets when they had any. The official report stated that the battle was fought with prodigious energy on both sides during a day and half, and that it ended with a complete victory for the American army. The completeness of the victory is established by this fact: that of the six hundred Moros not one was left alive. The brilliance of the victory is established by this other fact, to wit: that of our six hundred heroes only fifteen lost their lives." The soldiers were, Twain notes, carrying out Wood's orders to "kill or capture these savages. They had in effect been told to kill or capture according to taste, Twain says, and "their taste had remained what it has been for eight years in our army out there--the taste of Christian butchers."

In his essay, Twain goes on to compare casualty rates in such great conflicts as the Civil War, Waterloo, and in what he calls that "pathetic comedy" of the Cuban war. He goes on:

"Contrast these things with the great statistics which have arrived from that Moro crater! There, with 600 engaged on each side, we lost fifteen killed outright, and we had 37 wounded. The enemy numbered 600 (it was actually 900 by later count), including women and children--and we abolished them utterly, leaving not even a baby alive to cry for its dead mother. This is incomparably the greatest victory that was ever achieved by the Christian soldiers of the United States."

General Wood began by praising the courage of his men and the decisive results of his campaign against the Moros, but when Twain's blast appears and the sordid details reach the newspapers, he begins to feel uneasy and look for rationalizations. However, as Twain reminds everybody: "Doctor Wood will find that explaining things is not in his line. He will find that when a man has a proper spirit in him and the proper force at his command, it is easier to massacre nine hundred unarmed animals than it is to explain why he made it so remorselessly complete. The inference seems plain. We cleaned up our four days' work and made it complete by butchering these helpless people."

National memory is short. The Moros are quickly forgotten and progress marches on. Education is the device ultimately employed to make assimilation much easier than shooting everyone who wants freedom. Swarms of teachers come out from America to produce a high rate of literacy in the population. English becomes virtually a second language.

But somehow the Americans just can't seem to get out of the Philippines. It isn't until Franklin D. Roosevelt is in the White House that the islands get a constitution in 1935 and the last governor general, Frank Murphy (later a Supreme Court justice), changes the sign on his door and becomes the high commissioner, which seems to mean that he is an unanointed ambassador.

Before any further substantial progress can be made, World War II intervenes, and by May 1942 the American and Filipino forces under General Jonathan Wainwright are forced to surrender to the Japanese, who proclaim an "independent Philippine Republic," which is actually a cruel occupation. Once more, resisting Filipinos take to the hills and fight a guerrilla war against the invaders. General Douglas MacArthur's celebrated "return" to Leyte in October 1944 signals the resumption of the Philippines' tortuous road to independence. The American rescuers demand and get ninety-nine-year leases on a number of bases. Some Filipino politicians think there's no getting rid of these benevolent conquerors.

The sense of *déjà vu* has been enhanced during the war by the reappearance of Aguinaldo. In spite of having sworn allegiance to the United States, he hasn't forgotten who let him down, and after his capture by the Japanese, he becomes a collaborator, a kind of male Tokyo Rose who, on the radio, urges MacArthur to give up his untenable position on the Corregidor peninsula.

After the war ends, the Americans arrest him but then, inexplicably, he's pardoned and in 1950 he's still there, serving in President Elpidio Quirino's council of state. Only death can remove him from the scene, and that occurs in 1964.

Still ahead for the Philippines is a succession of governments that never quite succeed in bringing together this multitudinous people of so many different languages, ethnic backgrounds, and political convictions. Finally we come to our own time of Ferdinand Marcos and the shoe-happy Imelda, his wife, a popular virtual dictator who finally has to yield to a redoubtable woman, Corazon Aquino, under whose presidency the last American forces begin to withdraw, leaving the Philippines to face an unpredictable future.

Is there anything at all to be learned from the Spanish-American War, this cruel imperial venture in American history? Perhaps the best summary appears in the most unlikely publication imaginable, the *Army and Navy Journal* of January 22, 1906: "About the most unbeautiful thing in the general drama of American opinion is its contempt for small republics struggling with internal troubles."

SELECTIVE BIBLIOGRAPHY

AZOY, A. C. *Charge! The Story of the Battle of San Juan Hill.* (New York: Longmans, Green, 1961).

BEER, THOMAS. *Hanna, Crane and the Mauve Decade* (New York: Alfred Knopf, 1941).

BERLCOVE, LAWRENCE I. (ed.). *Skepticism and Dissent: SelectedJournalism, 1898-1901* (Ann Arbor: UMI Research Press, 1988).

BULLARD, F. LAURISTON. *Famous War Correspondents* (Boston: Little, Brown, 1914).

CAREY, JOHN (ed.). *Eyewitness to History* (Cambridge: Harvard University Press, 1987).

CRANE, STEPHEN. *The War Dispatches of Stephen Crane.* (New York: New York University Press, 1996). *Wounds in the Rain* (New York: Plainview Books, 1976).

CREELMAN, JAMES. *On the Great Highway* (Boston: Little, Brown, 1901).

DAVIS, RICHARD HARDING. *A Year From a Reporter's Notebook* (New York: Harper & Bros., 1898). *The Cuban and Puerto Rican Campaigns* (New York: Charles Scribner's Sons, 1898). *Notes of a War Correspondent* (New York: Harper & Bros., 1897).

FREIDEL, FRANK. *The Splendid Little War* (Boston: Little, Brown, 1958).

GEISMAR, MAXWELL. *Mark Twain: An American Prophet* (Boston: Houghton Mifflin, 1970).(ed.). *Mark Twain and the Three R's: Race, Religion, Revolution--and Related Matters* (Indianapolis: Bobbs-Merrill, 1973).

HEALY, DAVID F. *The United States in Cuba, 1898-1902* (Madison: University of Wisconsin Press, 1963).

JAMES, WILLIAM *Letters* (Henry James, ed.). Vol II (Boston: Atlantic Monthly Press, 1920).

JENNISON, PETER S. *Roadside History of Vermont* (Missoula: Mountain Press, 1989).

JOHNSON, EDWARD A. *History of Negro Soldiers in the Spanish-American War* (Raleigh: Capital Printing Co., 1899).

KAPLAN, JUSTIN. *Mr. Clemens and Mr. Twain* (New York: Simon and Schuster, 1966).

LEECH, MARGARET. *In the Days of McKinley* (New York: Harper & Bros., 1939).

LINDERMAN, GERALD F. *The Mirror of War* (Ann Arbor: University of Michigan Press, 1974).

MAY, ERNEST R. *Imperial Democracy: The Emergence of America as a World Power* (New York: Harcourt Brace, 1961).

MILTON, JOYCE. *The Yellow Kids: Foreign Correspondents in the Heyday of Yellow Journalism* (New York: Harper & Row, 1989).

MORISON, SAMUEL. MERK, FREDERICK; AND
FREIDEL, FRANK. *Dissent in Three American Wars* (Cambridge: Harvard University Press, 1970).

MUSICANT, IVAN. *The Banana Wars: A History of U.S. Military Intervention in Latin-America from the Spanish-Armerican War to the Invasion of Panama* (New York: Macmillan, 1990).

OSBORN, SCOTT. *Richard Harding Davis: The Development of A Journalist* (Unpublished dissertation, University of Kentucky, 1953).

OSBORN, SCOTT COMPTON, AND PHILLIPS,
ROBERT L., JR. *Richard Harding Davis* (Boston: Twayne Pub., 1978).

PERRETT, GEOFFREY. *A Country Made By War* (New York: Random House, 1989).

SCHIRMER, DANIEL B. *Republic or Empire: American Resistance in the PhilippineWar* (Cambridge: Schenkman Publishing, 1972).

SCHOTT, JOSEPH L. *The Ordeal of Samar* (Indianapolis: Bobbs-Merrill, 1964).

SNYDER, LOUIS L., AND MORRIS, RICHARD B. (eds.). *A Treasury of Great Reporting.* (New York: Simon and Schuster, 1949).

STOREY, MOORFIELD, AND LICHAUKO, MARCIAL P.
The Conquest of the Philippines by the United States, 1898-1925 (New York: G. P. Putnam's Sons, 1926).

SULLIVAN, MARK. *Our Times* (New York: Charles Scribner's Sons, 1926).

SWANBERG, WILLIAM A. *Pulitzer* (New York: Scribner's, 1967). --- *Citizen Hearst* (New York: Scribner's, 1967).

TOMPKINS, E. BERKELEY. *Anti-Imperialism in the United States:*
The Great Debate, 1890-1920 (Philadelphia: University of Pennsylvania Press, 1970).

WELCH, RICHARD E., JR. *Response to Imperialism: The United States and the Philippine-American War* (Chapel Hill: University of North Carolina Press, 1979).

WILKERSON, MARCUS M. *Public Opinion and the Spanish-American War: A Study in War Propaganda* (Baton Rouge: Louisiana State University Press, 1932).

INDEX